Discourse as Social Interaction

Discourse Studies:
A Multidisciplinary Introduction
Volume 2

edited by

Teun A. van Dijk

Los Angeles | London | New Delhi
Singapore | Washington DC

ISBN 978-0-8039-7846-1 (hbk)
ISBN 978-0-8039-7847-8 (pbk)
ISBN 978-0-7619-5320-3 Hardback set
ISBN 978-0-7619-5321-0 Paperback set
Preface and Chapter 1 © Teun A. van Dijk, 1997
Chapter 2 © Shoshana Blum-Kulka, 1997
Chapter 3 © Anita Pomerantz and B.J. Behr, 1997
Chapter 4 © Paul Drew and Marja-Leena Sorjonen, 1997
Chapter 5 © Candace West, Michelle M. Lazar and Cheris Kramarae, 1997
Chapter 6 © Teun A. van Dijk, Stella Ting-Toomey, Geneva Smitherman
and Denise Troutman, 1997
Chapter 7 © Dennis K. Mumby and Robin P. Clair, 1997
Chapter 8 © Paul Chilton and Christina Schäffner, 1997
Chapter 9 © Cliff Goddard and Anna Wierzbicka, 1997
Chapter 10 © Norman Fairclough and Ruth Wodak, 1997
Chapter 11 © Britt-Louise Gunnarsson, 1997
First published 1997
Reprinted 1997, 1998, 2000, 2003, 2004, 2006, 2007 (twice), 2009

SAGE Publications Ltd
1 Oliver's Yard, 55 City Road
London EC1Y 1SP

SAGE Publications Inc
2455 Teller Road
Thousand Oaks, California 91320

SAGE Publications India Pvt Ltd
B 1/11 Mohan Cooperative Industrial Area
Mathura Road.
New Delhi 110 044
India

SAGE Publications Asia-Pacific Pte Ltd
33 Pekin Street #02-01
Far East Square
Singapore 048763

British Library Cataloguing in Publication data
A catalogue record for this book is available from the British Library

Library of Congress Control Number: 96072299

Typeset by Mayhew Typesetting, Rhayader, Powys
Printed digitally in Great Britain by
the MPG Books Group, Bodmin and King's Lynn

Contents

Contributors

Shoshana Blum-Kulka is Associate Professor at the Department of Communication and the School of Education at the Hebrew University. Her research interests include cross-cultural pragmatics, interlanguage pragmatics, ethnography of communication and family discourse. She has published articles on these topics in *Text, Language in Society, Research on Language and Social Interaction, Journal of Narrative and Life History* and *Journal of Pragmatics*. Her most recent book is *Dinner Talk: Cultural Patterns of Sociability and Socialization in Family Discourse* (1997).

Paul Chilton is Professor of Language and Communication in the Department of Languages and European Studies at Aston University, Birmingham. He was a visiting fellow at the Center for International Security and Arms Control, Stanford (1988–90). His research is in the field of discourse analysis and the relationship between language, discourse and politics. His publications include *Language and the Nuclear Arms Debate* (as editor, 1985), *Orwellian Language and the Media* (1988), *Security Metaphors: Cold War Discourse from Containment to Common Home* (1996) and articles in numerous journals.

Robin P. Clair is an Assistant Professor in the Communication Department at Purdue University. She received her PhD from Kent State University and specializes in organizational communication with specific research interests in the areas of the meaning of work and the discursive practices surrounding the sexuality of organization.

Paul Drew lectures in Sociology at the University of York. His fields of research are the analysis of conversation, in which he has published on such topics as repair, teasing, invitation sequences, and the use of idiomatic expressions; and the application of conversation analysis to the study of courtroom interaction, and to the comparative analysis of institutional talk more generally. He is co-author (with Max Atkinson) of *Order in Court* (1979), co-editor (with Tony Wootton) of *Erving Goffman: Exploring the Interaction Order* (1988), and co-editor (with John Heritage) of *Talk at Work: Interaction in Institutional Settings* (1992).

Norman Fairclough is Professor of Language in Social Life in the Department of Linguistics and Modern English Language at the University of Lancaster. His main interests are in critical discourse analysis. His publications include *Language and Power* (1989), *Discourse and Social*

Change (1992), *Critical Discourse Analysis* (1995) and *Media Discourse* (1995). He has also edited *Critical Language Awareness* (1992).

B.J. Fehr is a Visiting Scholar in the Department of Communication Sciences at Temple University. Her main areas of interest include ethnomethodology, waymaking, and clinical practice. With Jeff Stetson and Yoshifumi Mizukawa, she prepared a bibliography of papers and books in ethnomethodology and conversation analysis for *Ethnomethodological Sociology* (edited by J. Coulter, 1990).

Cliff Goddard is a Senior Lecturer in Linguistics at the University of New England, Armidale, Australia. He has published a dictionary and grammar of the Yankunytjatjara language of Central Australia, where he has done extensive field work. His current research interests are in semantic theory and cross-linguistic semantics and pragmatics, with special reference to Yankunytjatjara and to Malay. He has published journal articles on the semantics of emotions, grammatical categories, and illocutionary particles, among other topics. His forthcoming book is titled *Semantic Analysis*. With Anna Wierzbicka, he is co-editor of *Semantic and Lexical Universals: Theory and Empirical Findings* (1994).

Britt-Louise Gunnarsson is currently Associate Professor in Scandinavian Languages at Uppsala University, where she is the founder and director of a research group on discourse in the professions. Her major fields of interest are text linguistics, sociolinguistics, discourse analysis, comprehensibility, writing and language for specific purposes. Since 1981 she has directed several large research projects (funded by the major Swedish research foundations) related to these fields. Her publications include books and articles in Swedish, some 30 articles in English (*TEXT, Written Communication, International Journal of Applied Linguistics*) and a handful in German and French. Books she has co-edited include *Text and Talk in Professional Contexts* (1994) and *The Construction of Professional Discourse* (1977).

Cheris Kramarae is a former Director of Women's Studies at the University of Illinois at Urbana-Champaign, and Professor of Speech Communication, Linguistics, Sociology, and Women's Studies. Her teaching and research are focused on sociolinguistic analysis (especially language and power issues, and Internet interaction). Books she has co-authored, edited, or co-edited include *Language and Power* (1984), *A Feminist Dictionary: Amazons, Bluestockings, and Crones* (1986, 1992), *Technology and Women's Voices* (1988), *The Revolution in Words* (1990), and *Women, Information Technology and Scholarship* (1993). She and Dale Spender are general editors of an international women's studies encyclopaedia which will be available on CD-ROM.

Michelle M. Lazar taught at the National University of Singapore and is currently engaged in full-time doctoral research at Lancaster University.

Her research interests are in critical discourse analysis, gender and the media. She has written an article, 'Equalizing gender relations: a case of double-talk', and has a chapter, 'Family life advertisements and the narrative of heterosexual sociality', in Phyllis G.L. Chew and Anneliese Kramer-Dahl (eds), *Reading Singapore: Textual Practices in Singapore Culture* (forthcoming).

Dennis K. Mumby is Associate Professor of Communication at Purdue University. His primary research interests lie in the study of power and discourse as they occur in organizational settings. He is the author of *Communication and Power in Organizations* (1988), and editor of *Narrative and Social Control* (1993). He is currently working on a book that addresses the relationships among feminism, postmodernism, and organization studies.

Anita Pomerantz is an Associate Professor in the Department of Communication Sciences at Temple University. Her main interest areas include conversation analysis, language and social interaction, and naturalistic field methods. Since 1990, she has been investigating the training and supervision of professionals in medical settings. Her published research includes work on strategies of information-seeking (*Communication Monographs, Sociological Inquiry*), on methods of presenting evidence and making accusation (*Journal of Pragmatics, Human Studies, Sociology*), and on methodological issues of combining conversation analysis and ethnography (*Research on Language and Social Interaction, Communication Monographs, Western Journal of Speech Communication*).

Christina Schäffner is a lecturer in German in the Department of Languages and European Studies at Aston University, Birmingham. Until 1992 she was at the Saxon Academy of Arts and Sciences at Leipzig where she conducted research on political vocabulary, text linguistics, and translation studies. Her research interests are political discourse, metaphors, intercultural communication, and translation. Her publications include *Gibt es eine prototypische Wortschatzbeschreibung?* (editor, 1990), *Language and Peace* (co-edited with Anita Wenden, 1995), *Conceiving of Europe: Diversity in Unity* (co-edited with Andreas Musolff and Michael Townson, 1996), and articles in journals such as *Discourse and Society* and *Target*.

Geneva Smitherman is University Distinguished Professor of English and Director of the African American Language and Literacy Program at Michigan State University. She is author or co-author of eight books, among which is the influential study *Talking and Testifying* (1977), and over 100 papers dealing with African American English and language variation. 'Dr G.', as she is popularly known, is a culture warrior and educational activist who combines academic and community work.

Marja-Leena Sorjonen holds an Assistantship at the Department of Finnish Language, University of Helsinki. She is currently working in a project on

Finnish doctor–patient interaction, funded by the Finnish Foundation for Alcohol Studies (principal investigators Anssi Peräkylä and Marja-Leena Sorjonen). Her doctoral dissertation (forthcoming, University of California at Los Angeles) examines meanings and usages of response forms in Finnish conversation. Her research interests include the interplay between grammatical forms and interaction, and interaction in institutional settings.

Stella Ting-Toomey is Professor of Speech Communication at California State University, Fullerton. Her research, focusing on facework negotiation and cross-cultural conflict styles, has appeared in a wide variety of communication and intercultural journals. Her recent books include *The Challenge of Facework: Cross-Cultural and Interpersonal Issues* and *Building Bridges: Interpersonal Skills for a Changing World*. She has held major leadership roles in international communication associations. She has also been actively involved in conducting effective intercultural communication workshops in the US and abroad.

Denise Troutman is an Associate Professor at Michigan State University in the Departments of Linguistics and American Thought and Language. Her sociolinguistic training informs her research on the language patterns of African Americans in the United States. She is one of the first sociolinguists to focus on developing a description and theory of the linguistic behaviour of African American women.

Teun A. van Dijk is Professor of Discourse Studies at the University of Amsterdam. After earlier work in literary studies, text grammar and the psychology of text comprehension, his research in the 1980s focused on the study of news in the press and the reproduction of racism through various types of discourse. In each of these domains, he published several books. His present research in 'critical' discourse studies focuses on the relations between power, discourse and ideology. He is founder editor of the international journals *Text* and *Discourse and Society*, and editor of the four-volume *Handbook of Discourse Analysis* (1985). He has lectured widely in Europe and the Americas, and has been visiting professor at several universities in Latin America.

Candace West is professor of Sociology at the University of California, Santa Cruz. Her research has focused on the relationship between gender and face-to-face interaction, especially conversation. Her recent articles include 'Women's competence in conversation', 'Doing difference' (with Sarah Fenstermaker), and 'Rethinking "sex differences" in conversational topics: it's not what they say but how they say it'.

Anna Wierzbicka was born and educated in Poland. She is now Professor in Linguistics at the Australian National University. She uses semantic analysis as a key to the understanding of cognition, emotion and culture. Her theory of meaning combines a search for the universals of language and thought with a 'radical relativism' in the study of cultures. Her forthcoming book *Diversity and Universals: Emotions across Cultures* illustrates well this dual focus of her work, as does her 1992 book *Semantics, Culture and Cognition*. Among her other books are *Cross-Cultural Pragmatics* (1991), *Semantics: Primes and Universals* (1996) and *Understanding Cultures through their Key Words* (1997).

Ruth Wodak is Full Professor and Head of the Department of Applied Linguistics at the University of Vienna. Her areas of research include racism and ethnicism in discourse, communication in diverse institutions (medical, educational, bureaucratic), problems of discursive identity formation (on the individual, group and national levels) as well as gender studies. Very widely published, her books include *Die Sprache der 'Mächtigen' und 'Ohnmächtigen'* (with F. Menz, B. Lutz and H. Gruber, 1985), *Language, Power and Ideology* (1989) and (as co-author) *'Wir sind alle unschuldige Täter!' Diskurshistorische Studien zum Nachkriegsantisemitismus in Österreich* (1990). Her most recent books are *Disorders of Discourse* (1996) and (as co-author) *Zur diskursiven Konstruktion nationaler Identitäten* (1997).

Preface

This book offers a first introduction to discourse studies, a new cross-discipline that comprises the theory and analysis of text and talk in virtually all disciplines of the humanities and social sciences. For the main areas of discourse studies, the respective chapters feature literature reviews, explanations of theoretical frameworks and many concrete discourse analyses.

Besides providing a current state of the art, the chapters in this book have especially been written for newcomers to the field: students who take a special course in discourse analysis or choose this topic as part of their own discipline, as well as scholars from other disciplines who (finally) want to know what this study of discourse is all about. Esoteric jargon has been avoided in favor of a style of presentation that is accessible to all students and scholars in the humanities and social sciences.

There are several other introductions to the study of discourse. Most of them are now dated, or suffer from other limitations, such as very partial (and sometimes partisan) coverage of only a few domains of this new discipline. The chapters in the two volumes of the present book offer insight into a broad range of topics and areas, ranging from linguistic, stylistic and rhetorical approaches, to psychological and especially also social directions of research. Some deal with written texts, others with informal as well as institutional dialogue in a multitude of social contexts. Some focus on abstract structures of discourse, others on the orderly organization of ongoing talk by language users as well as on the broader social, political and cultural implications of discourse. The book highlights most important dimensions and levels of discourse description, and the authors do so from different theoretical perspectives. And in addition to more theoretical and descriptive approaches, critical and applied perspectives are represented here. In sum: this is the most complete introduction to discourse studies to date.

However, the study of discourse is a huge field, and it is being practiced by many scholars in many countries. Thus, despite their comprehensive set-up, even two volumes are unable to cover everything. For instance, there was no space for a chapter on the sound structures of discourse. Of the many discourse genres discussed as examples throughout the various chapters, only two important ones, namely argumentation and storytelling, could be dealt with in separate chapters.

The same is true for the various social domains and issues of discourse analysis: space limitations only allowed us a separate chapter on political discourse analysis, so that no special treatment could be given to, for example, medical, legal and educational discourse, among many other discourse domains. But again, the variety of the examples in the various chapters amply makes up for this limitation. Of the pressing social issues dealt with in separate chapters, we have focused on those of gender and ethnicity, although discourse is obviously involved in the reproduction of many other forms of domination and inequality, such as those of class, age, nationality, religion, language, sexual orientation, and so on.

The authors who contribute to this book are among the most prominent in the discipline, worldwide. Women and men from several countries were invited to join this project, so as to guarantee theoretical, analytical and cultural diversity – a criterion that is often ignored or impossible in one-author monographs. For the same reason, several chapters are co-authored by well-known senior as well as bright junior scholars in the field.

Despite this variety, however, many theoretical approaches, in many countries and many languages, are not represented by separate chapters here. Thus, as is so often the case, the requirement of English as a dominant academic language prohibited contributions from prominent discourse scholars who only write in, for example, Japanese, Chinese, Russian, French, Spanish, German and Italian, among other languages. Linguistic limitations and lack of cross-cultural data also prevented most authors from analysing more examples from more languages and more cultures, an aim that only an ideal book with multilingual authors can ever realize.

The book has been divided into two separate volumes that may be read independently of each other. The first focuses on the analysis of verbal structures and cognitive processes, the second on discourse as interaction in society. This division roughly corresponds to the traditional separation between the study of discourse in the humanities and psychology on the one hand, and in the social sciences on the other. As several chapters show, this division has become increasingly arbitrary, and there are several chapters that precisely aim to integrate these different approaches. Despite the inevitable specialization of each mature discipline, I hope that increasing integration will overcome the current divisions in the field.

I would like to see this book as an ongoing project, in which future editions in several languages follow the developments in the field, and in which new versions of chapters realize as much as possible the scholarly and social ideals of theoretical, analytical and cultural diversity. Readers from all over the world have a special responsibility in such an endeavor, and are invited to send me their critical comments as well as suggestions for improvement. I hope that teachers will provide feedback about their experiences with the use of this book in class. It is only in this way that the book may become a joint project of the growing global community of students and scholars of discourse.

Teun A. van Dijk

1

Discourse as Interaction in Society

Teun A. van Dijk

On 4 June 1991 the 102nd US House of Representatives debated the Civil Rights and Women's Equity in Employment Act, a bill submitted to the House by the Democratic majority, and violently opposed by Republicans. They argued that, whatever it explicitly formulated, its upshot would be quota and spurious litigation against employers. Here is a fragment of the debate, a contribution by Mr Rohrabacher, Representative from California (*Congressional Record*, vol. 137, no. 84, H3857):[1]

> MR HYDE. Mr Chairman, I am pleased to yield 3 minutes to the gentleman from California [Mr Rohrabacher].
> MR ROHRABACHER. Mr Chairman, there is already legal recourse for the victims of discrimination. Legal suits can be brought or, in employment cases, complaints can be filed with the EEOC [Equal Employment and Opportunities Commission]. We just don't need any more laws in this area. We have civil rights legislation and regulations up the ying-yang. Federal, State, county and local laws. The only ones who are going to benefit from this unneeded legislation are those who will benefit from unnecessary legislation. This is right, the lawyers are the ones that are going to benefit.
> Of course, politicians and political activists who cannot find work doing anything else also expect to gain from this legislation. And who will not be helped by this obtrusive civil rights bill? The less fortunate or our fellow citizens. That is who will not be helped.
> We have an underclass of people of all races trapped in poverty, living in wretched conditions, enveloped in helplessness and hopelessness. We need economic growth, business expansion, not more civil rights legislation that is redundant and useless.

This volume is about the kind of speech pronounced by Mr Rohrabacher in the US House of Representatives, as well as about many other forms of talk and text that characterize the myriad of informal and institutional situations that make up our societies. It focuses on the properties of what people say or write in order to accomplish social, political or cultural acts in various local contexts as well as within the broader frameworks of societal structure and culture.

Thus, Mr Rohrabacher is not merely uttering words or grammatical sentences of English. He does so in the context of a parliamentary debate between speakers of two political parties, at a specific date and historical moment. He is doing so in order to argue against a bill with the ultimate purpose to help defeat it. Many would agree that at the same time he is doing so also to defend the business community against (more) civil rights legislation, as may be expected from a conservative legislator. In sum, Mr Rohrabacher is doing many things by addressing the House, in fact much more than briefly summarized here. In this chapter, we'll use some of the properties of his speech in order to illustrate the discussion of some main concepts used in this volume. For now, the fragments of his speech just quoted illustrate the main point of this volume, namely that people do many social and political things while engaging in text and talk.

From Structure and Process to Social Action in Context and Society

The first volume of this book has shown that discourse may be described at various levels of *structure*. These structures are variously accounted for in, for example, syntax, semantics, stylistics and rhetoric, as well as in the study of specific genres, such as those of argumentation and story-telling. It was also shown that in addition to these more abstract structural approaches, discourse may be studied in terms of the actual cognitive (mental) *processes* of its production and comprehension by language users.

Thus, in the example of Mr Rohrabacher's speech, such an approach would explain how his sentences semantically hang together, such as by referring to different aspects of legislation. It would point out the rhetorical means of repetition, irony and metaphor (like 'being trapped in poverty'), or the stylistic implications of using popular expressions (such as 'ying-yang') in a formal speech. And it would of course pay special attention to the structures of the argumentation that so typically characterizes speeches in the House, and many other dimensions of structure that organize this fragment of speech, as well as text and talk in general. From another perspective, a cognitive study would examine the knowledge, attitudes and other mental representations that play a role in the production and understanding of his speech, and how his speech would influence the opinions of his audience on civil rights legislation.

Discourse as Action

Discourse, however, has another fundamental dimension that has received less attention in the first volume and that will be the special focus of this second volume, namely the fact that it is also a *practical, social* and *cultural*, phenomenon. As we have seen in our example of the parliamentary speech, language users engaging in discourse accomplish *social acts* and participate in *social interaction*, typically so in *conversation* and other forms of *dialogue*. Such interaction is in turn embedded in various social and cultural *contexts*, such as informal gatherings with friends or professional, institutional encounters such as parliamentary debates.

Such a focus on discourse as action in society does not mean that we are no longer interested in *structure*. On the contrary, the analysis of discourse as ongoing, social action also focuses on *order* and *organization*. Discursive language use consists not only of ordered series of words, clauses, sentences and propositions, but also of *sequences* of mutually related acts. Some of the structures and processes described in the first volume were also analysed from this more active point of view. For instance, stories and arguments not only have abstract structures and not only involve mental processes and representations (such as knowledge), but are at the same time a dimension of the communicative *acts* of storytelling and arguing by real language users in real situations, such as representatives arguing against civil rights legislation in the House.

In the same way, also word order, style or coherence, among many other properties of discourse, may be described not only as abstract structures, as we do in linguistics, but also in terms of the strategic *accomplishments* of language users in action: for instance, speakers and writers are constantly engaged in *making* their discourses coherent. And what holds for structures of discourse is also true for their mental processing and the representations needed for production and understanding: cognition has a social dimension and is acquired, used and changed in verbal and other forms of interaction.

Language Users and Context

Language users actively engage in text and talk not only as speakers, writers, listeners or readers, but also as *members* of social categories, groups, professions, organizations, communities, societies or cultures. As the chapters in this book show, they interact as women and men, blacks and whites, old and young, poor and rich, doctors and patients, teachers and students, friends and enemies, Chinese and Nigerians, and so on, and mostly in complex combinations of these social and cultural *roles* and *identities*. And conversely, by accomplishing discourse in social situations, language users at the same time actively *construct* and *display* such roles and identities.

Thus, in our example, Mr Hyde, Mr Rohrabacher and the Speaker of the house act and are addressed as men, that is, with the conventional form 'Mr'. The (unnamed) person addressed as 'Mr Chairman' implicitly acts as Speaker of the House, Mr Rohrabacher has the roles of current speaker, of Representative from California, of member of the Republican Party, among other roles and identities. And by saying and implying the kinds of things he does, Mr Rohrabacher is at the same time actually displaying and constructing himself as a conservative and as an opponent of more civil rights legislation.

As is also the case for Mr Rohrabacher in the House, speakers generally accomplish their actions in different communication settings, on the basis of various forms of social and cultural knowledge and other beliefs, with various aims, purposes and results. Their discourse usually shows or signals these features: relative to their contexts, talk and text are therefore said to be *indexical*. For instance, formal address forms in the House of Representatives may precisely index the formality of this legislative event. In sum, discourse manifests or expresses, and at the same time shapes, the many relevant properties of the sociocultural situation we call its *context*.

These examples of what typically constitutes the context of discourse also show that context analysis may be as complex and multi-layered as that of text and talk itself. Whereas the structures of an informal conversation between friends may be controlled by only a few contextual parameters (such as the setting, their knowledge and their social roles as friends), news reports, parliamentary debates or courtroom interaction may need to be analysed in relation to elaborate social, political and cultural conditions and consequences.

Talk and Text

The emphasis on the interactional and practical nature of discourse is naturally associated with a focus on language use as *spoken* interaction. Indeed, as is also the case in this volume, most work on discourse as action focuses on conversation and dialogue, that is, on *talk*.

It should, however, be obvious that writing and reading are also forms of social action, and most of what has been said so far therefore also applies to producing and understanding written *texts*. One crucial difference, however, is that talk (except conversations on the phone) takes place in *face-to-face* encounters between language users engaged in immediate interaction organized by changes of *turns*. That is, in talk speakers generally react to what the previous speaker has said or done. However, turn-taking during on-line e-mail 'talk' blurs even this distinction between written and spoken discourse.

Much everyday talk is *spontaneous*, and has many properties of impromptu speech: pauses, errors, repairs, false starts, repetitions, overlaps, and so on. Writing texts will mostly be more controlled, and especially on the computer writers have many means to correct and change text that was written before. That is, whereas spoken language is 'linear' or 'on-line', the act of writing may combine linear, on-line writing with other forms of 'composition', of going back and rewriting.

Yet, even this difference should not be taken absolutely: formal genres of oral discourse, such as academic speeches or lectures, as well as the speeches in the House like the one we have encountered here, may well be prepared just like written text and then simply read, with or without improvised, spontaneous parts. Conversely, notes, letters or e-mail may also be more or less spontaneous and show many elements of unprepared writing. More or less prepared or spontaneous speeches in the House may be recorded and then published as text in the *Congressional Record*. In sum, the study of discourse as action may not be identified simply with the analysis of spontaneous conversation, or even with spoken language: many genres combine monologue and dialogue, written and spoken parts, and may be more or less spontaneous.

Hierarchies of action

When writing or speaking, we of course accomplish the acts of writing and speaking, but the point is that *thereby* we accomplish such acts as making assertions and accusations, replying to questions, defending ourselves, being polite, or engaging in strategies of positive self-presentation. That is, discourse may be constituted by a complex *hierarchy of different acts* at different levels of abstractness and generality, whereby we do X *by* or *while* doing Y. Thus, while speaking, Mr Rohrabacher is at the same time representing California, arguing against a bill, and defending the position of the Republican Party.

Social Practices and Functions

Less used in conversation analysis, and more in social and political discourse analysis, the notion of *social practice* usually implies a broader social dimension of discourse than these various acts accomplished by language users in interpersonal interaction. For instance, an interaction between doctor and patient, between teacher and student, as well as a parliamentary debate or a courtroom session, are not only complex forms of institutional dialogue. They constitute, or are inherent parts of, the more complex discursive and social practices of teaching, providing health care, legislation and 'doing' justice. Similarly, an informal, everyday conversation about immigrants may at the same time be part of the complex social practice of communicating ethnic stereotypes, a practice which in turn may contribute to the reproduction of the social system of racism.

Thus, by arguing against the extension of civil rights legislation, Mr Rohrabacher at the same time serves the interests of the business community (also by explicitly advocating 'business expansion'), and indirectly contributes to a perpetuation of ethnic and gender inequality in the United States. Of course he will do so with a disclaimer, that is by presenting himself at the same time in a positive light, namely as being concerned about the 'underclass of people of all races trapped in poverty'.

These examples show that the study of discourse as action may focus on the interactive details of talk (or text) itself, but also take a broader perspective, and show the social, political or cultural *functions* of discourse within institutions, groups, or society and culture at large. As was the case for hierarchies of action, we may therefore also speak of a hierarchy of functions: an assertion may function as a verdict when made, at an appropriate moment, by a jury or a judge in court, and this verdict may in turn function as imparting justice (or injustice, for that matter) in a specific legal system.

It should be borne in mind though that although our *analysis* may identify different acts or social functions at various levels, language users are 'doing' all these things at the same time, sometimes even without being aware of that. An integrated social approach to discourse should not exclude one of these levels as less relevant or as less social: for instance, 'doing justice' is not limited to trials and their indictments or verdicts, but also involves taking turns, asking questions, making accusations, describing past actions, using a legal style, and so on. Also the more detailed micro-actions of complex social practices are *social* acts in their own right: they are acts *by which* the higher level social practices are being accomplished.

That is, both the more *local* and the more *global* aspects of discourse are involved in the accomplishment of social practices. Thus, in social discourse analysis we also find that social reality may be constituted and analysed anywhere between a more *micro* and a more *macro* level of description, for instance as (details of) acts and the interaction of social actors, and as what whole institutions or groups 'do', and how both thus contribute to the production and reproduction (or challenge) of *social structure*. Thus, at the micro level Mr Rohrabacher's speech is constitutive of a debate of the House, which in turn is part of the acts of legislation and government at a macro level. However, as is also the case in this volume, different researchers may of course at any one time rather focus on the micro or the macro levels of discourse and social organization. Increasingly, however, social discourse analysis precisely focuses on the interrelations between the local and the global properties of social text and talk.

Aims

We now have a first impression of a crucial dimension of discourse analysis, namely the fact that discourse should be studied not only as form, meaning and mental process, but also as complex structures and hierarchies of interaction and social practice and their functions in context, society and culture.

The chapters that follow provide the details of some major approaches to the study of discourse in society. In order to understand some of the concepts, presuppositions, concerns and aims of these chapters, I shall try to go beyond the 'first impression' given above, and briefly introduce some of the fundamental concepts used in the sociocultural analysis of discourse, including approaches not represented in this volume.

The point of this conceptual analysis is to discuss notions that are needed to establish *theoretical* links between discourse and society. We may of course simply follow common sense and assume that discourse is a form of action and interaction and hence declare discourse to be social. But the few examples briefly referred to above suggest that the links between discourse and society are much more complex, and need theoretical analysis in their own right. The concepts I have selected for further analysis have been chosen because they regularly appear in several chapters of this volume and in many other social approaches to discourse.

1   *Action*   We have defined discourse as action, but what exactly is action and what makes discourses a form of social interaction?

2 *Context* Social discourse analysis typically studies discourse in context. However, although frequently used, the notion of context is not always analysed in as much detail as text and talk, although contexts are so to speak the interface between discourse as action on the one hand and social situations and social structures on the other. So what exactly is context?

3 *Power* Both action and discourse contexts feature participants who are members of different social groups. Power is a key notion in the study of group relations in society. If any feature of context and society at large impinges on text and talk (and vice versa), it is power. It is therefore important, especially for more critical approaches to discourse, to briefly analyse this fundamental notion.

4 *Ideology* At another level, ideologies also establish links between discourse and society. In a sense, ideologies are the cognitive counterpart of power. As is the case for social knowledge, ideologies monitor how language users engage in discourse as members of (dominant, or dominated, or competing) groups or organizations, and thus also try to realize social interests and manage social conflict. At the same time, discourse is needed in the reproduction of the ideologies of a group.

Although fundamental, these are not the only notions that relate discourse with the many dimensions or structures of society. If we recall the brief characterization of context given above, other important properties of the discourse–society interface might have been discussed, for example groups, roles, knowledge, rules, norms, goals, organizations and institutions, among others. However, the concepts discussed below allow us to pay at least some attention to these other dimensions of society that define how discourses are social. Note that the literature, in several disciplines, that deals with these fundamental notions is vast, so that we can barely highlight some of their relevant features. Further theoretical details, discourse examples and references are provided in the chapters that follow.

Action

Few notions are used more often in this volume than the concepts of *act, action* and *interaction*. As is the case for the notion of discourse itself (see Chapter 1, Volume 1), these notions are hardly problematic in their everyday, common-sense uses, but theoretically rather complex as soon as we start to look at them more closely.

Intentionality

Intuitively, actions are the kinds of things people *do*. However, people do many things that we would hesitate to call actions, such as falling from the stairs, dreaming, or seeing something. Conversely, in some situations we may socially, morally or legally *act* although we don't *do* anything, for instance when we keep silent, remain seated, or refrain from smoking.

At first analysis, this observation suggests that 'doings' or 'activities' (or refraining from doing something) by human beings tend to be called 'acts' only if they are (interpreted as) *intentional*. Falling and dreaming are events of our body or mind that 'occur' to us, but which we usually do not do on purpose: they are largely beyond our *control*. Moreover, most actions are intentionally accomplished in order to realize or bring about something else, that is, other actions, events, situations, or states of mind: they have *goals* that make these actions meaningful or have a 'point', and that make their actors appear to be *purposeful*.

According to this analysis, *discourse* is obviously a form of action, as we have claimed before. It is mostly intentional, controlled, purposeful human activity: we do not usually speak, write, read or listen accidentally or just to exercise our vocal chords or hands. Or if we do, like speaking in our sleep or under hypnosis, this is a rather special case – in which we may not be held responsible for what we do.

The same is true for many of the higher level acts we accomplish *by* speaking or writing: asserting or asking something, accusing someone, promising something, avoiding an answer, telling a story, defending ourselves, being polite or persuading an audience, are among the many things we 'do with words' that we usually accomplish more or less intentionally and purposefully. These actions may have very different properties, but they are all *communicative acts*. Although intentions and purposes are usually described as mental representations, they are socially relevant because they manifest themselves as social activity, and because they are ascribed or attributed to us by others who interpret this activity: others thus construct or define us as more or less rational *persons* and at the same time as social *actors*.

Perspective

If we push this analysis somewhat further, we soon run into difficulties. That is, people *do* a lot when using language or accomplishing text or talk, but at some level it is not so clear anymore whether such 'doings' are intentional or under their control. Take insults, for instance. Undoubtedly, an insult is a communicative act, at least for the recipient, who will typically hear what we say as an insult if he or she assumes that it is our purpose to insult. We may, however, dramatically disagree, and deny any such purpose, and such disagreement may be the core of a familiar social conflict. In other words, we here encounter discursive doings that may be acts only for recipients, for example if the speaker categorically denies having accomplished the act of insulting. We may be sure for instance that Mr Rohrabacher would be offended to read that at least some people in his audience (and probably many women and minorities who would hear about what he said) would interpret his speech as contributing to gender and ethnic inequality in the United States.

That is, the analysis of action may depend on the *perspective* we take, namely that of the speaker or that of the recipient. For a speaker, awareness, consciousness, intentionality and purposes may be associated with 'real' action. For the recipients what count are what is said and its social consequences, that is, what is being *heard* or *interpreted* as (intentional) action. That is, more or less in the same way as language users assign meanings to discourses, they ascribe intentions to other people, and thus define them as social actors. This is one of the reasons why most social discourse analysis focuses less on speakers, and even less on their (non-observable) intentions, than on how discursive doings can be reasonably heard or interpreted, that is, inferred as actions from what is actually said, shown or displayed. In such analysis, it is usually the perspective and the interpretation of the other(s) that prevail: discursive activity becomes socially 'real' if it has real social consequences.

Thus, people do many things 'with' discourse that they are not aware of, that they do not intend, that is beyond their control, or that is only interpreted as such by others. As is the case with all social action, we may nevertheless be responsible for some of such less intentional acts, simply because we *could* or *should* have known about their possible or likely social consequences if we had thought about them a bit more. Thus Mr Rohrabacher will of course deny that his speech contributes to social inequality, but it would be much more difficult for him to argue against the fact that if this civil rights bill is defeated, gender and ethnic discrimination in the US will be much harder to fight in court than if it is adopted.

Speakers may thus be expected to think at least about the more likely implications and consequences for others of what they do with talk and text. *Responsibility* for discursive action may involve norms and values about how 'thoughtful' they should be. In sum, intentions and purposes that are ascribed to discourse may be of variable scope: some consequences of text and talk are actually and inherently (understood as) intended, purposeful and under control of the speaker, whereas others are less so.

Implications, Consequences and Components

By making these statements about the theory of action I intentionally explain something to my readers, and thus intentionally engage in academic discourse or teaching, and thus hope to educate others, and contribute to the social reproduction of knowledge. But when writing or speaking we are usually only aware of the first 'levels' of such action, and may need more thought, or indeed sociological analysis, in order to understand all the implications or consequences of what we do.

Similar remarks hold not only for the (following) *consequences* of discourse for recipients, or for their (higher level) *implications* in society, but also for their *components*. If discourse is an action, it might be assumed that the production or comprehension of sentences, words, style, rhetoric or argumentation should also be understood as action. In order to accomplish discourse as social action, we need to accomplish not only illocutionary acts (or speech acts) such as assertions and promises, but also locutionary or graphical acts of actual speech or writing, as well as propositional acts such as meaning something when we speak or write (see Chapter 2, Volume 2, by Shoshana Blum-Kulka).

So far so good. But what about the details of pronunciation, syntax and semantics? Is 'having an accent' an act, or rather something that occurs to us (even if we may consciously 'do' an accent sometimes)? And the same may be asked for 'using' a specific word order, or selecting a specific word, or establishing coherence, or taking a next turn in a conversation. In other words, when analysing overall discursive acts into their components, we do not always wind up with acts that are (understood as) intentional, even if we *may* do them intentionally in some situations. That is, in the analysis of discourse as action, we may also need to assume some level of (component) *basic actions*, below which linguistic or mental activity is no longer intentional but more or less automatic and 'below' our control.

Interaction

The next step makes things even more complex: indeed, when are the actions of several people defined as *interaction*, and not simply as subsequent but unrelated acts of different people? Again, do people have to be intentionally interacting and have the purpose of acting with, for or against someone else? Must we be aware of the other person, and actually hear or see him or her? Do we need to *understand* the other's actions in order to interact with him or her? Indeed, how do we know what others want or intend, and how do we manage such *mutual knowledge*? Do others have to *cooperate*, at least in some respects? And if so, what are the rules or criteria of such cooperation? Do others have to *react* to our act before we can speak of interaction? For instance, is simply greeting another person a form of interaction if the other does not greet back or otherwise acknowledge us? If social actors do act with and for each other, how exactly do they manage to *coordinate* these actions into interaction? And when exactly does the interaction begin or end? Does it have to be in the same situation, and more or less at the same time? Is a response next year to a question of today still part of the 'same' interaction? If all of Mr Rohrabacher's hearers walk out on him but he continues to speak, can we then still call his speech a contribution to a debate, and would there still be a session of the House?

We will leave all these questions unanswered here, but they suggest that some of the familiar notions used in this book may need much conceptual, cognitive, social and cultural analysis, an analysis which can, however, be offered only partly in an introductory book. Our first steps in the analysis of action, and the following questions about the further complexities in the definition of interaction, merely show that our seemingly unproblematic initial claim that discourse is a form of social action and interaction involves much more than common sense.

Context

Above, as well as in the chapters that follow, the notion of *context* is used many times. As we already suggested, the concept of context is also not as straightforward as its common-sense uses in everyday life might suggest. Intuitively, it seems to imply some kind of environment or circumstances for an event, action or discourse. Something we need to know about in order to properly understand the event, action or discourse. Something that functions as background, setting, surroundings, conditions or consequences.

In the study of discourse as action and interaction, contexts are crucial. Indeed, the main distinction between abstract discourse analysis and social discourse analysis is that the latter takes the context into account. It was provisionally suggested that this context may involve such parameters as participants, their roles and purposes, as well as properties of a setting, such as time and place. Discourse is being produced, understood and analysed relative to such context features. It is therefore taken that social discourse analysis defines text and talk as *situated*: discourse is described as taking place or as being accomplished 'in' a social situation.

However, not all properties of a social situation are part of the context of discourse. Human participants seem to be crucial elements of contexts, and so are some of their action roles, such as being speakers and recipients of verbal acts. Other properties of participants are often (but not always) relevant, such as being a man or a woman, being young or old, or having power, authority or prestige. We take these properties to be contextual because they may influence the production or interpretation of (the structures of) text and talk, such as the use of pronouns or special verbs, the choice of topics or the use of forms of politeness. In sum, we may provisionally define a context as the structure of those properties of the social situation that are systematically (that is, not incidentally) *relevant* for discourse. Let us examine some of these relevant context features.

Participants

Although there are social and cultural variations of contextual relevance, it was assumed that some situational features are always or often relevant, and some others seldom or never. Gender, age, class, education, social position, ethnicity and profession of participants are often relevant, as many chapters in this book show. On the other hand, height, weight, eye color or having a driver's license are seldom or never relevant. The same is true for social roles: some roles and social relations are often relevant, such as being friend or foe, powerful or powerless, dominant or dominated, whereas others seem to have less systematic impact on text and talk and its understanding, such as being first or last, moviegoer or theatre lover. We have already seen that in order to understand and to analyse the speech of Mr Rohrabacher, we need to know that he is a member of the House of Representatives, a member of the Republican Party and a delegate from California. Indeed, the previous speaker explicitly addresses him in terms of this last role, and he is able to take the floor only because he is a member of the House. In other words, relevant properties of participants constitute contextual *conditions* of specific properties of discourse.

In sum, participant categories are often part of the theoretical definition as well as of the common-sense understanding of context: people *adapt* what they say – and how they say it, and how they interpret what others say – to at least some of their roles or identities, and to the roles of other participants. This is precisely the point of context analysis: discourse structures *vary* as a *function* of the structures of context, and may at the same time be *explained* in terms of these context structures. And conversely, contexts may themselves be shaped and changed as a function of discourse structures. In sum, we study contexts not merely for their own sake, as social scientists would do, but essentially also to better understand discourse.

Setting

There is little dispute that context must also embody a number of 'setting' dimensions of a social situation, such as time, place or speaker position and perhaps some other special circumstances of the physical environment. As for time, many discourse genres are 'set' for specific time slots, as is the case for meetings, sessions or classes. Mr Rohrabacher is allocated exactly three minutes by the previous speaker.

And as to location: some participants are typically more in front (like teachers and lecturers) or higher placed (like judges or Speakers of the House) than others, and will signal this with appropriate verbs, pronouns or other expressions, such as the well-known request 'Please approach the bench!' directed by a judge to attorneys in US courts. More generally, deictic expressions of place and time (today, tomorrow, here, there, etc.) need these contextual parameters in order to be interpretable.

The setting may also be private or public, informal or institutional, as when discourses are marked by the fact that they are accomplished at home or in the office, in court, in hospital or in the classroom. Some discourse genres can only be validly accomplished in such an institutional environment. An accusation is a legally valid indictment only in court. Many utterances of doctors and teachers would not be comprehensible outside the operating room or the classroom. Mr Rohrabacher's speech is only part of a parliamentary debate when pronounced on the floor of the House. In general, institutional environments are so closely linked to institutional discourse genres that they multiply interact with the structures of text and talk.

Props

Institutional contexts further feature typical props or objects that may be relevant for formal text or talk, such as uniforms, flags, special furniture, instruments, and so on. The courtroom, the classroom and the newsroom, among many 'sites' of special discourse genres, are full of such typical objects. Note though that while they are undeniably relevant in the social situation, they become defining parts of the context only when their presence is systematically marked in the verbal interaction or discourse genres of such a situation. Just talking *about* them of course does not count, because in that case anything that can be talked about would be part of the context. Systematic relevance thus means that special structural properties of talk, such as different word order, different style, special speech acts, etc., are required in the presence of such situational objects.

Thus, meetings or sessions may sometimes only be closed with a special formula and the use of a gavel; christening someone requires (holy) water, and christening a ship a bottle of champagne. Probably a phone is crucial in the context of a conversation on the phone, and a computer terminal or PC relevant as part of the context of interaction by e-mail. Mr Rohrabacher almost certainly speaks into a microphone, as do most speakers for large audiences. However, by definition, the presence of microphones is a systematic context feature of a parliamentary debate only if they play a role in the very organization of such talk. Thus, in the Dutch Parliament, for instance, there is a special microphone, called the 'interruption microphone', which does seem to have just such a role: it only serves to allow special changes of turns, namely interruptions.

Action

What else do contexts and their participants need for text and talk to be comprehensible, appropriate or valid? Obvious candidates are the other, non-verbal acts being accomplished in the situation. Most directly involved, while in a sense part of the communicative event itself, are such non-verbal meaningful acts as gestures, face-work and body movement. An accusation may be accompanied by an angry face, and a command with an outstretched arm; military speech acts may require salutes, and some speech acts (like oaths) need to be performed while standing up and raising one's hand. Indeed, Mr Rohrabacher almost certainly was standing up when pronouncing his speech, and his eventual vote against this bill will probably involve raising his hand.

But also the action structure in which discourse is so to speak structurally embedded is obviously relevant in the description and understanding of context. Doctor–patient interaction is not limited to talk, but also involves examination and other medical acts that make such talk relevant. A host of institutional genres thus combine text, talk and other acts, in such a way that discourse may be a structural condition or a consequence of such acts.

Knowledge and Intentionality

The analysis of action given above suggests various socio-cognitive dimensions, such as socially shared or personal knowledge and other beliefs. All explanations about implied meanings, presuppositions or interpretations of discourse or language users crucially assume some form of knowledge of the participants. Similarly, understanding action, as we have seen, presupposes that we also attribute intentions, plans or purposes to speakers or writers. While being relevant properties of participants, we should also admit them to the definition of the context.

Thus, without knowledge of English and knowledge and other beliefs about US society, Mr Rohrabacher would be unable to say what he does, and we would be unable to understand what he says or implies. And since he does so with obvious purposes (namely, to get this bill defeated), such intentions or purposes also need to be included in the context, as well as many other relevant beliefs, such as his attitudes towards civil rights, women and minorities. These are not simply cognitive components of the context that explain what he says or how he does so, but rather (also) social ones: it is thus how his audience, and we as analysts, understand him and make sense of what he says. Such understanding (or lack of understanding) may routinely be expressed in talk itself, as in 'You don't know what you are talking about!', or 'Why are you telling me that?'

Higher Level Action

Contexts need not only structural elements at the same level as discourse, such as other acts, but also a *higher level* definition of the *whole situation* or event. An indictment and a verdict thus make sense only as structural parts of a trial. That is, discourse as action may be structurally relevant as part of higher level events and actions such as a class, an interrogation, a visit to the doctor, a board meeting or a press conference. Most of the examples of talk and text studied in this volume are studied with respect to their contextual functionality at this higher level.

Without aiming to account for all possible details of contexts, this discussion confirms what we assumed above: context analysis may be as complex as discourse analysis itself. Depending on our theoretical perspective, we may limit the definition of context to a small number of immediately relevant features of participants, settings and other acts.

But there is of course no *a priori* limit to the scope and level of what counts as being relevant context: a verdict is defined as part of a trial, which, however, in turn takes its social and legal meaning in a system of justice, and the same is true for teaching in education and parliamentary debates in legislation and, even more broadly, within a democratic system. A speech may be intended and understood as a crucial part of a campaign, which in turn is functional in a system of elections, and so on. And a speech like Mr Rohrabacher's, besides contributing to the higher level act of legislation, was suggested to also contribute in a specific way to race and gender relations in the United States. Interpreting his speech as prejudiced only makes sense within that broader context. In other words, contexts thus naturally take their place in complex institutional and societal arrangements, structures and systems.

Local and Global Contexts

Many discourses find their ultimate rationality and functionality in social and cultural structures. For this reason, it makes analytical sense to distinguish between *local* or *interactional* context and *global* or *societal* context. These are not easy to delimit exactly. Intuitively, the local context of a trial, and its relevance for the structures of the discourse genres being performed in such a court session, might rather easily be defined (by specific participants, actions, time and place) and thus distinguished from the complex and more abstract system of criminal justice.

This may be true for many forms of institutional talk and text, but what about everyday conversations, storytelling, jokes or many other mundane forms of discourse? Like all talk they are locally occasioned and contextualized, but are such contexts always embedded in a more global, societal order or situation? Is such a global situation relevant for discourse, so that it can be defined as a global *context?*

Examples discussed in this volume suggest it often is. Stories in corporate business may be told in order to manage a company and to reproduce corporate culture and ideologies (see Chapter 4, Volume 2, by Paul Drew and Marja-Leena Sorjonen, and Chapter 7, Volume 2, by Dennis K. Mumby and Robin P. Clair). They may also be relevant in racist arguments that reproduce prejudice, racism and hence social inequality, as we also have suggested in our first analysis of Mr Rohrabacher's speech (see also Chapter 6, Volume 2, by Teun A. van Dijk, Stella Ting-Toomey, Geneva Smitherman and Denise Troutman). Similarly, whether simple or elaborate, greetings and forms of address make sense in the complex system of politeness, deference and power that defines each community and culture (see Chapter 9, Volume 2, by Cliff Goddard and Anna Wierzbicka). In sum, local discourse and context is often produced and understood as a functional part of global contexts. This dependence should therefore also be studied in social discourse analysis.

Constructing Contexts

There are two further aspects of context analysis that need to be attended to. First, no more than discourse itself, contexts are 'fixed' or 'given'. They may be flexible and changing and may need to be negotiated, especially in conversational interaction (see Chapter 3, Volume 2, by Anita Pomerantz and B.J. Fehr). Discourses may be conditioned by them, but also influence and construct them. That is, discourses are a structural part of their contexts and their respective structures mutually and continually influence each other.

Secondly, contexts, just like discourse, are not objective in the sense that they consist of social facts that are understood and considered relevant in the same way by all participants. They are interpreted or constructed, and strategically and continually *made* relevant by and for participants.

From a more cognitive perspective, one might indeed say that contexts are (socially based) *mental constructs*, or models in memory. Since meaning and other discourse properties are also mentally managed, this also explains the vital link between discourse and context: as subjective representations, mental models of contexts may thus directly monitor the production and comprehension of talk and text. Indeed, without such subjectivity of language users and their minds, the 'same' social contexts would have the same effect on all language users in the same situation, which they obviously have not. That is, besides their customary social definition, contexts also need a cognitive definition in order to account for personal variation and subjectivity and in order to explain how social structures can influence discourse structures 'via' the mind of social members.

Trivially, the objective social facts of my age or my profession do not *cause* my interlocutors to use the pronouns of polite address. Rather it is their socially based but subjective interpretation or construction of these social 'facts' that are used as *reasons* to be polite. It is at this point that cognition and context meet, and indeed become mutually relevant. Hence also the frequent reference made in the chapters in this volume to the fact that language users are not simply engaging in discourse and thereby acting in some situation, but are basically trying to *make sense* of it.

Finally, it should be stressed that contexts may need more components than discussed above. For some of these components it is theoretically not entirely clear whether we should consider them as properties of discourse itself or of its context. Take for instance the *modality* of communication, such as whether discourse is spoken or written (or recorded on disk) and indeed the whole (multi-media) 'environment' of talk or text. The same may be asked about the *genres* of discourse, such as stories, news reports or everyday conversations. And what about the *rules* and *norms* that govern the discourse? Thus, if we take rules as social, then they could be part of the global social context, but if we take them as some kind of knowledge, we may also see them as (socially shared, but) mental properties of participants. In sum, some properties of situated discourse may be part of a theory of context, others of a theory of discourse structure, depending on our perspective or theory. Indeed, some theories may treat them as properties of the relationship between discourse and context.

Power

One of the concepts that organize many of the relationships between discourse and society is that of *power*. Several chapters in this volume implicitly or explicitly deal with power, for example:

1 *Corporate power* in the dominant discourses of a business company (see
   Chapter 7 by Dennis K. Mumby and Robin P. Clair)
2 *Male power* in sexist discourse (see Chapter 5 by Candace West,
   Michelle M. Lazar and Cheris Kramarae, and also Chapter 7)
3 *White power* in racist text and talk or forms of counter-power or
   resistance in the discourse of African American women (see Chapter 6
   by Teun A. van Dijk, Stella Ting-Toomey, Geneva Smitherman and
   Denise Troutman, and Chapter 10 by Norman Fairclough and Ruth
   Wodak)
4 *Political power* in the discourses of governments, parliaments, dictators,
   dominant parties, politicians, and political institutions (see Chapter 8 by
   Paul Chilton and Christina Schäffner).

In other words, if we want to understand some of the fundamental functions of discourse in interaction and society, further insight into the nature
of power is needed. Since the literature on the concept of power is vast, we
only highlight some of its main characteristics and then especially examine
the ways discourse is related to power.

The kind of power we focus on is *social* power, defined as a specific
relation between social groups or institutions. That is, we here ignore
various forms of personal power between individuals, unless such power is
based on group membership.

Control of Action and Mind

The explanatory concept we use to define social power is that of *control*.
One group has power over another group if it has some form of control
over the other group. More specifically, such control may pertain to the
actions of the (members of the) other group: we control others if we can
make them act as we wish (or prevent them from acting against us).

The question then is *how* we are able to make others act that way. One
option is plain *force*: we force others bodily to do what we want, whether
they like it or not. Such *coercive* power is typical for say the power of the
police, the military or of men with respect to women and children. In this
case, force is a power *resource* (or power *basis*) of the powerful group.

Much power in society, however, is not coercive, but rather *mental*.
Instead of controlling the activities of others directly by bodily force, we
control the mental basis of all action, as explained above, namely people's
intentions or purposes. Typically, powerful groups may make others act as
desired simply by *telling* them to do so, for instance by commands, orders
or similar directive speech acts. In other words, one of the crucial means
used to influence others people's minds so that they will act as we want is
text or talk. We here have a first, rather obvious, relationship between
power and discourse.

Commands 'work' if other people comply with them. That is, if
recipients do what we want. Our command has the function to let them

know what we want. Explicitly or implicitly, we may at the same time communicate or presuppose that there is no alternative but to comply: if you don't do X then we may do Y, and you probably would like that much less than to comply with our command. Thus, the exercise of power limits the options for action, and thereby the freedom, of others. Moreover, usually we will only thus exercise our power over others if we assume that the others will not act as desired our of their own free will.

This simple analysis yields one basic form of the power–discourse link. Note that in the exercise of this kind of discursive power, we need three elements: discourse, action and cognition (intention, purpose, motivation, etc.). A discourse (such as a command) is being understood in such a way that actors form an intention to act as we want and it is this intention that is being acted upon. (Of course, the mental representations and processes involved here are much more complex than our elementary summary of them suggests.)

In the example of exercising power through commands, the power resource that allows (members of) a powerful group to exercise its power is symbolic, namely special *access* to special speech acts, such as commands, orders or other directives. A police officer, a judge, a teacher, a superior or a parent may thus have special access to directives, whereas friends, peers or subordinates have not. Obviously, besides discourse, such powerful groups also have other power resources, such as social position, access to force, and the authority derived from these. That is, symbolic power resources may be based on socio-economic, legal or political ones.

Persuasive Power

In discourse analysis, this elementary case of controlling the minds of others, so that they will act as we want, needs further extension towards the more complex and sometimes more subtle ways people control others through text and talk. Instead of ordering others, we may *persuade* them to do something. In this case, compliance is based not on an implicit threat, but rather on arguments or other forms of persuasion.

But here also, the option to act as required is chosen because the alternative (not to act, or to act differently) is less attractive for the actor. As in the case of commands, the alternative may have unwanted consequences, such as being given less (access to) wanted social resources controlled by the powerful group: money, salary, a job, a house, and other material resources, or more symbolic resources such as knowledge, education, residence, or esteem.

Thus, parents, bosses or teachers will often simply *ask* or even *suggest* others to do something for them, without any explicit threat, and their power precisely consists in the fact that others will tend to comply in order to avoid negative consequences. The discourses of control may get quite subtle in this case. But here also, discourse (or other acts of control) enacts power if it presupposes control over a material or symbolic power resource.

If we return for a moment to Mr Rohrabacher and his speech, we also encounter various forms of power. That is, as a member of the House he has the power to 'take' the floor (and the Speaker of the House the power to give or deny permission to do so on any specific occasion). He thus has special access to the symbolic resource of influencing other House members, and (through the media) other citizens, with his arguments. Of course, he has no direct sanctions when his opponents, the Democrats, do not accept his arguments. However, he obviously also represents corporate business, and by implying that this bill is 'bad for business' (except that of lawyers), he does of course invoke corporate power by spelling out dire economic consequences for the country in general, and for the poor inner cities in particular, if this bill should be adopted.

Hegemony and Consensus

Mind control and the actions that derive from it may be based on even more subtle and indirect forms of text and talk. Instead of letting others know what we want through commands, requests, suggestions or advice, we may shape their minds in such a way that they will act as we want out of their own free will. That is, the discourses of a powerful group may be such that others will form the intentions and accomplish the acts as if they were totally without constraints, and consistent with their own wants and interests. If our discourse can make people believe in this way and we thus indirectly control their actions such that they are in our best interest, we have successfully manipulated them through text and talk. In this case, the term *hegemony* is often used to refer to social power: hegemonic power makes people act as if it were natural, normal, or simply a consensus. No commands, requests or even suggestions are necessary.

Again, the crucial question is how such forms of hegemonic, discursive power are being implemented. Obviously, we need to know much about the subtleties of discourse structures, as well as about those of the mind, action, and society, in order to be able to describe and explain how text and talk may thus manipulate people into doing what the powerful group prefers. This may happen through education, information campaigns, propaganda, the media, and many other forms of public discourse (see Chapter 10, Volume 2, by Norman Fairclough and Ruth Wodak).

For instance, Western governments, by 'informing' citizens about the allegedly dire economic and social consequences of immigration, may influence popular attitudes about immigration. These attitudes may in turn influence the intentions or motivations of people to act as the government or other elites prefer – expressing resentment and staging protests against immigration, so that the politicians can claim that there is no 'popular support' for liberal immigration policies. This may seem cynical, but this is largely how discourse about immigration is managed in many Western countries (see Chapter 6, Volume 2, by Teun A. van Dijk, Stella Ting-Toomey, Geneva Smitherman and Denise Troutman).

It should be emphasized that this control can hardly to total: people use many sources of information, and also otherwise may make up 'their own mind', and often disregard the discourse of the powerful. That is, mind control is only possible under very specific conditions, for example when there are no other sources of information and opinion, and when the preferred attitudes, intentions and actions are not obviously inconsistent with the interests of those who are thus manipulated. In other words, in real social situations the exercise of power through discourse is much more complex than suggested here.

Access

This analysis roughly shows that in order to exercise hegemonic power, and in order to establish a consensus, powerful groups control the actions of others through controlling the minds (knowledge, attitudes, ideologies) of groups, and they largely do so through discourse. This, however, pre-supposes another fundamental aspect of the relations between power and discourse, namely *access*. Indeed, as suggested before, the powerful have access to and control over not only scarce material resources but also symbolic ones, such as knowledge, education, fame, respect and indeed public discourse itself. That is, discourse is not only a *means* in the enactment of power, as are other actions of the powerful, but at the same time itself a power *resource*. Thus, the various power elites control (the access to) many types of public discourse, for instance in politics and the administration, the media, education, and so on.

In order to control other minds through control over discourse, the powerful also need to control the most effective discursive features to influence others. Such control is not limited to content or form, but also applies to the context, as analysed above. For instance, a socio-economic analysis is required if we need to explain how ownership of the means of discursive production (such as of the mass media) is related to control over discourse. Again, the simplest case here is based on directives: media owners (or the state, or the party, etc.) may tell editors what (not) to publish, or else.

Although this happens daily all around the world, it is crude and resented by journalists, who cherish the freedom of the press. In most democratic societies, therefore, controlling the media and its public discourses is much more indirect and subtle. Indeed, as we have seen for hegemony above, it is much more effective if we can let journalists believe that they are free to write what they want, but at the same time manipulate their minds in such a way that in fact they write (more or less) what we want.

That is, the relation between discourse, mind and power as explained above now also applies in the production phases of public text and talk: either speak and write directly to the audience (through political meetings, own publications, etc.) or provide such discourses to journalists (through documentation, press conferences, reports, etc.) that they will naturally write what you want, or at least will consider the issues or topics you find crucial (crime, immigration, etc.) as more negative and newsworthy than others (racism, sexism, poverty, etc.). If the media hire journalists who have similar ideologies and attitudes as you have, then no mind control may be needed at all: there simply will be a consensus about what is interesting, what is newsworthy, and how topics and issues need to be dealt with. Thus, by continuing to refer to the scare word 'quota' in Congress, Mr Rohrabacher and his Republican colleagues, as well as President Bush, were able to draw on the general consensus against quota.

In sum, preferential access to public discourse is a vital power resource. This access is managed in many subtle ways, beyond ownership and direct control of discourse content. Access may be routinely organized and institutionalized, for example through information campaigns, interviews, press conferences, press releases and other discourse genres directed at journalists. Thus, seemingly objective information may be released in many different ways so that it will seem credible and will actually be believed and reproduced. What holds for the media is more generally true for the control of discourse by powerful social groups.

Controlling Context

Given the analysis of context provided above, we may assume first that if we control context, we also control much of the structures of discourse. Thus, the powerful may control the nature of the overall communicative event, for example by imposing its definition: this is a hearing and not an interrogation; this is a press conference and not an indoctrination session of the president; etc. The powerful may similarly control the context by controlling the participants and their roles: who may be present, who may speak or listen, and who may speak (or must speak) as what. For instance, a secretary will probably be required to be present at traditional board meetings, but only in a listening role, that is in order to prepare the minutes, or to respond to questions when asked, but not to actively participate in corporate decision making. Similarly, those in power may define the overall aims or goals of the event, schedule it (set time and place), provide the agenda, and control other circumstances of text and talk. As we have seen, the Speaker of the US House of Representatives thus controls parts of the context by distributing turns at talk. In sum, the first set of strategies that are used to control public discourse as a means to exercise social power consists in controlling the parameters of the context.

Controlling Discourse Structures

The next set of strategies pertains to talk and text structures themselves, including preferences for a specific language or genre. Nationalist policies may demand non-Anglo US citizens not to speak in Spanish, for instance, and judges may tell defendants to 'answer the question' instead of telling their own versions of their experiences.

Similar forms of more overt and more subtle control may extend to all levels and dimensions of discourse: graphical layout, intonation, lexical choice, word order, details of local meanings, coherence, topics, rhetorical devices, speech acts and so on.

The examples, also discussed in this volume, are manifold and need not be spelled out here. Men may control topics or topic change in conversations with women. White elites may prefer some topics or headlines (for example, about minorities as criminals, immigration as a big problem) over others (such as racism) in the media, textbooks, scholarly research and public policy documents. Besides such control over overall content, even local details of meaning and form may be crucial, such as when to use the words 'terrorist' or 'freedom fighter', or the use of specific metaphors (for example, immigration as 'invasion') over others.

Thus, the powerful will usually tend to emphasize all information that portrays them positively, and to de-emphasize the information that does so negatively, and the opposite will be the case for the discourse representation of their opponents, enemies or any other outgroup. These may be communists, Arabs, fundamentalists, drug barons or others, depending on the historical and political situation. Thus Mr Rohrabacher presents himself and his party as concerned about the people 'trapped in poverty', and later in his speech claims that 'Our hearts break and we really feel a terrible pain for these people who are living a painful existence.' At the same time he represents his opponents in negative terms, that is as 'politicians and political activists who cannot find work', and later as 'so-called liberal leaders'.

The powerful are thus able not only to control communicative events, but also to set the agenda, to define the situation and even the details of the ways groups, actions and policies are represented. If recipients have no alternative information or no access to other discourses, the credibility and persuasive rhetoric of public discourse may be such that many recipients will adopt the beliefs expressed by these biased discourses.

Closing the Circle of Control

We have come full circle in the analysis of the discursive exercise of power and are back where we started with the discussion of power and discourse: power is control of action, which requires control of personal and social cognitions, which presupposes control of public discourse, which is possible only through special forms of access, which may in turn be based on political, economic, social or academic power resources (position, ownership, income, knowledge, expertise, etc.). Traditional power, based on force (the military, the police), money (corporations), or political position, may have become less compelling, in much contemporary discourse directed at skeptical gatekeepers of public discourse, than symbolic power resources, such as expertise, control over information, propaganda strategies, and so on.

The Division of Power

At this point, we also see that the analysis provided thus far needs an important correction. The very example of the media and leading journalists and their relation to other elites shows that power is not simply imposed, but often shared and distributed over several powerful groups. Politicians, corporate managers or academics usually do not tell journalists what (not) to write or say. The mainstream media have their own power, if only by managing the public image of the other elites, and by being in the key position of having control over public discourse and hence indirectly over the public's mind. Similarly, academics may largely control the vital resource of knowledge and expertise, but for their funding they again depend on politicians or corporate business, both of which, however, in turn need knowledge and expertise from academics.

Power relations thus get very complex. Instead of straightforward top-down coercion or persuasion, we find various patterns of sharing, negotiating, colluding with, and hence dividing power among powerful groups. Similarly, as soon as others (opponents, dissidents) acquire partial access to public discourse, they will also acquire at least some counter-power.

A typical example is the counter-power of Amnesty International against governments that violate human rights. This power is largely based on expertise (detailed knowledge about such violations) and access to public discourse, in which such governments are accused and thus portrayed negatively, which again influences 'world opinion', that is the minds of the public at large.

In similar ways, power based on class, gender, ethnicity, political allegiance, sexual orientation, religion or origin, among others, is not always straightforwardly defined as between totally powerful and totally powerless groups. Apart from counter-power through counter-discourse, there are complex patterns of negotiation, collusion and the co-production of social relationships, for example in the formation of consensus and the manufacture of consent.

This complexity should, however, not obscure the overall tendency in the relationships of power, as is the case for most forms of gender or ethnic power, in which one group (male, white) is clearly dominant, and has more power because it controls most economic, social and symbolic resources, including preferential access to public discourse. That is, the complexity of the relationships, or even collaboration or, in everyday life, the 'joint production' of power differences, should not make us conclude, as is sometimes done, that there 'is' no social power, or that the notion has become largely meaningless in modern Western society.

Yet, we should bear in mind that social power of groups is not monolithic, permanent or without contradictions. It is daily being exercised and
enacted by group members, also through text and talk. Such individual
enactment allows for variation, dissent and even change, which also partly
explains historical changes of power: members may collude with opponent
groups, and thus contribute to a change in the balance of power between
groups. Thus some whites sympathized with the civil rights movement and
some men with the women's movement and thus supported social change.

Power Abuse

Finally, another addition to this analysis is needed. It may have been
understood above that power, as such, is bad. Such a conclusion, however,
would be wrong, as many examples of acceptable power enactment show,
for example, between parents and their children, teachers and students,
superiors and subordinates, judges and defendants, and elected politicians
and citizens.

The real ethical problem we need to focus on in critical discourse
research is not power, but the *illegitimate* exercise of power, that is, *power
abuse* or *domination*. The analysis provided above for power in this case
should be complemented with the provision that power is being exercised
primarily in the interest of the powerful, and against the interest of the less
powerful. Again, such interests may range from economic to more symbolic
resources, including freedom and safety.

In order to define the illegitimate forms of power abuse, we may opt for
the notion of *violation*. At the highest level, this is the violation of human
and social rights of individuals and groups, for example as codified by
the UN Charters. At other levels, power abuse may involve violations
of national, local or community laws, rules and agreements, as well as of
accepted norms and values, although these may again be in violation
of more general or universal human rights if they were established by
dominant groups in their own best interests. Crucial in power abuse, thus,
is not only the violation of basic principles, but also the nature of its
consequences defined in terms of the interests of groups, such as unequal
access to resources. Thus, racism is a system of ethnic or 'racial' power of
which the enactment through prejudice and discrimination leads to social
inequality of minority groups or immigrants.

These definitions also apply to discursive domination, that is, when
control of text and talk, and hence indirectly of the minds of others, is in
the best interest of the powerful, against the interests of the less powerful,
and resulting in social inequality. Thus, if the elites control public discourse
and thus also (subtly or overtly) racist text and talk, they may manipulate
the dominant ethnic group into a consensus by which everyday discrimination of minorities may be officially rejected, but implicitly condoned.
Thus, Mr Rohrabacher and his Republican colleagues not only have
powerful control over public discourse, but may also abuse such power by

misrepresenting, as they did, the provisions and the intentions of the Civil Rights Bill, by negatively portraying those who are in favor of it, and by claiming that their main concern is the economic position of minorities and women, instead of the freedom of employers to hire whom they want.

Ideology

There is another fundamental notion that establishes a link between discourse and society: *ideology*. Seldom studied in the microsociology of everyday interaction and conversation, it has been a staple concept in more critical approaches to discourse. There is a vast literature in most of the humanities and the social sciences. This does not mean, however, that the nature of ideology – or its relations to discourse – is well understood. Whether Marxist, neo-Marxist or other, the traditional approaches are mostly philosophical, either with little interest in detailed studies of text and talk and other ideological practices, or ignoring the important cognitive dimensions of ideology. Within the perspective of the discussion in the chapters of this volume, our introductory account of the nature of ideology is merely a blueprint for one of the bridges that need to be built between the respective studies of discourse, cognition and society.

Social Functions

To understand what ideologies are and how they relate to discourse, we may start answering the basic question of their *social functions* or accomplishments. Why indeed do people need ideologies in the first place? What do people *do* with ideologies? The classical answer to that question is that ideologies are developed by dominant groups in order to reproduce and legitimate their domination. One of the strategies to accomplish such legitimation is for instance to present domination as God-given, natural, benign, inevitable or to otherwise persuade the dominated group to simply take such a social relation for granted. Implied in such an analysis is that dominated groups don't know what is good for them: as a result of propaganda and manipulation, they have a representation of their own position that is inconsistent with their own best interests, a state of mind traditionally referred to as 'false consciousness'. Discourse in this approach essentially serves as the medium by which ideologies are persuasively communicated in society, and thereby helps reproduce power and domination of specific groups or classes.

Although such an account is not fundamentally wrong, it is both one-sided and much too superficial. For one, at all points we need to ask: how exactly does this work? Secondly, it limits ideologies to social relationships of domination, suggests that dominated groups are merely ideological dupes and ignores that these may develop their own ideologies of resistance. As is the case for the notions of action and power introduced above, it is theoretically much more interesting to develop a general notion of ideology that can be applied in any kind of social analysis. In the same way as power abuse was above defined as a special case of power, a dominant ideology would then be a special case of ideology, so that we may continue to use the notion in a critical account of social inequality.

Against this background, then, let us attempt another, more analytical approach to ideology by first re-examining the question about the main social functions of ideologies and then analysing the role of discourse in that framework. As is the case for many related social systems, people develop ideologies in order to solve a specific problem: ideologies thus serve to manage the problem of the *coordination* of the acts or practices of individual social members of a group. Once shared, ideologies make sure that members of a group will generally act in similar ways in similar situations, are able to cooperate in joint tasks, and will thus contribute to group cohesion, solidarity and the successful reproduction of the group. This is especially relevant in situations of threat and competition, when lack of coordination and solidarity may lead to loss of power, disintegration or defeat. For the classical concept of ideology as a means of reproducing domination, this would mean that ideology serves to coordinate the social practices of dominant group members so as to perpetuate their dominant position as a group.

This still very general analysis of the social functions of ideologies has several important implications. First, ideologies are inherently *social*, and not (merely) personal or individual: they need to be *shared* by the members of groups, organizations, or other social collectivities of people. In that respect, they resemble natural languages, which also are inherently social, and also shared and used by social members of a community to solve a social problem of coordination, namely that of successful communicative interaction.

One fundamental difference between language and ideology, however, is that groups develop and use languages only for internal purposes, that is for communication among their own members, whereas ideologies serve not only to coordinate social practices within the group, but also (if not primarily) to coordinate social interaction with members of other groups. That is, ideologies serve to 'define' groups and their position within complex societal structures and in relation to other groups. It is this prevalent overall *self-definition* or social *identity* that is acquired and shared by group members in order to protect the interests of the group as a whole.

Thus characterized as shared self-definitions of groups that allow group members to coordinate their social practices in relation to other groups, ideologies show a number of basic dimensions. They feature representations of criteria of membership and group access (Who are we? Who belongs to us?), typical actions and aims (What do we do, and why?), norms and values (What is good and bad for us?), relative social position to other groups (Where are we?), as well as the special social resources of the group (What do we have?).

These are very general categories and so are their contents: in order to be able to function appropriately in many situations for most group members, ideologies must be fundamental as well as very general and abstract. They do not immediately tell each social member how to act in each situation, but rather serve groups to develop shared, general and mutually coherent representations for large domains or major problems of social and cultural life, such as life and death, illness and health, threat and survival, nature and culture, work and leisure, housing and clothing, settlement and migration, birth and abortion, dominance and subordination, crime and punishment, transgression and compliance, and so on.

More specifically, ideologies are developed to coordinate the socially shared representations that define and protect the 'answers' that each group provides to manage such fundamental social problems and issues in relation to, or in conflict with, those of other groups. Thus, their ideology suggests members of one group to represent themselves as pro-choice rather than pro-life in matters of birth and abortion and to act and talk accordingly, or to be or more less hospitable on matters of foreign immigration, or, as we have seen in our example, to be for or against the extension of civil rights legislation on litigation in cases of discrimination against women and minorities.

It is thus that social categories, groups, organizations, institutions or other social collectivities gradually acquire, develop, use (and occasionally change) a basic framework that allows their members to act as such, namely as group members who share a very general identity, aims, values, positions and resources in the general domains and conflicts of daily life. Thus, men and women, feminists and chauvinists, black and white, racists and anti-racists, rich and poor, the homeless and the home-owners, journalists and audiences, professors and students, doctors and patients, companies and employees, and many other groups and organizations each need to develop a basic system that allows their members to act as such, to know what is good and bad for them, and what to do in situations of conflict, threat or competition. In sum, socially ideologies function primarily to serve as an interface between collective group interests and individual social practices. Thus, it is the conservative ideology of his Republican Party that explains why Mr Rohrabacher argues against the extension of civil rights legislation, and why he is in favor of letting the market solve ethnic inequality.

Social Cognition

Having thus formulated a first general answer to the question *why* groups of people have ideologies, we need to attend to the details of *how* ideologies serve that function, a question that is largely ignored in traditional approaches. So far, the nature of ideologies has been left unspecified. We vaguely referred to them as systems people share. We have compared them to natural languages, which are also socially shared by communities and also allow the social practices of text and talk of individual members.

It is this comparison with language that may be instructive for our next step in the characterization of ideology: ideologies are, as such, *both* social systems, while shared by groups, as well as *mental representations*. Instead of comparing them with natural languages, we should perhaps rather compare them with the abstract grammars or systems of discourse rules of a language, which are also shared by a group while at the same time allowing group members to engage in text and talk. Metaphorically speaking, then, ideologies are group-specific 'grammars' of social practices.

Ideologies and Knowledge

In that respect ideologies also resemble the *knowledge* of a group, which is also socioculturally shared while at the same time known and usable by group members in their everyday practices. Indeed, both knowledge and ideologies are types of social belief. What is knowledge for one group may be seen as an ideology by others. Given the overall social function of coordination, however, ideologies must be more fundamental than knowledge: they represent the underlying *principles* of social cognition, and thus form the basis of knowledge, attitudes and other, more specific beliefs shared by a group.

The problem of the relations between ideology and knowledge has been at the center of much traditional debate about ideology: whereas knowledge is usually defined as true beliefs, that is, as beliefs that have been verified by some criterion or standard of truth (which may of course historically or culturally vary), ideologies have often been defined precisely as misguided beliefs. We do not follow this traditional distinction, however: ideologies may be 'objectively' true or false. Thus, from a liberal perspective, male chauvinist ideologies are wrong about the abilities of women, and feminist ideologies right about gender inequality.

Although probably not generally the case, this example suggests that the ideologies of dominated groups (minorities, women, poor people, etc.) may only be effective to organize opposition against dominant groups if these ideologies are more or less 'true to the facts'. Conversely, in order to legitimate of justify domination or social inequality, dominant ideologies may be inherently false, if only by denying such domination or social inequality. This also explains the well-known phenomenon of 'false consciousness': if a powerful group is able to manipulate the ideologies of dominated groups through disinformation campaigns (say about immigration or crime), for example through its control over the media, it may also be able to manage possible opposition into support. That is, the criterion of ideological validity is not truth, but social effectiveness: ideologies need to function in order to optimally serve the best interests of the group as whole.

Whether true or false, thus, ideologies do of course control what groups themselves usually hold to be true beliefs. Thus, ecological ideologies control what environmentalists believe to be the case about pollution, beliefs that may be thought erroneous or exaggerated by owners or managers of polluting plants. Similarly, we may assume that ideologies also monitor the *structure* of knowledge as well as its acquisition: environmentalists probably seek and have more detailed knowledge about the environment than people who could not care less about it, while at the same time possessing a different hierarchy of relevance or importance for all issues that have to do with pollution.

We see that although they are more fundamental than knowledge, ideologies at the same time are more *specific*, because they need to represent the specific concerns or interests of *one group* within society or culture. Thus, in our society and culture, we all know what nuclear energy, abortion and immigration are, but different ideologies control whether some groups will be for or against such social phenomena. In other words, and as we have seen in the examples above, ideologies control not only knowledge but especially also the *evaluative* belief systems (attitudes) groups share about certain social issues. Thus, in his speech Mr Rohrabacher hardly minces his words when it comes to formulating the ideological principles and attitudes of his group: no government interference with the job market, hence no detailed legislation on discrimination against women and minorities.

In sum, ideologies are the mental representations that form the basis of social cognition, that is of the shared knowledge and attitudes of a group. That is, besides a social function of coordination, they also have *cognitive functions* of belief organization: at a very general level of thought, they tell people what their 'position' is, and what to think about social issues.

The Structures of Ideology

Before we are able to spell out how ideologies organize social cognition, we need to know what they look like. Just as we expect linguistics to formulate the rules of grammar, or the general principles that underlie all grammars, we need to specify the internal structures and contents of specific ideologies and how ideologies in general are organized. Unfortunately, and again despite many decades of ideological analysis, no such basic structures of ideologies have as yet been found.

However, we must assume that these structures somehow reflect the social functions of ideologies discussed above: our mind is configured not merely as a function of the bio-neurological systems of the brain or in order to enable the many mental functions of thought, but also and especially as a function of the social practices and social interaction in which it is acquired, used and changed. Thus, if ideologies need to represent the interests and self-definition of each group, they should exhibit a group schema, featuring the mental counterparts of the social categories we postulated above to describe such group identity: membership, activities, aims, values, position and resources.

For instance, journalists thus acquire and use an ideology that consists of a self-schema that self-servingly defines them as people with special abilities, who professionally produce news and background articles in order to inform the public, by value standards such as objectivity, reliability and fairness, while being positioned independently between the public and the elites, and having special access to the resource of information. Note that these typically positive self-representations are not necessarily factual but ideological and hence self-serving. Similarly structured ideological self-schemata may be provided for professors, corporate managers, priests, feminists, anti-racists and environmentalists. Note that these are merely fundamental schemata, not detailed representations of all possible aims, issues or problems faced by group members.

The schema merely codifies the specific identity of a group and its relations to other groups. Special tasks and domains require special mental representations, such as attitudes or other beliefs, for instance – for journalists – how to deal with censorship or professional codes imposed by governments, or how to manage popular reactions in letters to the editor. Similarly, an overall feminist ideology will monitor feminists' opinions about abortion, equal pay, promotion at the job, gender discrimination, and sexual harassment. Such monitoring is very general though. The more specific the beliefs and circumstances, the more variation and differences of opinion may be expected within the group. As soon as individual members no longer share the basic ideological principles of their group, they no longer identify with the group, and may leave it or become a dissident.

From Group to Group Members

Socially based ideological schemata organize the other social beliefs of groups, and because these are generally shared, ideologies indirectly also control the general beliefs of individual members. In specific contexts of action, these members use these general beliefs in the construction of *specific* beliefs about events, actions and other people they are confronted with in their daily lives. In other words, we are now finally able to indirectly relate social ideologies with individual practices of group members, including discourse.

Conversely, we may in turn infer from their social practices the group membership and ideologies of social actors, and categorize someone as, for example, a liberal, feminist, black journalist. This example also shows that social members are usually members of *several* social groups, and therefore participate in several group ideologies. These are not always mutually consistent, so that the actual practices of social actors may show contradictions and variation, depending on the measure of identification with a specific group and ideology. The black, liberal, feminist journalist may in specific, professional situations give priority to attitudes monitored by a journalistic ideology, and in other situations prefer to act more as a black person, as a liberal, or as a feminist woman.

In other words, at the abstract level of the group, ideologies may well be generally coherent, but that does not imply that this will always show directly in the actual social practices of members. Specific beliefs and practices are a function of social situations, as well as of different group allegiances and self-identification, and may therefore vary accordingly. For empirical research into ideologies, this also means that they cannot always be directly 'read off' from individual social practices. Needed is insight into the overall tendencies and similarities across different group members and situations.

Ideology and Discourse

At this point we encounter the more detailed mechanisms involved in the relations between ideology and discourse. From the previous discussion we may first infer that such relations must be indirect, and involve both general beliefs as well as more specific, contextual ones. Secondly, language users are members of different social groups and may exhibit conflicting group identities and allegiances in their talk and text, again depending on context. Thus, we may recognize racist or chauvinist talk when we hear it, but racists and chauvinists do not always talk that way.

The detailed mental representations, processes and strategies involved in the ideological control of discourse are beyond the scope of this chapter and of this book (see, however, Volume 1, Chapter 11 and 12, for an account of the cognitive processes involved in text production and comprehension). Our point is, however, to present a blueprint of the structures and functions of ideologies and how they relate to discourse in order to understand how discourse is related to societal structure.

For the discussion in this volume this is also crucial as an example of how we can bridge the notorious divide between the social and the individual, the macro and the micro, the social and the cognitive. We have shown above how discourse as action and interaction is structurally part of local and global contexts. Thus, one link between the micro and the macro is through discourse participants engaging in text and talk both as individual persons and as group members. In a way, thus, groups act 'through' their members.

The same is true for the cognitive dimension: groups think through their members. Thus, ideologies of groups organize domain-related group beliefs, which in turn influence the specific beliefs of their members, and these finally form the basis of discourse. We thus relate a macro notion such as group ideology to the micro notion of the discourses and other social practices of its members. At the same time, we begin to understand how ideologies may in turn be acquired and reproduced by groups and their members, namely through discourse comprehension, sharing, abstraction and generalization.

Ideological Analysis

For the ideological discourse analyses that are part of the broader study of discourse in society, the theoretical framework sketched above also provides some suggestions for the study of the discursive manifestations of

ideology. What indeed is 'ideological' in text and talk, and in what context?
Let us summarize some of the criteria of such an ideological analysis.

The first conditions are contextual: language users must speak or write as
group members. Thus, an utterance that merely expresses personal desires,
such as 'I don't like this apple!', will generally be less ideological than one
that expresses group opinions, such as 'I am against further civil rights
legislation.' This is more generally the case for all expressions featuring
pronouns that represent social groups, most typically so for the polarized
pronouns *us* and *them*. Similarly, discourse structures that exhibit or realize
group goals and interests are more ideological than those that focus on
purely personal ones: 'We should oppose all forms of censorship' is more
ideological than 'I want to go to Amsterdam tomorrow.' Similarly, listen to
Mr Rohrabacher:

> We need economic growth, business expansion, not more civil rights legislation
> that is redundant and useless . . .
>   We care about these people living in horrible situations, whatever their race,
> and they come in all colors . . .
>   [Their horrible situation] Rarely is this a result of bigotry . . .
>   They were listening to so-called liberal leaders who were telling them that they
> should not try [to get jobs] because they did not have a chance rather than
> listening to conservatives who were telling them to go for it . . .
>   This first step is to recognize that racial discrimination plays only a minor role
> in the economic tragedy befalling our inner cities. We need to talk about our
> economy moving, creating new jobs and personal economic advancement of our
> citizens . . .
>   Let us defeat this legislation. It is going to hurt those it claims to help.

The ideological polarization expressed in these fragments of Mr Rohrabacher's speech manifests itself in several ways, for example through
references to different groups (conservatives and liberals) and their different
social views of the situation of minorities and the inner cities. All statements are general and abstract and deal with the economy and the causes
of minority unemployment. Twice the speaker denies that bigotry and
discrimination is the main cause, and at the same time he emphasizes the
conservative ideological position of personal responsibility. However, while
denying the relevance of racism, he must make sure not to be heard as
being anti-black, and hence repeatedly emphasizes that his group really
cares about 'these people' and wants them to get jobs. The ideological
opponents, on the other hand, are negatively represented as keeping
minorities from getting jobs. In other words, we see here how underlying
conservative ideologies monitor attitudes about civil rights legislation,
minority unemployment and discrimination. At the same time, the internal,
polarized structure of the underlying ideologies and attitudes appears in the
meaning of these fragments, as well as the conflicting values and aims:
social versus personal initiative to curb social problems.

Given the assumed structures of ideologies, we witness discourse
expressions of group identity, activities, values, position and resources.
Crucial in this case are the representations of social position, of *ingroups*

and *outgroups*, and their association with what is defined as good and bad. Thus, throughout discursive structures at all levels, we may expect to find emphasis on *our* good things and *their* bad things, and conversely the denial or mitigation of *our* bad things and *their* good things, as also has become clear in Mr Rohrabacher's speech.

This principle of the 'ideological square', that is, of positive self-presentation and negative other-presentation, may find expression at the following level of discourse description (using some examples from Mr Rohrabacher's speech):

1 *Topic* selection (for example, 'We tell them to go for it' vs 'They tell them they should not try').
2 *Schematic organization* (the overall argument against civil rights legislation: we oppose a redundant law, and instead propose better job opportunities).
3 *Local meanings*, coherence, implications and presuppositions (for example, 'a welfare system that provides the wrong incentives to people who need an inspiration to change, not pressure to remain the same' implies that the jobless don't want to work, and that their position is caused by welfare and not by employers who refuse to hire them); similarly we find disclaimers and denials of racism ('Rarely is this a result of bigotry').
4 *Lexicalization* implying our positive and their negative properties ('we care about these people' vs 'obtrusive civil rights bill').
5 *Style* (for example, imitation of popular oral argumentative style: 'The less fortunate of our fellow citizens. That is who will not be helped').
6 *Rhetorical devices*, such as contrasts, metaphors, hyperboles and euphemisms (see such euphemisms as 'less fortunate of our fellow citizens'; contrasts such as 'It [the bill] is going to hurt those it claims to help'; and metaphors such as 'The job explosion experienced throughout America during the Reagan years').

Similarly, we may expect information to be detailed, specific and highlighted when it serves us, and to be very general, vague or low level when it does not. Thus Mr Rohrabacher does not detail the facts and experiences of job discrimination in the USA, but instead simply denies that this is a major factor. More generally, as well as in semantic meaning itself, this may take place through variations of intonation, graphical display, word order or other means of making information more or less prominent, and hence more or less perceptible and memorable. Arguments may be specific but presuppose implied general premises that are derived from group attitudes, as is typically the case in Mr Rohrabacher's speech when he opposes liberal to conservative social philosophies. In sum, if the implicit goal of text or talk is to express and persuasively convey group impressions, we may generally assume that these are ideological.

Ideological inferences may be made of many other properties of discourse. A description of the negative consequences of immigration, for instance, usually implies that these consequences are negative for *us*, and thus expresses an ideological group opinion because our group interests are involved. In Rohrabacher's speech the negative consequences of civil rights legislation are emphasized for the groups (minorities, women) his party claims to protect, and which hence must be represented as 'wretched' victims of liberal policies. Similarly, a seemingly positive description of motherhood may imply that women should (only) strive to be good mothers rather than (also) good professionals. In sum, as soon as descriptions of events, situations, actions and people imply good and bad qualities of social groups, or involve conflicting interests between groups, discourse will generally be ideological.

Returning to the level of interaction and context, this ideological control of discourse also affects discourse as action. If male speakers frequently interrupt female speakers, or do not yield the floor, they may unwittingly enact ideologically based attitudes of male superiority or priority. That is, group power and control over discourse are themselves managed by ideologies. Since ideologies influence not only discourse, but social practices in general, also the action dimension of text and talk may be thus controlled. Conflicts, fights and disagreements in discourse may thus express, enact or encode ideologically based group conflicts. Speakers' representations of recipients may be based on group membership rather than on individual characteristics, and discourse will be multiply tuned to such biased models of recipients, for example in the use of pronouns, slurs, (lack of) politeness forms, pitch and intonation, and other properties of talk that imply participant evaluation. Indeed, Mr Rohrabacher's attack against liberals can only be understood when we assume that he knows that part of his audience in the House are liberal Democrats.

In sum, all levels and structural properties of discourse and context may 'code for' the ideologies of language users acting as group members. Often this happens in an indirect way, for instance through group opinions, personal opinions, or specific mental models of events and actions. An 'innocent' story about foreign neighbors may thus be an expression of a biased model about a conflict with foreign neighbors, which itself may be a concrete instantiation of more general, socially shared prejudiced attitudes and ideologies. Similarly, sometimes minute details of male talk may indirectly signal and reproduce gender ideologies. Members of an organization or institution will similarly reproduce or challenge the ideology of the organization in their work-related storytelling or argumentation.

Conclusions

This chapter has introduced some of the fundamental concepts that define the relationships between discourse and society. That discourse is also action is a standard principle of contemporary discourse studies. That text and talk are social and cultural has similarly become a trivial statement in the field. That discourse is contextual is taken for granted, and few discourse analysts will deny that discourse also enacts and reproduces power. The chapters in this volume provide many examples that illustrate these basic principles.

However, as we have tried to show in this chapter, the basic concepts involved are exceedingly complex and not yet fully understood. If discourse is action, we need to spell out in detail under what conditions this is so, and what types, levels or scope of action are involved. That context shapes the structures of text and talk, and vice versa, may have become trivial, but we are only now beginning to understand what the structures of context are and how they are able to affect discourse in the first place. Nothing is less obvious than the concept of power in a critical discussion of the role of discourse in the reproduction of social inequality. Yet, this requires a detailed analysis of what power is, what kinds of power are involved, and how such power is enacted, expressed, or reproduced in text and talk. And the same is true for the socio-cognitive counterpart of power, namely ideology, as the basis of shared social representations of groups.

In the introductory analyses of these notions, we appear to move between societal or group levels of analysis, on the one hand, and the sometimes minor properties of action and discourse, on the other hand, between the macro and the micro level of social analysis. At the same time, it appears necessary to relate the social and the individual, simply because language users speak and understand both as group members and as persons. Each speaker is as unique as her or his discourse, and besides the social similarities that define them as group members, we may therefore also expect individual variation, disparity and dissent. And finally, although the overall aim of social discourse analysis is to understand the relationship between discourse structures and these local and global social contexts, it appears that such a relation cannot be established without also dealing with another fundamental aspect of social interaction and society, namely the socially acquired and socially shared mental representations that define cultures and groups and that organize and monitor their beliefs as well as their social practices and discourses. It is this integration of the study of their cognitive and social dimensions that enables us to fully understand the relations between discourse and society.

Recommended Reading

The literature on the analysis of discourse in society and on the key concepts introduced in this chapter is vast. Therefore, we merely recommend some useful studies for further exploration of these topics. For more specific references, see the chapters that follow.

For a general discussion of the study of *discourse as interaction in society* see, for example, Atkinson and Heritage (1984), Boden and Zimmerman (1991), Drew and Heritage (1992) and Schiffrin (1993).

For an introduction to the *theory of action and interaction* see Danto (1973), Goldman (1976) and Turner (1988).

Although the notion of *context* is often used, there are virtually no book-length studies that present a general theory of that notion. See, however, Auer and Luzio (1992), Duranti and Goodwin (1992), Leckie-Tarry (1995) and Watson and Seiler (1992). Some of the components of the context discussed here have been introduced in early work by Dell Hymes, and are summarized in his SPEAKING model of context (Hymes, 1962; see also Chapter 9, Volume 2, by Cliff Goddard and Anna Wierzbicka). For a discussion of the discursive relevance context, illustrated in detail with the example of the speech of Mr Rohrabacher, see van Dijk (1996a).

There are many books on *power*. Here are some useful selections and overviews: Clegg (1989), Lukes (1986) and Wrong (1979). For a discussion of power and control over discourse defined as 'access', see van Dijk (1996b).

Among the hundreds of books on *ideology*, the following may be recommended: Aebischer et al. (1992), Billig (1982), Billig et al. (1988), CCCS (1978), Eagleton (1991), Larrain (1979), Rosenberg (1988) and Thompson (1984; 1990). For the theory of ideology presented here, see van Dijk (1995).

Notes

I am indebted to Philomena Essed and Lesanka Petiet for comments and suggestions about an earlier version of this chapter.

1 A year earlier, in 1990, President Bush had vetoed a similar bill, which focused only on employment discrimination against minorities: the Republican president agreed with the opposition that this bill was a 'quota' bill, which forced employers to hire 'by the numbers' in order to avoid costly litigation. The 1991 bill extended its application to women, and at the same time explicitly prohibited quotas. Nevertheless, the Republicans persisted in accusing the Democrats with the dreaded 'Q-word': according to them it still implied 'quota'.

References

Aebischer, V., Deconchy, J.P. and Lipiansky, E.M. (1992) *Idéologies et représentations sociales*. Fribourg: Delval.
Atkinson, J.M. and Heritage, J. (eds) (1984) *Structures of Social Action: Studies in Conversation Analysis*. Cambridge: Cambridge University Press.
Auer, P. and Luzio, A. di (eds) (1992) *The Contextualisation of Language*. Amsterdam: Benjamins.
Billig, M. (1982) *Ideology and Social Psychology*. Oxford: Basil Blackwell.
Billig, M., Condor, S., Edwards, D., Gane, M., Middleton, D. and Radley, A.R. (1988) *Ideological Dilemmas: a Social Psychology of Everyday Thinking*. London; Sage.
Boden, D. and Zimmerman, D.H. (eds) (1991) *Talk and Social Structure: Studies in Ethnomethodology and Conversation Analysis*. Cambridge: Polity Press.
CCCS (Centre for Contemporary Cultural Studies) (1978) *On Ideology*. London: Hutchinson.
Clegg, S.R. (1989) *Frameworks of Power*. London: Sage.
Danto, A.C. (1973) *Analytical Philosophy of Action*. Cambridge: Cambridge University Press.

Drew, P. and Heritage, J. (eds) (1992) *Talk at Work: Interaction in Institutional Settings.* Cambridge: Cambridge University Press.

Duranti, A. and Goodwin, C. (eds) (1992) *Rethinking Context: Language as an Interactive Phenomenon.* Cambridge: Cambridge University Press.

Eagleton, T. (1991) *Ideology: an Introduction.* London: Verso.

Goldman, A.I. (1976) *A Theory of Human Action.* Princeton, NJ: Princeton University Press.

Hymes, D. (1962) 'The ethnography of speaking', in T. Gladwin and W.C. Sturtevant (eds), *Anthropology and Human Behavior.* Washington, DC: Anthropological Society of Washington. pp. 13–53.

Larrain, J. (1979) *The Concept of Ideology.* London: Hutchinson.

Leckie-Tarry, H. (1995) *Language and Context: a Functional Linguistic Theory of Register* (ed. David Birch). London: Pinter.

Lukes, S. (ed.) (1986) *Power.* Oxford: Blackwell.

Rosenberg, S.W. (1988) *Reason, Ideology and Politics.* Princeton, NJ: Princeton University Press.

Schiffrin, D. (1993) *Approaches to Discourse.* Oxford; Blackwell.

Thompson, J.B. (1984) *Studies in the Theory of Ideology.* Berkeley, CA: University of California Press.

Thompson, J.B. (1990) *Ideology and Modern Culture: Critical Social Theory in the Era of Mass Communication.* Stanford, CA: Stanford University Press.

Turner, J.H. (1988) *A Theory of Social Interaction.* Stanford, CA: Stanford University Press.

van Dijk, T.A. (1995) 'Discourse semantics and ideology', *Discourse and Society,* 5 (2): 243–89.

van Dijk, T.A. (1996a) 'Context models and text processing', in M. Stamenow (ed.), *Language Structure, Discourse and the Access to Consciousness.* Amsterdam: Benjamins.

van Dijk, T.A. (1996b) 'Discourse, power and access', in C.R. Caldas-Coulthard and M. Coulthard (eds), *Texts and Practices: Readings in Critical Discourse Analysis.* London: Routledge. pp. 84–104.

Watson, G. and Seiler, R.M. (eds) (1992) *Text in Context: Contributions to Ethnomethodology.* London: Sage.

Wrong, D.H. (1979) *Power: its Forms, Bases and Uses.* Oxford: Blackwell.

2

Discourse Pragmatics

Shoshana Blum-Kulka

Pragmatic Theory

In the broadest sense, pragmatics is the study of linguistic communication in context. Language is the chief means by which people communicate, yet simply knowing the words and grammar of a language does not ensure successful communication. Words can mean more – or something other – than what they say. Their interpretation depends on a multiplicity of factors, including familiarity with the context, intonational cues and cultural assumptions. The same phrase may have different meanings on different occasions, and the same intention may be expressed by different linguistic means. Phenomena like these are the concern of pragmatics. Formal definitions of pragmatics stress that 'pragmatics is the science of language seen in relation to its users' (Mey, 1993: 5); in other words, the focus of pragmatics is on both the processes and the products of communication, including its cultural embeddedness and social consequences.

Historically, pragmatics originates in the philosophy of language. The philosopher Charles Morris (1938), who was concerned with the general outline of the science of signs, or *semiotics*, distinguished three distinct fields of study: *syntax*, the study of 'the formal relations of signs to one another'; *semantics*, the study of 'the relations of signs to the objects to which the signs are applicable' (their referents); and *pragmatics*, the study of 'the relation of signs to interpreters' (1938: 6).

In this chapter we discuss a number of topics in current pragmatics research. As we point out the main theories, concepts, findings and problems, our aim will be to illustrate the relevance of each approach to the *analysis of discourse*. Such a focus is relatively new to pragmatics: much of early pragmatics research (especially speech act theory, discussed below) tended to focus on isolated utterances. In contrast, contemporary pragmatics bases its analyses mainly on discourse – extended sequences of actual text and talk – and sets as its goal the development of a comprehensive theory of the relations between language use and sociocultural contexts. To this end, current research in discourse pragmatics tends to go beyond traditional pragmatic theory, drawing also on theories and methods in the study of human communication being carried out in those related fields that focus on language as a social and cultural phenomenon, such as the ethnography of communication (see van Dijk, Ting-Toomey, Smitherman and Troutman, Chapter 6 in this volume).

Grice's Theory of Meaning

One of the basic philosophical insights about the nature of the relation of signs to interpreters is offered by H. Paul Grice's (1957) definition of intentional communication. For Grice, intentional linguistic communication involving the transmission of *non-natural meaning* (as distinguished from natural meaning as in 'That smoke means fire') is the process by which a speaker, by saying X, wishes to communicate a specific communicative intent and achieves his or her goal when this intent is recognized by the hearer, and becomes *mutual knowledge*.

Grice's (1957; 1971) theory of meaning stresses that what the speaker says does not necessarily encode his or her communicative intent explicitly. Thus when I say 'The door is open' I may be inviting you to come in or I may be asking you to close the door. The choice between these and other pragmatic meanings in practice will be minimally a matter of pairing the words with the context in which they are uttered. Processing the words on the basis of linguistic knowledge alone will provide *sentence meaning* (providing the information that 'the door is open'); considering the *circumstances* of the utterance (along with other types of pragmatic knowledge, to be elaborated below) will help in deciphering the *speaker meaning* (that is, deciding whether the utterance was meant as an invitation, a request or something else). Pragmatic theory is concerned with explaining how interlocutors bridge the gap between sentence meanings and speaker meanings; hence its units of analysis are not sentences, which are verbal entities definable through linguistic theory, but rather *utterances*, which are verbal units of communication in specific contexts.

The process by which interlocutors arrive at speaker meanings necessarily involves inferencing. According to Grice (1975), communication is guided by a set of rational, universal principles and sub-principles (called *maxims*) which systematize the process of inferencing and ensure its success. All communication is based first and foremost on the general tacit assumption of cooperation: in Grice's words, in any talk exchange interlocutors assume that all participants will make their contribution 'such as required, at the stage at which it occurs, by the accepted purpose or direction of the talk exchange' (1975: 45). Furthermore, to ensure efficient communication, interlocutors assume that all participants abide by the following four maxims: (a) the maxim of *quality*, whereby one does not say what one believes to be false, or that for which there is no adequate evidence; (b) the maxim of *quantity*, whereby conversational contributions need to be made neither more nor less informative than is required; (c) the maxim of *manner*, whereby speakers are required to avoid obscurity and ambiguity and be brief and orderly; and finally (d) the maxim of *relevance*, which Grice defines succinctly as 'make your contribution relevant.'

Now Grice is not suggesting that all of these principles are strictly adhered to in all communication. His point is more subtle: these conversational norms serve as a set of guidelines by which interlocutors judge each other's contributions to talk and make sense of what is said. Consider the following exchange, recorded at the dinner-table of an Israeli middle-class family. Three children participate: Danny, 11.5 years old; Yuval, 9; and Yael, 7.

(1)   Mother: Danny, do you have any homework?
      Danny: I've finished it already.
      Yael: Danny didn't answer Mommy's question.
      Yuval: He did, he did; and when he said that he's already
                done it, he saved her the next question.

                            (Blum-Kulka, 1989, translated from Hebrew)

Taken literally, Danny's reply fails to answer his mother's question, and thus seems to violate the maxim of relevance. To an adult such violations are hardly noticeable, since by social convention a parental query about having homework is bound to be interpreted as a check on performance. But to a younger child such inferencing is far from obvious, as evidenced by Yael's comment. Yuval, who is older, understands that a response may be relevant to what is *meant*, rather to what is *said*. Such *conventional implicatures* are part and parcel of everyday communication. Instead of replying 'Fine' or 'Not so good' to a 'How are you?' query, one can as easily reply 'I won the lottery' or 'I failed the test in pragmatics', and in either case the hearer will be able to infer the speaker's intention due to his knowledge of the world and the shared assumptions of cooperation and relevance.

Grice is interested in distinguishing cases like the above from what he calls *conversational implicatures*: a speaker may be suspected of intending to *imply* something conversationally when what he says *blatantly violates* one of the maxims but the hearer assumes that the cooperative principle is being observed. Certain figures of speech, such as tautologies ('Men are men') and irony (Grice's example is 'He is a good friend', said about a friend who has betrayed a secret), are the extreme examples of flouting the maxims. A tautology like 'men are men' is a blatant violation of the maxim of quantity since it is completely non-informative. The remark would be informative only on the level of what might be implied – if it were uttered by a woman to a woman friend in reference to a man's behavior on a particular occasion, for example. Notice that, whereas in tautologies the utterance means *more* than what it says, in the case of irony the implication is *at odds* with what is said. If both participants know about their mutual friends' betrayal, then calling him a 'a good friend' is a blatant violation of the maxim of quality and can be understood as cooperative and true only if it is meant ironically.

Grice speaks about the procedure by which conversational implicatures are generated as *exploitation*: the speaker intentionally 'exploits' a maxim (by blatant flouting) in order to imply something more or different from what he or she actually says. One of the strengths of Grice's proposal is that it also allows us to explain cases of potential misunderstandings: misunderstandings arise when it is not clear whether the speaker indeed intended the implicature which the hearer attributed to him or her. This lack of certainty is illustrated in the following conversation, overheard in an Israeli toyshop. The three speakers are a small child, an adult woman (probably the mother) and an adult man (probably the grandfather).

(2) Child: What's that?
     Woman: We can't buy up the whole store.
     Man: He is a good boy, he just wanted to know.

                                    (Blum-Kulka, 1989, translated from Hebrew)

The woman's reply suggests that she interpreted the child's apparent query for information as intended to generate a conversational implicature, namely as an indirect request to buy the toy. But as the adult male present on the scene notes, the conversational implicature of the utterance as a request to buy the toy is a matter of the mother's attribution. It is unclear what exactly the child intended; the child might, or might not, have meant to make a request (Blum-Kulka, 1989).

As these examples show, the application of Grice's maxims *is subject to contextual variation*. Expectations for the degree of informativeness, for example, will vary with the social roles of the participants and other features of the interactional setting. Furthermore, in many institutionalized asymmetrical encounters (teacher–student, therapist–patient, interviewer–interviewee) the degree of adherence to the maxims is determined by the party in power. It is the teacher, the therapist, the interviewer who has the right to decide whether a response to a question is informative enough, and failure to meet his or her expectations may have serious social results, such as failing a test or not getting the job of one's choice.

It is also important to note that the interpretation of the maxims is *subject to cultural variation*. Cultures may vary in their expectations for degree of adherence to the maxims as required in different situations, as well as in the relative importance of the individual maxims. In the closely knit agricultural society of Madagascar, for example, all significant new information is considered a rare commodity that speakers are reluctant to part with. In this community a speaker is not necessarily required to meet the informational needs of his or her partner, and whether or not one is expected to 'be informative' at all will vary with the social situation and the type of information in question (Keenan Ochs, 1974).

Speech Act Theory

Grice's theory of meaning is concerned foremost with the ways in which interlocutors recognize each other's communicative intentions; speech act theory is concerned with providing a systematic classification of such communicative intentions and the ways in which they are linguistically encoded in context. The basic insight offered by the work of philosophers of language like John L. Austin (1962) and John R. Searle (1969; 1975) is that linguistic expressions have the capacity to perform certain kinds of communicative acts, such as making statements, asking questions, giving directions, apologizing, thanking and so on. Such *speech acts* are the basic units of human communication.

Austin laid the foundations for what became known as standard speech act theory. In his book *How to Do Things with Words* (1962) Austin moves from the basic insight about the capacity of certain linguistic expressions to perform communicative acts to a general theory of communicative actions, namely *speech acts*. Austin first noted that the utterance of certain expressions, such as 'I apologize', 'I warn you' or 'I hereby christen this child', cannot be verified as either true or false, since their purpose is not to make true or false statements, but rather to 'do' things with language. He termed such utterances *performatives*, to be distinguished from all other utterances in the language. He further noted that to achieve their performative function as an apology or a warning, such utterances need to meet certain contextual conditions, called *felicity conditions* (also sometimes called *appropriateness conditions*). Both the circumstances and the participants must be felicitous or appropriate for successful performance: an act – for example a marriage ceremony – must be executed correctly by all participants, using the appropriate words. Likewise, speakers must have the right intentions: if I say 'I promise to be there at five' but do not mean to keep the promise – if I am not sincere in uttering this sentence – then the utterance will be faulted and cannot count as a promise.

But Austin went a step further: he realized that performing communicative acts is not limited to the given subset of utterances, included under his original performatives, but is rather an inherent property of *every* utterance. Any utterance simultaneously performs at least two types of act:[1]

1 *Locutionary act*: the formulation of a sentence with a specific sense and reference. The locutionary act is what is *said*, typically containing a referring expression (such as 'John', 'the teacher, 'the government') and a predicating expression ('getting married', 'left her job', 'will negotiate a peace treaty') to express a proposition.

2 *Illocutionary act*: the performing of a communicative function, such as stating, questioning, commanding, promising, etc. The illocutionary act is what the speaker *does* in uttering a linguistic expression. For example, if a teacher says 'Open your books to page 20', the illocutionary act performed – the utterance's *illocutionary force* – is that of a directive (Austin, 1962).

Working from Austin's theories, Searle (1969; 1975) went several steps further in classifying types of speech acts and systematizing the nature of the felicity conditions needed for the performance of different speech acts. Another of his major contributions to speech act theory was in drawing attention to and elaborating on the phenomenon of indirect speech acts. Searle (1979) suggested that though there seem to be an endless number of illocutionary acts, such acts in fact may be grouped into five main types:

1 *Representatives*   A representative is an utterance that describes some state of affairs ('The sun rises in the east') by asserting, concluding, claiming, etc. Representatives commit the speaker to the truth of the proposition expressed.

2 *Directives*   A directive is an utterance used to get the hearer to do something, by acts like ordering, commanding, begging, requesting and asking (questions constituting a sub-class of directives). Examples include utterances such as 'Close the door, please' as well as 'What time is it?'

3 *Commissives*   Commissives are utterances that commit the hearer to doing something, and include acts like promising, vowing, and pledging alliance.

4 *Expressives*   Expressives include acts used to express the psychological state of the hearer, such as thanking, apologizing, congratulating and condoling ('I'm very sorry to hear that').

5 *Declarations*   A declaration is an utterance which effects a change in some, often institutionalized, state of affairs. Paradigm examples are christening a baby, declaring peace, firing an employee, and excommunicating (the types of acts included originally in Austin's 'performatives').

Searle's classification is far from being universally accepted. Some critics are mainly concerned with the principles of classification (Bach and Harnish, 1979), while others reject Searle's claim that speech acts operate by universal pragmatic principles, demonstrating the extent to which speech acts vary across cultures and languages in their conceptualization and modes of verbalization (for example, Rosaldo, 1990; Wierzbicka, 1985).

Despite these criticisms, Searle's theory of speech acts has had a major impact on several domains in the study of natural discourse: on *cross-cultural pragmatics*, in studies concerned with cross-cultural variation in modes of speech act performance; on *developmental pragmatics*, a field of study following the acquisition of pragmatic skills by children in their first language; and on *interlanguage pragmatics*, in studies concerned with the acquisition and performance of pragmatic skills in a second language.

Searle advocated the principle of expressibility: 'anything that can be meant can be said' (1969: 18ff). But for any act of expression to be successful, it needs to meet its *specific contextual conditions*. These conditions are *constitutive* of the different illocutionary forces performable, and their realizations *vary systematically with the type of speech act performed.*

Thus for Searle the grouping of speech acts is closely tied to the set of preconditions proposed for the performance of speech acts, and the exact nature of these preconditions serves as a grid for distinguishing between different speech acts. Searle proposed four such conditional parameters:

1 *Propositional content*, specifying features of the semantic content of the utterance. For example, requests usually contain reference to the future, whereas apologies (most of the time, but not exclusively) refer to an act in the past.
2 *Preparatory conditions*, specifying the necessary contextual features needed for the speech act to be performed, such as the ability of the hearer to perform a requested act (for directives), or the assumption that some offense has been committed (for apologies).
3 *Sincerity conditions*, specifying the speaker's wants and beliefs, such as his wish that the hearer does the requested act (for requests), or his belief that an offense has been committed, and recognized as such by the hearer (for apologies).
4 *Essential condition*, the convention by which the utterance is to *count* as an attempt to get the hearer to do something (for requests) or as an undertaking to remedy a social imbalance (for apologies).

Indirect Speech Acts

Indirectness is one of the most intriguing features of speech act performance. Whereas of course one may issue a request directly, specifying communicative intent and the nature of the act to be carried out in unambiguous terms ('Please close the door'), one may attempt to achieve the same communicative intent indirectly, uttering any of the following:

(3)   May I ask you to close the door?
(4)   Could you please close the door?
(5)   It seems a bit chilly in here.

Although examples (3), (4), and (5) all encode communicative intent indirectly, they vary in their degree of indirectness, both in terms of whether the utterance is *meant* as a request (its *illocutionary transparency*) and in terms of the *nature* of the request (what exactly is being requested and who is supposed to carry out the act, namely its *propositional transparency*: Weizman, 1993). Note that utterances (3) and (4) address the potential performer of the act and name the act to be performed, whereas these elements are missing from the wording of (5). Empirical research (Blum-Kulka et al., 1989) shows the prevalence of forms like (3) and (4) in several languages, including French, German, Spanish and Hebrew:

(6)   Pourriez-vous me déposer chez vous en passant? (Could you drop me at your place on your way?)
(7)   Können Sie den Wagen wegfahren? (Can you move the car?)
(8)   ¿Me prestas tus apuntes de ayer? (Will you lend me yesterday's notes?)

(9) ulay ata muxan lenakot velesader? (Perhaps you'll be prepared to clean and tidy up?)

As in all indirect strategies, the literal meaning of these utterances does not convey their illocutionary force. This is also true of example (5) ('It seems a bit chilly in here'); yet examples like (6)–(9), as well as (3) and (4), seem to be more closely dependent on the exact words used than does example (5). There have been several attempts to explain this difference. The debate around indirect forms involves at least three issues. Firstly, can speech act theory point to any systematic method that specifies the types of utterances that can be used to convey indirect speech acts? Secondly, to what degree is the encoding of indirect speech acts dependent on the use of specific linguistic expressions? And thirdly, how do participants in an interaction interpret indirect speech acts in context?

These issues are discussed here from the viewpoint of the *conventionality* thesis suggested originally in speech act theory (Searle, 1975; Morgan, 1978) and further developed within the framework of cross-cultural studies of speech acts across different languages (Blum-Kulka et al., 1989; Blum-Kulka, 1989).[2]

In elaborating his theory of indirect speech acts, Searle (1975) suggests a basis for a solution to the problem of systematicity: specific conventions linking indirect utterances of a given speech act type with the specific preconditions needed for the performance of the same act. This link is clearest in the case of directives: *conventions of usage* allow one to issue an indirect request by questioning the preparatory condition of the hearer's ability to carry out the act ('*Can you* do it?'), or by asserting that the sincerity condition obtains ('*I want* you to do it'). Such conventions of usage hold true at least for English, Spanish, German, French and Hebrew: in all of these languages one can perform an indirect request by reference to the hearer's ability ('*Could* you do this?': preparatory condition), or by predicting that the hearer might do the act in the future (as in '*Will* you/ *would* you help me clean up?', referring to the propositional content condition) (Blum-Kulka, 1989).

Though Searle (1975) claims that the phenomenon is not specific to directives (Searle's example is 'I intend to do it for you', an utterance concerning the sincerity condition for commissives, which counts as a promise), examples for other speech acts are much harder to come by, and most of the available literature on conventionality in indirect speech acts uses directives as its paradigm example for this type of systematicity.

What role does language play in carrying the pragmatic meaning of such conventionalized indirect forms? Notice that the requestive meaning in an ability question is carried by specific conventionalized wording: 'can you' and 'are you able to' are semantically synonyms, but only 'can you' carries the pragmatic force of a request. Languages may differ as to which specific linguistic expressions become conventionalized as indirect requests. In Hebrew, for example, an indirect request referring to the future is standardly realized by asking about the *possibility* of doing something. Thus in actual use the Hebrew equivalent to 'Can you pass the salt?' is 'efshar lekabel et hamelax?' ('Is it possible to get the salt?').

It is important to note that not all indirect forms are governed by such wording conventions: for instance, 'It's a bit cold in here', or 'It's very cold here', or 'It's freezing', though not equivalent semantically, may all be intended as requests, carrying the same requestive pragmatic force potential. Based on such considerations and on request realizations in five different languages, it is essential to distinguish between two types of indirectness in requests: *conventional indirectness* (as in examples (3), (5)–(9)) and *non-conventional indirectness* (as in examples (1), (2), and (5)) (Blum-Kulka, 1989).

The interpretation of indirect speech acts seems to be closely tied to degree and type of conventionality: the higher the degree of convention-ality in content and form, presumably the narrower the range of potential interpretations. Thus *conventional indirectness* like that in (3) in inherently ambiguous; a requestive interpretation is part of the utterance's meaning potential, and it is co-present with the literal interpretation. Due to this *pragmatic duality* (Blum-Kulka, (1989) such strategies are negotiable in context in *specific* ways. Potentially speakers can deny – and hearers ignore – the requestive interpretation. For example, if a child says to a parent 'Can you mend this toy for me?' and the parent replies with 'Not now', the child may say 'I only wanted to know', denying any requestive intent.

On the other hand, in *non-conventional indirectness* as in example (5), interpretation is much more open-ended. An utterance such as 'I'm hungry', depending on the context, may be: coming from a beggar, a request for money; coming from a child at bed-time, a request for prolonged adult company; or, said entering the dining room, an anticipatory statement for gastronomic pleasures to come. Thus, the mother in example (1) might wish to remind her son of his school work, while at the same time – if she suspects him of not yet having done it – she might wish to register a reprimand. The child in the store (example (2)) might only be intending to ask for information, or might be intending to make a request as well. We can see that unless they are conventionalized, indirect utterances may carry (simultaneously) multiple pragmatic forces and be ambiguous as to the speaker's meaning.

For Searle (1975), the interpretation of indirect speech acts is governed by the Gricean principle of cooperation and by conversational maxims, as well as by speech act conventions of use. Building on Grice (1975), Sperber and Wilson (1986) account for the way indirect meanings are encoded and decoded in context on the basis of general pragmatic principles, claiming that the principle of *relevance* supersedes all others. But the issue of interpretation – of how interactants match information encoded by the utterance with relevant features of the co-text and context – is far from being resolved. For example, it is a matter of debate among psycholinguists as to whether in order to understand conventional indirectness we need first to process the literal meaning of the utterance before arriving at the indirect meaning, or whether the literal meaning is bypassed completely in assigning the requestive intent (cf. Clark and Lucy, 1975; Gibbs, 1981). Furthermore, it has become increasingly clear that an overall pragmatic theory of the interpretation of indirectness needs to pay closer attention to the role of *context*, where context includes both the situation and co-text, as well as the wider sociocultural context.

In summary, the main contributions of speech act theory to the study of discourse are in drawing attention to four major phenomena:

1 Utterances serve not only to express propositions but also to perform linguistic actions ('speech acts') in context.
2 Languages provide their speakers with a variety of linguistic means, ranging in levels of illocutionary and propositional transparency (that is, 'directness'), for the performance of every single speech act.
3 The same utterance, depending on context, may serve to perform different pragmatic functions.
4 Speech acts can be differentiated by specifying the types of contextual preconditions needed for their successful performance.

The following questions raised by speech act theory remain contestable in pragmatic research:

1 Is there a universal set of speech act types? And is such a set to be identified at the level of cultural conceptualization and/or linguistic expressibility?
2 What is the exact nature of the links between the linguistic form and content of utterances and their pragmatic force potential?
3 What is the scope of the contextual dimensions – co-textual, situational, sociocultural – needed for the interpretation of indirect pragmatic meanings in context? And what is the nature of the process by which interactants arrive at interpretations?

Sample Analysis: Speech Acts in Discourse

The major problem in applying speech act analysis to discourse is how to map what is said into what is done: namely, how we can identify the illocutionary force of utterances in context given that (a) an utterance in context may carry multiple functions and (b) the speech act interpretation we assign to any given utterance derives at least in part from where it is placed sequentially and in part from our familiarity with the context in which it appears. Another problem concerns the delimiting of units of analysis: are speech acts necessarily definable at the level of single utterances, or can we assign speech act functions ('macro speech acts') to larger segments of discourse (van Dijk, 1977)? These issues are discussed in the following analysis of a short segment from a dinner conversation in an Israeli middle-class family.

(10)   Gaddi and Sarah are having supper with their two children (Nadav
       and Yoram) and Rachel, who came to dinner as a research assistant
       to collect data on conversations during family meals. Several dishes of
       food are laid out on the table.

1   Gaddi: What's on the menu?
2   Sarah: Rice, at the request of Nadav.
3   Gaddi: The truth is I have not had lunch today, so I'm hungry.
4   Sarah: So Gaddi, do you want me to warm you up some
             chicken?
5   Gaddi: No, what I thought was to . . .
6   Sarah: Yes?
7   Gaddi: . . . make myself some eggs and such, but I don't feel
             comfortable in this formal atmosphere.

(Weizman and Blum-Kulka, 1992, translated from Hebrew)

The first problem in the analysis is to determine the speech act function of
'What's on the menu?' Is it indeed a 'question' speech act, as suggested by
its surface form and pattern of intonation? According to Searle (1969: 66),
for an utterance to be assigned the illocutionary force of a question it needs
to satisfy speech act conditions as follows. The *preparatory condition* of
questions requires that the speaker does not know the answer, and it is not
obvious to the speaker and the hearer that the information will be provided
at that time unless it is specifically asked for. The *sincerity condition*
requires that the speaker wants this information; according to the *essential
condition* the utterance counts as an attempt to elicit this information.
Given that there are several dishes of food already laid out on the table, it
is not obvious at all that Gaddi does not know the answer to this question,
or that the information is not being provided (non-verbally) without being
asked for. Since the literal meaning of the utterance does not seem to
match the speaker's meaning, the utterance may be meant as an indirect
speech act. Given the context, and the common use of information seeking
questions as requests, the most likely interpretation is that the utterance is
meant as an indirect request. As Searle notes, the interpretation of indirect
speech acts is informed by the application of Grice's theory of conversational implicature. And indeed, Gaddi's question seems to violate at least
the maxim of quantity, because it asks for superfluous information. Yet at
this stage of the conversation we have no way of knowing if indeed Gaddi
means his utterance as a request, or, if he does, what he is requesting. The
analysis so far shows the potential multifunctionality of utterances in
context; without considering subsequent utterances, Gaddi's move may be
interpreted either as an information seeking question or as a requestive hint
or as both.
    Sarah's response in utterance 2 shows *the importance of position* in the
assignment of speech act categories: the assignment of illocutionary force is
dynamically negotiated in context, with elicited speech acts like 2 providing

evidence for the actual interpretation of eliciting speech acts like 1. The response here ostensibly relates to the first utterance as an information seeking question only, either misinterpreting or ignoring the possibility that Gaddi intended his utterance as an indirect request. Yet it is also possible that Sarah suspects an indirect meaning and that this is why she adds a comment justifying the choice of rice for dinner (otherwise we might see in the phrase 'at the request of Nadav' a violation of the maxim of quantity).

In his next utterance (utterance 3), by completely ignoring Sarah's response to his question, Gaddi violates the maxim of relevance, and thereby suggests a hidden meaning. The utterance has the form of the speech act of assertions, but due to its placing – its relation to the prior utterance and context – it is 'suspect' of being meant as a different, indirect speech act. And in fact, Sarah's offer in utterance 4 clearly indicates that Sarah, at least, understands the rejection in 3 (and retrospectively also 1) as a repeated *indirect request* targeted at her, meant to get her to provide some other dish of food. We can now see that utterance 3 is a repeated try of the requestive hint in 1, and utterance 4 is an attempt for compliance on the part of Sarah.

But negotiations about indirect requests may be further complicated by an indeterminacy of meaning with regard to the purpose of the request. Gaddi's rejection (utterances 5 and 7) of Sarah's offer in 4 indicates that he indeed intended utterance 1 as an indirect request, but the purpose of this request does not have the purpose assigned to it by Sarah. In technical terms, the illocutionary act of utterance 1 as an indirect request becomes clear by turn 4, but its propositional content (what is being requested) and exact illocutionary force remain obscure and in need of further negotiation. It is only after two further unsuccessful attempts by Gaddi to clarify his intentions (which prolong the exchange for another 14 turns) that the meaning of his (repeated) indirect request becomes clear:

Gaddi: So is it all right for me to go and prepare something for myself?

This phrase (turn 21 of the exchange) indicates that the indirect request in turn 1 was actually meant as a *permission request*: Gaddi seems to feel that in the given circumstances – in the presence of a guest – his wife might be offended by his leaving the table to prepare food for himself, and hence he asks her permission to do so. The indirect meaning made explicit in 21 is already hinted at in turn 7 ('but I don't feel comfortable'), but needs to be repeated due to lack of appropriate response (from Gaddi's point of view) on Sarah's part.[3]

Analysing the exchange from the point of view of speech act theory allowed us to gain some insight into a few of the ways in which participants in actual conversations negotiate implicit meanings, yet did not suffice to unveil all the intricacies involved in such negotiations. A full pragmatic account would need to consider the various linguistic and paralinguistic signals by which *both* participants encode and interpret each other's utterances, as well as the way in which politeness is taken into consideration. The last topic is taken up in the next section.

Politeness: the Pragmatic Perspective

The discussion on indirectness suggests that languages around the world provide their speakers with alternative modes for the achievement of communicative goals. Furthermore, in actual usage, in many situations speakers do not express their intentions in the clearest and most explicit ways possible: indirectness and the flouting of Gricean maxims are the norm rather than the exception. Grice realized that adherence to the maxims may clash with considerations of *politeness*; in subsequent research the notion of 'politeness' has been developed as a theoretical construct presumably capable of explaining both the social motivations for indirectness and its social implications.

The most influential pragmatic theory of politeness to date was proposed by Penelope Brown and Stephen Levinson (1987). Since the first publication of Brown and Levinson's theory in 1978, politeness has became a major concern in pragmatics, generating a wealth of theoretical and empirical studies. In essence, research in the pragmatics of politeness aims at explaining contextual and cultural variability in linguistic actions: what social motivations are inherent in and what social meanings are attached to the choice of verbal strategies (that is, 'politeness strategies') for the accomplishment of communicative goals. As will be elaborated, for Brown and Levinson *politeness* is the intentional, strategic behavior of an individual meant to satisfy self and other face wants in case of threat, enacted via positive and negative styles of redress.

As Erving Goffman suggested, when individuals interact they are concerned with presenting and maintaining a public image of themselves, that is 'face': 'the positive social value a person effectively claims for himself by the line others assume he has taken during a particular contact' (1967: 5). Following Goffman, Brown and Levinson claim that maintaining *face* is a basic motivation of human interaction and has two dimensions. One is *positive face*, which is the person's concern that he or she be thought well of by others, as positively contributing to the social world. At the same time, a person wishes to preserve a certain degree of autonomy, a 'space' within which he or she has freedom of action and the right not to be imposed upon. This aspect of face, because it claims the right for non-imposition, is *negative face*. In Brown and Levinson's view social interaction is based on a person balancing the satisfaction of their own positive and negative face needs with the face needs of other interactants.

The need to balance face needs, according to this theory, derives from the fact that most acts of communication are inherently imposing, or *face threatening*. For example, all directives challenge the hearer's need for freedom of action (*negative face*, whereas warnings and criticisms constitute a threat to the hearer's *positive face*. In a parallel fashion, the speaker's positive face is threatened by the admission of guilt involved in an apology, or by the commitment to some undesirable future action involved in making an unwilling promise. Politeness strategies are the means by which interactants fend off and *redress* such risks to face. They fall into five main categories.

Bald On-Record Strategies   If the risk is minimal, or if there are overwhelmingly good reasons for ignoring face risks, speakers *go on record* in realizing the communicative act in the most direct way possible. For example, the teacher's language of control in classroom discourse might rely heavily on the use of imperatives ('Open your books on page . . .', 'Sit straight') both for reasons of efficiency and because, in asymmetrical relations like teacher–pupil, there is an accepted licensing of the suspension of politeness considerations.

Positive Politeness Strategies   Positive politeness strategies enhance the positive face needs of the interlocutor, by such means as attending to the hearer, stressing reciprocity, displaying a common point of view and showing optimism. For example, attending to the hearer's interests or needs is a positive strategy that might be used to preface a request for a favor from a neighbor ('Uncle Jim inquires about your health and would like to know if he can borrow your hammer'), and in-group identity markers may be used to mitigate a command ('Let's take off our glasses' addressed by a hairdresser to a client who is wearing glasses). Other typical positive politeness strategies include the use of slang, jokes, endearments and nicknames.

Negative Politeness Strategies   Negative politeness strategies are geared to satisfy the hearer's negative face, that is, his or her need for freedom from imposition. They are realized by asking about (rather than assuming) cooperation: by giving options to the hearer not to do the act, by adopting a pessimistic attitude and by various kinds of hedging. Conventional indirectness in requests is a prime example of negative politeness: by saying 'Could you do X for me', the speaker leaves himself an option to deny any requestive intent ('I only wanted to know if . . .', thereby protecting his or her own positive face while simultaneously enhancing the hearer's negative face by asking rather than saying, namely by not presuming compliance. Other negative politeness strategies include hedging ('*I wonder if* you know whether Bill has been around'), minimizing the imposition on the hearer ('You might consider introducing a few tiny changes such as . . .', said by an academic criticizing a colleague's paper), and explicit linguistic marking of deference ('*Your honor* might wish to consider . . .', in arguing with a judge in court).

Off-the-Record Strategies   In cases where the risks to face are estimated as very high, speakers can realize the act in a way that leaves maximal options for deniability. Going *off the record* means realizing the act so indirectly that the speaker cannot be made accountable for any specific communicative intent. Non-conventional indirect requests are good examples: if I say 'It's a bit chilly in here' I cannot be held accountable for a requestive intent, and my hearers are just as excusable if they do not understand that I did intend a request.

Opting Out   If the risk is considered too great, the speaker may decide not to say anything at all. For example, the possibility of complaining to a neighbor about the loud music coming from her house at odd hours needs to be weighed against the risk of severing an amicable neighborly relation through the threat to her positive face, and consequently may be abandoned.

The choice between these five options in context is determined, according to Brown and Levinson, by the configuration of three contextual variables: the social distance (D) between the speaker and the hearer, in effect their degree of familiarity; the relative power (P) of the speaker and the hearer; and the absolute ranking (R) of the various impositions in the given culture.

The degree of politeness (face saving) that will be encoded in any linguistic act will depend on the 'weightiness' of the face loss involved, as determined by the combined estimates for the above three variables. Such assessments of the context of the utterance need to be viewed as constantly changing between individuals, since they depend on given types of relationships, on social role and specific situational constraints and, most importantly, on the way all these and other perceptions of the social world are constructed and negotiated through talk.

The list of five strategic options is claimed by Brown and Levinson to represent a scale of politeness. The movement from *bald on-record* strategies that show no concern for face, through *positive* and *negative* modes of redress, to the opaqueness of *off-the-record* strategies presumably represents a universally accepted principle of politeness: the more indirect the utterance, the more considerate and the more polite it is considered to be. This conceptualization of politeness as the expression of autonomous, rational individuals striving to avoid conflict and preserve interactional harmony through indirectness is shared by many other Western politeness theories (for example, Lakoff, 1975; Leech, 1983), but has been strongly contested by scholars studying other than Western cultures (see Kasper, 1990 for a review of this literature).

Politeness in Discourse

The analysis of politeness phenomena in discourse shows the way in which variation in choice of politeness strategies reflects and constructs the social world, and how the cross-cultural variation in politeness systems can be informative about deep-set differences between cultures.

Social Variation Research in the *sociopragmatics* (that is, the social dimensions of pragmatics: Leech, 1983) of diverse societies shows, as predicted by Brown and Levinson (1987), that the values of social power, social distance and degree of imposition indeed play a role in determining the choice of politeness strategies. Speakers of different status, in asymmetric power relations, will differ in the degree to which they encode politeness. For example, in Shakespeare's *King Lear*, the doctor and Cordelia (who at this stage of the play is Queen of France) exchange directives:

(11) Doctor: So please your Majesty
                 That we may wake the King; he hath slept long.
      Cordelia: Be governed by your knowledge, and proceed
                 I'th' sway of your own will.

                                        (*King Lear*, IV. vii. 17–20)

Both speakers are polite, but the doctor, who is the less powerful, is more polite: he uses an indirect request ('So please . . . that we'), a term of deference ('your Majesty') and an inclusive 'we' (a positive politeness strategy). Cordelia's response is polite in that it expresses respect for the doctor's knowledge and uses the passive voice. As Brown and Gilman (1989) note in analysing this example, stripped of redress to face the doctor is asking 'May I waken the king?' and Cordelia is responding 'Use your own judgement.'

Politeness can also play a role in the striving for symbolic power of one speaker over another, as in the following conversation between two 12-year-old African-American children, both girls:

(12) S: Gimme that ruler.
      A: Huh?
      S: Gimme that ruler, girl.
      A: Huh?
      S: Will you please gimme that ruler before I knock you down.

                                        (Mitchell-Kernan and Kernan, 1977)

Social variables may affect not only the choice of politeness strategies, but also the sequential structure of the discourse. Thus an increase in the degree of imposition involved may lead to an increase in the number of turns needed for the performance of the speech act, as seen in A's request pattern in the following conversation between two Israeli students on campus:

(13) A: Say, how is your English?
      B: Okay. Why?

A: There are a few [difficult] things in this article. I wondered
    (pause)
B: Yes?
A: Would you have time [to help me]?

                        (Blum-Kulka et al., 1985, translated from Hebrew)

The negative politeness strategy finally used by A ('Would you have time
[to help me]?') is preceded first by a question checking whether the
preparatory condition for the request obtains, and then by a hedge ('I
wondered'), both devices signalling redress to face.

Empirical research shows that a speaker's estimates of power, distance
and imposition interact with other factors, such as communicative goals,
the medium of the interaction and the degree of affect between interactants,
in determining his or her choice of politeness strategies (Blum-Kulka et al.,
1985; Brown and Gilman, 1989). Gender is another important factor in
accounting for social variation in the use of politeness. There is no simple
answer to the question of whether women are more polite than men; rather,
any observed gender differences in styles of politeness should be seen as
tied to gender differences in social power on the one hand, and to gender-
biased cultural conceptions of politeness on the other (Keenan Ochs, 1974).

Cultural Variation Cross-cultural research on politeness seriously challenges claims for the universality of politeness models. Cultures differ widely
in their interactional styles, so that whereas indirectness is the accepted
polite behavior in a given situation in one culture, directness is the norm in
the same situation in another. Such variation can be understood as representing cultural preferences for positive or negative styles of politeness.
Thus in a culture that tends to minimize social distance and stress collectivism, like Israel, for example, the prevalent style is that of positive politeness, stressing in-group bonding rather than non-involvement. A closer look
at presumably positive politeness cultures which emphasize involvement and
cordiality rather than distancing, such as Slavic and Mediterranean cultures
(for example, Wierzbicka, 1985), suggests that directness in such cultures is
not necessarily impolite. In Israeli culture, for instance, an emphasis on
sincerity and truthfulness in interpersonal relations overrides the importance
of avoiding infringement of the other, licensing (especially in the private
sphere) high levels of directness (Katriel, 1986; Blum-Kulka, 1992). It
follows from examples like these that Brown and Levinson's scale of
politeness is not necessarily valid for all cultures.

Cross-Cultural Pragmatics

Studies in cross-cultural pragmatics are informed by advances in pragmatic
theory, focusing on a specific discourse pragmatics phenomenon, singling it

out from the flow of discourse and comparing it across languages both analytically and empirically, as manifest in actual use. A widely researched area in cross-cultural pragmatics concerns contrastive pragmatics: cross-linguistic comparisons of particular types of linguistic actions. The speech act types studied from this perspective include directives, compliments, questions, thanks and apologies. For example, Coulmas (1981) contrasts the functioning of such highly routinized speech acts as thanks and apologies in Japanese with a number of European languages, and Chen (1993) compares responses to compliments by English and Chinese speakers.

The main issues in this type of research can be exemplified by the studies carried out within the framework of the Cross-Cultural Speech Act Realization Project (CCSARP: Blum-Kulka et al., 1989). We investigated two speech acts – requests and apologies – in eight languages and language varieties: Australian English, American English, Argentinian Spanish, British English, Canadian French, Danish, German and Hebrew. To ensure comparability, a written discourse-completion test was used, requiring the (student) respondents to fill in the request or apology missing from a given dialogue. The following example contains sample responses (a) to (e) from Australian English, Argentinian Spanish, Canadian French, German and Hebrew, respectively:

(14) *At the university*
      Ann missed a lecture yesterday and would like to borrow Judith's notes
      Ann: (a) Would you mind if I borrowed your notes from the last class? [Australian English]
            (b) ¿Podes prestarme los apuntes? (Can you lend me your notes?) [Argentinian Spanish]
            (c) Judith, accepteras-tu de me prêter tes notes de cours? J'étais absente hier. (Judith, will you be willing to lend me your notes from the course? I was absent yesterday.) [Canadian French]
            (d) Kannst du mir bitte deine Aufzeichnungen zum Kopieren geben? (Can you give me your notes for copying?) [German]
            (e) haim at muxana lehashil li et hamaxberet shelax lekama yamim sheuxal leha'atik et hashiur? (Are you willing to lend me your notebook for a few days so that I can copy the lesson?) [Hebrew]
      Judith: Sure, but let me have them back before the lecture next week.

A cross-linguistic comparison of the speech act data provided this way allows for two types of analyses. In the terms used by Leech (1983) these are: first, *pragmalinguistic* studies of the degree of cross-linguistic variability in strategy form, examining the linguistic repertoire available in a particular language for conveying a specific pragmatic function (for example, requesting strategies in English); and second, *sociopragmatic* studies of the degree of cross-cultural variation in the choice of strategies across different situations, examining the way in which pragmatic performance is subjected to social and cultural conditions.

The overwhelming majority of respondents chose to use conventionally indirect strategies to formulate their request to borrow notes (as in example (14)). These request realizations allowed us to examine the degree of pragmalinguistic diversity in the formulation of conventionally indirect requests in the languages studied. All of these languages, we found, shared certain conventions of use, but *differed in specific modes of realization.*

For instance, only Canadian French and Spanish speakers standardly use the politeness formula 'Will you be kind enough to?', as in 'Serais tu assez gentille de me prêter tes notes?' ('Will you be kind enough to lend me your notes?'), a formula that might sound overelaborate or even invite conversational implicatures if it were translated literally into English. Similarly, only Hebrew speakers standardly request by asking whether others are 'prepared' (literally 'Are you prepared to lend me your notes?') or by prefacing their commands with 'perhaps' (literally, 'Lady, perhaps you'll move the car').

Sociopragmatic variability was studied by considering situational variation. The situations in the test varied systematically in the degree of social distance and social dominance. The results revealed that speakers of all the languages studied vary their strategies according to situational variables: requests from a policeman were phrased more directly than requests from a student to a teacher, and apologies from a waiter to a customer were less elaborate than apologies between friends. But, at the same time, the responses also reveal a high degree of cultural variability, which can be construed as further evidence for the claim that speech communities develop culturally distinct *interactional styles* (Hymes, 1974). Thus, in asking a roommate to clean up the kitchen in a shared apartment, only 12% of Australian respondents used direct *bald on-record* strategies, as compared to 74% of the Argentinians. This result is consistent with the general pattern that showed the Australian English speakers as preferring the least direct strategies in all situations and the Argentinian speakers the most direct.

Cross-linguistic differences in pragmatic systems have important implications for two domains of language contact: translation and second language acquisition.

Translation

Since pragmatic meaning in a given text might be encoded through language-specific pragmalinguistic means, translators may and do sometimes fail to provide pragmatic equivalents (such as expressions that carry the same pragmatic meaning potential) in the target language. For example, the phrase 'I beg your pardon' may be used in American English to signal lack of comprehension, to express indignation, or as an apology. In context, the phrase may be deliberately ambiguous, as it is when used by a (married) female character in John Updike's novel *Rabbit, Run* after her offer of coffee to a (married) male character has been turned down in a way that makes clear his interpretation of her offer ('No, look . . . You're a doll . . . but I have got this wife now') (Updike, 1960: 223). The Hebrew translator of the phrase opted for a literal translation, 'I'm asking for your forgiveness.' Since in Hebrew this phrase serves usually as a formal apology, and hardly carries the potential for other meanings, the translation loses the pragmatic meaning potential of the original and renders the hero's later deliberations (was the woman offended because he had turned her down, or because he made clear to her his interpretation of her offer of coffee?) completely meaningless.

Second Language Acquisition: Interlanguage Pragmatics

Learners (and speakers) of a second language run into similar difficulties when trying to express their pragmatic meanings in the target language. Studies in *interlanguage pragmatics* (Kasper and Blum-Kulka, 1993) show that learners, unaware of the fact that the pragmatics of their native tongue do not match that of the target language, may transfer pragmatic strategies from their first to their second language; even when they are aware of differences, they may still formulate wrong hypotheses about the pragmatics of the second language. Such processes may in turn result in *pragmatic* failure (Thomas, 1983; Blum-Kulka and Olshtain, 1986), namely, a failure on the part of the speaker to express his or her intended meaning accurately and/or appropriately.

In native/non-native communication, the transfer of sociopragmatic norms from the source culture may combine with other factors in yielding miscommunication and/or negative stereotyping of the non-native speaker. It is important to note that, whereas grammatical deviances from target language norms are easily recognizable, lending their producers a protective 'non-native' identity, pragmatic deviances are not: pragmatic failure at the pragmalinguistic and sociopragmatic levels carries the risk of being attributed to flaws of personality or ethnocultural origins and may carry grave social implications. Yet when non-active speakers communicate in a style different from native speakers, their degree of accommodation to the target culture may be as much a matter of choice as ability. On the other hand, from the native speakers' point of view, a different way of speaking pragmatically is rarely recognized and treated positively as a marker of cultural identity, being viewed instead frequently in a negative vein.

Conclusions

This chapter has discussed a selected set of topics in pragmatics, chosen for their relevance to discourse pragmatics. They are the concepts and methods offered by pragmatic theory and related fields for the analysis of discourse in its sociocultural context. To this end, in addition to classical pragmatic theory that originated in the philosophy of language (for example, Grice, Austin and Searle), we have also discussed theories of politeness (Brown and Levinson), and empirical work in cross-cultural pragmatics. Though these (and other) different perspectives on discourse tend to overlap and merge in current pragmatic research, as witnessed by the papers published in the leading journals in pragmatics such as the *Journal of Pragmatics* and *Pragmatics*, all work in pragmatics as a discipline shares a set of theoretical assumptions with regard to the nature of human communication. In this concluding section I focus on the major insights that this pragmatic perspective brings to the understanding of human verbal communication and point out further issues and domains in current pragmatic research.

Language and Context

We have seen that the pragmatic perspective on human communication focuses on language users and conditions of use, rather than on abstract linguistic systems or on the (possibly) innate capacity to speak a language. One of the basic tenets of this approach is the focus on the inherently contextualized nature of communication.

Research in pragmatics has been much concerned with teasing out the types of presuppositions needed for interpretation (Levinson, 1983). As formulated by Mey (1993: 173), 'pragmatic presuppositions in a culture constitute the link between the spoken word and the world of the users.' Yet the pragmatic approach has been often criticized for failing to account for the full role of context in the process of communication. One of the main arguments has been that by focusing on single speech acts, it under-estimates not only the role of situational and socio-cultural contexts as frames of reference for interpreting speech, but also the role of context in shaping the talk or text that emerges on any given occasion. Other approaches, like the *ethnography of communication* developed by Gumperz and Hymes, stress this double role of context as a field of action within which talk is embedded as well as a focal event (a *speech event*) constituted through talk (see Schiffrin, 1994 for a review). What should be stressed is that assigning context a central role in social interaction – along the lines suggested by the ethnography of communication – does not rule out a discourse pragmatics approach to the study of the negotiation of meaning enfolding within the event. In fact, future research in discourse pragmatics may be much enriched by incorporating ethnographic viewpoints and procedures in its study of social interaction.

Human Communicators in Search of Meaning

Pragmatics views understanding as an interactive, inferential process which necessarily involves a constant matching of what is said with what is meant. Thus Grice's account of human verbal communication relies heavily on the notion of rationality. Communication is a goal oriented activity, and interpreting a communicative act amounts to trying to determine the interlocutor's communicative aims. Communication proceeds in a loop-like fashion, with each interlocutor searching in sequence, as the conversation proceeds, for signals that show understanding of his or her communicative intents. What is said does not necessarily always reflect what is meant, and therefore communication necessarily proceeds through inferences: one turn of talk or sentence in a text is linked to the previous one, often through (inferred) messages absent from the actual words said or written.

In Grice's account human communicators are rational beings who presume that others preserve the principle of cooperativeness, and hence if anyone ostensibly violates any of the conversational maxims, such violations must be explained away as intentionally produced. In this search for meaning, conversational implicatures (attributed and intended) serve the interpreter as bridges for coherence: one turn of talk may be linked to the previous one not through direct linguistic means, but rather through an inference with regard to indirect meaning.

Speech act theory has gone a long way towards systematizing the notions of intended and indirect meanings. For one thing, it provides us with a mapping of performable communicative intents (*speech acts*) specifying the conditions of use necessary for their performance. For another, it clearly distinguishes between direct and indirect speech acts, providing pragmatic criteria for sorting out different types of indirectness.

Empirical research on speech acts has been most fruitful when applied to the study of single speech acts, both intra- and inter-culturally, and has drawn most criticism when applied to the study of discourse. Thus to date there is a wealth of literature on speech acting in various languages and cultures, but no generally accepted, speech act theory informed, discourse analytical model for the analysis of conversation. As a result, some accounts of pragmatics (for example, Levinson, 1983) recommend incorporating *conversation analysis*, a field of study based on theoretical premises different from those of pragmatics, into the study of discourse (see Pomerantz and Fehr, Chapter 3 in this volume).

The Gricean approach to communication is still the basis for much of current theorizing in pragmatics; less studied are the societal and cultural applications of the theory. For instance, many institutionalized worlds of discourse, such as medical interviews, educational practices, and job interviews, seem to be governed by speech-event specific sets of Gricean norms, the understanding of which may determine success for the patient, the student or the job applicant. For example, the set of norms a child brings from home may be linked to her specific social background and/or culture and in turn clash with the institutional norms of her school (as in determining what type of response is considered informative enough). Thus considering speech events as basic units of communication, as advocated by ethnographers of speaking, is of paramount importance for understanding the negotiation of pragmatic meanings.

Communication and Miscommunication

Negotiations over pragmatic meaning are part and parcel of everyday communication even when interlocutors share language and culture. But when interlocutors come to the communicative event from different linguistic and cultural backgrounds, with possible mismatches in cultural and contextual presuppositions – as well as in the interpretative frameworks for the linguistic means of signalling pragmatic meanings – the chances for miscommunication abound. Such miscommunication in turn can lead to mutual negative stereotyping, and have grave social implications for further inter-group relations.

In its applications to actual discourse, the pragmatic perspective has proved invaluable in explaining cases of miscommunication in intra-cultural, native/non-native, inter-ethnic and cross-cultural communication. Once the pragmatic dimension is incorporated in a description of the human communication process, we are alerted to the multi-level nature of meaning embodied in verbal messages and have a much better grasp of what can go wrong.

Recommended Reading

Seminal Papers and General Introductions

The two most widely quoted theoretical papers in pragmatics are probably Paul Grice's (1975) article 'Logic and conversation' and John Searle's (1975) article 'Indirect speech acts'.

Other important primary sources are books by John Austin (1962) and Searle (1969), as well as Searle's (1979) article on the classification of illocutionary acts. For comprehensive overviews of pragmatics see Geoffrey Leech (1983), Stephen Levinson (1983), Jacob Mey (1993) and Jenny Thomas (1995); for a more philosophically oriented discussion see Marcelo Dascal (1983). The collection of papers in the volume edited by Jeff Verschueren and Marcella Bertuccelli-Papi (1985) offers a wide scope of pragmatic issues investigated during the 1980s.

Two European journals, the *Journal of Pragmatics* and *Pragmatics* (formerly called *IPRA Papers in Pragmatics*), publish current research in the field.

Social Dimensions of Pragmatics

The 1987 edition of Penelope Brown and Stephen Levinson's seminal work on politeness contains an introduction that reviews work on politeness since the article's first publication in 1978. For a more recent overview see Gabriele Kasper (1990).

Robin Lakoff's (1990) book provides a highly readable discussion of the issues of language and power from a pragmatic perspective.

Cross-Cultural Communication

For brief and lucid introductions to issues in cross-cultural communication see the papers by Deborah Tannen (1985) and Nessa Wolfson (1983).

For further reading in cross-cultural communication (in addition to references mentioned in the text, namely Blum-Kulka et al., 1989; Gumperz, 1982) see the collection of papers edited by Donal Carbaugh (1990) and Ron Scollon and Susan Scollon Wong's (1995) most recent book.

Notes

I would like to thank Teun van Dijk, Talya Habib, Sherna Kissilevitz and Eric Saranovitz for their helpful comments and suggestions on earlier versions of this chapter.

1 Austin also posited a third type of act, called a *perlocutionary act*, which specifies the effects on the hearer(s) caused by uttering an expression in given circumstances. But in further development of speech act theory, perlocutionary acts drew less attention than illocutionary acts.

2 For a review of other positions on indirectness, see Levinson (1983).

3 Further analysis of this exchange would need to consider whether the exchange can be assigned a *macro speech act* (van Dijk, 1977) which takes into account the overall purpose of the negotiation and its content at the macro, collective level, rather than from the point of view of each individual speaker (see Weizman and Blum-Kulka, 1992 for an analysis along those lines).

References

Austin, J. (1962) *How to Do Things with Words*. Oxford: Oxford University Press.

Bach, K. and Harnish, R.M. (1979) *Linguistic Communication and Speech Acts*. Cambridge, MA: MIT Press.

Blum-Kulka, S. (1989) 'Playing it safe: the role of conventionality in indirectness', in S. Blum-Kulka, J. House and K. Kasper (eds), *Cross-Cultural Pragmatics: Requests and Apologies*. Norwood, NJ: Ablex. pp. 37–70.

Blum-Kulka, S. (1990) '"You don't touch lettuce with your fingers": parental politeness in family discourse', *Journal of Pragmatics*, 14: 259–89.

Blum-Kulka, S. (1992) 'The metapragmatics of politeness in Israeli society', in R. Watts, R.J. Ide and S. Ehlich (eds), *Politeness in Language: Studies in its History, Theory and Practice*. Berlin: Mouton de Gruyter. pp. 255–81.

Blum-Kulka, S., Danet, B. and Gerson, R. (1985) 'The language of requesting in Israeli society', in J. Forgas (ed.), *Language and Social Situation*. New York: Springer Verlag. pp. 113–41.

Blum-Kulka, S., House, J. and Kasper, G. (eds) (1989) *Cross-Cultural Pragmatics: Requests and Apologies*. Norwood, NJ: Ablex.

Blum-Kulka, S. and Olshtain, E. (1986) 'Too many words: length of utterance and pragmatic failure', *Studies in Second Language Acquisition*, 8: 47–67.

Brown, P. and Levinson, S. (1987) *Politeness: Some Universals in Language Usage*. Cambridge: Cambridge University Press. First published as 'Universals of language: politeness phenomena', in E. Goody (ed.), *Questions and Politeness*. Cambridge: Cambridge University Press, 1978. pp. 56–324.

Brown, R. and Gilman, A. (1989) 'Politeness theory and Shakespeare's four major tragedies', *Language in Society*, 18: 159–212.

Carbaugh, D. (ed.) (1990) *Cultural Communication and Intercultural Contact*. Hillsdale, NJ: Lawrence Erlbaum.

Chen, R. (1993) 'Responding to compliments: a contrastive study of politeness strategies between American English and Chinese speakers', *Journal of Pragmatics*, 20: 49–77.

Clark, H. and Lucy, P. (1975) 'Understanding what is meant from what is said: a study of conversationally conveyed requests', *Journal of Verbal Learning and Verbal Behavior*, 14: 56–72.

Coulmas, F. (1981) 'Poison to your soul: thanks and apologies contrastively viewed', in F. Coulmas (ed.), *Conversational Routines*. The Hague: Mouton. pp. 273–88.

Dascal, M. (1983) *Pragmatics and the Philosophy of Mind*, vol. 1. Amsterdam: John Benjamins.

Gibbs, R.W. (1981) 'Your wish is my command: convention and context in interpreting indirect requests', *Journal of Verbal Learning and Verbal Behavior*, 20: 431–44.

Goffman, E. (1967) *Interaction Ritual: Essays on Face to Face Behavior*. New York: Doubleday.

Grice, H.P. (1957) 'Meaning', *Philosophical Review*, 66: 377–88.

Grice, H.P. (1971) 'Meaning', in D. Steinberg and L. Jakobovits (eds), *Semantics: an Interdisciplinary Reader in Philosophy, Linguistics and Psychology*. Cambridge: Cambridge University Press. pp. 53–9.

Grice, H.P. (1975) 'Logic and conversation', in P. Cole and J. Morgan (eds), *Syntax and Semantics 3: Speech Acts*. New York: Academic Press. pp. 41–58.

Gumperz, J. (1982) *Discourse Strategies*. Cambridge: Cambridge University Press.

Hymes, D. (1974) 'Ways of speaking', in R. Bauman and J. Sherzer (eds), *Exploration in the Ethnography of Speaking*. New York, London: Cambridge University Press.

Kasper, G. (1990) 'Linguistic politeness: current research issues', *Journal of Pragmatics*, 14: 193–219.

Kasper, G. and Blum-Kulka, S. (eds) (1993) *Interlanguage Pragmatics*. New York: Oxford University Press.

Katriel, T. (1986) *Talking Straight: Dugri Speech in Israeli Sabra Culture*. Cambridge: Cambridge University Press.

Keenan, E. Ochs (1974) 'Norm-makers and norm-breakers: uses of speech by men and women in Malagasy community', in R. Bauman and J. Sherzer (eds), *Explorations in the Ethnography of Speaking*. New York: Cambridge University Press. pp. 125–43.

Lakoff, R.T. (1975) 'The logic of politeness, or minding your p's and q's', *Chicago Linguistics Society*, 9: 292–305.

Lakoff, R.T. (1990) *Talking Power: The Politics of Language in Our Lives*. New York: Basic Books.

Leech, G. (1983) *Principles of Pragmatics*. London, New York: Longman.

Levinson, S. (1983) *Pragmatics*. Cambridge: Cambridge University Press.

Mey, J. (1993) *Pragmatics: an Introduction*. Oxford: Blackwell.

Mitchell-Kernan, C. and Kernan, T.K. (1977) 'Pragmatics of directive choice among children', in S. Ervin-Tripp and C. Mitchell-Kernan (eds), *Child Discourse*. New York: Academic Press. pp. 189–211.

Morgan, J. (1978) 'Two types of convention in indirect speech acts', in P. Cole and J. Morgan (eds), *Syntax and Semantics 9: Pragmatics*. New York: Academic Press. pp. 261–81.

Morris, C.H. (1938) 'Foundations of the theory of signs', in *International Encyclopedia of Unified Science*, vol. 2 no 1. Chicago: University of Chicago Press.

Rosaldo, M. (1990) 'The things we do with words: Ilongot speech acts and speech act theory in philosophy', in D. Carbaugh (ed.), *Cultural Communication and Intercultural Contact*. Hillsdale, NJ: Lawrence Erlbaum. pp. 373–407. First published in 1982.

Schiffrin, D. (1994) *Approaches to Discourse*. Oxford: Blackwell.

Scollon, R. and Scollon Wong, S. (1995) *Intercultural Communication: a Discourse Approach*. Oxford: Blackwell.

Searle, J. (1969) *Speech Acts*. Cambridge: Cambridge University Press.

Searle, J. (1975) 'Indirect speech acts', in P. Cole and J. Morgan (eds), *Syntax and Semantics 3: Speech Acts*. New York: Academic Press. pp. 59–82.

Searle, J. (1979) 'The classification of illocutionary acts', *Language in Society*, 5: 1–24.

Sperber, D. and Wilson, D. (1986) *Relevance: Communication and Cognition*. Cambridge, MA: Harvard University Press.

Tannen, D. (1985) 'Cross-cultural communication', in T. van Dijk (ed.), *Handbook of Discourse Analysis*, vol. 4. London: Academic Press. pp. 201–17.

Thomas, J. (1983) 'Cross-cultural pragmatic failure', *Applied Linguistics*, 4: 91–112.

Thomas, J. (1995) *Meaning in Interaction: An Introduction to Pragmatics*. London and New York: Longman.

Updike, J. (1960) *Rabbit, Run*. New York: Fawcett Crest.

van Dijk, T. (1977) *Text and Context: Explorations in the Semantics and Pragmatics of Discourse*. London: Longman.

Verschueren, J. and Bertuccelli-Papi, M. (eds) (1985) *The Pragmatic Perspective*. Amsterdam: John Benjamins.

Weizman, E. (1993) 'Interlanguage requestive hints', in G. Kasper and S. Blum-Kulka (eds), *Interlanguage Pragmatics*. New York: Oxford University Press. pp. 123–38.

Weizman, E. and Blum-Kulka, S. (1992) 'Ordinary misunderstandings', in M. Stamenov (ed.), *Current Advances in Semantic Theory*. Amsterdam and Philadelphia: John Benjamins. pp. 417–33.

Wierzbicka, A. (1985) 'Different cultures, different languages, different speech acts', *Journal of Pragmatics*, 9: 145–63.

Wolfson, N. (1983) 'Rules of speaking', in J.C. Richards and R. Schmidt (eds), *Language and Communication*. London, New York: Longman. pp. 61–89.

3

Conversation Analysis: An Approach to the Study of Social Action as Sense Making Practices

Anita Pomerantz and B.J. Fehr

Conversation analysis (CA) originated in the mid 1960s within sociology, in the work of Harvey Sacks and his colleagues, as an approach to the study of the social organization of everyday conduct. During the ensuing thirty years, CA has produced a substantial body of rigorous and informative analyses of human action and interaction. In this chapter we will: (1) provide an initial characterization of CA and its relation to other forms of discourse analysis (DA); (2) briefly discuss CA's early history; (3) describe CA's assumptive base and analytic commitments; and (4) most importantly, provide a set of tools for conducting analyses. Experience has taught that an understanding of CA is particularly enhanced by actually attempting analytic work.

An Initial Formulation of Conversation Analysis and its Relation to Other Forms of Discourse Analysis

At the outset, it is important to point out that the name of this research tradition, conversation analysis, is something of a misnomer and can lead to some confusion as to the phenomena under investigation and their analytic conception.[1] One source of confusion arises from the term 'conversation'. Some researchers discriminate between the informal talk of everyday life (for example, chats with a friend) and talk occurring within formal institutions (for example, the presentation of evidence in a court of law). These researchers argue that interaction in formal organizations seems to be governed by different orders of constraint than informal conversation. Since they view 'conversation' as referring to informal talk in everyday social settings and 'institutional talk' to formal talk in institutional contexts, they expect conversation analysts to study only the former domain. Conversation analysts, however, are concerned with conduct or action in both contexts, and an *a priori* distinction between the two is regarded as analytically unnecessary.

Secondly, the name 'conversation analysis', or even 'talk-in-interaction',[2] may wrongly suggest that only the verbal aspects of interaction ('talk') are of interest. Conversation analysts from the outset have been interested in both the verbal and the paralinguistic features of talk (that is, sound quality, pauses, gaps, restarts, etc.). In fact, the actions constituted in and through speaking can be difficult or impossible to identify without attention to both. Moreover, a number of researchers have expanded the scope of CA to include the visually available features of conduct, such as appropriate orientation, hand-arm gestures, posture, etc. (C. Goodwin, 1981; 1986; M. Goodwin, 1980; 1990; Heath, 1986; Schegloff, 1984).

The organization of talk or conversation (whether 'informal' or 'formal') was never the central, defining focus in CA. Rather it is the organization of the meaningful conduct of people in society, that is, how people in society produce their activities and make sense of the world about them. The core analytic objective is to illuminate how actions, events, objects, etc., are produced and understood rather than how language and talk are organized as analytically separable phenomena. This point was made by Harvey Sacks in one of his early lectures:

> So the question was, could there be some way that sociology could hope to deal with the details of actual events, formally and informatively? . . . I started to work with tape-recorded conversations . . . *It was not from any large interest in language or from some theoretical formulation of what should be studied* that I started with tape-recorded conversations, but simply because I could get my hands on it. (1984: 26, emphasis added)

We propose neither that the study of talk is unimportant nor that studies which focus exclusively on talk are inadequate in any way. We merely claim that the analytic approach of CA is not limited to an explication of talk alone but is amenable to analyses of how conduct, practice, or praxis, in whatever form, is accomplished. Studies within this tradition which do focus on talk view talk, nonetheless, as social action.

Since roughly the 1940s, many disciplines have moved toward a more socially based, interactive and pragmatic understanding of human action and interaction. This does not signify adoption of a radically new approach to the study of human conduct. Rather it reflects the steady ascendancy of a minority position which has been voiced within a broad array of disciplines since at least the Middle Ages (Vico, 1975) or, as some would argue, from the pre-Socratics forward (Coulter, 1991). Given the discursive turn across disciplines, CA has family resemblances to a number of other approaches. One commonality is a shift away from the search for causes of human conduct and toward the explication of how conduct is produced and recognized as intelligible and sensible.

Within linguistic philosophy, for example, Austin (1962) proposed that language not only is a means of representation but also is used to perform social actions, such as making a promise. Sociolinguistics arose within linguistics and sociology to highlight the variations found in different social contexts of speaking (for example, formal vs informal) and among various cultural and ethnic groups (Labov, 1972a; 1972b; Bernstein, 1975). In anthropology, Hymes (1962) developed an approach which he called 'the ethnography of speaking' in order to examine talk-in-interaction as an activity system in its own right, usefully subject to ethnographic description as is any other part of cultural life. Discourse analysis emerged in linguistics in an attempt to characterize talk and texts longer than the sentence or clause, which had been the upper limit of linguistic analysis prior to this innovation (Coulthard and Montgomery, 1981; Stubbs, 1983). Greater attention was given to the pragmatic aspects of language use in semiotics, which had formerly emphasized syntactics and semantics (Levinson, 1983). Under the influence of critical theory and feminism, scholars became interested in the power of words to beguile and entangle people in webs of understanding which limit their potential development beyond traditionally defined boundaries. These scholars argue that power is an unequally distributed resource and that language serves to legitimate and maintain established hierarchies without the awareness of those disadvantaged by the system (Fowler et al., 1979).

Each of these initiatives has spawned productive streams of research which, over time, have become intertwined in complicated ways, each borrowing concepts and methods from the others as the need and interest arose. It has become increasingly difficult to crisply characterize their distinctiveness because they have converged on a number of issues.[3] All of these projects (including CA) arose partially in response to the emerging conception of language and speaking as involving more than a representation of the world. They all agree that language can be used to enact social actions. All have come to record and analyse instances of talk-in-interaction and to display a concern for the role of context in sense production. All have argued in various ways for attempting to capture the perspective of the participants in interactive sequences.

CA, however, may be differentiated from these various perspectives by its particular approach to certain analytic issues. First, it rejects the use of investigator-stipulated theoretical and conceptual definitions of research questions. Instead, conversation analysts attempt to explicate the relevances of the parties to an interaction. Conventionally, for example, a researcher with an interest in the relations between men and women might decide to code, as part of the analysis, those who are female or male. Such codings treat gender as an omnirelevant matter for analysis, but they may or may not be so for the parties to the interaction. Gender may be relevant for some interactions and not for others. A similar set of concerns would obtain for the a priori analytic importation of the concept of 'power', that is, presuming that power and/or status relations are a central component of all social relations prior to an analysis of their relevance for the parties to an interaction. Persons who occupy different positions in some status or power hierarchy do not necessarily make that difference the basis for all and every interaction between them.

Secondly, conversation analysis gives particular attention to the details of the temporal organization of, and the various interactional contingencies that arise in, the unfolding development of action and interaction. In important ways, the sense or intelligibility of an action is provided for by its location in an ongoing series of actions. For example, consider the following utterance extracted from a naturally occurring conversation:[4]

Heather: I did too=I took two of everything.

What Heather 'did', what 'everything' she took two of, and the interactional significance of this utterance, are not given in what she said. However, if we return the utterance to its natural interactional home in an ongoing series of actions, its sense and significance become apparent:

Don: .hh I got my uh (1.2) I <u>did</u> get my tax forms today
Heather: Yea
Don: Yea I walked inta the post office an' mail my thing and I <u>took</u> one of everything hhh
Heather: I did too=I took two of everything.
Don: For me?
Heather: Yea
Don: That's my baby.

Like Don, Heather got tax forms on the day of this conversation, and further, that she got two copies of each form was significant because the 'extra' copy was intended for Don.[5,6]

Thirdly, the perspective taken by CA leads to a different understanding of the concept of rules than that held by other research traditions. Rather than a theoretically given form of explanation for human conduct, CA treats rules as situationally invoked standards that are a part of the activity they seek to explain. For example, Wieder (1974) analysed the ways in which residents of a correctional half-way house invoked rules (for example, 'Above all else, do not snitch.') to account for their disinclination to report on certain activities of their co-inhabitants. The invocation of the rule becomes part of the activity, in this case, refusing to snitch.

Historical Background

Conversation analysis arose primarily through the impetus and insights of Harvey Sacks in close collaboration with colleagues (initially fellow graduate students), Emanuel Schegloff and David Sudnow, among others. All three were students of Erving Goffman at Berkeley who was championing the ordinary, mundane activities of everyday life as legitimate inquiry for sociology. Also, Sacks had met Harold Garfinkel, the founder of ethnomethodology, during the latter's sabbatical at Harvard in 1959. Sacks continued to meet with Garfinkel at UCLA and to read his published and unpublished manuscripts. Sacks found some resonance between his questions about what provided for certain social forms, for example, law, and Garfinkel's (1967) foundational explorations of the basis of social order in the details of everyday conduct. He began to probe the possibility of an empirically based, naturalistic, descriptive study of human conduct. In the next few years, Sacks attracted students of his own who importantly contributed to the enterprise: Gail Jefferson, Anita Pomerantz, and Jim Schenkein, among others.[7]

In 1963, Sacks became a fellow at the Los Angeles Suicide Prevention Center. There, audio recordings and transcriptions of telephone calls to the clinic hotline were routinely made. The recordings provided a resource for beginning to examine the details of interactional conduct. Two noticings based on these materials formed the basis of the initial work in conversation analysis. One dealt with the terms callers used to refer to and describe themselves and others. The other had to do with the sequential placement of utterances by the parties to the calls.

Callers to the Suicide Prevention Center hotline mentioned, referred to, and described themselves and others during the course of their calls. Given that there are many correct ways to categorize oneself and others (for example, wife, socialist, tall, Latino, opera buff, she, nut case), Sacks wondered if there was an orderliness or organization to the use of categorizations. Consider the following transcript excerpt (from Sacks, 1972: 64):

A: You don't have anyone to turn to?
C: No.
A: No relatives, friends?
C: No.

In asking about people to turn to, the Suicide Prevention Center's staff person inquired about 'relatives' and 'friends'. Sacks wanted to begin to explicate our everyday understandings of the human social world by considering such uses. 'Relatives' and 'friends' are the categories of persons that one should be able to expect assistance from in a time of trouble. It would seem nonsensical in such a situation to inquire: 'No Toms, Sylvias?', 'No men, women?', 'No socialists, republicans?' Sacks showed that in the ways we use categorizations, we display our understanding of the rights and obligations of persons to whom certain categories apply. This does not mean that any particular person will actually have individuals in such categories available. Even if there are individuals in such categories, these persons may or may not be willing, able, etc. to be the ones turned to. That itself could provide for a person having troubles, warrantably and intelligibly so.

A second observation Sacks made was that the sense or intelligibility of utterances was tied to their particular sequential location in a stretch of talk. Recall that the intelligibility of Heather's utterance 'I did too=I took two of everything.' was provided for by its position in a particular, ongoing series of utterances.

As time went on, the interest in and investigation of sequential organization took precedence over categorization in the work of conversation analysts (see, for example, Sacks et al., 1974). As Sacks (1975: n. 1) notes, this should not be seen as a rejection of the importance of categorization in human interaction. In fact, a number of subsequent analysts again have turned attention to the connection between categorization and sequential analysis (Jayyusi, 1984; Watson, 1976; 1983).

Assumptions and their Methodological Implications

Conversation analysis, like ethnomethodology,[8] treats the conduct of everyday life as sensible, as meaningful, and as produced to be such. This assumption implies a distinction between conduct treated as 'behavior' (as noise making and bodily movement) and conduct treated as 'action' (as intelligible activity). If a person raises his or her arm, the everyday understanding typically is centered on the fact not that an arm that was down is now up but rather that someone is calling for a turn, hailing a cab, stretching, or perhaps greeting an acquaintance. If a person speaks, it is not noise but rather meaningful utterances directed at some other or range of others.

It is further assumed that meaningful conduct is produced and understood based on shared procedures or methods. People's conduct is not wholly idiosyncratic. If it were, coordinating activities with others, especially previously unknown others, would be impossible. However, it is a routine feature of our everyday lives that we can interact and coordinate our conduct with others. CA's goal is to explicate the shared methods interactants use to produce and recognize their own and other people's conduct.

The sense or meaning conduct has thoroughly depends upon the context of its production in at least two ways. One sense of context involves the temporal organization of actions and interaction. Conduct is produced and understood as responsive to the immediate, local contingencies of interaction. What an interactant contributes is shaped by what was just said or done and is understood in relation to the prior. Over the course of an interaction, the context continually changes: each contribution provides a new context for the next.

There is another sense in which conduct depends upon context: to understand conduct we need to know the type of occasion, who is interacting with whom, where and when. For example, our understanding of conduct as lecturing and note-taking is derived from the fact that the participants are instructor and students and a lesson is taking place in a classroom. Rather than treating the identities of the participants, the place, the occasion, etc., as givens, conversation analysts and ethnomethodologists recognize that there are multiple ways to identify parties, the occasion, etc. and that the identifications must be shown to be relevant to the participants. A person may speak as a member of a seminar and then, in some next utterance, as a woman – and be taken as so doing by others. The forward progress of a seminar may halt momentarily while the assembled parties discuss the health of a friend. Furthermore conversation analysts and ethnomethodologists maintain not only that the identifications of who, what, where, etc., are part of producing and understanding conduct but that the conduct helps to constitute the identities of the participants, the type of occasion, etc., as they are. That is, the context is in part brought into being by the actions people produce. By speaking 'informally', one not only is responsive to an 'informal' setting but also helps to constitute the setting as 'informal'.

These assumptions carry with them corollary methodological implications relating to the types of interaction studied, the role of the analyst in the interaction, and the recording and transcription of interaction.

In CA, any sort of interaction may be studied, for example chats among acquaintances, consultations with physicians, job interviews, broadcast news commentaries, political speeches, etc. In each case, the interest is in explicating the methods or procedures people employ to make sense and be understood by others.

In observing conduct, a researcher may or may not be a participant/ observer in the scene and/or may or may not use a recording device. However a researcher observes conduct, it is important to consider whether and how the researcher's and/or the recording device's presence may be related to the observed conduct. For example, if the participants know they are being recorded during their dinner conversation, they may alter some of their conduct (for example, they may choose to avoid a sensitive topic) but not other conduct (such as making a report coherent).

Conversation analysts strongly prefer to work from recordings of conduct. First, certain features of the details of actions in interaction are not recoverable in any other way. Second, a recording makes it possible to play and replay the interaction, which is important both for transcribing and for developing an analysis. Third, a recording makes it possible to check a particular analysis against the materials, in all their detail, that were used to produce the analysis. Finally, a recording makes it possible to return to an interaction with new analytic interests.

One last note on recordings. In cases where the interactants are co-present, it is preferable to have a videotaped recording so that at least some of the conduct visually available to the interacting parties also is available for review by the analyst. In cases where the parties are not co-present (such as telephone calls), audiotaped recordings generally have been employed. A great deal of early CA work dealt with recordings of telephone calls, not because of any special interest in phone calls but because audio recordings could be easily and inexpensively produced.

Conversation analysts generally transcribe their tapes using transcript conventions developed and elaborated by Gail Jefferson.[9] These conventions cannot reproduce what is on the audiotape or videotape but are meant to remind the reader of the details of the conduct that can be heard or seen on tape. The best way to develop analyses is to use both a tape and a transcript. It is harder to isolate and study phenomena when working only with a tape, and much information is lost when working only with a transcript. Also, without hearing/seeing the tape from which a transcript was derived, one cannot know how much confidence to have in a transcript.

Tools for Analysis: Questions to Ask and Areas to Consider

In this section, we offer tools to help you develop your conversation analytic skills. The tools consist of questions to ask and areas to think about as you attempt to analyse conduct rendered on your tapes and transcripts. In the next section we offer two demonstrations of how the tools may be used when you work with tapes and transcripts.

An analysis should illuminate the understandings that are relevant for the participants and the practices that provide for those understandings. Analysing a practice involves describing both the knowledge that the participants use, and when and how they use it. What analysts find interesting or noticeable depends upon, and plays off of, their own tacit knowledge, expectations, and interests. Drawing upon one's knowledge of language use and interaction is a necessary resource in developing analyses.

Conversation analysts use different approaches in developing analyses; there is no one right way. This presents a challenge in teaching others to do analyses since there are many paths to the final destination. We offer five questions to ask, or areas to consider, to help you get started in your analyses. Consider the tools offered here as representing one of many ways into analysis.

1 Select a Sequence When watching or listening to a tape, choose a place on which to start focusing. Initially you might notice the way something is said or what someone is doing. Identify the *sequence* in which whatever interests you occurs. In order to identify a sequence, look for identifiable boundaries. For the start of the sequence, locate the turn in which one of the participants initiated an action and/or topic that was taken up and responded to by co-participants. For the end of the sequence, follow through the interaction until you locate the place in which the participants were no longer specifically responding to the prior action and/ or topic.[10] When looking at (or for) sequence openings and closings, treat them as products of negotiation. While one party may offer a possible start or finish, the start or finish usually is not fully accomplished without the ratification of the co-participant.

A sequence will contain a variety of phenomena that can be investigated. It is like a very rich mine with different ores: you can mine for some ores now and return later to mine for other ores. It is quite common to identify new areas of interest as you work on materials. You may be tempted to choose sequences that are funny or novel or topically interesting. In our experience, however, the quality of one's findings is unrelated to the apparent interest of the sequence.

2   Characterize the Actions in the Sequence   A basic analytic concept for conversation analysts is an *action*. Actions are central to the way that participants, themselves, produce and understand conduct; they are a fundamental part of the meaningfulness of conduct. When we say, 'Want to go to lunch?', we intend, and are understood as intending, for the recipient to understand that we are inviting him or her to lunch. Moreover, we expect an action in response, that is, an acceptance or a declination of the invitation. One identifies actions by answering the question, 'What is this participant doing in this turn?' A few examples of actions include: greeting, announcing news, acknowledging news, complaining, disagreeing, correcting, telling a joke, and telling a story.

For each turn in the sequence under study, characterize the action or actions that the interactant performed. Sometimes you will see several actions being performed within a turn: that is fine. There is not one right characterization; rather there may be several that appropriately capture a sense of the conduct. Furthermore, these characterizations are provisional; they are first attempts to capture something of the action. Analysts may change their characterizations as they proceed when better characterizations come to mind.

When you characterize the action or actions performed in each turn, you will end up with characterizations of the actions that comprise the sequence. Now consider the relationship between the actions. Actions are not islands unto themselves: most are offered with an expectation of a response (such as requesting information) and/or as a response to a prior action (such as supplying the requested information).

3   Consider How the Speakers' Packaging of Actions, Including their Selections of Reference Terms, Provides for Certain Understandings of the Actions Performed and the Matters Talked About. Consider the Options for the Recipient that are Set Up by that Packaging   By *packaging* we mean the ways in which speakers form up and deliver actions.[11] With respect to any given action, there are multiple ways to package it. On actual occasions of interaction, speakers package the actions that they perform in particular ways. Conversation analysts often say that speakers *select* the packages, formulations, or formats that they use. The problem with this metaphor is that it suggests that interactants consciously consider the multiple ways to perform their actions and then choose among the options. Actually, however, much of the time interactants perform their actions without deliberating on the manner in which they do it, without considering the alternatives. In a given context, a speaker may not consider the options that an analyst proposes are alternatives. Analysts use the metaphor 'the speaker *selects* . . .' as a shorthand way of reminding themselves to consider alternative items in a class, not necessarily as an accurate description of the actors' decision making processes.

For a given action, consider how the speaker formed it up and delivered it. Consider the understandings that are tied to the packaging that the speaker used in relation to alternatives that might have been used but were not on this occasion. Also, consider the options that the packaging the speaker used provided for the recipient. Alternative ways of packaging an action may set up different options for the recipients.

As an example, consider the many ways you can invite someone for lunch. The way you invite a person helps to establish what kind of invitation it is and what the options are for the recipient. If you issue an invitation with the inquiry 'Have you had lunch yet?', you allow the recipient to give information which would imply rejection (for example, 'Yes I have') without actually having to reject an invitation. The use of this type of package has been well researched by a variety of conversation analysts, including Drew (1984) and Schegloff (1980; 1988).

Part of packaging an action involves selecting ways to refer to persons, objects, places, activities, etc. For example, when a speaker says 'Let's grab a bite', he or she may be referencing not only having lunch but also time constraints on one or both parties. The interactants may understand that in 'grabbing a bite', some but not other food places will be considered. Since the terms the speaker uses in part provide for the recipient's understanding, the terms selected may provide for the greater or lesser desirability of an offer, request, or invitation. A recipient with time constraints may agree to 'grab a bite' yet hesitate to 'go out to lunch'.

To summarize, the following questions may be useful in trying to identify the packaging of a given action and to understand its consequentiality. What understandings do the interactants display (and you have) of the action? Do you see the interactants treating the matter talked about as important, parenthetical, urgent, trivial, ordinary, wrong, problematic, etc.? What aspects of the way in which the action was formed up and delivered may help provide for those understandings? What inferences, if any, might the recipients have made based on the packaging? What options does the package provide for the recipient? In other words, what are the interactional consequences of using this packaging over an alternative? Finally, what are the circumstances that may be relevant for selecting this packaging over another for the action?

4 Consider How the Timing and Taking of Turns Provide for Certain Understandings of the Actions and the Matters Talked About For each turn in the sequence, describe how the speaker obtained the turn, the timing of the initiation of the turn, the termination of the turn, and whether the speaker selected a next speaker. *Obtaining the turn*: did the speaker select him or herself to speak or was he or she selected by the previous speaker? How does this fit with the actions being performed? *Timing the start of the turn*: relative to the prior turn, where did the current speaker start to speak? Did he or she wait for a possible completion, or start prior to a possible completion point, or did a gap emerge? Do you think the timing of the turn is connected to the participants' understandings? *Terminating the turn*: did the current speaker continue to speak until he or she was definitely finished?

possibly finished? not finished? Did any recipients start up while he or she had the floor? *Selecting next speaker*: to whom did the current speaker address his or her talk? What were the intended recipients doing during the current speaker's turn? How did the current speaker show the intended recipients that he or she was addressing them?

5 Consider How the Ways the Actions were Accomplished Implicate Certain Identities, Roles and/or Relationships for the Interactants What rights, obligations, and expectations between the parties may be gleaned from the discourse? Are the ways that these interactants talked and acted appropriate across a wide range of relationships, roles, statuses, etc. or do they implicate particular relationships, roles, statuses? Do the ways that the speakers referred to persons, objects, places, activities, etc. implicate particular identities and/or relationships between them? Do the ways they packaged their actions implicate particular identities, roles, and/or relationships? Do the ways that the interactants took their turns (or declined to) implicate particular identities, roles, and/or relationships?

Two Demonstrations of the Tools

In order to show how you might use these tools, we offer two demonstrations. In the first demonstration, the points are followed in the order in which they are described above: choose a sequence, characterize the actions, examine the packaging of the actions, explore the timing and taking of turns, and consider the implications of the packaging and turn-taking for identities, roles and relationships. While analysts do not necessarily keep these areas distinct as they work, we address each in turn to clarify the domains. In the second demonstration, we show the inter-relationship between the points and develop a more unified analysis.

The materials we use in our demonstrations consist of a portion of a telephone conversation between two young adults, Don and Heather (these are pseudonyms). For the two demonstrations, we selected two contiguous sequences. While readers do not have access to the audiotape, the transcript allows us to demonstrate how the tools might be used. The portion of the transcript that contains both sequences is replicated below:

[BJF/Bisco:]

1	Heather:	He shoulda bought a water bed.
2	Don:	Na::
3	Heather:	Much more comfort[able
4	Don:	[.hh I got my uh (1.2) I <u>did</u> get my tax forms today
5	Heather:	Yea
6	Don:	Yea I walked inta the post office an' mail my thing and I <u>took</u> one of everything hhh
7	Heather:	I did too=I took two of everything.

8	Don:	For me?
9	Heather:	Yea
10	Don:	That's my baby
11		(1.0)
12	Don:	How was school today
13	Heather:	Okay
14		(3.6)
15	Don:	Hhhh Just okay?
16	Heather:	Ayup
17	Don:	Why what happened?
18	Heather:	Nothin. It was kinda boring. We left for lunch though
19	Don:	Who did
20	Heather:	Me and Maria an' Sean an' ( ) an' Max Clancey
21	Don:	Sean who?
22	Heather:	Sean ah (1.0) Peters. Maria's – You know Abruzzi
23	Don:	Yeah
24	Heather:	Maria's new boyfriend.
25		(2.4)
26	Don:	And who?
27	Heather:	A:h his best friend Max
28		(2.0)
29	Heather:	We just went to Dunkin's I had to have a croissant
30	Don:	Yea well you better tell Max that uh:
31	Heather:	Max has a girlfriend
32	Don:	Yea
33	Heather:	Plus he (has disgusting earrings)
34		(4.0)
35	Don:	Hhhh Me and Vic did a lota talking tonight

First Demonstration of the Tools

1 Select a Sequence In listening to the tape and reading the transcript, our attention initially was drawn to Heather's reply in line 7: 'I did too=I took two of everything.' It attracted our attention because of the possible implication that Heather had been considerate while Don had not been. We wondered if we could make a case for her talk as a put-down, test, and/or lesson.

To identify the sequence of which Heather's talk in line 7 was a part, we need to identify boundaries: a beginning and an end. In lines 1, 2, and 3, Heather and Don were continuing a discussion about Don's father's purchase of a bed. In line 4, Don made a report about one of his activities during the day. Heather acknowledged Don's report, thereby ratifying his bid to share this news report. Hence we identify the start of the sequence occurring in line 4.

The actions/topics that follow Don's report (line 4) can be seen to be part of the same sequence in as much as they directly respond to prior actions.

Don's elaborating on his report, Heather's offering a related report, and Don's responding to her report with an expression of appreciation (line 10) are all actions which respond to prior actions. Following Don's expression of appreciation, there was a 1 second gap which was broken by Don's inquiry about how school was that day. We claim that the sequence ends on lines 10 or 11. The last turn of talk clearly within the sequence is line 10. The 1 second gap that emerged on line 11 was a place where the interactants could have continued with talk that responded to the prior but elected not to. When Don took a turn to speak in line 12, he started a new topic. The 1 second gap in line 11 was transitional: within it the participants discontinued responding to the prior talk.[12]

2   Characterize the Actions in the Sequence   The transcript of the interaction is on the left; the characterization of the actions are on the right.

4	D:	I got my uh (1.2) I <u>did</u> get my tax forms today	D announces the successful outcome of an activity.
5	H:	Yea	H acknowledges.
6	D:	Yea I walked inta the post office an' mail my thing and I <u>took</u> one of everything hhh	D elaborates on the circumstances and outcome.
7	H:	I did too=I took two of everything.	H reports the same activity but with variation.
8	D:	For me?	D checks H's motives, offering as a possibility that she was serving D's interests.
9	H:	Yea	H confirms D's possibility.
10	D:	That's my baby	D displays appreciation.

In the sequence above, there are many things that may be examined. We chose to explore three actions: Don's reporting that he successfully picked up his tax forms, Heather's reporting that she picked up two copies of each form, and Don's displaying appreciation. We will analyse these actions – how they are accomplished and their implications – by using the questions that we discussed in the tools section.

3   Consider How the Speakers' Packaging of Actions, Including their Selections of Reference Terms, Provides for Certain Understandings of the Actions Performed and the Matters Talked About   Apparently both Don and Heather had picked up the tax forms that day, so each had a report, or news, that he or she could tell. Yet whether, when, and how each one would share the report was influenced, to some extent, by interactional contingencies. First we will examine how the packaging of Don's report provides for our understanding of his news; then we will analyse how the packaging of Heather's report provides for our understanding of her news.

We understand the news that Don reported in line 4 to be newsworthy but not of great importance. It was the kind of news that people share when they talk to each other frequently and report on how their day was, what they did that day, etc.[13] How do we get this sense of the news from its packaging? In the way that a speaker delivers a report or news, he or she implicitly proposes its importance (Sacks, 1992). The timing of the report is a way to provide for an understanding of its importance. Reporting news as the first topic proposes its importance; contacting someone at a time that he or she usually is unavailable for contact proposes even more importance (Sacks, 1992). In this telephone call, Heather and Don had been talking for 2 minutes 20 seconds about events of the day before Don reported that he picked up his tax forms. Consistent with reporting just a daily activity (that is, not big news), Don did not use any introduction that would mark the report's importance. He did not preface the telling with something like 'Guess what?' or 'Do you know what I did today?' Rather he announced or reported the outcome of the activity.

One way Don increased somewhat the importance of the activity was by referencing its history. Don started to report his activity using the term 'got' (in 'I got my uh') but stopped before completing it. After a gap of slightly over 1 second, he restarted his report with 'I did get my tax forms today.' Had he completed the first version ('I got my tax forms today'), he would have reported simply the outcome of an activity. With the repaired version, 'I did get . . .', Don acknowledged a history of attempts or previously unrealized intentions to get the forms. The emphasized 'did' provides for the current referent to be seen in relation to referents that contrast with it. With the formulation 'I did get . . .', Don referenced a history possibly known in common by Don and Heather. The activity referenced was not simply picking up his tax forms but rather his finally picking them up.

With the formulations that he incorporated, Don implied that he picked up the tax forms just as he should have, that he did a good job of it. We already discussed how, by including the emphasized 'did' in 'I did get my tax forms today', Don invoked a history of previous unsuccessful attempts or unrealized intentions that contrasted with this successful outcome. In elaborating the circumstances and manner in which he picked up his tax forms (line 6), Don further portrayed his activity as a success.[14] Rather than referring to what he took as 'one of each', he referred to it as 'one of everything'. In using the extreme case formulation 'everything' (Pomerantz, 1986) he seemed to claim a thoroughness in picking up the forms: he has any form he could possibly need. In his description of his activity, he portrayed his having done it just as it should have been done.

Heather's subsequent report of her picking up tax forms proposed that she considered Don's needs whereas Don considered only his own needs. How does the packaging of Heather's report provide for this understanding?

Once Don reported that he picked up his tax forms (line 4), Heather was no longer in the position of making her report as an initial announcement or a new topic. Rather she was in the position of seconding his report, that is, of casting her activity as similar or dissimilar to Don's activity.

Just after Don reported having picked up his tax forms, Heather had the opportunity to give her report. In fact, the slot immediately following his report is a 'natural' place in which to offer her report. However, at this point in the interaction, Heather merely acknowledged Don's report, inviting him to elaborate (line 5).[15] In his elaboration ('. . . and I took one of everything'), Don described the circumstances and manner in which he picked up his tax forms. While he may have intended to portray a successful outcome and a job well done, Heather could have heard the elaboration as firmly establishing that he picked up forms for himself only.

In line 7, Heather started her turn by reporting that she had accomplished the same activity as the one Don just reported having done ('I did too'). She continued the turn with an elaboration that contrasted with Don's prior elaboration ('I took two of everything'). To display a contrast, Heather reused Don's formulation ('I took one of everything'), though she incorporated one alteration ('I took two of everything'). Reusing the formulation provided the frame within which to highlight the contrast or difference. With the replication plus alteration format, she exhibited a difference between their actions. When interactants exhibit a difference, they invite co-interactants to make something of that difference.

In the way in which she reported her activity, she implied that her picking up two copies of each tax form was appropriate behavior. Individuals have ways of portraying actions as 'mistakes', 'blunders', 'errors', 'incompetencies', etc. Heather incorporated no such markers, for example, no explanation or laughter to indicate that her action was deficient or troublesome. In packaging her report to exhibit the difference between their performances while at the same time implying that her performance was the appropriate one, Heather handed Don a puzzle. If Don had assumed that success involved picking up one copy of each form, he would need an explanation as to why she picked up two of each. Heather did not offer a reason; she relied on Don to supply it. By not supplying it, she gave him the opportunity to recognize her thoughtfulness. And in recognizing her thoughtfulness, he provided for his contrastive behavior to be seen as not particularly thoughtful.

4 Consider How the Timing and Taking of Turns Provide for Certain Understandings of the Actions and the Matters Talked About Rather than analysing the timing and taking of all of the turns in the sequence, this discussion is limited to just two points within it: how the timing and taking of turns at the beginning and the end of the sequence provide for certain understandings.

We have claimed that the sequence started with Don's turn, '.hh I got my uh (1.2) I did get my tax forms today' (line 4). We would like to show how Don's timing and taking of the turn provided for the understanding that the prior topic was finished and that Don was not receptive to any further arguments for water beds.

Prior to the sequence about picking up tax forms, Don and Heather had been talking about Don and his father's moving to a condominium. As part of that discussion, Don itemized the new furniture that his father bought, including a king size bed. After reporting that his father bought the bed, Don listed the other items that he bought and planned to buy. Several turns later, Heather returned to the topic of beds with her own recommendation (line 1):

1 Heather: He shoulda bought a water bed.
2 Don: Na::
3 Heather: Much more comfort[able
4 Don: [.hh I got my uh (1.2) I did get my tax
              forms today

Don's immediate response was to reject Heather's recommendation (line 2). He did so with an elongated negative token. In producing the negative token as the entire turn, he indicated his rejection of Heather's recommendation without engaging in argument or discussion about it. In response to his rejection, Heather offered a reason supporting her recommendation. This could serve as a bid to have an exchange of reasons in support of their respective positions.

As Heather approached the end of this turn, Don took an in-breath and, with no gap between the end of her turn and the beginning of his, reported that he picked up the tax forms that day. In response to a recommendation with which he apparently had no desire to further engage, Don started speaking with latched timing, reporting different news of the day. He timed his report in a way that was non-interruptive yet provided no room for Heather's continuing to support her water bed recommendation. His starting a new topic at just that point was a way of displaying that he was unconvinced by her argument and had no interest in further discussion of the point.

In sum, the practice Don used involved showing respect for a fellow-interactant's right to speak while attempting to close down his or her line of argument. This practice requires both precision timing of one's turn (Jefferson, 1973) and the initiation of a topic appropriate to the local and immediate circumstance. By starting one's turn with virtually no overlap, an interactant can display respect for a fellow-interactant's right to speak. By leaving no gap, the interactant can attempt to eliminate the fellow-interactant's continuing on with his or her argument. By initiating a new topic, the interactant implies that the previous matter is finished.

At the close of the sequence, Don expressed appreciation of Heather's thoughtfulness. We understand that Don's expression of appreciation was an adequate and sufficient expression of appreciation of Heather's thoughtfulness. How did Don's and Heather's timing and taking of turns help provide for this understanding? In particular, we want to claim that the 1 second of silence that occurred in line 11 helped provide for this under-standing.

7	Heather:	I did too=I took two of everything.
8	Don:	For me?
9	Heather:	Yea
10	Don:	That's my baby
11		(1.0)
12	Don:	How was school today

In saying 'That's my baby', Don showed that he recognized and appreci-ated Heather's thoughtfulness in picking up additional forms for him. Upon his uttering the appreciation, the sequence was not definitely closed. Either Don or Heather could have continued or extended it, though in different ways. Don could have added more to his expression of appreci-ation or modified it in some way. By not adding to or modifying what he said, by not continuing or resuming his turn at talk, Don treated his expression of appreciation as adequate and complete. Heather could have responded to Don's expression of appreciation in a number of coherent ways. She could have acknowledged his appreciation, disputed it, expressed appreciation back, etc. In responding with no talk, Heather implied that Don's expression of appreciation needed no reply. By not responding with talk, she treated Don's expression of appreciation as completing the matter on the floor, as showing that he understood and appreciated Heather's picking up extra forms for him.

The sense that participants make of the absence of talk depends on the immediate and local circumstances in which it is done. In this case, Heather and Don's silence followed Don's expression of appreciation. Don's expression of appreciation was an action that allowed for further comment but set up no expectation or relevance of a next action. In this environ-ment, their lack of an immediate response implied that the prior matter or business was finished.

5   Consider How the Ways the Actions were Accomplished Implicate Certain Identities, Roles and/or Relationships for the Interactants   Through what he said and the way in which he said it, Don implied that he was a certain kind of person: one who liked to play a certain kind of character from the movies. Don acted as if he were a 'tough guy' or macho character when he showed appreciation of Heather's picking up extra forms for him. With the expression 'That's my baby' (line 10), Don displayed pride in Heather and/or in the relationship. Don's delivery was not with the same voice as he had used in the sequence up until then. His voice dropped into a gutteral register and seemed scripted as if he were Humphrey Bogart in a 1930s gangster movie.[16] He presented himself not as a tough guy but as someone who likes to occasionally play the role, or sound like, the tough guy.

In his conduct, Don implied that Heather was a certain kind of person, a considerate person, particularly in attending to his needs. This can be illustrated in two of his turns. In his initial response to hearing that Heather picked up two copies of each tax form, Don attempted to find out why she picked up two instead of one of each. There are various ways he could have inquired about her reason or motive. One way could have been to ask for the reason or motive, 'Why two?' However, the way Don asked was to offer a possible reason or motive within a question, that is, to guess. Conceivably, there were many possible reasons why Heather would have taken two copies of each form. (She might have picked up the duplicate copies in case she made mistakes or to have one set to keep for her own records.) In incorporating a particular reason or motive within the question, Don cast that motive as familiar and expected (Pomerantz, 1988). In other words, in specifically asking if Heather picked up the additional forms for him, Don implied that her thinking of him was in character. The second bit of Don's conduct that implied that Heather was thoughtful and considerate was his expression of appreciation. In saying 'That's my baby', Don registered no surprise at the deed; rather the expression implied that what she did was consistent with her previous conduct.

Related to the prior points, Don's conduct can be seen as a bid for defining their relationship as follows: it is a relationship in which it is right, appropriate, and desirable for Heather to be attentive to Don's needs and for Don to appreciate her attentiveness. We just proposed that in guessing 'For me?', Don showed his familiarity with Heather's thinking about his needs. Yet a person's familiarity with someone's motives or conduct does not say how that person regards the motives or conduct. For example, it would be possible for Don both to expect Heather to be attentive to his needs and to be annoyed each time it occurred. The attitude Don displayed was approval and appreciation of Heather's thinking about his needs. Don treated Heather's report as an occasion to express pride in her and in the relationship. When Heather confirmed his guess about her motives, Don honored those motives, displaying appreciation for the caring deed. One can easily imagine how Don's honoring or dishonoring Heather's motives, particularly when her motives involved a concern for him, would be part of their negotiations in establishing their relationship.

Second Demonstration of the Tools

Our first demonstration of analytic work was organized in terms of, and in the same order as, the suggested list of 'tools' or questions. In this second demonstration, the discussion is organized around three topics derived from the characterizations of actions in the sequence. In each, we address the same issues as in the first demonstration though we feel in a more integrated way. This may serve to make our point that these questions are intended as suggestions rather than as a blueprint for analysis.

1   Select a Sequence   For the second demonstration, we selected the sequence that immediately followed the sequence we just analysed.

2   Characterize the Actions

12	D:	How was school today	D asks for an assessment of school that day.
13	H:	Okay	H replies with moderately or weakly positive assessment, passing opportunity to elaborate.
14		(3.6)	3.6 second gap in which time D may be waiting for elaboration and H may be declining to offer any.
15	D:	Hhhh Just okay?	D queries H's assessment, treating it as less than a positive report.
16	H:	Ayup	H confirms with no elaboration.
17	D:	Why what happened?	D requests report which would explain the less than positive report.
18	H:	Nothin. It was kinda boring. We left for lunch though	H claims no such event occurred. She gives characterization of school day consistent with the less than positive report. She reports an activity which is contrastive with the prior report of no interesting activities.
19	D:	Who did	D queries the identity of the participants.
20	H:	Me and Maria an' Sean an' ( ) an' Max Clancey	H names the participants.
21	D:	Sean who?	D queries further identification of the participant, Sean.
22	H:	Sean ah (1.0) Peters. Maria's– You know Abruzzi	H supplies Sean's surname. She begins to identify Sean relative to Maria, cuts off, and supplies Maria's surname.
23	D:	Yeah	D acknowledges (claiming to know which Maria).
24	H:	Maria's new boyfriend.	H completes identification of Sean in relation to Maria.
25		(2.4)	2.4 second gap in which D may have been waiting for further elaboration on the participants and H not offering to elaborate.
26	D:	And who?	D inquires about the fourth participant.

27	H:	A:h his best friend Max	H identifies him in relation to Sean.
28		(2.0)	2 second gap in which D may have been waiting for a further report on Max and H declining to give more.
29	H:	We just went to Dunkin's I had to have a croissant	H reports where they went for lunch and what she ate.
30	D:	Yea well you better tell Max that uh:	In a tough-guy tone, D advises H to tell something to Max, though what she should tell is left unsaid.
31	H:	Max has a girlfriend	H states that Max already is in a relationship.
32	D:	Yea	D acknowledges.
33	H:	Plus he (has disgusting earrings)	H adds an unfavorable description of Max.

The three topics we selected to focus on are: Don's attempts to get Heather to tell about her school day's experiences; Heather's casting the lunch excursion as not very exciting, as barely reportable; and Don's display of possessiveness and/or jealousy.

Don's Attempts to Elicit Information about Heather's School Day   In several ways, Don prompted Heather to share her day's experiences. The first attempt involved asking Heather for an assessment or a report of her experiences at school that day (line 12: 'How was school today'). This type of question allows the recipient to report on experiences or to indicate that he or she has no experiences to report. The recipient can offer an assessment to indicate whether or not he or she intends to report any experiences. As Sacks (1975) demonstrated, moderately positive assessments (for example, 'fine') are offered and understood to indicate that the recipients have nothing to report, while markedly positive or negative assessments are offered and understood as indicating the recipient has experiences to report.

Whereas Don's initial attempt to elicit information about Heather's school day was made with no previous talk on the topic, his subsequent attempts were designed to elicit more of a report from Heather than her initial 'Okay'. The first of these attempts involved not responding verbally for about 3½ seconds. During this period, Don declined to acknowledge or comment upon Heather's assessment. In not taking a turn at speaking, Don treated Heather's 'Okay' as incomplete, as needing some follow-up or elaboration. This emergent gap can be seen as a negotiational period, one in which Don implied that Heather's response was incomplete or inadequate and, as will be discussed shortly, Heather implied that it was adequate and complete. The interactants' timing and taking of turns do not operate independent of their actions, meanings, and sense-making. Whether and when interactants take their turns are part of both performing and understanding actions. Don's not taking a speaking turn served as an action, a claim that Heather's response was inadequate.

Line 15 contains Don's next attempt to elicit more of a report. In this turn, he queried Heather's assessment. One way of querying or challenging what someone has just said is to repeat it with a questioning intonation, such as 'Okay?' Another way is to incorporate a commentary, an indication of the basis for the query or challenge. Don included such a commentary. By including 'Just' in his query 'Just okay?', he cast Heather's 'Okay' as less than a positive report. In querying whether her response was really only 'Just okay', Don drew upon and invoked a contrast between 'Just okay' and an assessment which would indicate nothing problematic. The formulation or reference 'Just okay' was part and parcel of the activity that Don accomplished in the turn. By checking on the meaning of Heather's 'Okay' by questioning whether it was equivalent to 'Just okay', Don created the occasion to elicit more of a report from Heather. He attempted to elicit a further report by 'checking his understanding' of her assessment. He performed the understanding check by reformulating her reply 'Okay' as possibly meaning 'Just okay'.

The last attempt that Don used to elicit more of a report was to prompt Heather to explain the basis of the now confirmed less-than-positive assessment (line 17). He prompted her by coupling a request for an explanation ('Why') with an inquiry about the event responsible for her less-than-positive assessment ('what happened?').

The four attempts that Don used can be seen as strategies, strategies that are interactionally and sequentially not equivalent. The first strategy ('How was school today?') was used as a potential topic opener; it allowed Heather to satisfy the request for an assessment by giving an assessment or report. While satisfying the request, she also had the opportunity to indicate whether she had any newsworthy experiences to share. Don's second strategy, not taking a turn at talk after Heather's reply of 'Okay', was a way of implicitly claiming that Heather's response was problematic. Don's third strategy was a way of more explicitly claiming that Heather's response was problematic. Don queried the meaning of Heather's reply, checking whether she intended it to be less than positive. Finally, Don's fourth strategy was to ask Heather to tell about the experience that was responsible for the less-than-positive assessment. When viewing the four strategies as a series, one notices that they moved from a strategy that allowed Heather the choice of determining whether she had newsworthy experiences to report to a strategy that presupposed a negative experience and directly asked Heather to report it.

Heather's Casting the Lunch Excursion as Not Very Exciting, as Barely Reportable The timing and manner in which Heather reported on her lunch excursion (line 18) framed it as not very important or interesting. We consider four bits of her conduct that provided for this sense of the excursion.

The first piece of conduct occurred in the slot following Don's question, 'How was school today?' Don's question provided an opening for Heather to report on events or experiences during the school day. One consideration in selecting materials to report is whether any are newsworthy, interesting and/or important. *In telling an event, an interactant implicitly proposes that it is worth telling.* Heather responded with 'Okay', an assessment used to indicate 'nothing newsworthy to report'.

The second bit of Heather's conduct that provided for the sense of the lunch excursion as not interesting or important was in her declining to elaborate during the next 3.6 seconds. While Heather warrantably could infer that Don saw her answer as problematic in some way, she attempted no remedy. In waiting for Don to offer more talk, she passed up opportunities to further elaborate on her experiences of the day. In remaining silent, she implicitly claimed to have had no experiences worth telling.

The next bit of conduct that provided for that sense of the lunch excursion was Heather's confirmation of Don's query about the meaning of her 'Okay' (line 16). It is possible that Heather interpreted Don's 'Just okay?' somewhat differently than he may have intended it. If Heather's 'Okay' was a way of indicating that nothing newsworthy happened, she might have heard the 'Just okay' as invoking the distinction between having nothing to report ('Just okay') versus having positive experiences to report (for example, 'good'). In confirming 'Just okay', Heather may have been confirming that she indeed had nothing to report. This interpretation of Heather's sense of Don's 'Just okay' finds support in her next response.

The last bit of Heather's conduct that cast the lunch excursion as a barely reportable event occurred in response to Don's 'Why what happened?' In line 18, Heather's initial response was to claim that no newsworthy event occurred. She continued on with a characterization of the school day that was consistent with both the less-than-positive assessment and the claim that no newsworthy experiences occurred. Having several times in several turns implied or affirmed that nothing interesting happened, Heather then found an event to report. In adding 'though' to her report of the event, she marked the event as contrastive with her previous position that nothing interesting happened. Offered as it was only after affirming that nothing interesting happened, her report seemed to have been offered to satisfy Don's pursuit rather than to share an interesting event. Thus, in her conduct, Heather framed the lunch excursion to be heard as only marginally interesting and the only item worth mentioning in an otherwise boring day.

Don's Display of Possessiveness or Jealousy: Don's Macho Role-Playing
There is some conduct which persons see as instancing jealousy; they have confidence in reading/knowing the motives of the actor. Other conduct poses more ambiguity for the reading of motives. In this sequence, some of

Don's conduct was consistent with his being jealous or possessive but not definitively so. Other of his conduct appeared to instance his acting or role-playing the jealous boyfriend. We will discuss both the conduct associated with ambiguous jealousy and that in which Don role-plays jealousy.

One way of being jealous and/or displaying jealousy is to monitor and check on possible competitors. If Don were jealous or displayed jealousy with respect to Heather, he might monitor Heather's reactions to persons who might replace him as her boyfriend. To learn whether there were potential competitors, Don might have a strong interest in eliciting reports from Heather about her daily experiences, paying close attention to the identities of persons who participated and observing how she talks about them.

We have already discussed Don's successive attempts to elicit a report from Heather on her experiences during the school day. Leaving that aside, we will now discuss how Don's responses to Heather's lunch excursion report were ambiguous with respect to displaying jealous motives. Upon hearing Heather's report of the lunch excursion ('We left for lunch though'), Don actively elicited information on the identities of the participants ('Who did'). There are at least two interpretations of his motives for asking. The first sees Don's inquiry as consistent with jealous motives. A report of a lunch sojourn can include details on where it took place, the kind and quality of the food and service, the cost of each lunch item, the participants, etc. Don's asking about the identity of the participants rather than other aspects of the lunch event was consistent with his screening Heather's activities for potential competitors. The second view involves attributing 'innocent' motives to Don. When Heather reported on the lunch sojourn, she referenced the participants with a 'we': 'We left for lunch though'. By using a pronoun, she implied that Don would have some sense of the participants. In such a circumstance, it was reasonable for Don to inquire after their identities.

Don's next inquiry was to ask for further identification of Sean ('Sean who?'). We view his motives for asking as ambiguous here as well. On the one hand, it might be seen to instance jealously in that he was inquiring about the first male mentioned. Alternatively, Heather identified Sean by first name only, indicating that she expected Don to recognize Sean without further elaboration (Sacks and Schegloff, 1979). If Don failed to recognize him, it was quite appropriate that he ask for additional descriptors.

Don's next inquiry was about the fourth participant ('And who?'). Again Don's motives for this inquiry are ambiguous. On the one hand, it could be seen to be based on the jealous motive of screening possible competitors; on the other hand, it could be seen to be motivated by simply an interest in hearing more about the event.

Two features of Don's conduct in line 30 can be read as less ambiguous as to motives, as more likely motivated by jealousy. The first feature is that Don maintained a focus on Max across a bid by Heather to change the focus (line 29). In response to Don's inquiry about Max, Heather identified him, waited 2 seconds, and then reported where they went to lunch and what she ate. In the next turn, Don returned the focus to Max. We suggest that maintaining a focus on a competitor rather than picking up on Heather's report is less ambiguous with respect to jealousy motives. The second feature involves what kind of talk he did in relation to Max. In line 30, he acted or role-played the possessive, jealous boyfriend ('Yeah well you better tell Max that uh:'). In a tough-guy tone, Don advised Heather to tell something to Max, though what she should tell him was left unspecified. As evidenced by her retort ('<u>Max</u> has a girlfriend'), Heather had no problem figuring out the uncompleted utterance: what she took Don to leave unstated was that she should tell Max that she was Don's girlfriend. Don acted out being macho, possessive, and/or jealous. In starting out with the words 'you better', Don was doing tough-guy talk; he used an expression associated with threats. Yet the intonation in his delivery was one of acting out or playing a role.[17]

Concluding Comments

In our guidelines, we included five areas to consider in developing analyses. We selected these five because we feel they are fundamental. One area we omitted is topical organization. Our decision to omit it rests upon the complexity that is involved in studying it. For a discussion of some of the complexity, see Schegloff (1990), Jefferson (1984a; 1993), Button and Casey (1984; 1985; 1988/89), and Maynard (1980) have produced analyses of some features of topical organization.

We conclude by noting that analysis is a slow process of becoming increasingly aware of features of conduct and practices of action. It can and often does start with listening to your tape and transcribing it. In listening closely enough to transcribe something of what you hear, you will have thoughts about the conduct to explore further. As you continue to listen or watch your tape and makes notes, your beginning analytic thoughts will gradually take on more shape. We know of no one, experienced conversation analysts included, who produces a finished analysis the first time around. This type of work lends itself to successive revision and refinement. Producing the demonstrations for this chapter involved this sort of slowly evolving work. The versions published here look quite different from the early passes through the materials, and they could be developed further.

Coming to the end of reading these demonstrations is approaching the beginning of gaining a deeper understanding of CA. The next step is to apply the perspective to your own materials.

Recommended Reading

We have tried to select materials that would give you access to the widest range of analytic work in the fewest number of citations.

Sacks (1992): Sacks's lectures, delivered between 1964 and 1972, were edited by Gail Jefferson and published in 1992, with an introduction by Emanuel Schegloff. Given Sacks's untimely death in 1975, and the relatively few papers he published during his life, these lectures provide an invaluable insight into his analytic thinking. Although entitled *Lectures on Conversation*, they include discussion and analysis of a much wider range of topics on 'the social organization of mind, culture and interaction' (Schegloff, 1992).

The following provide brief descriptions of seven edited books containing important papers in CA:

Sudnow (1970): this reader contains a collection of early CA work from the 1960s. There are two important papers by Sacks, and others by Schegloff, Sudnow, Moerman, Jefferson and Turner.

Schenkein (1978): contains an expanded version of the famous 'turn-taking' paper by Sacks, Schegloff and Jefferson originally published in *Language* in 1974, and others by Schenkein, Pomerantz, Ryave, Jefferson, Goldberg, Sharrock and Turner, and Atkinson et al.

Psathas (1979): contains papers by Sacks, Schegloff, Jefferson, C. Goodwin, Heritage and Watson, Coulter, Schenkein, Psathas, Pollner and Atkinson. Those by Coulter and Pollner have more broadly ethnomethodological interest, and the paper by Psathas deals with non-conversational materials: hand sketched maps.

Atkinson and Heritage (1978): an excellent collection of later CA work displaying emergent interest in, for example, topic organization and preference structure. Also very helpful general introduction and section introductions which aid reading of the analyses. Papers by Sacks, Schegloff, Pomerantz, Davidson, Drew, Button and Casey, Jefferson, Goodwin, Heath, Heritage and Atkinson.

Button and Lee (1987): contains two chapters (one by Lee and the other by Sharrock and Anderson) which discuss CA and its relation to DA. Two early papers of Sacks and others by Schegloff, Jefferson, Button, Goodwin, Pomerantz, Sharrock and Anderson, and Watson.

Helm et al. (1989): this collection was edited by four former ethnomethodology/CA graduate students from the Sociology Department at Boston University. It contains a number of interesting papers by the editors and their fellow students, as well as papers contributed by Frankel, Maynard, Pomerantz, Morrison and Schwartz.

Psathas (1990): contains analytic papers by Jefferson, Button, Davidson, Coulter, Psathas, Frankel and Watson. Includes a reprinting of a Schegloff, Jefferson and Sacks paper on the preference for self-correction. Psathas prepared a quite complete appendix describing a recent version of the transcription system which includes helpful examples.

Notes

The authors would like to thank David Bates, Paul Drew, Hanneke Houtkoop, William Husson, Douglas Maynard, Jody Morrison, Teun van Dijk, Stanley Yoder, and Alan Zemel for their helpful commentary and suggestions on earlier versions of this chapter.

1 'Conversation analysis' came into common usage before the confusions it could give rise to became fully evident. Changing the name of the approach at this time would seem to produce greater confusion than clarification.

2 'Talk-in-interaction' was a term that was proposed to avoid the confusion that could result from the term 'conversation analysis', namely that it concerns the study of *only* informal talk.

3 See Schiffrin (1994) for a recent survey of the original impetus and recent work in many of these research traditions.

4 See transcription conventions in the Appendix to this volume.

5 An analysis of this segment is worked up in more detail later in the chapter.

6 Conversation analysis has on occasion been characterized as *principally* concerned with the analysis of sequences. Although the analysis of the temporal organization of interaction provides a distinction between CA and other forms of DA, it is not its defining feature.

7 See Emanuel Schegloff's (1992) 'Introduction' to the Blackwell publication of Harvey Sacks's transcribed lectures for a more elaborated discussion of the early history of CA.

8 The commonalities and differences between CA and ethnomethodology have received detailed and innovative treatment in recent literature. See, for example, Lynch (1994), Maynard and Clayman (1991), and Whalen (1992).

9 See transcription conventions in the Appendix to this volume.

10 When participants perform new actions/topics and respond to prior actions/topics, they do so in ways such that their co-participants can see what they are doing. In as much as beginning, responding, and/or closing an action/topic are recognizable to the interactants, they also are recognizable to analysts.

11 While turn organization certainly is part of packaging, we discuss the timing and taking of turns as a separate point.

12 Further discussion of the timing and taking of turns at the boundaries, and the understandings provided by that turn organization, is contained in step 4 in this demonstration.

13 The tellability of a report may depend upon when it occurred relative to the time of the interaction. Sacks analysed how the vast majority of stories are of events that occurred 'today' and 'yesterday' (Sacks, 1992). He argued that items that are tellables on the day they occur may no longer be tellables several days or a week later.

14 In his elaboration, Don portrayed the accomplishment as having happened almost serendipitously. His formulation implies that he went to the post office to mail something, then saw the forms and took them.

15 We could not determine what actions Heather's utterance was accomplishing by only reading the transcript. We needed to rehear the audiotape to hear the intonation of the 'Yeah'. It was on the basis of hearing it as flat that we claim that she 'merely acknowledged' the news. With a livelier 'Yeah', a speaker may show surprise or even skepticism. For a richer and more subtle analysis of acknowledgment tokens, see Jefferson (1984b).

16 This characterization is derived from hearing the way Don delivered 'That's my baby'. Unfortunately, readers do not have the opportunity to evaluate our characterization.

17 Again, it is unfortunate that readers cannot hear the intonation.

References

Atkinson, J.M. and Heritage, J. (eds) (1984) *Structures of Social Action.* Cambridge: Cambridge University Press.

Austin, J.L. (1962) *How To Do Things With Words.* Cambridge, MA: Harvard University Press.

Bernstein, B. (1975) *Class, Codes, and Control. Vol. 3: Towards a Theory of Educational Transmission.* London: Routledge and Kegan Paul.

Button, G. and Casey, N. (1984) 'Generating topic: the use of topic initial elicitors', in J.M. Atkinson and J. Heritage (eds), *Structures of Social Action: Studies in Conversation Analysis.* Cambridge: Cambridge University Press. pp. 167–90.

Button, G. and Casey, N. (1985) 'Topic nomination and topic pursuit', *Human Studies*, 8 (1): 3–55.

Button, G. and Casey, N. (1988/89) 'Topic initiation: business-at-hand', *Research on Language and Social Interaction*, 22: 61–92.

Button, G. and Lee, J.R.E. (1987) *Talk and Social Organization.* Clevedon: Multilingual Matters Ltd.

Coulter, J. (1991) 'Logic: ethnomethodology and the logic of language', in G. Button (ed.), *Ethnomethodology and the Human Sciences.* Cambridge: Cambridge University Press. pp. 20–50.

Coulthard, M. and Montgomery, M. (1981) *Studies in Discourse Analysis*. London: Routledge and Kegan Paul.

Drew, P. (1984) 'Speakers' reporting in invitation sequences', in J.M. Atkinson and J. Heritage (eds), *Structures of Social Action*. Cambridge: Cambridge University Press. pp. 129–51.

Fowler, R., Hodge, B., Kress, G. and Trew, T. (1979) *Language and Control*. London: Routledge and Kegan Paul.

Garfinkel, H. (1967) *Studies in Ethnomethodology*. Englewood Cliffs, NJ: Prentice-Hall.

Goodwin, C. (1981) *Conversational Organization: Interaction between Speakers and Hearers*. New York: Academic Press.

Goodwin, C. (1986) 'Gesture as a resource for the organization of mutual orientation', *Semiotica*, 62 (1/2): 29–49.

Goodwin, M.H. (1980) 'Processes of mutual monitoring implicated in the production of description sequences', *Sociological Inquiry*, 50 (3/4): 303–17.

Goodwin, M.H. (1990) *He-Said-She-Said: Talk as Social Organization among Black Children*. Bloomington, IN: Indiana University Press.

Heath, C.C. (1986) *Body Movement and Speech in Medical Interaction*. Cambridge: Cambridge University Press.

Helm, D.T., Anderson, W.T., Meehan, A.J. and Rawls, A.W. (1989) *The Interactional Order: New Directions in the Study of Social Order*. New York: Irvington Press.

Hymes, D. (1962) 'The ethnography of speaking', in T. Gladwin and W.C. Sturtevant (eds), *Anthropology and Human Behavior*. Washington, DC: Anthropology Society of Washington.

Jayyusi, L. (1984) *Categorization and the Moral Order*. Boston: Routledge and Kegan Paul.

Jefferson, G. (1973) 'A case of precision timing in ordinary conversation: overlapped tag-positioned address terms in closing sequences', *Semiotica*, 9 (1): 47–96.

Jefferson, G. (1984a) 'On stepwise transition from talk about a trouble to inappropriately next-positioned matters', in J.M. Atkinson and J. Heritage (eds), *Structures of Social Action: Studies of Conversation Analysis*. Cambridge: Cambridge University Press. pp. 191–222.

Jefferson, G. (1984b) 'Notes on a systematic deployment of the acknowledgement tokens "yeah" and "mm hm"', *Papers in Linguistics*, 17 (2): 197–216.

Jefferson, G. (1993) 'Caveat speaker: preliminary notes on recipient topic-shift implicature', *Research on Language and Social Interaction*, 26 (1): 1–30.

Labov, W. (1972a) *Language in the Inner City: Studies in the Black English Vernacular*. Philadelphia: University of Pennsylvania Press.

Labov, W. (1972b) *Sociolinguistic Patterns*. Philadelphia: University of Pennsylvania Press.

Levinson, S.C. (1983) *Pragmatics*. London: Cambridge University Press.

Lynch, M. (1994) *Scientific Practice and Ordinary Action*. Cambridge: Cambridge University Press.

Maynard, D.W. (1980) 'Placement of topic changes in conversation', *Semiotica*, 30: 263–90.

Maynard, D.W. and Clayman, S.E. (1991) 'The diversity of ethnomethodology', in W.R. Scott (ed.), *Annual Review of Sociology*, vol. 17. pp. 385–418.

Pomerantz, A. (1986) 'Extreme case formulations: a way of legitimizing claims', *Human Studies*, 9 (2/3): 219–29.

Pomerantz, A. (1988) 'Offering a candidate answer: an information seeking strategy', *Communication Monographs*, 55: 360–73.

Psathas, G. (ed.) (1979) *Everyday Language: Studies in Ethnomethodology*. New York: Irvington Press.

Psathas, G. (ed.) (1990) *Interaction Competence*. Washington, DC: University Press of America.

Sacks, H. (1972) 'An initial investigation of the usability of conversational data for doing sociology', in D. Sudnow (ed.), *Studies in Social Interaction*. New York: The Free Press. pp. 31–74.

Sacks, H. (1975) 'Everyone has to lie', in M. Sanchez and B.G. Blount (eds), *Sociocultural Dimensions of Language Use*. New York: Academic Press. pp. 57–79.

Sacks, H. (1984) 'Notes on methodology', in J.M. Atkinson and J. Heritage (eds), *Structures of*

Social Action: Studies in Conversation Analysis. Cambridge: Cambridge University Press. pp. 21–7. From a lecture originally delivered in Fall 1967; transcribed, edited and compiled by Gail Jefferson.

Sacks, H. (1992) *Lectures on Conversation*, vols I and II. Oxford: Basil Blackwell. Edited by Gail Jefferson, with an introduction by Emanuel Schegloff.

Sacks, H. and Schegloff, E.A. (1979) 'Two preferences in the organization of reference to persons in conversation and their interaction', in G. Psathas (ed.), *Everyday Language: Studies in Ethnomethodology*. New York: Irvington Publishers. pp. 15–21.

Sacks, H., Schegloff, E.A. and Jefferson, G. (1974) 'A simplest systematics for the organization of turn-taking in conversation', *Language*, 50 (4): 696–735.

Schegloff, E.A. (1980) 'Preliminaries to preliminaries: "Can I ask you a question?"', *Sociological Inquiry*, 50 (3/4): 104–52.

Schegloff, E.A. (1984) 'On some gestures' relation to talk', in J.M. Atkinson and J. Heritage (eds), *Structures of Social Action*. Cambridge: Cambridge University Press. pp. 266–96.

Schegloff, E.A. (1988) 'Presequences and indirection: applying speech act theory to ordinary conversation', *Journal of Pragmatics*, 12: 55–62.

Schegloff, E.A. (1990) 'On the organization of sequences as a source of "coherence" in talk-in-interaction', in B. Dorval (ed.), *Conversational Organization and its Development*. Norwood, NJ: Ablex. pp. 51–77.

Schegloff, E.A. (1992) 'Introduction', in H. Sacks, *Lectures on Conversation*. Oxford: Basil Blackwell. pp. ix–lxii.

Schenkein, J.N. (ed.) (1978) *Studies in the Organization of Conversational Interaction*. New York: Academic Press.

Schiffrin, D. (1994) *Approaches to Discourse*. Oxford: Blackwell.

Stubbs, M. (1983) *Discourse Analysis: the Sociolinguistic Analysis of Natural Language*. Chicago: University of Chicago Press.

Sudnow, D. (ed.) (1970) *Studies in Social Interaction*. New York: Free Press.

Vico, G. (1975) *The New Science of Giambattista Vico* (1744) (ed. and trans. T.G. Bergen and M.H. Fisch). Ithaca, NY: Cornell University Press.

Watson, D.R. (1976) 'Some conceptual issues in the social identification of victims and offenders', in E.C. Viano (ed.), *Victims and Society*. Washington, DC: Visage Press. pp. 60–71.

Watson, D.R. (1983) 'The presentation of victim and motive in discourse: the case of police interrogations and interviews', *Victimology*, 8 (1/2): 31–52.

Whalen, J. (1992) 'Conversation analysis', in E.F. Borgatta and M.L. Borgatta (eds), *Encyclopedia of Sociology*, vol. 1. New York: Macmillan. pp. 303–10.

Wieder, D.L. (1974) *Language and Social Reality*. The Hague: Mouton. Reprinted by University Press of America.

4

Institutional Dialogue

Paul Drew and Marja-Leena Sorjonen

Institutional Dialogue: the Field of Study

When people visit the doctor, appear as witnesses in court, hold meetings at their workplaces, negotiate business deals, call railway stations for information, as faculty meet their students in office hours, or as counsellors or clients participate in AIDS counselling sessions, they are talking, communicating and interacting in institutional 'contexts'. They are using language to conduct the kinds of affairs in which we are all engaged when dealing with the variety of organizations we encounter in our daily lives, either as professional members of those organizations, or as their clients (customers, students, patients and the like). Language – in the form of talk-in-interaction – is the means by which the participants perform and pursue their respective institutional tasks and goals. Of course, other forms of language such as written documents and computer messages also play a part in institutional communication; but here we focus specifically on spoken dialogue. The study of 'institutional dialogue' is, then, the study of how people use language to manage those practical tasks, and to perform the particular activities associated with their participation in institutional contexts – such as teaching, describing symptoms, cross-examining, making inquiries, negotiating and interviewing. Thus when investigating institutional dialogue, we are focusing on linguistic resources at various levels – lexical, syntactic, prosodic, sequential, etc. – which are all mobilized for accomplishing the interactional work of institutions.

Institutional interactions may be conducted face-to-face or over the telephone. And although they frequently occur within designated physical settings, such as hospitals, post-offices and schools, it is important to emphasize that they are not restricted to such locations. Thus, places not usually considered 'institutional', for example, a private home, may well become the setting/arena for institutional or work-related interactions. Similarly, people in a workplace may talk together about matters unconnected with their work. Thus, the institutionality of talk is not determined by its occurrence in a particular physical setting.

Hence research in this field is confronted with the issue of what precisely constitutes 'institutional' interactions. There is probably no clear definition which would precisely delimit the scope of the field of institutional dialogue (for the difficulty of defining contexts in general, see Goodwin and Duranti, 1992). We can illustrate the complexities involved in identifying what might be and what might not be institutional by considering the following extract from the beginning of an internal telephone call between personnel in a US State administrative office.[1]

(1)   [J1MORE: 12: 4]
```
    1   Kate:  Hey Jim?
    2   Jim:   How are you Kate Fisher
    3   Kate:  How are you doin'
    4   Jim:   Well I'm doin' all right [thank you very [much
    5   Kate:                           [We-              [Well goo:d
    6   Jim:   And a lo:vely day it is.
    7   Kate:  Oh:, isn't it gor[geous=
    8   Jim:                    [Yes
    9   Kate:  =I snuck out at lunch
   10          its [really [difficult to come [back
   11   Jim:       [.hhh  [You(h)oo        [.hhh that was not-
   12          good
   13   Kate:  See it (was[ese-)
   14   Jim:              [You're s'pose to stay in your office
   15          and work work work [h e h ha:h
   16   Kate:                     [Well-
   17   Kate:  Jean and I went- she- she works in our office too
   18          we went together too: uh- .hhhh u:h do some
   19          shopping
   20   Jim:   [Um hum
   21   Kate:  [A:nd we each made each other come ba:ck,
   22   Jim:   Atta girl, ye:s I know what you mean
   23   Kate:  So maybe that's the ke(h)y of going [like that
   24   Jim:                                       [Huh huh huh
   25   Jim:   That's it
   26   Jim:   pt .hhhhh [What's up
   27   Kate:            [Well-
   28   Kate:  Well, I've had a call from Paul toda:y and after
   29          he called, I checked with your- terminal over
   30          there and they said our order's not awarded . . .
```

Lines 28–30 display that Kate has called a colleague, Jim, in order to conduct some work-related business; the call is in a general sense concerned with these participants' institutional tasks. But before they come to dealing with the call's official business, they converse for a brief interlude in a way that might be considered 'merely being sociable' (lines 1–25). Thus within a single encounter participants may engage in, and move between, 'sociable' and 'institutional' talk.

Notice, though, that the institutionality of this interaction might not be restricted to the phase in which they begin the call's official business. For example, even in these initial, sociable pleasantries in lines 1–25, their orientation to their institutional identities (namely colleagues in an administrative office) is manifest through the ways in which the topics of the weather and shopping are set in the context of office routines and employees' duties (for example, Jim's tease in lines 14–15). It is possible also that an institutional flavour is imparted to their talk by certain linguistic and sequential features in this phase (for example, their abbreviated greetings in lines 1–4; Jim's use of repetition rather than ellipsis in his response in line 4; and the somewhat unusual word order, fronting of the subject complement *a lovely day*, in Jim's comment about the weather in line 6). Moreover, they attend explicitly to their identities as co-workers in the administrative agency (see, for example, lines 14, 17–18 and 21). So on the one hand participants may fluctuate between different kinds of discourse (such as sociable and institutional) within a single conversation; and on the other hand an apparently 'non-institutional' phase may be suffused with the institutionality of its context (and may indeed be necessary for constructing institutionally appropriate rapport with one's colleagues). Despite these fluctuations and indeterminancies, the dialogue which takes place in this call can be considered generally 'institutional' in so far as the participants engage in and accomplish institutionally relevant activities (for example, checking that an order has been placed); and in doing so, orient to the relevance of their institutional identities for the interaction.

To summarize, the boundaries between institutional talk and conversation are not fixed. The institutionality of dialogue is constituted by participants through their orientation to relevant institutional roles and identities, and the particular responsibilities and duties associated with those roles; and through their production and management of institutionally relevant tasks and activities. The study of institutional dialogue thus focuses on the ways in which conduct is shaped or constrained by the participants' orientations to social institutions, either as their representatives or in various senses as their 'clients'. Analysing institutional dialogue involves investigating how their orientation to and engagement in their institutional roles and identities is manifest in the details of participants' language, and their use of language to pursue institutional goals.

Development of the Field

The study of institutional dialogue has emerged as a distinctive field of research during the past 20 years from developments in a number of cognate disciplines and perspectives, notably in *sociolinguistics, discourse analysis, ethnography of speaking, microethnography of face-to-face interaction,* and *conversation analysis* (for an overview, see Drew and Heritage, 1992b). Traditionally, *sociolinguistic* studies have focused on language variation associated with such social variables as class, ethnicity, age and gender. However, about 20 years ago, studies began to be published which acknowledged and documented the kinds of language variation associated with the social situation of use, somewhat independently of other (speaker-related) sources of variation.

Interactional sociolinguistics has been particularly innovative in attempting to shift the sociolinguistic paradigm away from its traditional focus on speaker attributes to explain language variation and towards an alternative focus on the situational accomplishment of social identity (Gumperz, 1982a; 1982b; Tannen and Wallat, 1993). The key contribution of this approach is to recast speaker identities, not as background 'givens', but as interactionally produced in those contexts which are crucial strategic sites in modern bureaucratic industrial societies. This programmatic objective (see especially Gumperz and Cook-Gumperz, 1982) has been pursued in a series of studies based on recordings made in naturally occurring settings such as job interviews, committees, courtroom interrogations, counselling, industrial training and public debates.

The recognition that speech events are built out of particular component actions or *speech acts* has been fundamental to most perspectives concerned with institutional dialogue. But the approach that most directly builds on the notion of speech act (from the philosophy of language) in the analysis of spoken interaction is *discourse analysis*, developed by the Birmingham discourse analysis group. Their description of the standardized sequences of acts and moves which make up exchanges characteristic of particular settings, such as the classroom and medical interaction, represents a more dialogic approach to language in institutional settings (Sinclair and Coulthard, 1975; Coulthard and Ashby, 1975).

Studies associated with the *ethnography of speaking* have emphasized that part of a speaker's 'identity' is her membership of a speech community. They have shown that the distinctive cultural communication style associated with particular speech communities is one of the ethnographic factors to be taken into account when analysing talk in particular speech settings – thereby introducing a much broader sense of what constitutes the ethnographic context of a speech event. In this perspective, the analysis of communicative meanings requires a description and understanding of such sociocultural features as speakers' social identities; their past history and other biographical details; the states of knowledge and expectations, manifest in their talk, that they bring to speech events; and the rights, duties, and other responsibilities which are attached to participants' roles or positions in particular institutional events. Thus research in this area is characterized by an emphasis on integrating the analysis of utterance meaning with a description of such ethnographic particulars (see, for example, S.B. Heath, 1983; Ochs, 1988; Cicourel, 1992).

A similar emphasis is to be found in *microethnographic studies of face-to-face interaction* in institutional settings, for example a study by Erickson and Shultz (1982) of academic advice/counselling interviews. Such work attempts to show that the ethnographic particulars of an occasion –

including the social and cultural context of that occasion and the knowledge etc. which participants bring to it by virtue of their membership in speech communities, such as speech style – are reflected in and consequential for the fine detail of the organization of verbal and non-verbal action. This line of research is consonant with earlier microanalytic studies, for instance of psychotherapeutic sessions (Scheflen, 1973).

One of the distinctive features of such microethnographic studies is their attempt to account for the dynamic unfolding of particular interactions, in terms of the locally produced understandings, responses and moves within that interaction – and hence the coordination of sequences of communicative actions. Recognition of the key importance of investigating the characteristic sequential dynamics of dialogue in particular institutional settings has been, perhaps, one of the most significant developments in the field of institutional dialogue (Mehan, 1979; see also the work of Linell and his associates on the initiation-response model, for example Linell et al., 1988).

This development is owed principally to the work, largely within sociology, of *conversation analysis*. There have certainly been other trends within sociology which impinge on the emergence of the study of institutional dialogue over the past 20 years, most notably Goffman's (1972) focus on the interaction order in face-to-face encounters, including those in institutional settings such as mental hospitals and medical surgery. Developments in sociological ethnography have foregrounded the closer analysis of verbal interaction in such settings as, for example, paediatric clinics (Silverman, 1987). But undoubtedly the most significant exploration of the sequential character of interaction in institutional settings has been provided by studies informed by the conversation analytic perspective. Sacks (1992) originated conversation analysis in the course of his investigations into telephone calls made to a suicide prevention centre. Subsequent studies have developed that interest in unravelling how the participants, in and through the ways in which they construct their turns and sequences of turns, display their orientation to particular institutional identities, and thereby manage the practical tasks associated with any given institutional setting (Atkinson and Drew, 1979; Maynard, 1984; Heritage, 1985; C. Heath, 1986; Drew and Heritage, 1992a).

Developments in the areas outlined above have converged around three principal foci: (a) the expansion of the sociolinguistic notion of 'context' to include the sensitivity of language to a variety of social situations, including institutional settings; (b) the emergence of analytic frameworks that recognize the nature of language as action and which handle the dynamic features of social action and interaction; and (c) methodologically, the analysis of audio and video recordings of naturally occurring interactions in specific institutional and occupational settings. Of course each of these perspectives has given prominence to different kinds of analytic and substantive themes. These include such closely interrelated issues as institutional/professional authority and control (Fisher and Todd, 1993), asymmetry in discourse

(Markova and Foppa, 1991; Maynard, 1991); formality of setting; ideology, types of knowledge and belief systems put into play by participants (Conley and O'Barr, 1990; Mishler, 1984; Hein and Wodak, 1987); and miscommunication (Coupland et al., 1991; West, 1984).

Across these different foci of interest, the field of institutional dialogue is beginning to coalesce around a cumulative body of knowledge concerning (a) participants' orientations to their institutional roles and identities, (b) participants' management of institutionally relevant activities, and (c) comparative dimensions of language and interaction. We now turn to illustrate these themes with empirical examples.

Participants' Orientation to their Institutional Identities

Following from the observations above about recasting the sociolinguistic notion of 'speaker identity', participants' institutional identities can be viewed, not as exogenous and determining variables, but as accomplished in interaction. Hence a key focus of research into institutional dialogue is to show how participants' orientation to their institutional identities is manifest in the details of the verbal conduct through which they manage their institutional tasks. Here we review some of the linguistic resources which participants use in orienting to their institutional identities, namely *person reference, lexical choice, grammatical construction, turn-taking* and institutionally specific *inferences.*

Person Reference

In their selection of the particular way of referring to each other and to third parties, participants may display their orientation to their acting as incumbents of an institutional role, or as somehow representing an institution. They do so, for instance, by using a personal pronoun which indexes their institutional rather than their personal identity. An example is the following, taken from a call to the emergency services in the US:

(2)   [Whalen et al., 1988: 344]
      1   Desk: Mid-city Emergency
      2   .
      3   .
      4   Desk: Hello? What's thuh problem?
      5   Caller: We have an unconscious, uh: diabetic
      6   Desk: Are they insiduv a building?
      7   Caller: Yes they are:
      8   Desk: What building is it?
      9   Caller: It's thuh adult bookstore?
      10 Desk: We'll get somebody there right away . . .

In this fragment the caller refers to himself through the first person plural pronoun *we* (line 5), thereby indexing that he is speaking not in a personal capacity (for example, as a relative of the victim) but on behalf of the shop in which the victim happened to fall ill (line 9, _adult bookstore_). Similarly, the desk uses a third person plural pronoun in inquiring about the victim, previously referred to in the singular (cf. _an unconscious diabetic_ in line 5 vs _they_ in line 6), as well as the first person plural pronoun _we_ in line 10 when announcing the action he is ready to mobilize.

In the following example from a Finnish doctor–patient consultation, the person reference forms are also shaped by 'institutional' considerations although they do not directly index an institutional role as in example (2). In this fragment, the doctor, who has just completed the verbal and physical examination of the patient, begins to outline the treatment (for glossing conventions see the Appendix to this chapter):

(3)   [12B1:7 – High blood pressure]
     1   D: .mhh >Kyllä meiä-n   täytyy ny si-llä   tava-lla   teh-dä
                   surely we-GEN must   now it-ADE way-ADE do-INF
                .mhh >We do have to do so now

     2   että me alote-ta-an se vere-n-paine-°lää:kitys°.=
                that we start-PAS-4 it blood-GEN-pressure-medication
                that we'll start the blood pressure °medication°.=

     3   =Ja koete-ta-an edelleen si-tä   laihdutus-ta ja
                and try-PAS-4   still   it-PAR diet-PAR   and
                =And let's continue trying to diet and

     4   °.hh° ja jos koetta-isi-tte jättä-ä   vielä °a-°
                    and if try-CON-PL2 leave-INF still ?
                °.hh° and if you'd try to leave out even °(   )-°

     5   (0.4) vielä tiuke-mma-lle   se-n   suola   ja (0.2)
                    still strict-COM-ALL it-ACC salt(ACC) and
                (0.4) even more salt and (0.2)

     6   o- yrittä-is   ol-la   vaikka ilman
                ?be try-CON(SG3) be-INF say   without
                be- try to be say without

     7   alkoholi-a-ki   jos vaa #onnistu-u   ja#,
                alcohol-PAR-CLI if just   succeed-SG3 and
                alcohol see if that #works out and#,

Here, the doctor outlines four different things that the patient should do to reduce his high blood pressure, namely take some medication (lines 1–2), diet (line 3), reduce his intake of salt (lines 4–5) and cut out alcohol (lines 6–7). He does so by using three different devices for indicating whose responsibility it is to put this treatment in effect. In the first two utterances (lines 1–2, 3), the doctor uses the first person plural pronoun _me_ 'we' and/ or the verb form associated with it.[2] He thereby formulates the actions as their joint project. Then (line 4) he moves to using the second person plural verb form _koettaisitte_ 'you would try', with which he treats the next action as the responsibility of the patient. Finally, in suggesting that the patient should give up alcohol, he employs the verb in a third person singular form (*yrittäis* 'would try', line 6) without a subject pronoun – which in Finnish is a way of avoiding explicit personal reference in order to index, for example, the delicacy involved in raising the topic, in this case the patient's drinking habits (see Hakulinen, 1987). Thus here the doctor uses resources available for person reference in the language to index a particular stance toward each single element of the treatment, in terms of dimensions such as who has the primary responsibility for executing the action (that is, carrying out the treatment) and the possible delicacy of a topic.

These brief examples not only illustrate aspects of how participants exhibit and orient to their institutional identities through person reference forms; they also begin to show the inseparable constitutive relationship between the linguistic devices for person reference and managing institutional activities (for some other examples of this issue in a medical setting, see Silverman, 1987: Chapter 3; in a university physics laboratory, see Ochs et al., forthcoming; in Samoan *fono* meetings, see Duranti, 1994).

Lexical Choice

The issues raised above concerning the selection of person reference forms shade into a more general issue of lexical choice – that is, the selection of descriptive terms and other lexical items treated by participants as appropriate to, and hence indicative of, their understandings of the situation they are in. Plainly, this connects with linguistic notions of setting-specific, situationally appropriate registers, codes or styles. The point to be made here is that speakers orient to the institutionality of the context, in part through their selection of terms from the variety of alternative ways for describing people, objects or events. This can involve the 'descriptive adequacy' of lexical choice with respect to the type of institutional context concerned (legal, educational, medical, etc.).

We can begin to see how lexical selection might invoke institutional settings and tasks in the following extract from a call by the attendance clerk in an American high school (AC is the attendance clerk; M is mother, F is father):

(4) [Medeiros 5]
```
     1   AC:    Hello this is Miss Medeiros from Redondo
     2          High School calling
     3   M:     Uh hu:h
     4   AC:    Was Charlie home from school ill today?
     5          (0.3)
     6   M:     .hhhh
     7          (0.8)
     8   M:     ((off phone)) Charlie wasn't home ill today
     9          was he?
    10          (0.4)
```

```
11  F:        ((off phone)) Not at all.
12  M:        No:.
13            (.)
14  AC:       N[o?
15  M:           [No he wasn't
16  AC: →     .hhh (.) Well he wz reported absent from his
17       →     thir:d an' his fifth period cla:sses tihday.
18  M:        Ah ha:h,
19  AC:       .hhh A:n' we need him t'come in t'the office
20            in th'morning t'clear this up
```

Having first inquired whether their child was ill at home that day, the attendance clerk then informs the mother that her child has been *reported absent* that day (lines 16–17). Notice that the attendance clerk says that the child was *reported* absent, not simply that he *was* absent. Her use of the verb *reported* here in collocation with *absent* is cautious or equivocal – at least in so far as it avoids directly accusing the child of truancy, and instead leaves the determination of his possible truancy for subsequent investigation. Moreover, it alludes to the procedures in the school for reporting absences, the possible fallibility of these procedures, and hence their possible incompleteness. So whilst the verb *reported* is by no means restricted to institutional settings, its inclusion here is part of the proper management of the attendance clerk's task (see Drew and Heritage, 1992b: 45–6; Pomerantz, 1980). Furthermore, the selection of the complement *absent* to describe the child's non-presence at school activates a specifically institutional form of non-presence (for instance, one is 'absent' from school or a workplace, but not from a party).

The institutional relevance of lexical choice, manifested in the selection of *absent* in example (4), is perhaps more transparent in cases where participants use a terminology more clearly restricted in their situation-specific distribution (such as technical terminology). Many studies have documented the ways in which the use of technical vocabularies (for example in medical and legal contexts) can embody definite claims to specialized technical knowledge. Generally, such studies point to the interactional salience for participants of *professionals'* use of technical vocabularies (Meehan, 1981). Often this is related to asymmetries of knowledge between professional and lay participants; and to claims that their use of technical vocabulary is one of the ways in which professionals may variously control the information available to the clients, thereby possibly influencing what emerges as the outcomes of interactions (for a review of these issues in studies on medical interaction, see Roter and Hall, 1992). However, that kind of research, that is concerning professional control through the use of technical vocabulary, may turn out to rely on what is, perhaps, a rather oversimplified dichotomy between professionals' possession of professional/technical knowledge, and clients' (patients') possession of lay knowledge.

We should emphasize that issues of lexical choice go beyond technical vocabularies. Potentially, *any* lexical selection in institutional dialogue is investigable for its constitutive and situated relevance for the kind of discourse in which participants are engaged, and for the tasks which they are performing through their lexical choices. Thus any lexical selection is *informative* about participants' orientations to institutional contexts and their roles within them. Lexical choice connects with broader issues concerning turn design, and particularly how certain kinds of activities managed in turns at talk are designed; and also with the pragmatics of description (Drew and Heritage, 1992b: 29–32; Danet, 1980), epistemic stances displayed through modal expressions (He, 1993), and stylistic variation and register (Duranti, 1992).

Grammatical Forms

We noted above that a particular institutional activity may be constructed in alternative ways, including alternative grammatical forms. For instance, in giving dietary advice to a patient, a doctor may use in English a verb of obligation (*You should use less sugar*) or one of recommendation (*I'd recommend . . .*), an imperative (*Put less sugar in your cooking*), or a hypothetical (*If I were you . . .*) (cf. Ervin-Tripp, 1975; West, 1990; M.H. Goodwin, 1992; Heritage and Sefi, 1992).

Thus a range of alternative grammatical constructions is available for performing given actions (such as asking questions). The use of particular grammatical forms, such as modals, is not exclusive or restricted to institutional settings. However, various grammatical forms are the resources available to participants in managing their institutional tasks. In so far as those tasks are part of the interactional routine for a given setting (for example, giving advice about treatment is part of the routine in medical consultations; attempts at undermining the witness's evidence are part of the routine of cross-examination), particular grammatical forms are likely to have distinctive distributions in given settings. That is to say, certain grammatical forms may be prevalent in certain settings; or they may show characteristic patterns of use which are associated with the characteristic activities in which participants engage in a setting.

Studies have documented a variety of characteristic uses of particular grammatical forms in settings such as courts, classrooms, news interviews (Heritage and Roth, 1995), medical consultations, service encounters (Ventola, 1987) and formal meetings (Duranti, 1994). What emerges from some of this research is in part a picture of the distribution of grammatical forms in various settings. More importantly, they also reveal the interactional functions or dimensions of their selection, especially the interactional consequences which may be associated with the use of certain forms. For example, a number of studies have documented the ways in which different forms used by attorneys for asking questions in courtroom examinations, such as between WH-questions and yes/no questions, can have variable constraining power over witnesses' answers (Danet and Bogoch, 1980; Harris, 1984).

Another example is Kim's (1992) finding that WH-cleft construction in English (utterances such as *what I want to suggest is . . .*) is much more common in such formal institutional settings as university lectures, radio call-in talk shows and group therapy sessions than it is in conversation. Furthermore, even though WH-clefts in institutional dialogues and in conversation shared basic discourse functions (shifting talk, marking the gist or making a certain interactional point), there were also differences in their usage in these two types of setting. In formal lectures, the construction is used, for example, to resume formality and thereby to shift to the default register of the interaction after an informal and often humorous stretch of talk. This formality-resumption character of the construction is deployed in conversation to depart from the default register of conversation in order to formulate one's utterance as authoritative when asserting a point in response to a co-participant's prompt or challenge in 'problematic' contexts. Thus the examination of grammatical form lies at the interface between linguistic work on syntax, and the analysis of the pragmatic and interactional role of utterances in their sequential contexts in institutional settings.

Turn-Taking

One of the most significant themes to have emerged in this field is that, in various ways, participants' conduct is shaped by reference to constraints on their contributions in institutional dialogues. Perhaps the most evident constraint lies in turn-taking systems which depart substantially from the way in which turn-taking is managed in conversation (Sacks et al., 1974). Interactions in courtrooms (Atkinson and Drew, 1979; Philips, 1984), classrooms (McHoul, 1978), and news interviews (Greatbatch, 1988; Heritage and Greatbatch, 1991) exhibit systematically distinct forms of turn-taking which powerfully structure many aspects of conduct in these settings. These turn-taking systems involve the differential allocation of turn types among the participants; notably, the interactions are organized in terms of question–answer sequences, in which questioning is allocated to the professional (attorney, interviewer, teacher) and answering to the 'client' (witness, interviewee, pupil).

However, even institutional contexts in which there is no formal prescription governing the turn-taking system appear to be characterized by asymmetric distribution of questions and answers among the participants. This suggests that the question–answer structure of talk is an emergent property of the local management of interaction by participants (Frankel, 1990). Similarly, even if the turn-taking system is predetermined by an external prescriptive organization, nevertheless the task of analysis is to specify how it is locally managed, in ways which display the participants' orientations to what they should properly be doing in a setting, and hence to their institutional identities and roles. Thus we can view any specialized institutional turn-taking system as the product of participants' orientations to their task-related roles.

It is quite familiar that news interviews exhibit a question–answer structure. However, the following example begins to show how this structure is achieved through the local practices for managing the talk as asking and answering questions.

```
(5)  [Heritage and Roth 1995: 18]
    1   IE:   er The difference is that it's the press that
    2         constantly call me a Ma:rxist when I do not, (.)
    3         and never have (.) er er given that description
    4         myself. [.hh I-]
    5   IR:        [But I]'ve heard you- I've heard you'd be
    6         very happy to: to: er .hhhh er describe yourself as
    7         a Marxist. Could it be that with an election in the
    8         offing you're anxious to play down that you're a
    9         Marx[ist.]
   10   IE:       [er ] Not at all Mister Da:y.=And I:'m (.)
   11         sorry to say I must disagree with you,=you have
   12         never heard me describe myself .hhh er as a
   13         Ma:rxist.
```

The significant points here are, first, that the interviewer (IR) constructs his turn (lines 5–9) so that, whatever else he does (see the declarative in lines 5–7), he produces a question as the last element in his turn, through an interrogative – thereby constituting his local task as one of 'asking questions'. Second, although it is clear that the interviewee (IE) disagrees with the IR's statement in lines 5–7, he withholds his answer/disagreement until a question has explicitly been asked. Thus the ways in which IR constructs his turn, and IE only speaks after a question has been asked, thereby producing an answer, display both participants' orientations to their respective tasks in the interview. It is in this sense that we mean that the turn-taking organization is an emergent product of participants' locally managed interactional practices (for further explication of these issues, see Heritage and Greatbatch, 1991; Heritage and Roth, 1995).

Institutionally Specific Inferences

Participants orient to institutional settings through their recognition of and response to the particular meanings that they attribute to each other's turns at talk. Hence some studies in this area focus on analysing the inferences participants make about what the other is saying or doing, and the specific institutional salience of those inferences. 'Inference' refers to participants' understandings of the activities that each is performing and the situationally relevant meanings of their utterances; those understandings are based on normative expectations concerning the nature of the occasion and each other's roles within it.

In some respects what participants take one another to mean, that is, the inferences they make from what is said, is rooted in their orientations to the constraints about what will count as allowable contributions to given institutional activities (Levinson, 1992). For example, the kind of answer that one might give at the beginning of a medical consultation to the doctor's question *how are you* might be very different from one's answer to the same question asked by a friend at the beginning of a telephone call. These differences, of course, reveal speakers' inferences concerning, for example, what the doctor wants to find out in asking that question, and hence what would be an 'allowable contribution' as an answer to her inquiry (Coupland et al., 1992).

But the inferential basis for participants' recognition of what the other means or is doing in an utterance is rather broader than such constraints on allowable contributions: it includes more general expectations associated with each participant's relevant institutional activities. For example, in the following extract from a visit by a health visitor (HV), the mother (M) treats HV's observation that the baby is enjoying sucking something (line 1) as implying that the baby might be hungry (lines 3–4). In so doing she orients both to the HV's institutional task of monitoring and evaluating baby care, and to her own responsibility and accountability for that care (note that the father treats the action implicature of HV's observation very differently, line 2).

(6)   [Drew and Heritage 1992b: 33]
     1   HV: →   He's enjoying that [isn't he.
     2   F: [°Yes, he certainly is=°
     3   M: →   =He's <u>not</u> hungry 'cuz (h)he's ju(h)st (h)had
     4   →   'iz bo:ttle .hhh
     5   (0.5)
     6   HV: You're feeding him on (.) Cow and Gate Premium.

The following example further illustrates participants' orientation to institutionally specific inferences. The extract comes from the cross-examination by the prosecution attorney (DA) of a defendant (D) who is charged with being an accessory to a murder. Briefly, her boyfriend, Pete, shot dead a friend of theirs, after an altercation during which the friend and murder victim stabbed Pete. The charge is that she aided Pete by getting admission to the victim's apartment. Here the purpose of the cross-examination appears to be to establish her motive in aiding her boyfriend.

(7)   [Murder trial: Cheek: 35-A-1: 136]
     1   DA: And you had strong feelings over Pete at that time?
     2   D: Yes (.) I was his girlfriend at the time.
     3   DA: You were upset because he was stabbed?
     4   D: I wasn't upset.

```
 5  DA:  You weren't upset? You were happy?
 6  D:   No.
 7  DA:  You had no feelings at all about the wound that he
 8       had.
 9  D:   I was concerned about what was going on.
10  DA:  Did you feel sad that he was wounded?
11  D:   I don't know.
12  DA:  You don't know how you felt? I mean you could have
13       been happy?
14  D:   No.
15  DA:  You know you didn't feel happy.
16  D:   I gue::ss
17  DA:  But you don't know if you felt sad or not?
18  D:   I felt ba:d some. ((voice breaks))
19  DA:  You felt ba:d some. You do remember.
20  D:   Yes, I felt bad some.
21  DA:  You remember that.
22  D:   Yes.
23  DA:  You felt angry.
24  D:   Yes.
25  DA:  You felt anger towards the person who stabbed him.
26  D:   No.
27  DA:  You remember specifically that you had no anger at
28       all about the person who stabbed him?
29  D:   I felt angry about . . . ((confused and inaudible))
30  DA:  You weren't angry at him.
31  D:   No.
```

It is fairly clear that the DA's questioning here is designed to establish that the D's motive for assisting her boyfriend arose from her feelings about him having been stabbed by the victim. It is clear also that it is evident to the defendant that this is the line of questioning which the DA is pursuing (on witnesses' recognition of lines of questioning, see Atkinson and Drew, 1979: 112–21, 173–81). This is evident in her resistance to the DA's suggestions about how she felt, and to his attempts to cast doubt on, and undermine, her qualified versions of her feelings about the incident. In her answers she, for example, rejects the DA's suggestion that she was upset because her boyfriend had been stabbed (lines 3–4), or that she 'felt anger towards the person who stabbed him' (lines 25–26); and she responds to his suggestion that she 'had no feelings at all about the wound' by agreeing to a qualified version of her feelings, which was that she was 'concerned about what was going on' (line 9).

In these and other respects, her orientation to the implications of the DA's questions, and her strategic attempts to avoid those implications, are particularly transparent. Likewise, the ways in which the DA is alive to the implications of her answers, and his attempts to combat her resistance, are equally transparent. The participants therefore design their turns with respect to the inferences to be drawn from each other's descriptions, in the context of the charge and the attendant circumstances of the incident with which it is concerned. Each thereby orients to the *strategic* purpose underlying the other's descriptions and constructs her/his descriptions with a view of their strategic goals (Drew, 1990). This association between the inferential meaning and strategy is part of what might be referred to as the 'pragmatics' of institutional dialogue.

Comparative Analysis

In so far as it focuses on the distinctive features of language use in institutional interactions, and on the characteristic activities which are associated with them (activities such as diagnosing, cross-examining, advising), research in the field of institutional dialogue is, in one way or another, *comparative*. That is, we are investigating the various ways in which institutional forms of interaction show systematic variations and restrictions on activities, and the linguistic means through which they are designed relative to non- institutional interactions, for which ordinary conversation stands as a benchmark (Drew and Heritage, 1992b: 19).

All analyses of institutional interaction connect talk to its institutional context by citing extracts of interaction in order to exhibit features of action and social relations that are characteristic of particular settings. These are associated with distinctive *patterns of sequences* in institutional interactions, as compared with, for example, ordinary conversation. At the broadest level, studies which document the specialized turn-taking systems of courtroom examination, classroom teaching and news interviews all draw attention to the ways in which these turn-taking systems differ from the organization of turn-taking in conversation (see earlier section on turn-taking for references). They show, further, that such specialized turn-taking systems have consequences for the management of certain activities, in comparison with their management in conversation (see, for example, Greatbatch, 1992 on disagreement in news interviews; and McHoul, 1990 on repair in classroom talk).

But more generally, sequential patterns in institutional interactions involve discernible differences from ordinary conversation. For example, the interaction in many institutional settings is characterized by question–answer sequences in which the questioner routinely makes some form of response, in third position in the sequence, to the answer. The instructional phase of classroom lessons, for instance, is typically managed through Q–A sequences in which the teacher does some kind of evaluation of a pupil's answer. An example is the following:

(8) [Sinclair and Coulthard 1975: 21]
     1 T: Can you tell me why do you eat all that food
     2   Yes

3   S: To keep you strong
4   T: →   To keep you strong. Yes. To keep you strong.
             Why do you want to be strong . . .

Here the teacher's evaluation in line 4 consists of repeats of the answer combined with an acceptance *Yes*, through which she confirms the correctness of that answer. Certain phases of classroom interaction consist of a progression of such three-part sequences. This distinctive sequential pattern – in which the third position response is an evaluation specifically of the correctness of an answer – is characteristic of talk in classrooms, since it is associated with the core activity in that setting, namely instruction. Such third position evaluations are rarely found in conversation, precisely because pedagogic instruction is not a frequent conversational activity.

We can further illustrate the important constitutive properties of third position activities in Q–A sequences by considering a particular English response type which is common in conversation, but absent in many institutional interactions, namely *oh*. Heritage (1985) reports that *oh* is frequently used to indicate both that what the other has just said is 'news' to the speaker, and her or his acceptance of the truth or adequacy of that news. He shows that *oh* is largely absent from talk in such institutionalized settings as news interviews, classrooms and courtrooms, for the very reason that the questioners are expected to know what the answers are likely to be (for example, interviewers and lawyers are briefed beforehand, and therefore can anticipate the likely response by an interviewee or witness, respectively). Furthermore, the primary recipient of the answers is not the questioner, but the audience (radio or television audience, or the jury; Heritage and Greatbatch, 1991). In such contexts, *oh*-receipts are avoided, and in this way the questioners define themselves as the elicitors of the talk but not as its primary recipients, thereby maintaining a neutral stance towards the interviewee's comments. Instead, interviewers use 'formulations' as a means for responding to the prior answer as news so as to maintain an institutionally appropriate footing in relation to the 'overhearing' audience (including avoiding either affiliating or disaffiliating with the prior talk: Heritage, 1985).

Hence, something of the distinctiveness of talk in classrooms as compared with conversations, and compared also with news interviews and courtroom examinations, is visible in the different patterns of questioners' response types in third position in Q–A sequences in each setting. This further highlights the importance of comparative sequential analysis as a means of investigating the identifying characteristics of the activities associated with different institutional settings.

A further example of a distinctive sequential pattern associated with institutional dialogue is provided by Heritage and Sorjonen's (1994) analysis of the role and function of the English connective *and* as a feature of question design. While *and* as a question preface is rarely found in ordinary conversation between peers or acquaintances, it is a commonplace feature of interactions in such settings as courtrooms, survey interviews, and certain types of medical encounter, where the participants are occupied with a restricted set of tasks or address one another as incumbents of particular institutional roles. The following is one of the many examples they cite in which a health visitor is making enquiries about basic information concerning the parents, the birth itself and post-natal experiences:

(9)   [Heritage and Sorjonen, 1994: 3–4]

```
 1  HV:        Has he got plenty of wo:rk on,
 2  M:         He works for a university college.
 3  HV:        O:::h.
 4  M:         So: (.) he's in full-time work all the ti:me.
 5  HV:        °Yeh.°
 6             (0.4)
 7  HV:  →     And this is y'r first ba:by:.
 8  M:         Ye(p).
 9             (0.3)
10  HV:  →     .tch An' you had a no:rmal pre:gnancy.=
11  M:         =Ye:h.
12             (1.1)
13  HV:  →     And a normal delivery,
14  M:         Ye:p.
15             (1.4)
16  HV:        °Ri:ght.°
17             (0.7)
18  HV:  →     And sh'didn't go into special ca:re.
19  M:         No:.
20             (1.8)
21  HV:  →     °An:d she's bottle feeding?°
22             (2.2)
23  HV:  →     °Um:° (0.4) and uh you're going to Doctor White for
24             your (0.6) p[ost-na:tal?
25  M:                     [Yeah.
```

Of the seven questions in this fragment, six (arrowed) are prefaced by *and*. Heritage and Sorjonen argue that by prefacing her questions with *and*, the HV invokes a routine or agenda-based activity across a succession of question–answer sequences, and in this way a form of continuity or coherence is achieved across this group of *and*-prefaced questions.[3]

Heritage and Sorjonen go on to argue that the way in which *and*-prefaced questions invoke their sense of arising from an agenda can serve to imply a routine, task-centred motivation for asking questions. This design feature can thereby be exploited to normalize or detoxify questions which might otherwise be treated as troublesome by virtue of their content or placement in a sequence of talk. Thus this normalizing property of *and*-prefacing may be used strategically, for example, in the following extract from a criminal trial, in which an alleged victim of a rape is being cross-examined.

```
(10)  [Heritage and Sorjonen, 1994: 22–3; from Drew, 1992: 510]
      1   D:       Now (.) subsequent to this uh (0.6) uh you say you
      2            received uh (0.8) a number of phone calls?
      3            (0.7)
      4   W:       Ye:s.
      5            (0.4)
      6   D:       From the defendant?
      7            (1.2)
      8   W:       Ye:s
      9            (0.8)
     10   D:  →    And isn't it a fa:ct uh (.) Miss ((Name)) that you
     11            have an unlisted telephone number?
     12            (0.3)
     13   W:       Ye:s.
     14            (1.2)
     15   D:  →    An'you ga::ve the defendant your telephone number
     16            didn' you?
     17   W:       No: I didn't.
     18            (0.3)
     19   D:       You didn't give it to [him
     20   W:                             [No:.
```

Here the cross-examining attorney (D) asks questions which build towards constructing an inconsistency in the witness's (W) testimony. He asks two questions (lines 1–2, 6; lines 10–11), the answers to which are unproblematic. However, the crucial question in constructing the inconsistency is the one in lines 15–16, in which he asks something which, of course, is highly problematic; he attempts to disguise that by prefacing it with *and*, hence normalizing it through invoking an agenda-based link with the series of prior informational questions.

To recapitulate: *and*-prefaced questions are relatively rare in conversation, but frequently occur in a range of institutional settings. Through the use of the *and*-preface, professionals invoke the sense that questions are based on an agenda, and hence are routine. This device may be deployed strategically in order to neutralize the potential difficulties which may be associated with answering certain questions. Hence its use is characteristic of institutional settings in which questions have a progressive connection in a series and some of those questions may, for a variety of reasons, be troublesome.

One further comparative point is that many kinds of institutional encounters are characteristically organized into an overall standard 'shape' or order of phases. Conversations, however, are not: the locally contingent management of 'next moves' in conversation, and the options speakers have within sequences, ensure that there is no standard pattern for the overall organization of conversations. By contrast, the activities conducted in many institutional settings are often implemented in a recurrent – and relatively fixed – order, which lends to such encounters a distinctive overall shape. That order may be prescribed, for instance by a written schedule, pro forma or formal agenda of points which an enquirer may be required to answer when requesting a service (Frankel, 1989; and for an account of what can happen when enquirers' expectations about what information they ought to give are not congruent with the organization's pro forma, see Jefferson and Lee, 1992). The order, and hence the overall shape of certain institutional interactions, may also be the product of locally managed routines (Byrne and Long, 1976; Erickson and Shultz, 1982; Zimmerman, 1992). In either case, the existence of standard patterns in institutional encounters, and their emergent overall organizations, owe much to the direction and initiative of the institutional professionals – who participate in many such interactions during a day, and therefore tend to develop standard practices for managing the tasks of their routine encounters.

In this section we have argued that research into institutional dialogue is essentially comparative, particularly in so far as comparisons are made, implicitly or explicitly, between forms of language use in non-institutional settings (such as conversation) and those which are characteristic either of institutional settings in general, or of particular types of settings. This comparative perspective is fundamental to work in this area, and it is worth emphasizing that research efforts into 'ordinary conversation' and institutional discourse are mutually informative; therefore research into institutional discourse is best undertaken in conjunction with, or with reference to, research into non-institutional talk. This is in part because the only way of determining whether or not a pattern is distinctively 'institutional', or of investigating what interactional significance a certain linguistic item might have interactionally, is to ascertain whether or not that pattern or item occurs in non-institutional talk, and if so whether it has different or special interactional properties in institutional as compared with non-institutional contexts. Thus research in this field should be comparative in scope, encompassing knowledge about both ordinary conversation and institutional discourse (preferably from a range of institutional settings).

Summary and Current Developments

In summary, we should highlight a point which until now has, perhaps, only been implicit. Participants in institutional encounters employ linguistic and interactional resources which they possess as part of their linguistic and cultural competences: they use these resources, and the practices associated with them, in talk-in-interaction generally (that is, in non-institutional as well as institutional talk). Hence many of the linguistic practices which one may observe in institutional settings may not be exclusive to such settings. One of the principal objectives of research concerning institutional dialogue is, therefore, to show either that a given linguistic practice is specifically and specially characteristic of talk in a given (institutional) setting; or that a certain linguistic feature or practice has a characteristic use when deployed in a given setting. This Schegloff (1992) refers to as the aim of demonstrating that the context of talk (that it is in a hospital, a school, etc.) is *procedurally relevant*, that is it has special consequences for the details of the language through which participants conduct their interactions in such contexts.

This objective arises from the quite general issue which has informed our outline of this area of linguistic/interactional analysis: namely, the importance of demonstrating not merely that dialogue happens to occur in a certain institutional setting, but that through various details of their language use, participants orient to their respective institutional identities, roles and tasks in that setting, that is that participants' institutional identities and roles are *procedurally relevant* for their talk (cf. the discussion of extract (1) above; but see especially Schegloff, 1992 on these issues). Researchers working in this field in different disciplines have a common objective, around which their different theoretical perspectives cohere; that is, to explore the ways in which participants in institutional interactions manage their institutional goals, tasks and activities through their use of language. The investigation of language use in any of the respects (levels) outlined here – lexical selection (including person reference), grammatical/ syntactic, sequential (including turn-taking), and pragmatic inference – can reveal aspects of how participants themselves orient to their institutional identities and activities.

Current research into institutional dialogue continues to extend our knowledge about the linguistic and interactional practices characteristically associated with what might be regarded as 'core' institutional settings, in so far as they are some of the 'crucial sites' of modern social life. These include educational settings, courts, social welfare agencies, service encounters, media (including news interviews and political communication) (Atkinson, 1984; Clayman, 1992; 1993; Hutchby, 1996), business organizations (Boden, 1994) and negotiations (Firth, 1994), and especially medical interactions, in which there is a burgeoning research interest and literature. Additionally, there has recently been a notable growth in research into certain institutional forms which reflect contemporary social developments, for instance certain forms of counselling (such as AIDS counselling: Peräkylä, 1995; Silverman, 1990) and conflict mediation (Greatbatch and Dingwall, forthcoming).

There is a growing body of research concerned, very broadly, with situated, collaborative practices in the workplace. This research focuses on the practices through which colleagues manage and accomplish their work activities collaboratively – sometimes 'co-constructing' a joint activity across distributed systems, some of which may involve technologically mediated communication systems, including those linking participants who are not physically co-present (for example, interactions between aircraft pilots and air traffic controllers). This area of research is distinctive, in part, because perhaps the majority of studies into institutional dialogue hitherto have been concerned broadly with professional–client interactions; whereas these studies explore the collaboration between professionals who share specialized expert knowledge, and thus expectations about their joint operations, in more symmetrical, 'conversational' interactions (that is, interactions whose turn-taking systems are organized more conversationally). The focus in some of this research on technically mediated communication systems includes analysis of human–computer interaction. This research tends to be microanalytic in method, using video recordings of relevant sites of action: and it offers the prospect of some connections (perhaps even *rapprochement*) with cognitive science, despite having developed in part from a critical stance towards certain cognitive approaches (Suchman, 1987; see also Engeström et al., 1995; C. Goodwin, 1994; M.H. Goodwin, 1996; C. Goodwin and M.H. Goodwin, forthcoming).

Recommended Reading

The references cited in this chapter have been chosen as exemplars of the principal theoretical and methodological perspectives which have informed research in this area, and to represent the main institutional settings which have been studied. Hence they offer a preliminary guide to reading in this area.

This is a multidisciplinary field inhabited by diverse perspectives and research orientations, so that no textbooks or collections successfully represent the field as a whole. The collection edited by Drew and Heritage (1992a) is an attempt to bring greater theoretical coherence to the field, and a greater sense of the cumulativeness of research – through both an extensive introductory section, and the inclusion of studies of a variety of different institutional settings, the aim of which was to encourage a comparative perspective from which a range of analytical and thematic connections might be discerned (although the studies themselves are all conversation analytic). A multidisciplinary collection which similarly includes studies of a wide range of discourse settings is Coleman (1989). Most other collections focus on specific institutional domains, such as medical (Fisher and Todd, 1993; Morris and Cheneil, 1995) and legal (Gibbons, 1994; Levi and Walker, 1990). A collection which begins to represent recent work in the field mentioned at the end of the previous section, that is studies of collaborative work practices and technologically mediated communication, is Engeström and Middleton (forthcoming).

The monographs cited in the text which focus on language in specific settings are a key resource. One which focuses on a particular and important dimension of talk in a range of settings (namely, accounts) is Buttny (1993). Otherwise, much of the important work in the area is to be found in such journals as *Discourse Processes, Discourse and Society, Journal of Pragmatics, Language in Society, Research on Language and Social Interaction* and *Text*: almost every issue of these journals includes papers reporting relevant research into forms of institutional dialogue. Some (such as *Text*) have published special issues devoted to language in certain settings.

Appendix: Key for the Glossing Symbols in the Finnish Example

The morphemes have been separated from each other with a dash (–). The following forms have been treated as unmarked forms, not indicated in the glossing:

nominative case
singular
third person singular (except when there are special reasons for indicating it)
active voice
present tense.

Different infinitives and participial forms have not been specified.

Abbreviations being used in examples:

2   second person ending
3   third person ending
4   passive person ending

ACC   accusative case (object)
ADE   adessive case ('at, on')
ADJ   adjective
ADV   adverb
ALL   allative case ('to')
CLI   clitic
COM   comparative
CON   conditional
GEN   genitive case (possession)
INF   infinitive
PAR   partitive case (partitiveness)
PAS   passive
PL   plural

PPC   past participle
PRT   particle
SG   singular.

Notes

We are grateful to Brenda Danet, Christian Heath, John Heritage, Robert Hopper and Anita Pomerantz for giving us access to unpublished data which have been cited here. Their colleagueship in this respect is much appreciated. We would like to thank Auli Hakulinen, John Heritage and Anssi Peräkylä for their insightful comments on an earlier draft of this chapter.

1 The data extracts cited in this chapter have been transcribed using the transcription conventions within conversation analysis developed by Gail Jefferson, which have been widely adopted by researchers studying naturally occurring discourse, from a variety of perspectives. A glossary of these conventions will be found in the Appendix to this volume.

2 Utterances in first and second person need not have a separate personal pronoun since the verb form indicates person and number. The verb form regularly associated with the first person plural in colloquial Finnish is the so-called passive form, see lines 2 and 3.

3 In this case the basis for the HV's agenda is the pro forma part of filling in a form; the agenda consists of a list of items on a record card that the HV has previously introduced as having to be completed.

References

Atkinson, J.M. (1984) *Our Masters' Voices: the Language and Body Language of Politics.* London: Methuen.

Atkinson, J.M. and Drew, P. (1979) *Order in Court: the Organisation of Verbal Interaction in Judicial Settings.* London: Macmillan.

Boden, D. (1994) *The Business of Talk.* Cambridge: Polity Press.

Buttny, R. (1993) *Social Accountability in Communication.* London: Sage.

Byrne, P.S. and Long, B.E.L. (1976) *Doctors Talking to Patients: a Study of the Verbal Behaviours of Doctors in the Consultation.* London: HMSO.

Cicourel, A. (1992) 'The interpenetration of communicative contexts: examples from medical discourse', in A. Duranti and C. Goodwin (eds), *Rethinking Context: Language as an Interactive Phenomenon.* Cambridge: Cambridge University Press. pp. 291–310.

Clayman, Steven (1992) 'Footing in the achievement of neutrality: the case of news interview discourse', in P. Drew and J. Heritage (eds), *Talk at Work: Interaction in Institutional Settings.* Cambridge: Cambridge University Press. pp. 163–98.

Clayman, Steven (1993) 'Reformulating the question: a device for answering/not answering questions in news interviews and press conferences', *Text*, 13: 19–188.

Coleman, H. (ed.) (1989) *Working with Language: a Multidisciplinary Consideration of Language Use in Working Contexts.* Berlin: Mouton de Gruyter.

Conley, J.M. and O'Barr, W.M. (1990) *Rules versus Relationships: the Ethnography of Legal Discourse.* Chicago: University of Chicago Press.

Coulthard, M. and Ashby, M. (1975) 'Talking with the doctor', *Journal of Communication*, 23 (3): 240–7.

Coupland, J., Coupland, N. and Robinson, J.D. (1992) '"How are you?": negotiating phatic communication', *Language in Society*, 21: 207–30.

Coupland, N., Giles, H. and Wiemann, J.M. (eds) (1991) *'Miscommunication' and Problematic Talk.* London: Sage.

Danet, B. (1980) '"Baby" or "fetus": language and the construction of reality in a manslaughter trial', *Semiotica*, 32: 187–219.

Danet, B. and Bogoch, B. (1980) 'Fixed fight or free-for-all? An empirical study of combativeness in the adversary system of justice', *British Journal of Law and Society*, 7: 36–60.

Drew, P. (1990) 'Strategies in the contest between lawyer and witness in cross-examination', in J. Levi and A.G. Walker (eds), *Language in the Judicial Process*. New York: Plenum. pp. 39–64.

Drew, P. (1992) 'Contested evidence in courtroom cross-examination: the case of a trial for rape', in P. Drew and J. Heritage (eds), *Talk at Work: Interaction in Institutional Settings*. Cambridge: Cambridge University Press. pp. 470–520.

Drew, P. and Heritage, J. (eds) (1992a) *Talk at Work: Interaction in Institutional Settings*. Cambridge: Cambridge University Press.

Drew, P. and Heritage, J. (1992b) 'Analyzing talk at work: an introduction', in P. Drew and J. Heritage (eds), *Talk at Work: Interaction in Institutional Settings*. Cambridge: Cambridge University Press. pp. 3–65.

Duranti, A. (1992) 'Language in context and language as context: the Samoan respect vocabulary', in A. Duranti and C. Goodwin (eds), *Rethinking Context: Language as an Interactive Phenomenon*. Cambridge: Cambridge University Press. pp. 77–99.

Duranti, A. (1994) *From Grammar to Politics*. Berkeley, CA: University of California Press.

Engeström, Y. and Middleton, D. (eds) (forthcoming) *Cognition and Communication at Work*. Cambridge: Cambridge University Press.

Engeström, Y., Engeström, R. and Kärkkäinen, M. (1995) 'Polycontextuality and boundary crossing in expert cognition: learning and problem solving in complex work activities', *Learning and Instruction*, 5: 319–36.

Erickson, F. and Shultz, J. (1982) *The Counsellor as Gatekeeper: Social Interaction in Interviews*. New York: Academic Press.

Ervin-Tripp, S. (1975) '"Is Sybil there?": the structure of some American English directives', *Language in Society*, 5: 25–67.

Firth, A. (ed.) (1994) *The Discourse of Negotiation: Studies of Language in the Workplace*. Oxford: Pergamon.

Fisher, S. and Todd, A.D. (eds) (1993) *The Social Organization of Doctor–Patient Communication*, 2nd edn. Norwood, NJ: Ablex.

Frankel, R. (1989) '"I wz wondering – uhm could 'Raid' uhm affect the brain permanently d'y know?": some observations on the intersection of speaking and writing in calls to a poison control center', *Western Journal of Speech Communication*, 3: 195–226.

Frankel, R. (1990) 'Talking in interviews: a dispreference for patient-initiated questions in physician–patient encounters', in G. Psathas (ed.), *Interaction Competence*. Washington, DC: University Press of America. pp. 231–62.

Gibbons, J. (ed.) (1994) *Language and the Law*. Harlow: Longman.

Goffman, E. (1972) *Encounters: Two Studies in the Sociology of Interaction*. London: Penguin.

Goodwin, C. (1994) 'Professional vision', *American Anthropologist*, 96 (3): 606–33.

Goodwin, C. and Duranti, A. (1992) 'Rethinking context: an introduction', in A. Duranti and C. Goodwin (eds), *Rethinking Context: Language as an Interactive Phenomenon*. Cambridge: Cambridge University Press. pp. 1–42.

Goodwin, C. and Goodwin, M.H. (forthcoming) 'Formulating planes: seeing as a situated activity', in Y. Engeström and D. Middleton (eds), *Cognition and Communication at Work*. Cambridge: Cambridge University Press.

Goodwin, M.H. (1992) *He-Said-She-Said: Talk as Social Organization among Black Children*. Bloomington, IN: Indiana University Press.

Goodwin, M.H. (1996) 'Announcements in their environment: prosody within a multi-activity work setting', in E. Couper-Kuhlen and M. Selting (eds), *Prosody in Conversation: Interactional Studies*. Cambridge: Cambridge University Press. pp. 436–61.

Greatbatch, D. (1988) 'A turn-taking system for British news interviews', *Language in Society*, 17: 401–30.

Greatbatch, D. (1992) 'On the management of disagreement between news interviewees', in P. Drew and J. Heritage (eds), *Talk at Work: Interaction in Institutional Settings*. Cambridge: Cambridge University Press. pp. 268–301.

Greatbatch, D. and Dingwall, R. (forthcoming) 'Argumentative talk in divorce mediation session', *American Sociological Review*.

Gumperz, J.J. (1982a) *Discourse Strategies*. Cambridge: Cambridge University Press.

Gumperz, J.J. (ed.) (1982b) *Language and Social Identity*. Cambridge: Cambridge University Press.

Gumperz, J.J. and Cook-Gumperz, J. (1982) 'Introduction: language and the communication of social identity', in J.J. Gumperz (ed.), *Language and Social Identity*. Cambridge: Cambridge University Press. pp. 1–21.

Hakulinen, A. (1987) 'Avoiding personal reference in Finnish', in J. Verschueren and M. Bertucelli-Papi (eds), *The Pragmatic Perspective. Selected Papers from the 1985 International Pragmatic Conference: Pragmatics and Beyond*, CS 5. Amsterdam: John Benjamins. pp. 141–53.

Harris, S. (1984) 'Questions as a mode of control in magistrates' courts', *International Journal of the Sociology of Language*, 49: 5–28.

He, A.W. (1993) 'Exploring modality in institutional interactions: cases from academic counselling encounters', *Text*, 13: 503–28.

Heath, C. (1986) *Body Movement and Speech in Medical Interaction*. Cambridge: Cambridge University Press.

Heath, S.B. (1983) *Ways with Words: Language, Life and Work in Communities and Classrooms*. Cambridge: Cambridge University Press.

Hein, N. and Wodak, R. (1987) 'Medical interviews in internal medicine: some results of an empirical investigation', *Text*, 7: 37–65.

Heritage, J. (1985) 'Analyzing news interviews: aspects of the production of talk for an overhearing audience', in T. van Dijk (ed.), *Handbook of Discourse Analysis*, vol. 3. London: Sage. pp. 95–117.

Heritage, J. and Greatbatch, D. (1991) 'On the institutional character of institutional talk: the case of news interviews', in D. Boden and D. Zimmerman (eds), *Talk and Social Structure: Studies in Ethnomethodology and Conversation Analysis*. Cambridge: Polity Press. pp. 93–137.

Heritage, J. and Roth, A.L. (1995) 'Grammar and institution: questions and questioning in broadcast media', *Research on Language and Social Interaction*, 28 (1): 1–60.

Heritage, J. and Sefi, S. (1992) 'Dilemmas of advice: aspects of the delivery and reception of advice in interactions between health visitors and first time mothers', in P. Drew and J. Heritage (eds), *Talk at Work: Interaction in Institutional Settings*. Cambridge: Cambridge University Press. pp. 359–417.

Heritage, J. and Sorjonen, M.-L. (1994) 'Constituting and maintaining activities across sequences: *and*-prefacing as a feature of question design', *Language in Society*, 23 (1): 1–29.

Hutchby, I. (1996) *Confrontation Talk: Argument, Asymmetries and Power on Talk Radio*. Hillsdale, NJ: Lawrence Erlbaum.

Jefferson, G. and Lee, J. (1992) 'The rejection of advice: managing the problematic convergence of a "troubles-telling" and a "service encounter"', in P. Drew and J. Heritage (eds), *Talk at Work: Interaction in Institutional Settings*. Cambridge: Cambridge University Press. pp. 521–48.

Kim, K. (1992) 'WH-clefts and left dislocation in English conversation with reference to topicality in Korean'. Unpublished PhD dissertation, Department of TESL and Applied Linguistics, University of California at Los Angeles.

Levi, J. and Walker, A.G. (eds) (1990) *Language in the Judicial Process*. New York: Plenum.

Levinson, S. (1992) 'Activity types and language', in P. Drew and J. Heritage (eds), *Talk at Work: Interaction in Institutional Settings*. Cambridge: Cambridge University Press. pp. 66–100.

Linell, P., Gustavsson, L. and Juvonen, P. (1988) 'Interactional dominance in dyadic communication: a presentation of the initiative–response analysis', *Linguistics*, 26: 415–42.

Markova, I. and Foppa, K. (eds) (1991) *Dialogical and Contextual Dominance*. Hemel Hempstead: Harvester.

Maynard, D.W. (1984) *Inside Plea Bargaining: the Language of Negotiations*. New York: Plenum Press.

Maynard, D.W. (1991) 'On the interactional and institutional bases of asymmetry in clinical discourse', *American Journal of Sociology*, 92: 448–95.

McHoul, A. (1978) 'The organization of turns at formal talk in the classroom', *Language in Society*, 7: 183–213.

McHoul, A. (1990) 'The organization of repair in classroom talk', *Language in Society*, 19: 349–77.

Meehan, A.J. (1981) 'Some conversational features of the use of medical terms by doctors', in P. Atkinson and C. Heath (eds), *Medical Work: Realities and Routines*. Aldershot: Gower. pp. 107–27.

Mehan, H. (1979) *Learning Lessons*. Cambridge, MA: Harvard University Press.

Mishler, E. (1984) *The Discourse of Medicine*. Norwood, NJ: Ablex.

Morris, G.H. and Cheneil, R. (eds) (1995) *Talk of the Clinic*. Hillsdale, NJ: Lawrence Erlbaum.

Ochs, E. (1988) *Culture and Language Development: Language Acquisition and Language Socialization in a Samoan Village*. Cambridge: Cambridge University Press.

Ochs, E., Gonzales, P. and Jacoby, S. (forthcoming) '"When I come down I'm in the domain state": grammar and graphic representation in the interpretive activity of physics', in E. Ochs, E.A. Schegloff and S.A. Thompson (eds), *Interaction and Grammar*. Cambridge: Cambridge University Press.

Peräkylä, A. (1995) *AIDS Counselling: Institutional Interaction and Clinical Practice*. Cambridge: Cambridge University Press.

Philips, S.U. (1984) 'The social organization of questions and answers in courtroom discourse', *Text*, 4: 228–48.

Pomerantz, A. (1980) 'Investigating reported absences: catching truants', paper presented at the First Anglo-German Colloquium in Ethnomethodology and Conversation Analysis, Konstanz, Germany.

Roter, D.L. and Hall, J.A. (1992) *Doctors Talking to Patients/Patients Talking to Doctors*. Westport, CT: Auburn.

Sacks, H. (1992) *Lectures on Conversation* (1964–72), vols 1 and 2 (ed. G. Jefferson). Oxford: Blackwell.

Sacks, H., Schegloff, E.A. and Jefferson, G. (1974) 'A simplest systematics for the organization of turn-taking for conversation', *Language*, 50: 696–735.

Scheflen, A.E. (1973) *Communication Structure: Analysis of a Psychotherapy Transaction*. Bloomington, IN: Indiana University Press.

Schegloff, E.A. (1992) 'On talk and its institutional occasions', in P. Drew and J. Heritage (eds), *Talk at Work: Interaction in Institutional Settings*. Cambridge: Cambridge University Press. pp. 101–34.

Silverman, D. (1987) *Communication and Medical Practice: Social Relations in the Clinic*. London: Sage.

Silverman, D. (1990) 'The social organization of HIV counselling', in P. Aggleton, P. Davies and G. Hart (eds), *AIDS: Individual, Cultural and Policy Dimensions*. Lewes: Falmer Press. pp. 191–212.

Sinclair, J.M. and Coulthard, M. (1975) *Towards an Analysis of Discourse: the English Used by Teachers and Pupils*. Oxford: Oxford University Press.

Suchman, L. (1987) *Plans and Situated Actions*. Cambridge: Cambridge University Press.

Tannen, D. and Wallat, C. (1993) 'Doctor/mother/child communication: linguistic analysis of a pediatric interaction', in S. Fisher and A. Todd (eds), *The Social Organization of Doctor–Patient Communication*, 2nd edn. Norwood, NJ: Ablex. pp. 203–19.

Ventola, E. (1987) *The Structure of Social Interaction: Systemic Approach to the Semiotics of Service Encounters*. London: Francis Pinter.

West, C. (1984) *Routine Complications: Troubles with Talk between Doctors and Patients.* Bloomington, IN: Indiana University Press.

West, C. (1990) 'Not just "doctors' orders": directive–response sequences in patients' visits to women and men physicians', *Discourse and Society,* 1: 85–112.

Whalen, J., Zimmerman, D. and Whalen, M. (1988) 'When words fail: a single case analysis', *Social Problems,* 35: 335–62.

Zimmerman, D. (1992) 'The interactional organization of calls for emergency assistance', in P. Drew and J. Heritage (eds), *Talk at Work: Interaction in Institutional Settings.* Cambridge: Cambridge University Press. pp. 418–69.

5

Gender in Discourse

Candace West, Michelle M. Lazar
and Cheris Kramarae

Do women and men use different languages? How does being a woman or a man affect the ways we are talked to and written about? And what is the relationship between the structure of a language and the use of that language by the women and men who speak it? Although interest in these questions goes back at least 100 years (see, for example, issues of *The Revolution*, a newspaper published in New York between 1868 and 1871), it was not until the 1970s that gender and discourse emerged as a recognized field of inquiry. The new wave of the Women's Movement stimulated unparalleled interest in relationships between gender and language among researchers around the world (Aebischer and Forel, 1983; Cameron, 1990a; 1992; Hellinger, 1985; Kramarae et al., 1983: 163–5; Roman et al., 1994; Spender, 1980; Thorne et al., 1983a: 8; Trömel-Plötz, 1982). It also led them to realize that most studies of discourse (for example, of text grammars, the semantics of coherence and the psychology of text processing) had not addressed gender at all.

Since the 1970s, the study of gender and discourse has achieved not only recognition as a full fledged field of inquiry but as one that is growing by leaps and bounds (compare, for example, Henley and Thorne's 1975 bibliography with Kramarae et al.'s 1983 bibliography – or with the results of a computerized search on the subject in a college library today). Interest in the topic crosses many disciplinary boundaries (such as those between anthropology, linguistics, literature, philosophy, psychology, sociology, speech communication and women's studies), and scholars use a wide variety of methods to study it (including ethnographic observations, laboratory experiments, survey questionnaires, philosophical exegeses and analyses of text and talk).

In this chapter, we provide a broad but selective introduction to research on gender and discourse. We focus especially on questions that excite scholars today, but we also attend to the political and sociohistorical contexts in which these questions developed. Our thesis is that gender is accomplished *in* discourse. As many feminist researchers have shown, that which we think of as 'womanly' or 'manly' behavior is not dictated by biology, but rather is socially constructed. And a fundamental domain in which gender is constructed is language use. Social constructions of gender are not neutral, however; they are implicated in the institutionalized power relations of societies. In known contemporary societies, power relations are asymmetrical, such that women's interests are systematically subordinated to men's. The significance of power relations cannot be overemphasized, in as much as these 'determine who does what for whom, what we are [and] what we might become' (Weedon, 1987: 1).

We begin our discussion with the relationship between discourse and the construction of gender, noting the evolution of interest in this area from studies of gender and language. Next, we consider relations between gender and talk, drawing conclusions about how analyses of talk contribute to our understanding of relations between women and men in social life. Finally, we suggest directions for future research, including work on gender and electronic communications.

A word of caution is in order before we start. To date, much of the published research on gender and discourse focuses on white, middle-class heterosexuals speaking English in Western societies. While journals such as *Discourse & Society* are expanding the breadth of this focus and feminists are advancing new theoretical perspectives to encompass the diversity of women's experiences of subordination across the globe, the gaps in our knowledge are substantial. Moreover, few analytical frameworks treat differences among cultures, classes, sexual orientations and racial/ethnic categories as more enriching than divisive. By and large, *women* and *men* are treated as undifferentiated groups, and theories about them are based on empirical studies with a very limited scope. To highlight this problem and to avoid compounding it, we take the somewhat unusual step of specifying *which* women and men researchers actually focused on in the studies we review. Where we note that this information is noticeably absent, we suspect that the researchers are focusing on whites, heterosexuals, members of the middle class, English speakers, and Western societies.

Discourse and the Construction of Gender

Research on language and gender has grown alongside the broad field of discourse analysis. Since the late 1960s and early 1970s, researchers in both fields have recognized the central place of language in the organization of social action. While many other scholars have resisted the argument that language is deeply implicated in their data and in their lives, those who study language and gender consider the analysis of language practices as a central task in the study of human relationships. For them, power relations get articulated through language. Language does not merely reflect a pre-existing sexist world; instead, it actively constructs gender asymmetries within specific sociohistorical contexts.

Discourse analysts in general recognize that discourse is always embedded in a particular social context. For some scholars, this may mean studying a society's mode of social stratification in relation to the language practices of its members. For those concerned with gender, this means addressing the relationship between gender inequality and the language practices of a society. For example, Ann Bodine (1990) observes that prescriptive grammarians instituted *he* and *man* as the 'correct' forms for gender-indefinite referents in English only at the end of the eighteenth century, after which these became purportedly 'generic' terms. But contemporary studies of language use (Cameron, 1992; Martyna, 1983; MacKay, 1983) illustrate just how specific masculine pronouns are to men, and many feminists are fighting for the currency of gender-neutral alternatives (such as singular *they* and *he* or *she*, and the use of *she* as a generic). Deborah Cameron (1992: 226), who adopts the generic use of *she*, emphasizes that *all* choices symbolize political alignments. Through our choice of particular language forms, we can either tacitly accept and thereby help perpetuate the status quo, or challenge and thereby help change it.

For example, consider the following extract from the preface to *Satow's Guide to Diplomatic Practice*, a compendium of protocol for diplomats among the British white upper classes:

> We have been conscious that in the twentieth century for the first time in known history, diplomacy has become in many countries a profession open to both sexes. The English language has not yet provided a grammatically elegant way of dealing with this change. We have, therefore, used the compromise of occasionally employing the 'he (or she)' formula to show our absence of prejudice; but its constant repetition would be intolerably tedious, and for this edition, the male pronoun has had, once again, to serve both sexes. (Gore-Booth and Paenham, 1977: x)

While the authors claim an explicitly unbiased stand, their ultimate decision to use masculine pronouns nonetheless helps preserve the status quo.

Research on gender and language structure has demonstrated numerous ways that women are ignored, trivialized and deprecated by the words used to describe them (for an overview of these, see Thorne et al., 1983a). Women are denied an autonomous existence through titles that distinguish them on the basis of their marital status ('Mrs' vs 'Miss', 'Señora' vs 'Señorita', 'Madame' vs 'Mademoiselle'). Career choices for women and men are segregated through distinctive occupational terms (waiter vs waitress, actor vs actress, Congressman vs Congresswoman), with modifying markers (woman doctor) added to exceptions to the rule. And words associated with women tend to pejorate over time (for example, *woman* came to mean *mistress* or *paramour* in the nineteenth century, leading to the necessity for *lady* after that: see Lakoff, 1975; Schulz, 1975). Studies of such language practices show a broad pattern of sexism, in which women are conceived of as different from and unequal to men. But, since few of these studies focus on the systematic study of discourse *per se*, they do not offer much explanation of how this pattern comes about. Increasingly, however, researchers are focusing on actual instances of text and talk, in an effort to understand the conditions under which this pattern is produced.

Socio-Economic Analysis

Some researchers focus on the social and economic contexts that are relevant to generating texts and talk. For example, Linda Christian-Smith (1989), who analyses the discourse of femininity in US romance novels,[1] situated her study in the conditions under which these texts are produced and consumed. In two US middle schools and one junior high school, she examined how teachers use novels for instructional purposes. She found that teachers' selection of romance novels for girls and adventures and mystery books for boys encouraged 'gendered' reading practices among their students. Through their sex-categorical selections, teachers confer their authority on the novels and endorse the normative images of femininity and masculinity the novels espouse. Christian-Smith argues that the depiction of girls, for example, as consumers in romance novels, prepares girls for future roles as wives and mothers and helps reproduce the traditional division of labor. By tying consumption to the home – a place where girls are shown making themselves beautiful for boys and engaging in household chores – romance novels depict young women as mere consumers of commodities, 'never as worker[s] and acknowledged producer[s] of those goods' (1989: 25).

Dorothy Smith (1988) notes that the discourse of femininity in Western women's magazines and television shows necessarily puts girls and women in the position of consumers, since the fashion, cosmetics and publishing industries speak to women in this position. Smith argues that the discourse of femininity in these media not only is embedded in economic and social relations, but also *constitutes* 'a set of relations', which arise in 'local, historical settings' (1988: 55). She notes that images of femininity in magazines like *Bazaar*, *Seventeen* and *Mademoiselle* become the locus of social interaction and activity among women, influencing what they talk about, how they shop, and how they 'work' on themselves to resemble the textual images they see. Smith points out that, until recently, media images of femininity were images of *white* femininity and beauty (for example, women with blue eyes and straight, smooth hair), which, by implication, defined Black women and, we would add, other women of color, as lacking. She further observes that, at any given historical time, a prevailing discourse of femininity coexists and intersects with a corresponding discourse of masculinity. So, for example, in Western societies, a woman's success in conforming to prevailing textual images of femininity is significant for her chances of attracting a heterosexual partner. Her looks determine whether a man can proudly display her in public and so establish his status with other men.

On the basis of her interviews with a group of Australian girls in their early teens,[2] Patricia Palmer Gillard (in Cranny-Francis and Gillard, 1990) argues that girls are wont to make decisions about their own socio-economic futures based on the characterizations and actions of the women they see in television soap operas. As one of her interviewees put it, 'If it worked for her [a TV soap opera character], being a woman, it might work for me' (1990: 176). The problem, as Gillard points out, is that such programs depict women mainly as wives and mothers, thus offering girls a limited view of the options available to them as adults. Like the girls in Christian-Smith's (1989) study, Gillard's interviewees could see themselves as consumers of commodities but not as producers.

Such studies show how economic relations work together with other social relations in capitalist societies to define women and men in particular ways and to shape their identities and practices. Small wonder, then, that language practices within these societies define women primarily in terms of their marital status and perpetuate unequal occupational opportunities for women and men.

Content Analysis

Other studies examine the social construction of gender in the content of texts themselves. For example, Angela McRobbie (1982; see also Christian-Smith, 1989) adopts this approach in her analysis of picture stories in *Jackie*, a popular British magazine for adolescent girls. She found a specific repertoire of topics and images conveying the unambiguous message that romantic love is central to a girl's identity.[3] The content of the picture stories idealized heterosexual romantic partnerships, ruled out other forms of relationships between girls and boys, eliminated the possibility of strong supportive relationships among girls themselves, and obscured the option of being single and happy. In a quest for love to endow their lives with meaning, girls were defined narrowly through their emotions: rivalry toward other girls, possessiveness, and blind devotion to their boyfriends. McRobbie argues that the 'code of romance' in these texts is fundamentally concerned with maintaining power relationships between girls and boys. It encourages girls to be unassertive and passive, and to simply wait for boys to take the initiative. Moreover, it renders romance a personal experience, dislocated in time and disembodied from the larger societal context.

Of course, a devil's advocate might argue that the causal relationship implicit in McRobbie's (1982) analysis should be reversed: for example, that it is hardly surprising to find such normative conceptions of appropriate manly and womanly behaviors in a magazine for adolescent girls, since that's what adolescent girls like to read. But researchers also find normative conceptions of gender in texts that purportedly have nothing to do with the sex-categorical preferences of their readers. For instance, Roger Fowler (1991) reports that British newspapers categorize women and men very differently through the noun phrases used to describe them. Men in general are more often described in terms of their occupational roles, while women are typically described in relation to their marital and family responsibilities (for example, as 'wives' and 'mothers'). Paul Simpson's (1993) analysis, also of British newspaper extracts, shows further that it is not at all unusual to see noun phrases describing women *vis-à-vis* their relationships to men (for example, as 'spinster' or 'wife') but very unusual to see corresponding descriptions of men. Such findings suggest that the construction of gender inequality in the content of texts is very pervasive indeed.

Textual Analysis

Still other studies of discourse focus on how gender is constructed through the means of assembling texts, such as sentences, grammatical structures and genres. These studies are less concerned with the content of discourse than with its form. For example, moving beyond the level of words, Deborah Cameron (1990b: 16–18) addresses the sentence structure of British newspaper reports of violence against women. She argues that the historical conception of rape as a crime one man commits against another – robbing him of the chastity of a wife or daughter – is perpetuated in contemporary newspaper stories. Cameron's analysis of one such story in different newspaper reports shows that these reports depicted the man affected by the rape of his partner as the grammatical subject of main clauses, for example 'A man . . .' and 'A terrified 19-stone husband . . .'. By contrast, reports mentioned the woman who was raped at the ends of complex sentences and only described her in relation to the man, that is, as 'his wife'. The rape itself also appeared at the ends of sentences, only after descriptions of the man's personal injuries: 'A man who suffered head injuries when attacked by two men who broke into his home in Beckenham, Kent, early yesterday, was pinned down on the bed by intruders who took it in turns to rape his wife.' Through these means of assembling their ostensibly 'objective' reports, newspapers describe events from the point of view of the husband whose wife was raped – not the woman herself.

In a related study of rape reports (in the *Sun*, a British tabloid), Kate Clark (1992) observes that these texts tend to obscure the guilt of the rapist and transfer blame to the victim or someone else. For example, rape reports often use passive sentence structures that delete the rapist as the agent: 'Two of Steed's rape victims – aged 20 and 19 – had a screwdriver held at their throats as they were forced to submit' (1992: 215). They also use passive sentences that attribute responsibility for the rapist's actions to someone else: 'Sex killer John Steed was set on the path to evil by seeing his mother raped when he was a little boy' (1992: 216). They even describe the victim of rape in ways that might be read as 'excusing' the rapist, for example, as an 'unmarried mum' or a 'blonde divorcee' (1992: 211). Clark hypothesizes that, by manipulating blame in this manner, newspaper reports of rape suppress the question of why so many men assault women in the first place.

Textual analyses of the media reveal competing ways of representing social life, which work insidiously to maintain inequality between women and men. Michelle Lazar (1993) analyses a pair of Singapore government advertisements – one targeted at women, the other at men – promoting marriage between well-educated Asians. The ostensible purpose of these ads is to change the conservative attitudes of Asian men, who prefer not to marry their intellectual peers. Lazar (1993: 451–61) finds that, while parts of the texts appear to redress the issue of men's chauvinism and promote gender equality, the advertisements on the whole jointly reproduce the status quo. On the one hand, she notes, the advertisements achieve an egalitarian discourse by using 'real partner in life' to mean both 'spouse' and 'equality in relationship'. The ads appear to support women's career interests: 'It's wonderful to have a career and financial independence.' And, when speaking to men, they use complementary clauses to indicate a reciprocal relationship to women: 'someone you can be proud of (just as she's proud of you)'. On the other hand, the advertisements simultaneously present a sexist discourse. For example, they use 'but' – a disclaimer – to qualify their support of women's career interests: 'It's wonderful to have a career and financial independence. But is your self-sufficiency giving men a hard time?' They refer to women as 'girls' but not to men as 'boys'. Moreover, they blame women for men's chauvinistic impressions: 'Are you [women] giving men the wrong idea?' And they suggest, through the use of comparatives, that women must do something 'extra' to make themselves attractive to men: '[Be] more relaxed and approachable. Friendlier and more sociable.' Lazar shows that the juxtaposition of these contradictory discourses serves to subtly shift the origins of the problem and responsibility for change from men to women. It encourages women to readily adjust to men's expectations, despite the fact that the root of the problem and the remedy for the problem lie with men. Lazar concludes that this strategy is necessary to preserve Singapore's social system, in which (as in most societies) men hold more institutional power than women.

Textual analyses show the workings of power dynamics not only through the presence of particular textual markers, but also through their systematic absences. For instance, Gwendolyn Etter-Lewis (1991) examines elderly African-American women's experiences with sexism and racism by looking at what they don't say (in addition to what they do say) in the texts of their oral narratives. She finds that a key to understanding these texts lies in their characteristic silences, indirect responses, and deleted nouns and pronouns. Consider the missing pronouns (indicated by empty brackets) that would otherwise name the perpetrators of sexism and racism in the following narrative excerpts:

[Etter-Lewis, 1991: 428]
[   ] Told me they don't serve niggers here.

[Etter-Lewis, 1991: 431]
First it was the bus driver. [   ] Came to me and said . . . .

As Etter-Lewis observes, the deletion of the agents in these actions may render them less threatening, by making them appear less direct. For instance, one of the women she interviewed, while describing her experience of having been turned down for a university teaching position, avoided saying 'They didn't hire me' by falling silent (as indicated by the ellipsis):

> [Etter-Lewis, 1991: 435]
> And so they did not . . . they had . . . .

Etter-Lewis argues that the many silences and indirect references in these texts are not merely routine space holders or fillers; instead, they mark the suppression of criticism – a characteristic of the speech of people who are oppressed.

Textual analyses also show that particular genres (text-types) of discourse focus readers' or viewers' reading or viewing in specific ways. Like a wide-angle or 'zoom' lens on a camera, the genre determines what those who look through it will see and the angle from which they will see it. For example, Paul Thibault (1988) notes that, in women's magazines throughout Western societies, the genre of personal columns invites girls and women to petition 'experts' for advice on their sexual and emotional dilemmas. Simultaneously, it invites other girls and women to read both the pleas for advice and the responses to those pleas. This genre, says Thibault (1988: 205), serves to standardize and universalize women's behaviors and experiences in relation to dominant Western ideas about heterosexual relations. Cranny-Francis and Gillard (1990) agree, based on their study of Australian soap opera story lines. They find that, as in most Western narratives, the causal sequence of events in soap operas is premised on viewers' unproblematic acceptance of conservative ideologies about gender, race and class – ideologies which encourage viewers to take for granted that 'that's the way things are.' As they observe, soap operas typically portray characters and interpersonal relationships in 'contextless' fashion (1990: 184), thereby concealing the class conflicts, racial struggles, sexual ambiguities and sexist practices that occur in real life. In learning the conventions for viewing this genre, girls come to accept the ideologies it contains as unproblematic, and come to see soap opera characters and relationships as realistic models for planning their own futures (Cranny Francis and Gillard, 1990).

Coda

We have learned a great deal since researchers in the 1970s made their observations about gender and language structure. Beyond the broad pattern of sexism they documented – in which women are conceived of as different from and unequal to men – studies of discourse and the construction of gender have taught us much about the systematic ways this pattern is generated. From those who focus on the social and economic contexts of texts and talk, we have learned of the textual construction of women as consumers, and men as producers, in capitalist Western societies. We have seen how women come to be defined in relation to their marital and familial roles, and how men come to be defined in relation to their occupational roles – as well as how these definitions influence the hopes and aspirations of those exposed to them. From those who study the content of discourse, we have been given a richly detailed picture of the normative conceptions of appropriate womanly and manly behaviors that pervade a variety of mass media, ranging from newspapers for the general public to magazines for adolescent girls. And from those who analyse the formal features of texts – sentences, grammatical structures and genres – we have developed a deep appreciation for the power of specific practices that allow us to 'see' the world as a gendered place.

Uniting these approaches is an unremitting emphasis on the context in which discourse is embedded. Socio-economic approaches point to the significance of social and economic relations in constructing the discourse of femininity and discourse of masculinity that will prevail at a particular historical moment. Content analyses illuminate the broad array of media that feature the same idealized versions of femininity and masculinity, and show how sex categories can be made to matter in the most mundane descriptions of social doings. Textual analyses push our understanding one step further, by exposing the mechanisms that provide us, the readers and viewers of texts, with our sense of 'context' in the first place. They show, for example, how the arrangement of building blocks such as nouns and verbs, the choice between voices such as active and passive, and the juxtapositioning of competing discourses, can construct a background – against which existing patterns of gender inequality seem 'only natural' to those who look at them.

To this point, we have been focusing on textual analyses of how women and men are talked about. Studies of the form of texts, the content of texts, and the conditions under which texts are produced show how women are described, depicted, categorized and evaluated as different from and unequal to men. But talk *about* women and men is only part of the picture: there is also the issue of how women and men talk. Below, we address this issue, beginning with a brief history of the origins of interest in it.

Gender and Talk

In the early 1970s, research on how women and men speak came to occupy center stage in the study of discourse and gender. A primary focus of this research was what made the talk of women different from the talk of men. In the United States, Robin Lakoff (1973; 1975) stimulated much of the interest in this question through her description of a distinctive 'women's language' – a language that avoids direct and forceful statements, and relies on forms that convey hesitation and uncertainty. Although she based her description on her personal observations in a white, middle-class milieu, her description was very influential. Because researchers prior to the early 1970s tended to treat men's talk as the standard, and sometimes did not even include women in their research projects, the notion that there might be differences between women's and men's talk was potentially revolutionary.

Initially, however, this notion had the impact of modifying old ideas, rather than transforming them. What it spawned was a wide ranging reassessment of existing linguistic knowledge to see what happened to it when women were included. Often, this involved inventories of differences between women and men across isolated linguistic variables such as pronunciation, vocabulary, or grammar (see Kramarae et al.'s 1983: 233–64 annotated bibliography). For example, women were thought to use more fillers (*you know, uhm*) than men (Hirschman, 1973); to employ intensifiers (*quite, so, such*) more often than men (Key, 1975); and to make more use of terms of endearment (*sweetie, dear, honey*) in a wider range of settings (Eble, 1972). Women's speech behaviors were compared to men's, to see what, if anything, distinguished the two.

Only two areas of consistent difference emerged from these efforts (Thorne et al., 1983a: 12–13). The first was the finding (McConnell-Ginet, 1978; Sachs, 1975) that women display more variability in pitch and intonation than men do. The second was the finding (Labov, 1972; Trudgill, 1975) that women use standard or prestige pronunciations more than men do, for instance, retaining the full /ing/ endings of verbs in English ('wanting', not 'wantin').

As in the case of most descriptive research, the purpose of these efforts was to document differences, not to explain them. In so far as earlier linguistic theory had rarely taken gender into account, one could not look to that source for answers. 'Sex differences'[4] were not only the point of departure for many studies but also the explanation for any linguistic variations that were found. Currently, however, scholars are directing their efforts to understanding why differences appear, by inspecting more carefully the conditions under which they occur.

A Functional Approach to 'Sex Differences'

Some researchers are tackling the 'why' question through a *functional* approach to 'sex differences' in speech. Janet Holmes (1984; 1990) contends that the same linguistic form, such as a tag question, may serve a variety of functions, depending on the context of its use: to whom one is speaking, with what kind of intonation, the formality of the speech context and the type of discourse (for example, a discussion, argument or personal narrative) involved. Her quantitative analyses of carefully matched samples of middle-class women's and men's speech in New Zealand[5] offer a much different picture than the one Lakoff hypothesized. For example, contrary to Lakoff's (1975: 16) claim that women use tag questions which undermine their own opinions by expressing uncertainty ('The way prices are rising is horrendous, isn't it?'), Holmes (1990) finds that men employ many more such tags. By contrast, women use significantly more tag questions that fill a facilitative function for conversation, such as generating 'small talk' ('Sure is hot in here, isn't it?': Lakoff, 1975: 16).

Deborah Cameron, Fiona McAlinden and Kathy O'Leary (1988) take Holmes's (1990) functional approach one step further, contrasting distributions of women's and men's tag questions across different conversational roles and statuses. In their samples of conversation from the Survey of English Usage (based primarily on white, middle-class, southern London speakers), women use more facilitative tags than men do and men use more 'undermining' tags than women do. However, in their recordings of speech involving speakers in 'powerful' and 'powerless' speaking roles (for example, doctor vis-à-vis caller on a medical phone-in show), the pattern is very different. Among those in 'powerful' roles, both women and men use facilitative tags to generate talk from other participants; among those in 'powerless' roles, neither women nor men employ facilitative forms, relying exclusively on tags that seek reassurance for their opinions. The authors conclude that 'the patterning of particular linguistic forms may be illuminated by . . . a number of variables, not just gender' (Cameron et al., 1988: 91).

Another approach to explaining 'sex differences' is a thoroughgoing rethinking of the methods that have been used to assess them. Cameron (1988) observes that, traditionally, sociolinguistics has meant the quantitative study of correlations between linguistic and social variables.[6] As she points out, quantitative methods of gathering data and analysing them are often designed for the study of men's speech and are not necessarily the best means of studying women's. Moreover, sex stereotypes have pervaded researchers' explanations for differences that are found. For example, one widely respected explanation for women's use of more standard linguistic forms is the idea that women are more status conscious than men (Cameron and Coates, 1988, citing Labov, 1972 in the United States, and Trudgill, 1975 in the United Kingdom). From this perspective, women attempt to gain status through their speech patterns because society holds them to a more exacting standard of behavior than men while denying them opportunities to gain status through alternative means. But this explanation rests on stereotyped and culturally specific assumptions about the family as the primary unit of social stratification, including the notion that women's status comes primarily from their husbands' or fathers' occupations (Cameron and Coates, 1988). As Patricia Nichols (1983) demonstrates, differing economic conditions can produce dramatic differences among women with respect to the general pattern. Nichols's fieldwork on the use of Gullah (a 'low prestige' variety of English) and 'standard' American English among Black speakers in South Carolina shows that local labor market conditions are the key to speakers' linguistic choices. Older mainland women, with few job opportunities beyond domestic and agricultural work, rely heavily on Gullah –

which serves them well in their intracommunity contacts with other Gullah speakers. Younger mainland women, with new job opportunities in the service sector, show a dramatic shift toward English – a requirement for communicating with the white world outside their local community. The moral of the story is that 'women are not a homogeneous group, they do not always and everywhere behave in similar ways and their behaviour cannot be explained in global, undifferentiated terms' (Cameron and Coates, 1988: 23).

Women's and Men's Styles of Talk

Some scholars have abandoned the quantitative paradigm altogether, focusing instead on women's and men's styles of talk within distinctive speech communities. For example, drawing on John Gumperz's (1982) work on difficulties in communication between members of different ethnic groups, Daniel Maltz and Ruth Borker (1982; see also Tannen, 1982; 1990) argue that observed differences in the talk of US women and men arise from the distinctive norms, conceptions and interpretations of friendly conversation they learn in segregated subcultures (that is, girls' and boys' peer groups). The subculture of girls, they say, stresses cooperativeness and equality; thus, it would encourage the patterns of 'active listening' (including precisely timed insertions of 'um-hmm' and 'uh-huh') that Fishman (1978) observes in the talk of adult women. But the subculture of boys puts the emphasis on dominance and competition, say Maltz and Borker; thus, it would promote the patterns of interruption (violation of a current speaker's turn) that Zimmerman and West (1975) observe in the talk of adult men. And while girls learn to talk their ways around 'best friend' relationships and situations, boys learn to speak in ways that gain them positions in social hierarchies. Thus, by the time they grow up, women and men are likely to operate on the basis of differing conversational norms – resulting not only in 'sex differences', but also cases of miscommunication between them. Maltz and Borker (1982) advance no systematic evidence for their argument (basing their claims on personal observations and reinterpretations of existing research findings), but other researchers do. For example, Jennifer Coates (1988) finds considerable evidence of women's cooperativeness in conversations that took place over nine months in a women's support group (obviously, a likely site for verbal cooperativeness) in the United Kingdom.[7] Members of the group built progressively on one another's contributions to talk, arriving consensually at a joint definition of the situation. They employed monitoring responses (such as 'mm' and 'yeah': see discussions of these in Fishman, 1978; Zimmerman and West, 1975) to indicate active listening and support for the current speaker, and often spoke simultaneously to collaborate in the production of joint utterances. Coates suggests that 'the way women negotiate talk symbolizes . . . mutual support and cooperation: conversationalists understand that they have rights as speakers and also duties as listeners; the joint working out of a group point of view takes precedence over individual assertions' (1988: 120).

Many scholars have criticized the speech-styles approach, particularly for its neglect of questions concerning power and control (for example, Henley and Kramarae, 1991; Trömel-Plötz, 1991; West, 1995). As Trömel-Plötz points out, the fundamental assumption of this approach, that girls and boys grow up in separate subcultures, is extremely problematic: 'Girls and boys, women and men . . . live together in shared linguistic worlds, be it in the family, in schoolrooms, in the streets, in colleges, in jobs; they are probably spending more time in mixed-sex contexts than in single-sex contexts, and, above all, they are not victims of constant misunderstandings' (1991: 490). She contends that, by interpreting observed asymmetries in conversation as the result of subcultural misunderstandings, those who adopt a speech-styles approach trivialize women's experiences of injustice and conversational dominance: see, for example, Tannen's discussion of patterned asymmetries in interruptions between women and men (reported by West and Zimmerman, 1977), which she describes as 'a matter of individual perceptions of rights and obligations, as they grow out of individual habits and expectations' (1990: 192).

Some researchers advance a more nuanced version of the speech-styles approach, moving beyond the idea of gender subcultures. For example, Elinor Ochs (1993) argues that the issue is not so much the particular forms women use (such as tag questions) but the specific pragmatic work these forms can accomplish (such as demonstrating a speaker's stance) *and* the norms associated with the distribution of this work between women and men. Thus, 'sex differences' in talk result from habitual differences between women and men in the pragmatic work they must do – a way of mapping or *indexing* gender. Penelope Brown (1980) contends that, among Tenejapan women, members of a Mayan Indian community she studied in Mexico, the use of 'polite' linguistic forms, such as rhetorical questions, in amicable situations displays deference to others' feelings as well as consciousness of one's own position within the social structure. However, when these women find themselves in hostile confrontations (such as occur in a courtroom), 'this stance is evoked, but from a distance, ironically, in the sarcastic politeness of hostile pseudo-agreement' (1994: 336). Brown concludes that such sarcastic politeness is a means of gender indexing: 'Even when women are not being polite, characteristic female strategies of indirectness and politeness are manifested in their speech' (1994: 336).

Gender and Talk-In-Interaction

A third major approach to explaining 'sex differences' in talk is one that takes the context of interaction as its starting point. While many forms of discourse involve mediated relationships among participants (for example, the printed page that intervenes between writers and readers or the electronic screen that stands between senders and receivers), talk generally does not. For researchers who study talk-in-interaction, this fact has three important implications: people talk (1) in real time, (2) on a turn-by-turn basis, and (3) typically (though not always) face to face in the same social situation. Talk is thus a form of situated social action, and:

> The human tendency to use signs and symbols means that evidence of social worth and evaluation will be conveyed by very minor things, and these things will be witnessed, as will the fact that they have been witnessed. An unguarded glance, a momentary change in tone of voice, an ecological position taken or not taken can drench talk with judgmental significance. (Goffman, 1967: 33)

The significance of this for the study of 'sex differences' is that the meaning of any linguistic variation cannot be determined outside the interactional context in which it occurs. For example, Marjorie Goodwin's (1990) research on the talk of African-American, working-class boys and girls at play in a city neighborhood indicates that girls and boys tend to coordinate their activities in dramatically different ways. In organizing tasks such as making slingshots, boys use directives – 'utterances designed to get someone else to do something' (1990: 65) – that emphasize differences between themselves and the other boys they play with:[8]

[Goodwin, 1990: 103–4]

(48) Malcolm: *All* right. *G*imme some rubber bands.
      Chopper: ((*giving rubber bands*)) Oh.
(49) Malcolm: PL: IERS. I WANT THE PLIERS! (0.6)
                 Man y'all gonna have to get y'all own
                 wire cutters ⌈ if this the way 'y'all gonna be.
      Pete: ⌊ Okay. Okay.
(50) *Regarding coat hanging wire*
      Malcolm: *G*ive it to me man. Where's yours at.
                 Throw that piece of shit *out*.
      Chopper: ((*gives Malcolm his cut-off piece of hanger*))

Above, Malcolm advances his directives as imperatives, with syntax that stress the distinctions between himself ('me') and his addressees (Chopper and Pete). Goodwin notes that the purpose of such directives is evident from both their form (as imperatives) and their context (for example, in the stretch of talk where Malcolm orders Chopper to throw out 'that piece of shit'). Through these means, boys organize their play hierarchically, developing asymmetrical arrangements between their playmates and themselves.

By contrast, girls employ directives that minimize differences among playmates:

[Goodwin, 1990: 110]

(3)   *Girls are looking for bottles.*
      Martha: Let's go around Subs and Suds.
      Bea: Let's ask her 'Do you have any bottles.'

(4)   *Talking about bottles girls are picking out of the trash can*
        Kerry: Hey y'all. Let's use these first and
                     then come back and get the rest
                     cuz it's too many of 'em.

Above, Martha, Bea and Kerry organize their plans (to make rings from bottle rims) as a series of proposals, employing 'Let's' to invite one another's collaboration. Often, they downgrade their directives even further, modifying them with words like 'can', 'could' and 'maybe' (for example, 'We could go around lookin for more bottles': 1990: 111).

From a 'sex differences' perspective, Goodwin's (1990) results might be taken as an indication of what girls and boys 'are like' in this society: girls are more polite and boys, more aggressive. From a speech-styles perspective, these results might be seen to reflect the distinctive conversational norms of girls and boys (and subsequently, women and men): boys gain status 'by telling others what to do and resisting being told what to do' while girls 'formulate requests as proposals rather than orders to make it easy for others to express other preferences without provoking a confrontation' (Tannen, 1990: 154). But note that, although Goodwin's analysis focuses on the impact of alternative directive forms in the contexts of their use, sex differences and speech-styles perspectives imply that the differences she observes arise from fundamental differences in what girls and boys know how to do – as a consequence of either 'what they are like' or what they have learned (West, 1995). Goodwin's evidence indicates that neither of these interpretations is correct. For instance, when girls deal with infractions, negotiate the roles of teacher or mother, or get in arguments, they show considerable skill in the use of imperatives:

[Goodwin, 1990: 119]
(40)   *Ruby bounces on top of Bea.*
        Bea: Ouch girl. Stop. That hurt!
(41)   *Ruby is sitting on top of Kerry.*
        Kerry: Get off Ruby.

Moreover, they use imperatives with boys, as well as with other girls:

[Goodwin, 1990: 119]
(37)   *Boy steps on Ruby's lawn.*
        Ruby: Get out the way offa that-
                     get off that lawn!
(39)   Chopper: Get outa here you wench.
                     You better get outa here.
        Bea: No! You don't tell me to get out.

Thus, Goodwin concludes that girls' preferences for downgraded directives in their play groups do not derive from their greater politeness or distinctive style. Rather, they result from 'systematic procedures through which a particular type of social organization can be created' (1990: 137).

Why would speakers use systematic procedures to create distinctive types of social organization? Candace West and Angela Garcia's (West and Garcia, 1988; West, 1992) analysis of conversational 'shift work' suggests a plausible answer to this question. West and Garcia examined conversations between white, middle-class, US college students who met for the first time in a laboratory setting. They observed that women and men worked collaboratively to produce the majority of topic transitions: both speakers demonstrated, turn by turn, that they had nothing further to say about one topic-in-progress prior to initiating another. However, men initiated *all* of the apparently unilateral topic changes, and they did so in the vicinity of particular kinds of 'tellables'. For example, a woman's explanation of the relationship between her academic major and her plans for law school (perhaps an unwomanly aspiration) was cut off mid-utterance; a woman's discussion of her feelings about being 'too close' to family members (arguably, an unmanly course of talk) never took place; and, as we see below, a woman's assessment of herself as 'really an irrational person sometimes' met with no disagreement:

[West and Garcia, 1988: 566]
```
Andy:   There's discuss::ion an':: short- .h There's ya' know,
        written an' oral exams frequently. Er (.) once in awhile
        at least.
Beth:   Yeah, I'd like to take uh-  something like  Hist'ry (of)
        Philosophy 'r something where you don' afta do any of that
        kinda-
        (1.0)
Beth:   I don't thINK that way,
        (0.6)
Beth:   I'm not that logical.
        (0.4)
Beth:   Yuh know they go step by step.
        (1.2)
Beth:   'N I just- (0.5) I'm REally an irRAtional person sometimes.
        (.) So
        (0.6)
Andy:   Where do you li:ve in Eye Vee?
```

In interpreting these results, West and Garcia (1988) do not simply argue that women pursue certain courses of conversational activity, such as describing their feelings, which men prefer to avoid. Instead, they contend that women's pursuit of these activities and men's curtailment of them both draw on and demonstrate what it is to be a woman or a man in these contexts. They note:

Whenever people face issues of allocation – who is to do what, get what, plan or execute action, direct or be directed – incumbency in significant social categories such as 'female and male' seems to become pointedly relevant. How such issues are resolved conditions the exhibition, dramatization or celebration of one's 'essential nature' as a woman or man. (West and Zimmerman, 1987: 143; cited in West and Garcia, 1988: 551)

In other words, what men accomplish through their unilateral topic changes is the then-and-there determination of which activities will be pursued and which tellables will be told. Simultaneously, *both* men and women demonstrate their accountability to normative conceptions of attitudes and activities appropriate for their respective sex categories. Thus, given a cultural conception of supportiveness as an essential part of womanly 'nature', evidence of such a nature can be found in women's collaborative efforts to introduce and develop potential tellables. By contrast, given a cultural conception of control as an essential part of manly nature, evidence of it can be found in men's unilateral shifts from one set of tellables to another (West, 1992: 378).

Coda

We have come a long way since Robin Lakoff's (1973; 1975) initial claims about a distinctive 'women's language'. From those who take a functional approach to gender and talk, we have been given a much more systematic picture of the distribution of 'sex differences', and the various expressive functions these may serve. From those who focus on women's and men's styles of talk, we have been given a rich understanding of what goes on in talk *among* women and talk *among* men, and thus, of how 'sex differences' in communicative styles can reflect the distinctive kinds of pragmatic work women and men do. And, from those who study talk-in-interaction, we have developed a profound appreciation of the fact that the local context of any particular 'sex difference' in talk may well determine its status *as* a 'sex difference' in talk.

One thing that distinguishes these three perspectives is how they attend to the question of context. 'Functional' researchers tend to take 'a variable approach' to this question, assessing attributes of linguistic variables and social variables *across* particular populations. For these researchers, 'context' is a matter of deciding which variables (gender, status of participants, etc.) will be included in the analysis, given what we already know about those variables and the relationships among them. Those who focus on communicative styles look at linguistic variations *within* particular populations, and within the social context in which such variations occur. Hence, these researchers take elements of the social context into account (such as the setting, the situation) in so far as they seem relevant to the members of the particular communities they are interested in. For those who study talk-in-interaction, the temporal and sequential context of talk is most important: '[It] supplies the ground on which the whole edifice of action is built (by participants) in the first instance, and to which it is adapted "from the ground up", so to speak' (Schegloff, 1992: 125). As a consequence of these differing approaches to context, 'sex differences' in talk are explained as characteristics of particular populations (for example, women and men), as products of the distinctive conversational norms within speech communities (for example, girls' and boys' peer groups) or as situated accomplishments (for example, the demonstration of womanly and manly 'natures').

Clearly, another thing that distinguishes these approaches is how they conceptualize gender. For example, those who take a functional approach think of gender as inherent to the individual. From this perspective, gender can be treated as an independent variable, whose effects can be assessed on dependent variables. Those who take a stylistic approach to 'sex differences' conceive of gender as a role – one that is contingent on the individual's social structural position and the expectations associated with that position. From this vantage point, the emphasis is on how the roles that generate 'sex differences' in talk are learned and enacted. Both conceptualizations have been subject to considerable criticism in recent years. For example, conceiving of gender as an individual characteristic makes it hard to see how it can structure distinctive domains of social life (Stacey and Thorne, 1985). 'Sex differences' are still the explanation (as in many early studies of isolated linguistic variables) rather than the analytic point of departure. Conceiving of gender as made up of the 'male role' and the 'female role' implies a 'separate but equal' relationship between the two, obscuring dynamics of power and inequality (Thorne, 1980). The concept of 'sex roles' does not explain 'whose version of the communication situation will prevail; whose speech style will be seen as normal [and] who will be required to learn the communication style, and interpret the meaning, of the other' (Henley and Kramarae, 1991: 19; see also Trömel-Plötz, 1991).

By contrast, those who study talk-in-interaction see gender as 'a routine, methodical and recurring accomplishment' (West and Zimmerman, 1987: 126). From this perspective, the emphasis shifts from matters internal to the individual and focuses instead on interactional and, in the end, institutional arenas. Rather than as a property of individuals, these analysts view gender as an emergent feature of social situations: both an outcome of and a rationale for various social situations – and a means of legitimating one of the most fundamental divisions of society.

Directions for Future Research

As Barrie Thorne, Cheris Kramarae and Nancy Henley (1983a: 16) point out, 'Overviews necessarily look backwards, patterning and joining work that has already been done.' Previews, by contrast, look forward, searching for work still left to do. In concluding this overview of research on gender and discourse, we offer a preview of sorts, assessing the implications of existing work for studies yet to be done.

One implication of existing research is that much of what we 'know' about gender and discourse is really about white, middle-class, heterosexual women and men using English in Western societies. Studies like Etter-Lewis's (1991), Goodwin's (1990), Lazar's (1993) and Nichols's (1983) are the exceptions, rather than the rule. Much more work remains to be done addressing the possibility of considerable diversity in relations between gender and discourse around the world.

A second implication of existing research is that we must remain flexible about our theoretical frameworks and methods of data collection and analysis. Just as methods designed for the study of men's speech may not necessarily be the best means of studying women's (Cameron, 1988), so too, methods designed for the study of white, middle-class English discourse may not be the best means of studying anything else. In particular, we must take care to avoid reducing culture, class, race, and ethnicity to the status of mere variables, to be 'added' to what we already know in mechanical fashion (see West and Fenstermaker, 1995: 8–14).

A third implication of existing research is that we need to pay far more systematic attention to silence. As Etter-Lewis (1991) demonstrates, we can learn a great deal about people's experiences of subordination by looking at what they don't say in addition to what they do say. Silence is a relatively neglected dimension of inquiry into what's 'there' in discourse – as is an emphasis on readers rather than writers of texts and hearers rather than speakers of talk. Moreover, silence can mean different things in different situations, to different women and men in different cultures.

A fourth implication of existing research is that we need to know more about the potential of texts and talk to convey multiple meanings. For example, Lazar's (1993) analysis of governmental double talk about gender equality in Singapore shows that texts can appear to promote equality between women and men while simultaneously conveying sexist messages. Further research on the interaction of multiple meanings in texts and talk (and on the relationship between different modes, such as words and images) could help us understand much more about how discourse reproduces institutionalized power relations between women and men in different societies.

Finally, we note that electronic communications pose new challenges for existing analyses of gender and discourse. Use of the Internet, the global electronic network of computers, is accelerating in Western countries that already have highly developed telephone networks. In many countries without extensive or reliable telephone lines, educators and government officials are using satellites and relatively inexpensive computers to make the Internet accessible to millions more. This network is likely to dramatically alter the ways people in many businesses and institutions establish and maintain relationships, and it will certainly change the way we conduct and publish research. Preliminary work indicates that, just as we are developing the tools needed to study them, traditional power relations between women and men are being quickly established in cyberspace.

Gender Inequality in Cyberspace

Asymmetry in the use and control of the Internet (of current users, an estimated 85 percent to 90 percent are boys and men: Taylor et al., 1993) means that we are witnessing the growth of a system (arguably, the most important social and educational network of our time) in which boys and men are developing and administering the rules of conduct. Even in contexts where women are the purported authorities, for example, in an electronic discussion group focused on issues of concern to women, men appear to be in control: they make up 63 percent of the participants, their messages receive more responses than women's, and their interests dominate discussions. Thus, while the Internet has the potential for facilitating interaction across time and space, it seems to be emerging as a men's forum (Ebben, 1994). Future research might address the question of how exactly this is happening.

Electronic harassment and stalking of girls and women using the Internet is common, and the distribution of pornographic visuals and messages is increasing, as are the numbers of racist and ethnocentric 'jokes' circulating there (Kramarae and Kramer, 1995). In interactive 'communities' on the Internet, many women confess that, to avoid harassment, they often present themselves as men (in name and manner) and refrain from expressing their opinions (Balsamo, 1994). Some men electronically present themselves as women, in order to see what it feels like and get the increased attention they think women receive. What are the mechanisms for displaying oneself as a man or a woman under circumstances like these?

Many women report a general hostility on the Internet (see, for example, Hawisher and Sullivan, in press) that is difficult to document with existing research measures – since many of the features that mark inequality in face-to-face interaction are not readily visible in electronic exchanges. For example, participants in most electronic discussions are free from concerns about securing speaking turns and forestalling interruptions because their contributions are typed in isolation, seemingly at whatever speed and length they desire. This has led some researchers (for example, Herring, 1994) to explore electronic 'indices' of hostility (such as numbers of postings, assertions, instances of name-calling, personal insults, and remarks repeated out of context) and politeness (such as comments that praise others, hedges and apologies) in men's and women's electronic messages. However, the most important lesson we have learned from existing research offers a promising new direction for such efforts: to the extent that categories such as 'woman' and 'man' are accessible through the Internet, and to the extent these categories are omnirelevant to social action (Garfinkel, 1967: 118), they provide users with an ever-available resource for interpreting, explaining and justifying actions as 'womanly' or 'manly' behaviors. Rather than seeking new measures of 'manly' and 'womanly' behaviors, we hope that future studies will address the situated accomplishment of gender – in the discourse of cyberspace, as well as the discourse of everyday life.

Recommended Reading

Cameron (1990a)
Coates and Cameron (1988)
Goodwin (1990)
Graddol and Swann (1989)
Henley (1995)
Holmes (1984)
Houston and Kramarae (1991)
Roman et al. (1994)
Thorne et al. (1983a)
Thorne et al. (1983b)
Trömel-Plötz (1982)
West (1995)

Notes

For their helpful comments on an earlier version of this chapter, we thank Ida Barnett, Marilyn Chap, Norman Fairclough, Lynn Fujiwara, Sydney Hart, April Kleine, Gary Lasky, Rosalind Lazar, Christopher Niemitz, Katherine Rosellini, Elizabeth Turner, Aki Uchida, Teun A. van Dijk and Elizabeth Wheatley. We alone are responsible for the final version.

1 Christian-Smith (1989) reports that suburban white girls, 12 to 15 years of age, are the primary readers of these novels, with Black girls and Latinas comprising a much smaller proportion of readers.

2 Gillard does not specify the class backgrounds or racial/ethnic identities of these Australian girls.

3 McRobbie (1982: 265) notes that *Jackie*, like many magazines produced for adolescent girls, addresses 'girls' as a monolithic group, obscuring important differences among girls, such as class background and racial/ethnic identity.

4 We use quotation marks around this prevailing terminology, because it collapses *sex* (an assignment based on physiological evidence, such as hormones, chromosomes and anatomy) and *gender* (a social accomplishment).

5 Holmes (1990) does not provide a description of the racial/ethnic identities of those in her samples.

6 Aki Uchida (1992) argues that the correlational approach still prevails in many sociolinguistics studies today.

7 Coates does not describe the class backgrounds or racial/ethnic identities of the women in this group, although she identifies speakers in two conversations as white and middle class (1988: 122, n. 4).

8 Transcribing conventions used in the text are presented in the Appendix to this volume.

References

Aebischer, Verena and Forel, Claire (eds) (1983) *Parlers Masculins, Parlers Féminins?* Neuchatel, Switzerland: Delachaux et Niestlé.

Balsamo, Anne (1994) 'Feminism for the incurably informed', in Mark Dery (ed.), *Flame Wars: the Discourse of Cyberculture*. Durham, London: Duke University Press. pp. 125–56.

Bodine, Ann (1990) 'Androcentrism in prescriptive grammar: singular "they", sex-indefinite "he", and "he or she"', in Deborah Cameron (ed.), *The Feminist Critique of Language: a Reader*. London, New York: Routledge. pp. 166–86. Reprinted from *Language in Society*, 4, Cambridge: Cambridge University Press, 1975.

Brown, Penelope (1980) 'How and why women are more polite: some evidence from a Mayan community', in Sally McConnell-Ginet, Ruth Borker and Nelly Furman (eds), *Women and Language in Literature and Society*. New York: Praeger. pp. 111–49.

Brown, Penelope (1994) 'Gender, politeness, and confrontation in Tenejapa', in Camille Roman, Suzanne Juhasz and Cristanne Miller (eds), *The Women and Language Debate: a Sourcebook*. New Brunswick, NJ: Rutgers University Press. pp. 322–39.

Cameron, Deborah (1988) 'Introduction', in Jennifer Coates and Deborah Cameron (eds), *Women in their Speech Communities: New Perspectives on Language and Sex*. London: Longman. pp. 3–12.

Cameron, Deborah (ed.) (1990a) *The Feminist Critique of Language*. London: Routledge.

Cameron, Deborah (1990b) 'Introduction: why is language a feminist issue?', in Deborah Cameron (ed.), *The Feminist Critique of Language: a Reader*. London, New York: Routledge. pp. 1–28.

Cameron, Deborah (1992) *Feminism and Linguistic Theory*, 2nd edn. London: Macmillan.

Cameron, Deborah and Coates, Jennifer (1988) 'Some problems in the sociolinguistic explanation of sex differences', in Jennifer Coates and Deborah Cameron (eds), *Women in their Speech Communities: New Perspectives on Language and Sex*. London: Longman. pp. 13–26.

Cameron, Deborah, McAlinden, Fiona and O'Leary, Kathy (1988) 'Lakoff in context: the social and linguistic functions of tag questions', in Jennifer Coates and Deborah Cameron (eds), *Women in their Speech Communities: New Perspectives on Language and Sex*. London: Longman. pp. 74–93.

Christian-Smith, Linda (1989) 'Power, knowledge and curriculum: constructing femininity in adolescent romance novels', in Suzanne de Castell, Allan Luke and Carmen Luke (eds), *Language, Authority and Criticism: Readings on the School Textbook*. London: Falmer Press. pp. 17–31.

Clark, Kate (1992) 'The linguistics of blame: representations of women in the *Sun* reporting of crimes of sexual violence', in Michael Toolan (ed.), *Language, Text and Context: Essays in Stylistics*. London, New York: Routledge. pp. 208–24.

Coates, Jennifer (1988) 'Gossip revisited: language in all-female groups', in Jennifer Coates and Deborah Cameron (eds), *Women in their Speech Communities: New Perspectives on Language and Sex*. London: Longman. pp. 94–122.

Coates, Jennifer and Cameron, Deborah (eds) (1988) *Women in their Speech Communities: New Perspectives on Language and Sex*. London: Longman.

Cranny-Francis, Anne and Gillard, Patricia Palmer (1990) 'Soap opera as gender training: teenage girls and TV', in Terry Threadgold and Anne Cranny-Francis (eds), *Feminine/Masculine and Representation*. Sydney: Allen and Urwin. pp. 171–89.

Ebben, Maureen (1994) 'Women on the net: an exploratory study of gender dynamics on the soc.women computer network'. Unpublished doctoral dissertation, Speech Communication, University of Illinois at Urbana–Champaign.

Eble, Connie (1972) 'How the speech of some is more equal than others', paper presented at the Southeastern Conference on Linguistics, Georgetown University, Washington, DC.

Etter-Lewis, Gwendolyn (1991) 'African American women's legacy', *Discourse & Society*, 2 (4): 425–37.

Fishman, Pamela (1978) 'Interaction: the work women do', *Social Problems*, 25 (4): 397–406.

Fowler, Roger (1991) *Language in the News: Discourse and Ideology in the Press*. London: Routledge.

Garfinkel, Harold (1967) *Studies in Ethnomethodology*. Englewood Cliffs, NJ: Prentice-Hall.

Goffman, Erving (1967) *Interaction Ritual: Essays on Face-to-Face Behavior*. New York: Anchor/Doubleday.

Goodwin, Marjorie Harness (1990) *He-Said-She-Said: Talk as Social Organization among Black Children*. Bloomington, Indianapolis: Indiana University Press.

Gore-Booth, Lord and Paenham, Desmond (eds) (1977) *Satow's Guide to Diplomatic Practice*. London: Longman.

Graddol, David and Swann, Joan (1989) *Gender Voices*. Oxford: Basil Blackwell.

Gumperz, John J. (1982) *Discourse Strategies*. Cambridge: Cambridge University Press.

Hawisher, Gail and Sulllivan, P.A. (in press) 'Women on the networks: searching for presence in online discussions', in S. Jarratt and L. Worsham (eds), *Feminism and Composition*. New York: Modern Language Association.

Hellinger, Marlis (ed.) (1985) *Sprachwandel und feministische Sprachpolitik: Internationale Perspektiven*. Opladen: Westdeutscher Verlag.

Henley, Nancy (1995) 'Ethnicity and gender issues in language', in Hope Landrine (ed.), *Bringing Cultural Diversity to Feminist Psychology: Theory, Research and Practice*. Washington: American Psychological Association. pp. 361–95.

Henley, Nancy and Kramarae, Cheris (1991) 'Gender, power, and miscommunication', in Nikolas Coupland, Howard Giles and John M. Wiemann (eds), *'Miscommunication' and Problematic Talk*. Newbury Park, CA: Sage. pp. 18–43.

Henley, Nancy and Thorne, Barrie (1975) 'Sex differences in language, speech, and nonverbal communication: an annotated bibliography', in Barrie Thorne and Nancy Henley (eds), *Language and Sex: Difference and Dominance*. Rowley, MA: Newbury House. pp. 205–305.

Herring, Susan C. (1994) 'Politeness in computer culture: why women thank and men flame', in Mary Bucholtz, Anita Liang and Lauren Sutton (eds), *Communicating in, through, and across Cultures: Proceedings of the Third Berkeley Women and Language Conference*. Berkeley Women and Language Group. pp. 278–94.

Hirschman, Lynette (1973) 'Female–male differences in conversational interaction', paper presented at meeting of the Linguistic Society of America, San Diego, CA.

Holmes, Janet (1984) 'Women's language: a functional approach', *General Linguistics*, 24 (3): 149–78.

Holmes, Janet (1990) 'Hedges and boosters in women's and men's speech', *Language and Communication*, 10 (3): 185–205.

Houston, Marsha and Kramarae, Cheris (eds) (1991) *Women Speaking from Silence*, special issue of *Discourse and Society*, 2 (4).

Key, Mary Ritchie (1975) *Male/Female Language, with a Comprehensive Bibliography*. Metuchen, NJ: Scarecrow Press.

Kramarae, Cheris and Kramer, Jana (1995) 'Net gains, net loses', *Women's Review of Books*, 12 (5): 33–5.

Kramarae, Cheris, Thorne, Barrie and Henley, Nancy (1983) 'Sex similarities and differences in language, speech and nonverbal communication: an annotated bibliography', in Barrie Thorne, Cheris Kramarae and Nancy Henley (eds), *Language, Gender and Society*. Rowley, MA: Newbury House. pp. 153–331.

Labov, William (1972) *Sociolinguistic Patterns*. Philadelphia: University of Pennsylvania Press.

Lakoff, Robin (1973) 'Language and woman's place', *Language in Society*, 2 (1): 45–79.

Lakoff, Robin (1975) *Language and Women's Place*. New York: Harper Colophon.

Lazar, Michelle M. (1993) 'Equalizing gender relations: a case of double-talk', *Discourse & Society*, 4 (4): 443–65.

MacKay, Donald G. (1983) 'Prescriptive grammar and the pronoun problem', in Barrie Thorne, Cheris Kramarae and Nancy Henley (eds), *Language, Gender and Society*. Rowley, MA: Newbury House. pp. 38–53.

Maltz, Daniel N. and Borker, Ruth A. (1982) 'A cultural approach to male–female miscommunication', in John J. Gumperz (ed.), *Language and Social Identity*. Cambridge: Cambridge University Press. pp. 196–216.

Martyna, Wendy (1983) 'Beyond the he/man approach: the case for nonsexist language', in Barrie Thorne, Cheris Kramarae and Nancy Henley (eds), *Language, Gender and Society*. Rowley, MA: Newbury House. pp. 25–37.

McConnell-Ginet, Sally (1978) 'Intonation in a man's world', *Signs: Journal of Women in Culture and Society*, 3 (3): 541–59.

McRobbie, Angela (1982) '*Jackie*: an ideology of adolescent femininity', in Bernard Waites, Tony Bennett and Graham Martin (eds), *Popular Culture: Past and Present*. London: Croom Helm in association with Open University Press. pp. 263–83.

Nichols, Patricia (1983) 'Linguistic options and choices for Black women in the rural South', in Barrie Thorne, Cheris Kramarae and Nancy Henley (eds), *Language, Gender and Society*. Rowley, MA: Newbury House. pp. 54–68.

Ochs, Elinor (1993) 'Indexing gender', in Barbara Miller (ed.), *Sex and Gender Hierarchies*. Cambridge: Cambridge University Press. pp. 146–69.

Roman, Camille, Juhasz, Suzanne and Miller, Cristanne (eds) (1994) *The Women and Language Debate: a Sourcebook*. New Brunswick, NJ: Rutgers University Press.

Sachs, Jacqueline (1975) 'Clues to the identification of sex in children's speech', in Barrie Thorne and Nancy Henley (eds), *Language and Sex: Difference and Dominance*. Rowley, MA: Newbury House. pp. 152–71.

Schegloff, Emanuel A. (1992) 'To Searle on conversation: a note in return', in John R. Searle et al. (eds), *(On) Searle on Conversation* (compiled and introduced by Herman Parret and Jef Vershueren). Amsterdam: John Benjamins. pp. 113–28.

Schulz, Muriel (1975) 'The semantic derogation of woman', in Barrie Thorne and Nancy Henley (eds), *Language and Sex: Difference and Dominance*. Rowley, MA: Newbury House. pp. 64–75.

Simpson, Paul (1993) *Language, Ideology and Point of View*. London, New York: Routledge.

Smith, Dorothy (1988) 'Femininity as discourse', in Leslie G. Roman and Linda K. Christian-Smith with Elizabeth Ellsworth (eds), *Becoming Feminine: the Politics of Popular Culture*. London: Falmer Press. pp. 37–58.

Spender, Dale (1980) *Man Made Language*. London: Routledge and Kegan Paul.

Stacey, Judith and Thorne, Barrie (1985) 'The missing feminist revolution in sociology', *Social Problems*, 32 (4): 301–16.

Tannen, Deborah (1982) 'Ethnic style in male–female conversation', in John J. Gumperz (ed.), *Language and Social Identity*. Cambridge: Cambridge University Press. pp. 217–31.

Tannen, Deborah (1990) *You Just Don't Understand: Women and Men in Conversation*. New York: William Morrow.

Taylor, H. Jeanie, Kramarae, Cheris and Ebben, Maureen (1993) *Women, Information Technology, and Gender*. Urbana–Champaign: The Center for Advanced Study, University of Illinois.

Thibault, Paul (1988) 'Knowing what you're told by the agony aunts: language function, gender difference and the structure of knowledge and belief in the personal columns', in David Birch and Michael O'Toole (eds), *Functions of Style*. London: Frances Pinter. pp. 205–33.

Thorne, Barrie (1980) 'Gender . . . how is it best conceptualized?', unpublished manuscript. East Lansing, MI: Department of Sociology, Michigan State University.

Thorne, Barrie, Kramarae, Cheris and Henley, Nancy (1983a) 'Language, gender and society: opening a second decade of research', in Barrie Thorne, Cheris Kramarae and Nancy Henley (eds), *Language, Gender and Society*. Rowley, MA: Newbury House. pp. 7–24.

Thorne, Barrie, Kramarae, Cheris and Henley, Nancy (eds) (1983b) *Language, Gender and Society*. Rowley, MA: Newbury House.

Trömel-Plötz, Senta (1982) *Frauensprache – Sprache der Veränderung*. Frankfurt: Fischer.

Trömel-Plötz, Senta (1991) 'Review essay: selling the apolitical', *Discourse & Society*, 2 (4): 489–502.

Trudgill, Peter (1975) 'Sex, covert prestige, and linguistic change in the urban British English of Norwich', in Barrie Thorne and Nancy Henley (eds), *Language and Sex: Difference and Dominance*. Rowley, MA: Newbury House. pp. 88–104.

Uchida, Aki (1992) 'When "difference" is "dominance": a critique of the "anti-power-based" cultural approach to sex differences', *Language in Society*, 21 (4): 547–68.

Weedon, Chris (1987) *Feminist Practice and Poststructuralist Theory*. Oxford, Cambridge: Blackwell.

West, Candace (1992) 'Rethinking sex differences in conversational topics', *Advances in Group Processes*, 9: 131–62.

West, Candace (1995) 'Women's competence in conversation', *Discourse & Society*, 6 (1): 107–31.

West, Candace and Fenstermaker, Sarah (1995) 'Doing difference', *Gender & Society*, 9 (1): 8–37.

West, Candace and Garcia, Angela (1988) 'Conversational shift work: a study of topical transitions between women and men', *Social Problems*, 35 (5): 551–75.

West, Candace and Zimmerman, Don H. (1977) 'Women's place in everyday talk: reflections on parent–child interaction', *Social Problems*, 24 (5): 521–9.

West, Candace and Zimmerman, Don H. (1987) 'Doing gender', *Gender & Society*, 1 (2): 125–51.

Zimmerman, Don. H. and West, Candace (1975) 'Sex roles, interruptions and silences in conversation', in Barrie Thorne and Nancy Henley (eds), *Language and Sex: Difference and Dominance*. Rowley, MA: Newbury House. pp. 105–29.

6

Discourse, Ethnicity, Culture and Racism

Teun A. van Dijk, Stella Ting-Toomey, Geneva Smitherman and Denise Troutman

The ethnic and cultural diversity of human societies is reflected in language, discourse and communication. Members of ethnic groups routinely speak with, or about, members of other groups. Such intercultural discourse is a taken-for-granted form of everyday interaction and cooperation. Each group may have its own norms, values, language as well as ways of speaking, but in order to understand each other and work together people tend to mutually adapt themselves, more or less, to the others. They often learn each other's languages and about each other's special habits, and up to a point accept and respect each other's cultural identities. This is the good news, and therefore not very newsworthy: multiculturalism is nothing special in most parts of the world. It is not something we read about in the paper.

The bad news is that often multiculturalism, mutual respect and tolerance between different ethnic or 'racial' groups, is merely a social, political or moral ideal. Lip service is routinely being paid to this official norm ('We have nothing against X . . .'). In the real world, however (as we all know either from personal experience or from reading about it in the paper or seeing it on TV), cultural misunderstanding, ethnic conflict, prejudice, xenophobia, ethnocentrism, antisemitism and racism frequently characterize relations between groups that are somehow 'different' from each other.

This is especially the case when one group holds more power, has more privileges or more resources and uses the 'difference' (for example of color, language or religion) as a legitimation to dominate or marginalize others. This is for instance the case in Western Europe, North America and Australia where people of European descent ('whites') usually have more power than ethnic minorities or immigrants who originally came from Africa, Latin America or Asia, or who lived there (for instance in North America or Australia) before the Europeans came.

It is not surprising, therefore, that the standard disclaimer just mentioned ('We have nothing against X . . .') is usually followed by *but*, introducing something negative *we* say about *them*. At the same time, this example shows that ethnic or 'racial' inequality is also evident in the way 'we' speak and write to (or about) the others. Indeed, discourse is a prominent way in which ethnic prejudices and racism are reproduced in society.

Aims

This chapter examines how cultural and ethnic identities, differences, conflicts and inequalities are expressed and reproduced by talk and text. From this huge domain of study, we have selected three main topics for special attention:

1 *Intragroup discourse* The specific discourse characteristics of one ethnic group, namely, African Americans in the United States, in the context of racist inequality and dominance, and against the background of a history of slavery. This chapter will especially focus on a combination of the role of gender and 'race', that is on some discourse properties of African American women.

2 *Intergroup discourse* Intercultural discourse between different groups. How do people of one cultural or ethnic group speak *with* members of other groups? How do ethnically 'different' people understand each other, interact, adapt themselves, and how do they create or resolve possible communication conflicts?

3 *Intragroup discourse about others* How do members of dominant (majority) groups speak and write *about* non-dominant (minority) groups? More specifically, how do many white people in Europe, North America, South Africa or Australia (also) enact their prejudices and racism through their discourse, for instance about blacks, Mexicans, Turks, Moroccans, Arabs, Aborigines, refugees or others from (and in) the South?

These three topics are multiply related. Prejudice and racism may be reproduced in discourse *with* as well as *about* the others. And the ways members of one ethnic group speak among each other are of course related to their position in society, and how they are spoken to and spoken about by dominant group members.

Many other topics of the field of intra- and intercultural discourse remain unexplored here, such as second language learning and use, the way minority group members talk to or about majority group members, and of course the vast variety of numerous other ethnic groups in the world whose discourse characteristics and interaction need our attention (see also Goddard and Wierzbicka, Chapter 9 in this volume).

Although our examples are taken mainly from Europe and North America, we do not imply that ethnic specificity and variation of text and talk, cultural communication problems, ethnic stereotyping and conflict, or racism, only exist there. On the contrary, the media emphasize that serious ethnic conflict is especially prevalent 'elsewhere', for example in Bosnia, Somalia, India or Rwanda. Without denying these tragedies, we may also point our that, interestingly, this special media emphasis itself is a prominent feature of 'ingroup' discourse: *they* create more (serious) problems than *we* do. The 'Western' press may even imply (though it will seldom say so explicitly) that *their* 'ethnic strife' or 'tribal wars' are backward and primitive, while at the same time denying or mitigating *our* (and its own) stereotypes and racism. No wonder that the interethnic conflict in Bosnia was as much a humanitarian and political catastrophe as it was an ethnic embarrassment: fifty years after World War II, these were (again) Europeans massacring each other!

Terminology

Probably no domain of language use and academic study has given rise to so much terminological debate as that of ethnic group relations. The very creation and use (mostly by conservative white elites) of the accusatory label of 'political correctness' bears witness of this confusion and conflict (Williams, 1995). How we call ourselves and others is a crucial part of intra- and intercultural discourse.

However, we are unable in this chapter to discuss questions of terminology. We use the term 'racial' between quotes in order to emphasize that 'races' do not exist, at least not biologically: they are merely social constructions based on common-sense perceptions of superficial differences of appearance (mostly of skin color). On the other hand racism, based on such imaginary biological differences, *does* exist, and hence needs no quotes – although you'll often find it with quotes in the press in order to signal that journalists have doubts about an 'accusation' of racism.

We'll use the general (and hence not very precise) terms *cultural* and *ethnic* to refer to a number of properties of groups, peoples or nations, such as their language, religion, norms, customs and social practices. We may also use the terms 'majority' and 'minority', which express not only a numerical difference between groups, but often also a relation of power and dominance, and unequal access to social resources. For this reason, 'racism' should in fact be called 'ethnicism'. However, given the widespread use of the term 'racism', we shall also use it, although it must be borne in mind that it also includes various forms of ethnocentrism, Eurocentrism, xenophobia and antisemitism.

Theoretical Framework

The issues discussed in this chapter are so diverse that it would be difficult to deal with them within a unified theoretical framework, so we shall be brief and quite general on such a theoretical enterprise. In the broadest sense, the topics of this chapter can be studied in terms of general theories of culture and communication, and more specifically within the framework of a theory of ethnic and intergroup relations. Both these theories are multidisciplinary and involve virtually all of the humanities and social sciences. Intercultural perception and communication typically link social psychology with anthropology. Intracultural communication and discourse similarly connect communication studies, linguistics, ethnography and sociology. Precisely at these boundaries, therefore, interdisciplines such as ethnic studies, black studies (or African American studies), and communication and discourse studies were created. No wonder, therefore, that with scholars from so many disciplines, and with so many different methods, concepts and approaches, a unified theory may well be an illusion.

And yet, the general object of study of this chapter, namely *how people talk with and about others of the same and other ethnic groups*, is a characterization that should allow at least some measure of theoretical integration. As we shall see, one theoretical orientation is the integration of sociolinguistics, ethnography and discourse analysis in the systematic study of such text and talk. That is, if ethnic groups have specific ways of talking and communicating, and if there are communication difficulties between members of different cultures or ethnic groups because of such differences, these specifics and difficulties should be based on the theoretically relevant properties of the whole communication process.

These may involve purely linguistic (grammatical) differences, as well as discourse or conversational structures beyond the sentence boundary, such as topics, coherence, stylistic variation, rhetoric, narrative or argumentative schemata, conversational strategies, non-verbal features such as facework, gestures or distance, forms of self-presentation and politeness, and the many other properties of text and talk studied in this book and its companion volume. Explicitly or implicitly, studies of these and other discursive specifics of and differences between ethnic groups are of course comparative: if we want to study communication differences and conflicts between European, Latin and African Americans in the US, for instance, we need to examine and compare the typical ways of speaking of each of these groups.

Cultural differences that may give rise to communication conflicts are not merely discursive, however, but may have to do with different *contextual* matters, such as cultural knowledge, attitudes and ideologies, norms and values, power relations between and various roles of participants, as well as setting and other properties of the social situation that are relevant for the appropriate accomplishment of discourse as a social practice.

Whether in intercultural harmony and conflict, or in the framework of domination and resistance, as is the case for African American discourse, however, merely focusing on text and context would hardly be enough. Intercultural communication conflict and minority group discourse need a broader explanation in the socioeconomic, political and cultural terms of group relations, power and inequality. The same is obviously true for our understanding of the ways dominant group members speak about minorities and immigrants, and thus reproduce prevalent patterns of prejudice and racism. Similar remarks may be made for the study of intergroup perception, attitudes and attribution in social psychology.

In sum: when we study discourse and communication within and between groups that are defined in terms of their ethnic or cultural specificities and differences, the fundamental contextualizing framework of *societal structures, power and dominance* also needs to be accounted for. Indeed, as suggested, biased discourse is not merely a form of individual talk or an expression of personal prejudice, but reproduces social systems of ethnic inequality, such as racism and antisemitism. Moreover, these systems of dominance are not limited to biased perception and communication, but also involve unequal access to scarce resources, such as (a restriction of) access to the country and citizenship, adequate housing, a decent job, schooling, and many other material and symbolic resources. Thus, many of the specifics of African American discourse can only be understood against the historical background and present legacy of slavery and segregation and within the broader societal context of the continued unequal position of African Americans in US society.

Many properties of intra- and intercultural talk and text, thus, are apparent in and supported by *dominant institutions* such as the state and state agencies, governing bodies, the mass media, the schools and universities, the arts industries and of course corporate business. Or conversely, they may be articulated by the structures and organizations of *dissent and opposition*, as was (and is) the case for the Church, the civil rights movement and numerous other movements and action groups in the African American communities in the US. The same is true for the discourse of minority and (other) anti-racist organizations in Europe during the last decade.

It is within this broader, multidisciplinary framework of study that we now turn to the more detailed study of our three selected topics.

Black Women's Discourse

The Field

In terms of intracultural communication in North America, specifically the US, the most pervasive and dominant discourse variety is that engaged in by Americans of African descent. Although other subcultural groups have their own intragroup discourses, the variety of English spoken by American descendants of African slaves has the longest history and has had the most significant impact on public culture in the US.

This linguistic variety has been variously labelled 'Black English' (Baugh, 1983); 'Ebonics' (for example, Williams, 1975; Asante and Gudykunst, 1989); 'Negro English Vernacular' (for example, Dillard, 1972; Labov, 1972); 'English'/'Nonstandard Negro English' (for example, Harrison, 1884; Stewart, 1964; 1967); and 'Black Talk' (for example, Smitherman, 1994). The term in current usage by most scholars is 'African American Vernacular English' (for example, Rickford, 1992). For our purposes here, we shall use this term, in the form AAVE.

AAVE is the result of the mixture of West African language patterns and ways of speaking with Europeanized American English. This language mixture – US-based Pidgin English – dates from 1619 when the first cargo of African slaves landed at Jamestown on the Dutch vessel *The Good Ship Jesus*. This Pidgin English was used initially as a transactional language in communication between master and slave. However, the Pidgin quickly became the lingua franca during enslavement since it was the practice of slaveholders to mix Africans from different linguistic-cultural backgrounds in the same slave communities, so as to foil communication and thwart escape. Nonetheless, Africans in enslavement appropriated the foreign tongue and made it work for them as a counter-language, a symbolic bond of solidarity. This was accomplished by superimposing upon the white man's tongue discourse styles and linguistic-cultural practices that were known only to those born under the lash. For instance, when an enslaved African said 'Everybody talkin bout Heaben ain goin dere', it was a double-voiced form of speaking which referred to, or 'signified on', slaveholders who professed Christianity but practiced slavery (for example, Smitherman, 1977; Gates, 1988). Thus was African American Vernacular English born.

Specific Discourse Genres

There are three areas of linguistic uniqueness in AAVE: (a) morpho-syntax; (b) phonology; and (c) discourse in the form of surviving black verbal traditions. The characteristic discourse forms of AAVE may be grouped into the following speech acts: (1) call-response; (2) semantic inversion; (3) narrativizing; (4) proverb use; (5) signification. To treat each AAVE discourse form in depth is beyond the scope of this chapter. Here we shall focus on those discourse forms that highlight, in particular, differing aspects of black women's speech patterns. Such patterns are especially interesting, since they express the constraints of both gender and ethnicity.

Review of Earlier and Current Work

Morgan (1989; 1991a; 1991b) has conducted ongoing research on African American women's discourse, focusing particularly on the speech patterns of three generations of women living in Chicago. She establishes that a counter-language exists within the African American speech community, which developed in the US historically as an intragroup communication system, a secret language unknown by enslavers (Morgan, 1991a). This counter-language allowed enslaved Africans to express a positive, self-affirming reality, beyond the degrading enslaved reality. It is in use still today throughout Africa and African America, one form of which is *signifying* (a style of speaking where meaning is conveyed on two different levels, the said and the unsaid).

Based on her study of *indirect discourse* – speech that stems from counter-language – Morgan finds that African and European American women perceive and interpret indirect discourse differently. African American women operate from the maxim that you are responsible for what you actually say. For European American women, however, a speaker is held accountable not for what she says but for what she intended to say: 'It is permissible to reconstruct a speaker's intention or provide psychological explanations for possible ambiguities' (1991a: 440). A speaker's report of her intentions, for African American women, is only 'one of many factors which determine [speaker] intention and responsibility' (Morgan, 1991a: 440). Knowledge of the events and the culture, the role and status of participants, and ideology help to determine speaker meaning and intention also.

Overall, Morgan identifies a different social reality for the African American speech community due to its unique history, belief system, and relationships, which establishes a different set of speech norms, especially for African American women, who hold a central role in the expression of the social reality of the entire speech community.

Houston Stanback (1983) describes middle-class African American women's communicative style by focusing on their traditional social roles. Thus, she examines the relationship between social roles and language. Stanback establishes a 'frame' which may be useful in the analysis of African American women's communication. She concludes that African American women (1) use a register not used by African American men due to their domestic activities; and (2) communicate in an assertive, outspoken way (just as African American men) in public spheres due to work and other public commitments, yet must curtail their outspokenness in their community due to community standards.

In another study, Houston Stanback (1985b) compares perceived and real communicative styles of professional African American women with those of European American women with similar educational and professional statuses. She found that both pairs of women perceived their interracial conversations with acquaintances to be based on knowing them as individuals and not on their race. The actual speech behavior, however, did not align with the women's perception of their communicative styles. The African American women varied their communicative style based on the participant. They used fewer AAVE features and were more tentative in style when talking with their European American acquaintances than when talking with each other. The African American women took greater responsibility in making the interracial conversations work by using two different linguistic codes, AAVE and 'women's language', demonstrating Houston Stanback's larger assertion that the typical African American woman has a 'more complex communicative repertoire' (1985a: 31) that she must select from than does the typical European American woman.

Houston Stanback's (1985b) subsequent research presents findings on middle-class African American women's language in comparison to both white American women and African American men. She identifies differences in women's speech across race due to differences in their cultural and communicative experiences. For example, because African American women worked two shifts historically, one domestic and one public, they developed a style of speaking called 'smart talk', which reflects their assertiveness established from the tradition of working two shifts.

In a series of studies, Etter-Lewis (1991) collected oral narratives of African American women. She conducted lengthy interviews dealing with racism and sexism, using professional women between the ages of 60 and 95 in order to collect data. Etter-Lewis uses the interviews as a means of revealing the women's experiences through the power of their own words.

Characteristic Properties of African American Women's Discourse

To further highlight these cultural specifics of African American discourse, this section focuses on five typical discursive practices: signifying, the dozens, reading dialect, culturally toned diminutives, and smart talk. The latter two features characterize African American women's speech behavior more exclusively than the former features, yet this community of speakers uses all five features. All of the examples below originate from African American women's speech.

Signifying Also known as 'siggin', 'joanin', and 'soundin', signifying or here 'signifyin' is a form of ritualized insult in which a speaker puts down, talks about, needles – signifies on – the listener. This black verbal tradition is a culturally accepted method of talking about somebody or their behavior through indirection. The signifier always employs humor, which is a face-saving strategy for the person being signified on. Signifyin is engaged in by all age groups and by both males and females in the black speech community. It has the following characteristics:

1 indirection, circumlocution
2 metaphors, images (images rooted in the everyday real world)
3 humor, irony
4 rhythmic fluency
5 'teachy' but not 'preachy'
6 directness with respect to person(s) present in the speech situation (signifiers do not talk behind your back)
7 puns, word-play
8 semantic or logical unexpectness.

There are two types of signifyin. One type is levelled at a person's mother (and occasionally at other relatives). Traditionally, this first type was referred to as 'the dozens'/'playin the dozens'. The second type of signifyin is aimed at a person, action, or thing, either just for fun, or for criticism. Currently, the two types of signifyin are being conflated under a more general form of discourse, known as 'snappin'.

The Dozens In the example below, the conversationalists engage in the first type of signifyin mentioned above, 'the dozens':

> Linda: Girl, what up with that head. ((referring to her friend's hairstyle))
> Betty: Ask yo momma.
> Linda: Oh (.) so you going there, huh? Well I **did** ask my momma (.) and she said (.) caint you see that Betty look like her momma spit her out.

Both Betty and Linda signify on each other. Instead of answering Linda's question directly, Betty decides to inform Linda that the condition of her hairstyle is not of Linda's business by responding with 'Ask yo momma'. Betty's response is taken humorously since the normal expectation in a conversation is that a speaker's question is answered honestly and sincerely. The unexpected indirection, then, produces laughter from listeners. Linda clearly recognizes the entry into the ritualized insult as indicated by her response, 'Oh, so you going there, huh?'

Unskilled players, lacking a spontaneous, apposite, humorous retort, would have let the conversation end at this point. However, Linda shows adeptness in playing this game. She regroups momentarily ('Oh, so you going there, huh?') and fires back skillfully. She, in fact, 'caps' (wins) this exchange with a more clever retort. Betty's use of the intragroup expression, 'Ask yo momma', is humorous and sets up a challenge, but it is a simplistic, stylized form of signifyin. In this instance, it cannot and does not beat: 'Well I **did** ask my momma, and she said, caint you see that Betty looks like her momma spit her out.' First, the stressing of '**did**' indicates that Linda has gone a step ahead of Betty, which contributes to her capping the exchange. Essentially, Linda indicates here that 'I'm already ahead of you; you've got some catching up to do': 'Well I **did** ask my momma . . .'. Secondly, Linda wins due to the humorous insult that she instantaneously creates: '. . . she said, caint you see that Betty look like her momma spit her out.' Lastly, through skillfully contoured intonation, Linda engages in the Black English style of 'marking', that is, mimicking the speech of another person, in this case, an imitation of a momma's voice, with the words '. . . caint you see that Betty look like her momma spit her out.'

Speech act theory indicates that communication succeeds or fails as a result of the illocutionary, that is intended, and perlocutionary, that is received, effects of a message. The surface meaning of 'yo momma' for those outside the African American speech community is 'your mother/mom', which in this sense conveys possession or relatedness – not my mother, but your mother. Within the African American speech community, however, the utterance of the two words immediately communicates to listeners (and is intended by the speaker) that an insult is hurled. The intended and received meaning of 'yo momma' for this speech community is invective, and the game of ritual insult begins with participants creating the most apposite, humorous, spontaneous, creative, untrue, non-serious retorts that they can skillfully weave. The loser of the game-playing may appreciate the skill and ingenuity of the winner so much that she will engage in laughter along with other listeners, in this way yielding to the winner; or the loser may conceivably become infuriated (perhaps due to her inability to respond humorously and skillfully, or due to her interpretation of the remarks as true), in which case the game is over. The choice of the retort 'Ask yo momma' is understandable if interpreted directly. In US society, many growing, maturing humans tend to 'ask their mother' when decision-making arises. Some fathers may even respond to children's or teenagers' requests by saying, 'Ask your mother.' Thus, the derivation of the command is straightforward and the direct meaning is clear. In the appropriate context in the African American speech community, to tell a receiver to 'Ask yo momma' sends the message that a verbal fight is about to begin. 'Ask yo momma', just as 'yo momma', is intended and received as an insult. The speaker does not intend the direct meaning, 'You should go and ask your mother about this situation.' Rather, indirectly the speaker is saying, 'Let the game begin.'

Reading Dialect   Morgan (1991a; 1991b) has focused on signifyin through a feature she terms 'reading dialect', especially as used within African American women's speech community. Reading dialect occurs when speakers consciously select AAVE or European American English (EAE) to signify. Since AAVE and EAE have many words, grammatical rules, and discourse features that are similar, speakers select a contrasting feature in order to communicate an unambiguous point and, most importantly, to 'read' (that is, verbally denigrate) a conversational partner.

In the examples given below, speakers intentionally select AAVE forms to read a targeted receiver through the use of the AAVE dialectal feature. Among African American women, a common way of reading dialect is through use of the expression 'Miss Thang'. In order to communicate dissatisfaction, the first person refers to the targeted receiver as 'Miss Thang'.

Helen: Is the Mass Choir still going on our trip?
Barbara: Don't look like it. We was doing alright til Miss Thang decided she didn't want to go along wit the program.

The speakers have shared knowledge and prior experience regarding 'Miss Thang', a clear reference to the Director of the Mass Choir at the church. In this instance, the first person reads dialect via AAVE, communicating a negative point about the targeted receiver. The expression 'Miss Thang' within African American women's speech community is a direct put-down of a targeted receiver. Thus the expression accomplishes the goal of signifyin through reading dialect. The broader African American speech community, as well as the African American women's speech community, interprets 'thang' negatively since a thing is an object, lacking an identity and other human qualities. By not naming the person, but instead referring to her as 'Miss Thang', the signifier intensifies the objectification of 'Miss Thang'. AAVE dialect features are apparent in both words. 'Miss', within the African American speech community, has for years been the phonologically preferred address title, whether or not the targeted person is married. 'Thang' shows AAVE phonology, particularly with the vowel [ae] replacing the vowel [i] (similar to 'ring' and 'rang' usage, as in 'Rang the bell' not 'Ring the bell'). Further, 'Thang' ends in a weakened and devoiced nasal [n], as is characteristic of AAVE pronunciation.

Culturally Toned Diminutives Another major conversational feature resonant in African American women's speech community is what we refer to as 'culturally toned diminutives'. In other speech communities, words such as 'dinette', 'piglet', 'sonny', 'Gracie', and 'Tommy' show diminution. However, for generations, African American women have used the diminutive 'girl' (and others, such as 'honey'/'honey child', 'baby', 'precious', 'child') to refer to someone who is likeable, loveable, or familiarly known.

'Girl' is a highly visible, popular word used by African American females in all spheres of their existence, public and private, and in all age groups, to show solidarity. If they view themselves as peers, one African American female can and will call another African American female 'girl'. Thus, an African American five-year-old may say to her eight-year-old sister, 'Girl, you bed' stop dat' or 'Girl, you crazy.' These same sentences can be used by older African American females of any age. The females involved do not have to be blood relatives in order for this diminutive to be used appropriately. They may be cousins, neighbors, classmates, playmates, church members, club members, or colleagues.

African American women obviously do not see themselves diminished in any form through the use of this term, for it continues to be passed on to succeeding generations of women. In contemporary times, it has even expanded to 'girlfriend'. Both 'girl' and 'girlfriend' are words that establish solidarity and may be used to bridge social distance, even when the females engaged in a conversation are strangers. Both terms exist simultaneously and have a high frequency of use. However, many African American women over the age of 65 will use 'girl', not 'girlfriend', because they have a long history of using 'girl' and are not prone to switch to the new term. Reticence to use the new term is similar to the linguistic practice of older African Americans, males and females, who continue to use 'Negro' (or even 'colored') rather than 'black' or 'African American' as their preferred term of racial identification.

Smart Talk 'Smart talk' is an overall characteristic of African American women's speech behavior. Black women use language in an assertive, bold, outspoken manner. Since, historically, African American women have had to work two shifts, that is, both in and outside of the home, this discourse feature probably derives from their social role in two spheres, one domestic, the other public. In a conversation among three women friends, one woman remarked: 'I'm glad I don't have a man around 'cause I can do whatever the hell I want to do.'

Terry McMillan, in her novel *Waiting to Exhale* (1992), creates authentic black women characters through the use of smart talk. Her main character, Savannah, punctuates her sentences with this discourse feature from the novel's beginning: 'Sheila, my baby sister, insisted on giving me his [Lionel's] phone number because he lives here in Denver and her simple-ass husband played basketball with him eleven years ago at the University of Washington.' In the excerpt below (also from McMillan's novel), Savannah and three other women, who have become 'girlfriends', engage in smart talk. (Note: since this discourse example is excerpted from McMillan's novel and not conversation, notational devices are not included.) The four women meet at the home of Gloria in order to celebrate her birthday:

> 'Toast!' Bernadine said, after she'd poured all four glasses [of wine]. 'Wait,' Savannah said. 'Where's the hats and shit? . . . Okay, okay,' she said. 'I've got a good one. Gloria, I just want you to know that you're the best hairdresser in this town and I'm glad I met you and I hope turning thirty-eight is your best year yet!' 'That was tired,' Robin said, and stood up. 'I hope you find true love and get some that's so good it'll make up for all the years you didn't! Now.' 'Happy birthday, girlfriend,' Bernadine said. 'Here's to finding genuine happiness and peace of mind.' 'Thank you,' Gloria said, and they all drank up. 'I love this shit,' [Bernadine] said. 'Champagne makes me silly as hell.' 'You're already silly as hell,' Robin said. 'I'd rather be silly than dizzy,' she said. 'Go to hell,' Robin said. 'All right, let's not start this shit,' Savannah said. (1992: 322–3)

Many readers might assume that the speakers in the discourse example above are poorly educated, of low socioeconomic statuses, and uncouth or offensive. On the contrary, within the African American speech community, the speakers are accepted as real, natural, and non-offensive. Three of the speakers are professional women; the other is a college student. The women speak openly, directly, and assertively, without offending each other; that is, nobody gets mad! Speaking openly, directly, and boldly are features that characterize smart talk. After Savannah gives her birthday toast, which she claims is 'a good one', Robin, with immediacy, directness, and assertiveness, lets Savannah know that her toast ('Gloria, I just want you to know that you're the best hairdresser . . . I'm glad I met you and . . . hope turning thirty-eight is your best year yet!') 'ain't all that!' In order to show Savannah what a good toast is and in order to cap Savannah's toast, Robin has to 'go for the gold'. She creates, 'I hope you find true love and get some [that is, sex] that's so good it'll make up for all the years you didn't!', which tops Savannah's toast, as indicated by Robin's 'Now.' Robin 'caps' Savannah's toast since finding true love and 'getting some' relate to Gloria's personal experiences of emotional and sexual deprivation in a very relevant way. In this instance, Robin outsmarts Savannah and lets her know so directly and boldly. In the latter part of the excerpt, Robin again does not bite her tongue but quite boldly, directly, and very smartly responds to Bernadine's 'Champagne makes me silly as hell' with 'You're already silly as hell.' This response is a humorous retort, which may contain some degree of truth. Bernadine, though, is not the least affected by Robin's assertion, and, in the manner of a skillful signifier, she adeptly creates, 'I'd rather be silly than dizzy', implying that Robin is the latter (which in fact has a degree of truth to it). Importantly, Robin does not become angry although she has been signified on. Her retort, 'Go to hell', is not serious, but a limp defense in this game of verbal arts, used primarily when speakers lack a more spontaneous, creative retort.

Within the African American speech community, elders typically do not put up with smart talk from those who are younger. Among peers, however, smart talk is revered, applauded, and celebrated because of the mental skill and acuity required in outsmarting a conversational partner. This feature of African American women's discourse, as well as the others discussed here, suggests a different 'code of feminine politeness' (Giddings, 1984) than that for European American women. Instead of women who live in cages (Frye, 1983) or who know their 'places', African American women boldly assert their right to define their place in the world through the use of a unique black women's discourse style.

Of course, African American women's speech behavior is marked by other features not discussed here. Within speech act theory, for example, other linguistic forms can be identified. Data collection and research conducted on this particular speech community, as well as a cross-section of women's speech communities beyond white, middle-class European American women, are new and requisite, yet receive insufficient attention.

Intercultural Communication

The Emergence of the Field of Intercultural Communication

The study of intercultural communication is an interdisciplinary enterprise. Five major events have influenced the development of the field of intercultural communication in the US: (1) the establishment of the Foreign Service Institute; (2) the body of work by anthropologist Edward T. Hall; (3) the launching of intercultural organizations; (4) the proliferation of intercultural coursework in colleges and universities; and (5) the growth of a body of work in intercultural communication theory and research.

Establishment of the Foreign Service Institute (Mid 1940s to Late 1950s)
The field of intercultural communication emerged from the practical need of training people to function effectively in an overseas setting. After World War II, the US government began to assess problems that US diplomats encountered in their respective host cultures. This led to an awareness that many US diplomats were ill-equipped to deal with linguistic and communication problems *vis-à-vis* the local hosts. With a sense of urgency, in

1946 the US Congress passed the Foreign Service Act which reorganized the Foreign Service (FS), and established a Foreign Service Institute (FSI) to provide regular training for FS officers to function effectively in new cultures (Leeds-Hurwitz, 1990).

Work of Edward T. Hall (Late 1950s to Present)   Edward T. Hall worked for the Technical Cooperation Authority (TCA), in the Department of State, which consisted of a large number of anthropologists. He and his associates (such as Ray Birdwhistell and George Trager) also did work with the FSI (Leeds-Hurwitz, 1990). Hall argued that culture is communication, and communication is culture. He advocated the importance of studying the 'informal' aspects of a culture such as non-verbal spatial interaction (or proxemics), time (or chronemics), body movements (or kinesics), and tone of voice (or paralinguistics) that surround the use of language in everyday lives. The term 'intercultural communication' appears to have been first used by Hall in his book *The Silent Language* (Hall, 1959b; see also Hall, 1959a).

Launching of Intercultural Organizations (Early 1970s to 1980s)   The formation of the intercultural communication interest groups in 1970 in both the Speech Communication Association (SCA) and the International Communication Association (ICA) brought intercultural communication scholars together to exchange intercultural research-related ideas. Additionally, the development of intercultural communication workshops in major US universities (for example, Cornell University and University of Pittsburgh), sponsored by the National Association for Foreign Student Affairs (NAFSA) and the Institute for International Education, added a strong experiential component to the field of intercultural communication.

Proliferation of Intercultural Coursework (Early 1970s to 1980s)   Collaborative dialogues between the intercultural groups of SCA and NAFSA led to the development of intercultural communication courses and programs at the undergraduate and graduate levels in the US. From the mid 1970s to the mid 1980s, more than 50 basic intercultural textbooks were published. Most of the textbooks covered the following intercultural topics: value orientations, language and verbal behavior, non-verbal behavior, perception and stereotype, intergroup and interpersonal contact, and intercultural adjustment and effectiveness.

Growth of Intercultural Communication Theory and Research (Early 1980s to Present)   With the annual publication of the *International and Intercultural Communication Annual* (SCA/Sage), the field took a double-lane trajectory. One lane focused on intercultural theory and research. Another lane focused on intercultural training. Together with the annual publication, the journals

International Journal of Intercultural Relations and *Cross-Cultural Journal of Psychology* have provided publication outlets for intercultural communication research.

Theoretical Trends and Approaches

We can delineate three broad theoretical trends in the current literature that are relevant to our understanding of intercultural discourse. These three trends are: the cultural communication trend, the facework negotiation trend, and the intergroup communication trend. Each broad trend is identified based on the criteria of systematic theoretical development over the years and its implications for the study of intercultural discourse.

Cultural Communication Trend   The cultural communication trend is derived from Dell Hymes's 'ethnography of speaking' model (Hymes, 1962). We first discuss the basic components of the ethnography of speaking (ES) model and then review relevant concepts in the cultural communication (CC) approach.

The ES model traces its roots to anthropology and linguistics. While traditional anthropologists are interested in studying the cultural functions (for example, meanings) of language, traditional linguists are interested in examining the structural components (for example, grammar) of language. Both fields, however, share a common interest in the concept of 'communication'. Hymes (1962; 1974), in developing his ES approach, emphasizes the importance of looking at language whose rules and norms are an integral part of the larger culture. To Hymes (1974), culture is a system of knowledge that gives meaning to behavior in society. Within a culture, many distinctive speech communities exist with distinctive rules to uphold and guide the interpretation of different linguistic varieties. It is assumed that the 'spoken life of various people is so richly varied that knowledge of how spoken life is conceptualized, enacted, and interpreted in a given community' (Philipsen, 1989: 80) constitutes a fascinating area of study.

Integrating methods from both the anthropological and the linguistic disciplines, Hymes (1962) develops the SPEAKING classificatory grid. Each letter in SPEAKING is an abbreviation for a different possible component of communication. This grid is presented as follows:

S   setting or scene
P   participants
E   ends/goals/outcomes
A   act sequence
K   key/tonal coloring and manner of speech
I   instrumentalities/channels
N   norms of interaction
G   genre/larger textual categories

Hymes advocates the importance of using participant observation method in understanding the different 'ways of speaking' in a culture. He also directs our attention to the study of both the emic nature (that is, cultural-specific) and the etic nature (that is, cross-cultural generalizations) of discourse phenomena. Excellent examples that have followed closely the ethnography of communication traditions include Basso (1990) and Katriel (1986).

The cultural communication (CC) model is a natural development from the ethnography of speaking perspective with a stronger emphasis on the term 'communication' from an individual-community dialectical perspective. According to Philipsen (1987), the term 'cultural communication' can be used as an umbrella term to understand the role of discourse forms (such as talk and silence, native terms, speech events, stories, and speech rituals) in relationship to the larger cultural conceptions of personal/social identity and community membership.

The CC model (Carbaugh, 1990; Philipsen, 1987; 1989) seeks answers to the following questions. How does communication reflect and create group membership identity? How is group membership being reinforced via interpersonal discourse? How does communication deal with issues of personal and communal identity in particular situations?

For example, Katriel (1986) has systematically described and interpreted the concept of Hebrew *dugri speech* (or 'direct talk') and illustrated the concept with 'thick-descriptive', cultural examples. She explores the cultural meanings of dugri speech along dimensions such as sincerity, assertiveness, and solidarity. The use of dugri markers is a way of speaking within the subculture of the Sabras (native-born Israelis of Jewish heritage, mainly of European descent). 'To speak dugri,' as one of Katriel's informants put it, 'is to act like a Sabra.' The Sabra represents the construction, in Israel, of a new Jew who had 'come to the Land of Israel to build and be both personally and communally rebuilt in it' (1986: 17).

Dugri speech, which consists of one person speaking to another in such a way as to suspend the usual requirements of politeness and decorum, reflects the larger Sabra cultural agenda. Katriel ends her dugri speech study with the following recommendations in discovering a cultural way of speaking: (1) a way of speaking can be identified in terms of its characteristic mode such as direct–indirect, formal–informal, serious–playful, etc.; (2) native discourse terms should be routinely consulted in describing particular ways of speaking; (3) a natively 'named' way of speaking should be analysed in conjunction with the meanings and the discourse contexts; and (4) cultural ways of speaking can be uncovered in interpersonal rituals, myths, and social dramas of a culture's life.

The ES approach and the CC approach offer us a conceptual framework to look at the interdependent relationship between communication and culture. Furthermore, they emphasize the importance of understanding everyday discourse within a social context. Both approaches advocate the importance of using an emic perspective (that is, cultural insider's viewpoint) in examining cultural discourse. The combined CC framework emphasizes the importance of analysing different discourse forms (such as, storytelling, metaphor analysis) in a wide range of speech communities (for example, in different gender, ethnic, social class communities) within a culture. From the discussion of a cultural indigenous approach in examining cultural discourse, we now turn to a discussion of the facework negotiation trend in understanding cross-cultural comparative discourse.

Facework Negotiation Trend As social beings, most of us have the experiences of blushing, feeling embarrassed, feeling awkward, feeling shame, feeling insulted, or feeling pride. Many of these feelings are face-related issues. When our social poise is attacked or teased, we feel the need to restore or save face. When we are being complimented or given credits for a job well done in front of others, we feel our self-respect is enhanced and caressed. Losing face and saving face are some of the key concepts under this 'face negotiation' umbrella. Additionally, we can use discourse strategies such as 'preventive facework' and 'corrective facework' strategies (Cupach and Metts, 1994) in dealing with face-threatening or face-losing situations. Preventive facework refers to the use of discourse tactics such as topic switch, hedging ('I may be wrong, but . . .'), and disclaimer ('I know this sounds crazy, but . . .') when the speaker realizes that the discourse appears to be moving in a face-threatening direction. Corrective facework, on the other hand, refers to discourse repair tactics such as quick verbal glossing ('I don't mean to call them Japs . . .'), verbal humor, apologies, and use of accounts (such as excuses and justifications) to repair face damage that has occurred because of a social transgression. We focus our discussion on the face negotiation theory (Ting-Toomey, 1988; 1994b). The theory emphasizes the influence of culture on the meanings of face and facework.

Relating individualism and collectivism to the study of facework, Ting-Toomey (1988) proposes a theoretical model of facework under the label of face negotiation (FN) theory. According to Ting-Toomey (1988; 1994b), face is conceptualized as an individual's need for a claimed sense of positive image in a social context. More specifically, face is: (1) a claimed sense of favorable social self-worth (for example, perceived credibility or competence issues) that a person wants others to have of her or him; (2) a vulnerable discourse resource in social interaction because this resource can be threatened, enhanced, maintained, and bargained over; and (3) a resource that is situated in the webs of interpersonal 'and sociocultural variability. Facework refers to the discourse strategies to protect/defend one's face and to enhance/support the other's face. Both face and facework can only be meaningfully interpreted within the values and situational norms of the culture (Brown and Levinson, 1987).

In a nutshell, Ting-Toomey's (1988) face negotiation theory posits that: (a) people in all cultures try to maintain and negotiate face in all communication situations; (b) the concept of 'face' is especially problematic in uncertainty situations (such as request, embarrassment, insult, or conflict situations) when the situated identities of the communicators are called into question; (c) the cultural variability dimension of individualism-collectivism influences members' selection of one set of facework strategies over others (such as autonomy face vs approval face); and (d) cultural values in conjunction with other individual, relational, and situational variables influence the use of various facework strategies in intergroup and interpersonal encounters. Individualism refers to 'I-oriented' values and the emphasis on individual goals over group goals. Collectivism, on the other hand, refers to 'we-oriented' values and the emphasis on ingroup goals over individual goals. While many Northern European cultures have been identified as 'individualistic-oriented cultures,' many Asian, African, Middle Eastern, and Latin American cultures have been identified as 'collectivistic-oriented' cultures (Hofstede, 1980; 1991; Triandis, 1995).

Overall, research by Ting-Toomey and associates (Ting-Toomey et al., 1991; Trubisky et al., 1991) indicates that while European Americans tend to use more self-oriented face-saving strategies, Taiwanese tend to use more other-oriented face-saving strategies. In addition, European Americans tend to use more direct, face-threatening conflict discourse, and Asian collectivists (that is, Taiwan and China respondents) tend to use more indirect, mutual face-saving conflict discourse. The concepts of 'social face' (concern for approval from others) and 'perceived self-pride' (concern for self-oriented pride) have been found to influence facework strategy selection in Japan and the US (Cocroft and Ting-Toomey, 1994). Japanese tend to emphasize the social facework dimension, and European Americans tend to emphasize the self-pride facework dimension. Males (from both Japan and the US) also report the use of more antisocial and competitive facework strategies than females.

From a conversational constraints perspective, the line of research by Kim et al. (1994) on construal of self and conversational constraints also provides additional evidence for FN theory. For example, Kim et al. (1994) uncover that individuals with independent self have higher perceived importance of conversational clarity than individuals with interdependent self. Additionally, interdependent self persons have higher perceived importance of not hurting the hearer's feelings and avoiding devaluation by the hearer in conversation than independent self persons. While the independent self concepts reflect individualistic value tendencies, the interdependent self concepts reflect group-oriented value tendencies.

We believe that the face negotiation theoretical trend can help to explain a wide range of discourse phenomena. The facework framework can help to explain polite to impolite discourse phenomena, conflict and prejudiced discourse phenomena, etc. Individuals in any cultures who have to deal with self-respect and other-consideration, dignity and humility, approval and disapproval, competence and incompetence issues have the notion of 'face'. However, how they strategically and stylistically manage facework issues would differ from one speech community to the next. From cross-cultural comparative theory of facework, we move to a discussion of intercultural or intergroup communication theories.

Intergroup Communication Trend Two theories can be identified under this broad intergroup communication trend: the anxiety/uncertainty management (AUM) theory (Gudykunst, 1988; 1995) and the communication accommodation theory (CAT) (Gallois et al., 1988; 1995).

Anxiety/uncertainty management (AUM) theory (Gudykunst, 1988; 1995) suggests that effective intergroup or interpersonal communication is a function of the amount of anxiety and uncertainty individuals experience when communicating with others. Anxiety refers to the feelings of discomfort or awkwardness when two strangers (from different cultural groups or ethnic groups) try to relate to each other. Uncertainty refers to the perceived unpredictability of the various intergroup situations. The concept of 'management' refers to the importance of cultivating awareness or 'mindfulness' (Langer, 1989) in dealing with unfamiliar values and discourse scripts. Being a 'mindful' communicator means one has to learn to monitor one's verbal/non-verbal interaction in dealing with unfamiliar situations and one has to learn to use different communication strategies to gather information about the cultural stranger.

Gudykunst and associates (for a detailed review, see Gudykunst, 1995) have been testing and refining AUM theory for the last ten years. Selected AUM axioms have been tested in intergroup settings. For example, Gudykunst and Shapiro (1996) show that greater anxiety is experienced in intergroup (that is, interethnic and intercultural) encounters than in intragroup encounters. Anxiety is associated positively with the degree to which social identities (that is, group membership identities) are activated in the interaction, and the amount of uncertainty experienced. In addition, they also find that there is greater uncertainty in intergroup encounters than in intragroup encounters. Uncertainty is associated negatively with positive expectations, communication satisfaction, and quality of communication. Finally, the ways that individuals gather information to reduce uncertainty differ in individualistic and collectivistic cultures. Members of individualistic cultures (such as European Americans) seek out person-based information to reduce uncertainty about strangers, and members of collectivistic cultures (such as Asians and Latinos) seek out group-based information to reduce uncertainty (Gudykunst and Nishida, 1986). In sum, Gudykunst (1995) claims that anxiety and uncertainty exist in all cultures. However, how people define these two terms varies across cultures. Cultural variability dimensions such as individualism–collectivism and power distance (Hofstede, 1991) have been integrated into the AUM theory to explain social and personal encounters across cultures.

Communication accommodation theory (CAT) (Gallois et al., 1988; 1995) emphasizes the importance of understanding speech convergence and speech divergence to increase or decrease communicative distance between members of different groups. For example, francophones and anglophones working in bilingual work settings in Montreal and Quebec often complained about each other's French/English language use. Korean shopkeepers and African American customers in central Los Angeles often reported frustrations about each other's use of 'English'. CAT focuses on explaining the motivations, the strategies, and contexts which group members employ to converge with their partners or diverge from their partners linguistically.

CAT is based on an earlier body of work by Giles and associates (see Giles and Coupland, 1991; Giles and Johnson, 1987) on ethnolinguistic identity theory and ethnolinguistic vitality theory, and the related work by Tajfel and Turner (1986) and Abrams and Hogg (1990) on social identity theory. According to Giles and associates, speakers move through their linguistic repertoire so as to linguistically converge or diverge based on the following three motivations: to gain approval from their discourse partners vis-à-vis linguistic similarity, to show distinctiveness and thus accentuate their own group membership, and to achieve clearer and smoother communication. Gallois et al. (1988) extend this model and add the components of: initial orientation (that is, whether speakers are predisposed to view the encounter as solely intergroup, interpersonal, or both), intergroup discourse situation, and the positive/negative evaluation that communicators take away with them concerning the discourse encounter.

The most recent version of CAT (Gallois et al., 1995) incorporates the cultural variability dimension of individualism and collectivism in its theoretical propositions. Factors such as sociohistorical context, the immediate context (goal orientation, tactical, and labeling/attribution factors), and evaluation and future intentions are incorporated in the theory. Gallois et al. (1992) tested some of the propositions in a videotaped scripted project (portrayed by actors) containing interactions between Chinese or Australian students and faculty members. The actors on the tapes engaged in accommodating or non-accommodating scripted behavior, using discourse management and interpersonal control strategies to treat the other person as an equal individual or as a subordinate. Judges were asked to evaluate the non-verbal behavior and the appropriateness of the behavior in general. Results indicated that non-accommodating students and faculty members were rated less favorably than accommodating ones. In addition, the perception of non-verbal behavior (both vocal and non-vocal) outweighs other factors in inducing a favorable or unfavorable reaction. In another study, Jones et al. (1994) tested the CAT model with videotaped naturalistic conversations between Australian and Chinese students and academic staff. The researchers found that the multiple roles (student vs faculty member, gender, and ethnicity) of the speakers and the judges all exert influences on perceived accommodation.

Both AUM and CA theories deal with the linkage among social cognition, interaction, and culture. While AUM theory focuses on how people can manage their anxiety and reduce their uncertainty via different communication strategies in the initial intergroup encounter process, CA theory focuses on speech convergence/divergence issues and the evaluative reactions by observers. Issues such as ethnocentrism and prejudice need to be incorporated more tightly in both theories because ethnocentrism is one way to deal with intergroup anxiety, uncertainty, and divergence. Prejudice is another form of biased cognitive beliefs that are presented and strategically managed in concrete discourse situations.

Intergroup Discourse: Conclusions

To be a competent communicator in intergroup discourse, we have to work on widening the knowledge net of ethnocultural values and norms. We have to understand how our own cultural values and norms condition our everyday behavior and interactional style. Additionally, we have to understand how our everyday talk or discourse shape and form our everyday intergroup experience. To be an effective intercultural communicator, we have to apply our knowledge strategically in constructive discourse practice. Without culturally grounded knowledge, group members cannot learn to uncover the ethnocentric lenses they use to interpret and evaluate intergroup discourse process. Some intergroup discourse situations can trigger intense misunderstandings because of verbal/non-verbal stylistic differences. Other intergroup discourse situations (such as prejudiced discourse) can accomplish clear understanding but retain intense intergroup friction and hostility. To manage intergroup discourse effectively, we must understand the underlying theories, assumptions, and vocabularies of diverse ethnic/cultural members in a diverse range of societies from multiple disciplinary perspectives.

Discourse and Racism

Text and Talk about 'Them'

Like all group relations in society, ethnic group relations are also partly managed by text and talk. We have seen above how group members culturally produce and reproduce their own identity – and hence their group – by using the group's own language variety and special discourse forms, and how intergroup relations are enacted by talking to people of other ethnic groups. These group relations are also established and maintained by writing or talking *about* such relations, and *about* the others.

It is in this way that ingroups express and acquire knowledge and attitudes about the outgroups, about ethnic relations, and about ethnic affairs in general. Prevalent prejudices of dominant groups may be expressed in parent talk during socialization, children's books, textbooks, news and advertising in the press and on TV, parliamentary debates, political propaganda and scholarly discourse, among many other discourse types. Such beliefs are crucial in the management of ethnic perception and interaction, and the enactment of dominance in multicultural societies.

In our analysis of such dominant discourse in Europe and the United States, it will appear that such expressions are not limited to the meaning or 'content' of talk and text. All levels and structures of discourse may be involved, and have several mental, interactional and social functions in the strategic accomplishment of 'doing' everyday racism. One main strategy, as we shall see, is to enact ethnic conflict, polarization and dominance by presenting the others in negative terms and us in positive terms (while at the same time denying or downplaying our negative characteristics, especially racism).

The analysis takes place within the broader framework of a theory of racism, defined as a complex system of ethnic or 'racial' domination, in this case, historically, of white Europeans over peoples from Asian, African or South American and Native American descent. Such racism may be blatant or more subtle, symbolic and mundane. It involves a social system of discriminatory practices, as well as a system of prejudiced ethnic attitudes and ideologies supporting and monitoring such discrimination. It may include discrimination and prejudice against 'racial' minorities, as well as other forms of ethnocentrism and xenophobia, such as antisemitism. The crucial consequence of racist domination is socially inequality, namely unequal access to material or symbolic social resources, such as (good) income, jobs, housing, health, education, status, respect, citizenship as well as public discourse, the media, politics, etc. (for details on racism, see, for example, Braham et al., 1992; Dovidio and Gaertner, 1986; Essed, 1991; Miles, 1989).

Discourse plays a crucial role in the enactment as well as in the reproduction of this system. Thus, racist talk and text themselves are discriminatory practices, which at the same time influence the acquisition and confirmation of racist prejudices and ideologies. This is especially the case for white elite groups and institutions, such as politics, the media, scholarship and corporate business, whose prestige, power and influence have played a prominent role in the 'pre-formulation' of racism at large (van Dijk, 1993a). Analysis of such discourse reveals the everyday communication practices of dominant groups in multicultural societies, while at the same time showing how ethnic beliefs are strategically expressed, acquired and distributed throughout the dominant group, that is as part of managing ethnic affairs and reproducing elite power and white group dominance.

Similarly, discourse plays a role in various forms of resistance and counter-power, in protest songs, banners, ethnic media, dissident scholarly work, and so on. However, since minority groups and (other) anti-racists seldom have as much access to the dominant media or other forms of public discourse as the mainstream elites, their discourse is usually effectively marginalized, problematized or ridiculed. Indeed, as is the case in much of the media, and not only in the conservative press, anti-racist discourse may be discredited (for example, as 'radical', 'crazy') more emphatically than the more 'appropriate' forms of racist text and talk.

Earlier Research

Within discourse analysis, as well as within the study of racism in the social sciences, the relations between discourse and racism have received relatively little attention. Most research has been done on the 'portrayal' of minorities in textbooks and in the mass media, for instance in movies, TV programs and news in the press. However, this work is largely 'content analytical' and focuses on a quantitative account of occurrences and topics, for example which ethnic groups appear in the TV programs or news, how often, and in relation to what topics or issues. The result of most of these studies was that minorities tend to be portrayed in terms of problems or in highly stereotypical roles and settings (Hartmann and Husband, 1974; Preiswerk, 1980; Wilson and Gutiérrez, 1985).

More qualitative, discourse analytical studies of more detailed properties of text and talk about ethnic events and ethnic relations were rare until the 1980s. Most of them have been carried out in the broader perspective of the directions of research known as critical linguistics and critical discourse analysis.

Thus, in a seminal study about the role of power and control in language, Fowler et al. (1979) also examined the ways the press accounts for an 'ethnic' event such as the disturbances occurring during the yearly Notting Hill festival in London. It was found, among other things, that the syntactic structures of sentences may reflect the dominant (white) group perspective of journalists in the description of such events. If white group members such as police officers are responsible for negative actions, their active agency and hence their responsibility may be mitigated by expressing such agency less prominently in sentences or news headlines, for instance by a passive form such as the (also ambiguous) 'blacks killed' instead of 'police killed blacks'. On the other hand, if minority actors are seen to engage in negative actions, their agency and responsibility will be emphasized syntactically, for example by expressing it in the prominent, first ('topical'), subject position of the sentence. And conversely: 'our' *positive* actions and actors will be syntactically prominent, whereas 'theirs' will be structurally played down.

Several studies have later come to similar conclusions about the role of grammatical form in the textual presentation of us and them (see, for example, Sykes, 1985). Indeed, we shall see that at all levels of discourse, this overall principle will remain the same, namely a strategy that combines positive self-presentation with negative other-presentation. Obviously, it is this strategy that plays a primary role in the sociocognitive function of discourse about others, namely the formation of negative cognitions (specific mental models of concrete events, as well as more general group prejudices and ideologies) about outgroups. Here we see again, as we have assumed before, that the structures of discourse may be tuned to their cognitive and social functions.

With the increasing prominence of the social and political issue of immigration and ethnic relations in Europe and North America, discourse analysis in the 1980s finally started to pay attention to this issue. Thus, in a series of studies, briefly summarized and illustrated below, van Dijk examined the ways majority group members in the Netherlands and the USA talk and write about minorities and ethnic relations in everyday conversations, textbooks, the press, parliaments, business corporations and scholarship (van Dijk, 1984; 1987; 1991; 1993a). This work was not intended as another 'application' of discourse analysis, but as a multi-disciplinary approach to the study of the reproduction of racism in society, involving the complex relations between discourse structures, cognitive representations and societal structures. The discourse analysis involved in this research mainly focused on preferred types of topic (such as those of difference, deviation and threat), story development, news structures, argumentative and local semantic moves (as in the well-known denial 'I have nothing against blacks, *but* . . .'), as well as stylistic and rhetorical properties of such discourse. Below we shall give some examples of such forms of ingroup text and talk about outgroups (for analysis of media discourse and ethnic relations, see also Smitherman-Donaldson and van Dijk, 1987; McGarry, 1994).

Jäger and his associates in Duisburg (Germany) followed and extended this paradigm by examining in detail the ways Germans spoke and wrote about minorities and refugees around 1990, and they arrived at essentially similar conclusions. This suggests that some of the modes of text and talk about others are fairly general, and characteristic of several European and North American countries (Jäger, 1988; 1992; Jäger and Link, 1993).

Similarly, as part of a vast program of critical discourse studies, Wodak and her associates in Vienna engaged in a series of inquiries into anti-semitic discourse in Austria on the occasion of the Waldheim affair, that is the election of a president suspected of Nazi war crimes during the Second World War. In addition to a detailed discourse analytical study of news in the press, TV talk shows, and everyday 'street talk', Wodak et al. also examined the cognitive, social, political and historical dimensions of anti-semitic discourse. Again, many of the results are in agreement with findings by Jäger and van Dijk for Germany, the Netherlands, Britain, France and the USA (Wodak, 1991; Wodak et al., 1990; for details, see also Fairclough and Wodak, Chapter 10 in this volume).

And finally, within the framework of a broad research program on the pragmatics of nationalist discourse, Blommaert and Verschueren (1992) examined how white people in Belgium talk about minorities and immigrants.

Discourse Structures

When analysing 'our' text and talk about 'them', we may in principle focus on *any* property of discourse and its contextual conditions and consequences. Yet, some discursive structures and strategies are more typical or influential than others in the reproduction of racism. The crucial criterion is that discourse structures play a role in the expression and persuasive communication of polarized underlying attitudes and ideologies that represent 'us' as good and 'them' as bad. Such meanings may be emphasized by a specific intonation in talk as well as by a banner headline in the press or a picture in a textbook. Among all these discourse structures, we shall focus on a few significant ones.

Topics Perhaps the most obvious common-sense property of discourse is its overall meaning or topics: if dominant group members or institutions speak or write about 'them', *what* do they speak or write about? An analysis of such discourse topics is important, since they also largely determine how people understand and recall such text and talk. Thus, prevailing topics in the media will influence the agenda, that is, what the public thinks and talks about.

Analysis of such topics in conversation, the media, textbooks, and political discourse reveals that they largely express and reproduce dominant stereotypes (van Dijk, 1984; 1987; 1991; 1993a). Unlike discourse about 'us', we do not find the usual variation of topics, but a short list of preferred 'ethnic topics', such as immigration, crime, cultural differences and deviance, discrimination and socioeconomic problems. Further analysis of topical propositions reveals that they often have negative implications. Thus, immigration is never topicalized as neutral, or as a contribution to the economy, but at least as a major problem, if not as fraud, an invasion or a threat to 'us'. Crime invariably appears in the top five (often first) of the 'ethnic' topics, and usually involves what is seen as typical 'ethnic crime', such as mugging, drugs or violence (riots). On the other hand, 'our' crime against 'them' (such as discrimination) tends to be mitigated or mainly associated with deviant individuals, the radical right wing or skinheads: racism is *never* dealt with as a problem of 'us' (our newspaper, company, politicians). If apparently more positively represented, as in the coverage of sports and entertainment, minorities (especially blacks) are still categorized in stereotypical terms (Johnson, 1987). Cultural differences, such as Islam, tend to be overemphasized and also portrayed as deviance from the dominant Western norms and values.

In the media, topics are typically expressed in headlines and leads (van Dijk, 1988a; 1988b). A systematic analysis of such headlines for news reports on ethnic affairs in the Dutch and British press in 1985 and 1989 confirms the general tendencies summarized above. Thus, we find the following kinds of headline, all taken from the British press in 1985 (van Dijk, 1991):

(1) POLICE BLAME RIOT ON DRUG DEALERS (*The Guardian*, 16 September 1985)

(2) RIOTING MOB SHOOT POLICE. Officer dies after being slashed in neck (*Daily Mail*, 7 October 1985)
(3) SECOND BLACK ON MURDER CHARGE (*The Daily Telegraph*, 14 December 1985)
(4) BLACK BRIXTON LOOTERS JAILED (*The Daily Telegraph*, 14 December 1985)
(5) RACIST? NO, I'M BEING VICTIMISED FOR SPEAKING OUT (*Daily Mail*, 14 October 1985)
(6) BRITAIN INVADED BY AN ARMY OF ILLEGALS (*The Sun*, 2 February 1986)

Thus, ethnic events are defined as aggression, invasion, riots, caused by drug dealers, killings, looting, and so on, whereas racism is being denied and converted towards the 'victimization' of those who 'speak out' (that is, 'tell the truth' about minorities). Whereas these few examples might have been selected for their negative topics, systematic research of more than 4000 headlines in the British and Dutch press has shown that ethnic events and minorities are seldom defined in a way that is positive for them or negative for us, and conversely, in a way that tends to attribute blame to us while denying or mitigating theirs. It is thus how the press, through its topical headlines, defines the 'ethnic situation', in which 'they' are a problem, if not a threat.

Local Semantics Although a topical analysis of discourse is crucial to establish what dominant groups think, speak and write about, it hardly goes beyond superficial content analysis. A more detailed semantic analysis is necessary for the local meanings of discourse; it focuses on coherence, implications, presuppositions, descriptions and other properties of propositions and their relationships in discourse (see Chapters 1 and 3 in Volume 1).

As may be expected, the local meanings of discourse about ethnic minorities first of all detail the overall topics, and do so just as negatively, for instance as follows in some British newspapers:

(7) [Four Asians acquitted] They were among a mob of 50 Asians who smashed up an East London pub after a series of hammer attacks on other Asians. (*The Sun*, 14 August 1985)
(8) [A discrimination case] A club manager banned a coloured singer after he had been mugged three times by blacks, an industrial tribunal heard yesterday. (*Daily Mail*, 16 August 1985)

Note in these examples how syntax, meaning and the choice of words in the conservative press emphasize the aggression or crimes of minorities, while mitigating or excusing the racist actions of majority group members and institutions.

Though generally in somewhat more subdued style, parliamentarians may also thus engage in negative talk about immigrants and minorities (see also Reeves, 1983). This is shown in the following fragment of a debate on immigration in the British House of Commons, where immigration is described in terms of a threat to 'our' country:

(9)   . . . one in three children born in London today is of ethnic origin . . .
      That is a frightening concept for the country to come to terms with. We
      have already seen the problems of massive Moslem immigration . . . .
      (UK, Mr Janman, 20 June 1990, *Hansard*, columns 293–4)

Rather typical of racist talk are a number of moves that combine the overall strategies of positive self-presentation and negative other-presentation. Well known is the move of *apparent denial*, in which a positive first clause denies prejudice or racism, and is followed by a contrasted *but* clause invariably saying or implying something negative about minorities, as in the classical phrase 'We having nothing against blacks, but . . .'. This move is called one of apparent denial because the denial is immediately flouted by the following clauses, or in fact the rest of the discourse, as is the case in the following example taken from an interview (see van Dijk, 1987):

(10) [these] people have their own way of life, and I have *absolutely*
      nothing against that, *but*, it *is* a fact that if their way of life begins to
      differ from mine to an extent that . . . . (interview with a Dutch
      woman)

Similarly, we may find an *apparent concession*, when it is conceded that we have done something wrong (or they have done something well), but it is then added that our negative action is excused or mitigated, or that their positive action is not that positive after all. In the following example, taken from a speech in the French parliament by conservative cabinet member Pascua (again responsible for strict immigration rules in the conservative government in 1993), we find a combination of denial ('The French are not racist') and various forms of mitigation or euphemism:

(11) The French are not racist. But, facing this continuous increase of the
      foreign population in France, one has witnessed the development, in
      certain cities and neighborhoods, of reactions that come close to
      xenophobia. (France, Mr Pascua, 9 July 1986, *Journal Officiel*, p. 3053)

Note how racism first of all gets mitigated to 'reactions that come close to xenophobia'. Secondly, there seems to be a good reason for such 'reactions', namely the 'continuous increase of the foreign population', which suggests that in fact the immigrants are themselves the cause of this form of popular resentment. The mitigation is combined with a form of restriction: 'in certain cities and neighborhoods', which at the same time is a typical move of *transfer*: there may be racism, but *they* (in the poor inner cities) are responsible for that. This is close to the typical transfer move, 'I have nothing against blacks, but my customers . . .'.

In sum, a local semantic analysis may reveal underlying opinions and attitudes about minorities, or contextual goals of face-keeping, by paying attention to topic specifications, implications, mitigation, and strategic moves such as apparent denials, apparent concessions or transfer. Whether more blatantly in less well self-monitored speech, or more subtly in official discourse, the semantic implications are usually the same: we are (doing) good, and they are (doing) bad.

Style Style, defined as the variable expression of meanings as a function of context, obviously is a major site for the formulation of ethnic opinions, for example through the selection of special words. Consider how a conservative Member of Congress, Mr Dannemeyer, talks about the Civil Rights Bill of 1990:

(12) This nonsense about quotas has to stop because when we begin to hire and promote people on the basis of their race, we are going to bring to our society feelings of distress, feelings of unhappiness, and these emotions will accumulate and ultimately explode and destroy us. (*Congressional Record*, 2 August 1990, p. H6332)

Here strong opposition against the bill (accused of being a 'quota bill') is combined with the usual semantic strategies of mitigation and euphemism ('feelings of unhappiness' instead of, for example, 'racial resentment'). At the same time, this fragment exemplifies an argumentative move of face-keeping, namely that the speaker implies he is against discrimination, but in fact argues against a bill that intends to make discrimination by employers harder.

The British conservative press, in particular, does not mince words, for example about 'the loony left' as well as about (other) anti-racists, who may be called 'snoopers', 'fanatics', 'the multi-nonsense brigade' or 'left-wing crazies' (for details, see van Dijk, 1991). Such and other lexical expressions typically categorize anti-racists among the mentally ill, as intolerant oppressors, if not as threatening animals ('bloodhounds').

Similarly, by the use of *pronouns*, speakers may signal their group membership and identification, and stress their social distance, disapproval or resentment against minorities. The fundamental opposition between *us* and *them* is a well-known stereotypical example of such a pronominally coded form of contrast, opposition and social conflict, as well as of a form of ethnocentrism. This is also clear in such distancing demonstratives as 'those people'. What is remarkable in some uses of pronouns is that 'they' is sometimes used in situations where a description or a name would have been more appropriate. Apparently, to avoid naming people is one of the moves in a strategy of ethnic distancing.

Finally, stylistic variation in the expression of meaning may also show in syntactic structures, such as word order, active or passive sentences, or other structural means to make the agency or responsibility of specific actors more or less prominent, as we have seen in the example of the police killing blacks above. Here is a typical example taken from *The Times*:

(13) On Saturday, police were petrol-bombed, shops looted and cars
      burned after the shooting of a West-Indian woman. (*The Times*,
      30 September 1985)

In this example it is not explicitly said that the West Indian woman was
shot by the police, although this may become clear elsewhere in the article.
On the other hand, neither is it said explicitly who petrol-bombed, looted
and burned, but in *that* case again, 'everybody knows' that black youths
are meant (as is also clear from the photographs). Such surface forms
apparently code for the ways ethnic events are represented in the mental
models of the speakers or writers, and their analysis may be a powerful
instrument in the reconstruction of such models, especially since such
syntactic structures are much less well monitored than the choice of specific
words.

Argumentation Organizing larger stretches of text or talk, argumentative
structures are frequently used to support an ethnic opinion, both in everyday conversations and in parliamentary debates or newspaper editorials.
Generally, the moves in such debates leave no doubt about 'our' tolerance,
hospitality, goodwill and help on the one hand, and the many negative
characteristics attributed to minorities or immigrants on the other. As a
general argumentative introduction, most debates in Western parliaments
about immigration, minorities or civil rights begin with *national self-
glorification*, so as to make sure that the negative measures proposed are
not seen as ethnocentric or racist. Here are the ways four debates on
immigration and civil rights are initiated in the UK, the USA, France and
Germany, showing that nationalist rhetoric is a rather general feature of
parliamentary discourse, especially when ethnic relations and immigration
are discussed:

(14) I believe that we are a wonderfully fair country. We stick to the rules
      unlike some foreign Governments. (UK, Sir John Stokes, 15 May
      1990, *Hansard*, columns 842–4)
(15) Our country has for a long time been open to foreigners, a tradition of
      hospitality going back, beyond the Revolution, to the *Ancien Régime*.
      (France, Mr Mazeaud, 9 July 1990, *Journal Officiel*, p. 3049)
(16) I know no other country on this earth that gives more prominence to
      the rights of resident foreigners as does this bill in our country.
      (Germany, Mr Hirsch, Bundestag, 9 February 1990, *Stenographischer
      Bericht*, p. 16,279)
(17) This is a nation whose values and traditions now excite the world, as
      we all know. I think we all have a deep pride in American views,
      American ideals, American government, American principles, which
      excite hundreds of millions of people around the world who struggle
      for freedom. (US, Mr Foley, 2 August 1990, *Congressional Record*, p.
      H6768)

Another argumentative move to make negative actions or decisions seemingly less harsh is to emphasize that they are in fact beneficial to the victims, an argumentative move we may call one of *apparent empathy*:

(18)   Any honest liberal would have to admit that affirmative action has been a dismal failure . . . Instead of advancing the cause of blacks, affirmative action has hurt the cause of blacks. Why? Because racial preference implies inferiority. And this implied inferiority actually aggravates the white racism affirmative action was designed to eradicate. That is why there has been an increase in racial incidents, for instance on college campuses, around the country. (USA, Mr Dornan, House of Representatives, 2 August 1990, *Congressional Record*, p. H6334)

(19)   . . . An uncontrolled increase of foreigners from non-European cultural backgrounds would further exacerbate the integration of non-European citizens, which is already difficult enough. (Germany, Mr Schäuble, Bundestag, 9 February 1990, *Stenographischer Bericht*, p. 15,035)

Apart from presenting immigration restrictions or limitations of human and legal rights as beneficial to the victims, these passages at the same time blame the victims for these negative decisions as well as the general racist reactions in the country. Thus racial incidents on campus are attributed not to racist students or staff, but to the attempt to combat racism by affirmative action. Similarly immigration and hence immigrants in Germany, rather than racist resentment from Germans, are taken as the main cause of integration difficulties. The argumentative move involved in this case is thus at the same time one of *reversal*, often found in text and talk about minorities and ethnic relations: not they, but we, are the victims; not they, but we, are discriminated against. In the same vein, we find frequent arguments referring to 'black racism', as if blacks would be the dominant group in the country and as if whites are systematically discriminated against (by blacks in dominant positions) throughout society.

Storytelling   In a similar way, many other structures of text and talk may be systematically examined for the ways they express, imply and persuasively communicate subtle or blatant stereotypes and prejudices. As may be predicted from our discussion of topics, everyday storytelling by whites in North America and Europe about minorities exhibits the dominant topics, also prevalent in the media, of problems, cultural deviance, neighborhood decay and crime. Moreover, in an analysis of 144 stories collected in Amsterdam it was shown that the narrative structure of these stories expressed and persuasively conveyed a negative view of ethnic relations: whereas stories generally have a resolution category following the complication category (Labov, 1972), about 50 per cent of these typically complaint stories did not have a resolution, thus signalling that ethnic problems are a predicament that cannot be resolved (van Dijk, 1984; 1993b).

Conversational Structures   Conversational analysis allows an even more subtle study of strategies of talk about the others. We have seen that topics and stories in everyday conversations tend to express and confirm stereotypes and prejudices. But also typical properties of spontaneous talk, such as hesitations, false starts, errors and repairs, indicate underlying uncertainties in the choicé of 'correct' words to name and describe minorities, for instance in the following interview of a student with a realtor in the San Diego area (van Dijk, 1987):

> (20)   Student: Uh hu, are there a lot of **um you know** races, cultural groups around here?
>   Realtor: NOT MUCH, in fact the other day I was noticing a couple of **um** Blacks waiting for the bus . . . . (LG2, 51–3)

Such hesitations may be accompanied by the usual *you know* phrases that signal shared knowledge about local situations, avoid redundancy, and implement a strategy of allowing oneself to remain implicit in contexts of awkwardness and insecurity, as is also the case for the realtor's reply (see also Erman, 1987). Naming minorities, thus, is morally and interactionally risky (at least among people who don't know each other), and therefore needs extra care and monitoring, and hence more time and mental processing, which are signalled by *um* and similar 'fillers'.

Related Research   Based on van Dijk's work on prejudiced discourse, Wang (1995) conducted 108 in-depth interviews with European Americans concerning their prejudices about outgroup members. Her research question also asks: how do people talk about outgroup members?

Wang uncovered eight topical themes in prejudiced discourse in her interview data. These eight topical themes include: intergroup difference, outgroup cohesiveness/clustering, intergroup competition, language and communication, outgroup stereotypes and self-stereotypes, social problems, cultural and social norms, and contacts and sources of information. These discourse themes basically revolve around 'difference, threat, and deviance' (van Dijk, 1987) posed by outgroup members. Wang basically found the same strategies being used (such as disclaimers) as did van Dijk (1987). However, in one respect her data show a difference: her interviewees sometimes had no compunction in admitting that they were saying racist things, a form of bold 'honesty' that does not occur in the Dutch data.

Talk about Others: Conclusion

From these few examples we may conclude that at all levels of discourse we find protypical expressions of ethnic opinions and attitudes. From topics to local meanings, style, rhetoric, argumentation, storytelling and conversational strategies, we thus find the implementation of the overall strategy of positive self-presentation of 'us' and negative other-presentation of 'them'. Obviously, such strategies are not merely mental, in that they express such polarized attitudes, or persuasively try to influence the mental models and attitudes of the recipients. They should be understood also as sociocultural and political forms of interaction in a social context of ethnic inequality, that is as the enactment and reproduction of dominant group power.

Conclusion

The analysis of some features of talk of African American women, the survey of issues in intercultural communication, as well as the study of dominant talk and text about others, show how social and especially ethnic identities influence social practices in general, and discourse in particular. Historical, social and cultural factors play a role in the development of diverse ways of talking and communicating, which in turn are associated with intergroup perception as well as marginalization and dominance. Discourse, thus, is not merely a reliable expression of cultural identity or ethnic intergroup relations, but also enacts and reproduces ethnic dominance. Especially where such expression is subtle and indirect (as is often the case for 'modern' racism) or where communication conflicts are ignored, sophisticated discourse analysis may offer insight not only into properties of intra- or intercultural discourse as such, and not only into underlying ethnic attitudes or ideologies, but more generally into ethnic relations and societal structure. Once we have obtained such insights, anti-racist counter-discourse and alternatives may also be formulated in view of more equitable ethnic and cultural relations.

Recommended Reading

On African American Discourse

Dillard (1972), Labov (1972), and Smitherman (1977) provide general, introductory reading on features in AAVE. Baugh (1983), Dillard (1972), Labov (1972), and Smitherman (1977) provide detailed descriptions of AAVE. Smitherman (1977) is the classical source for work on signifying. Etter-Lewis (1991), Houston Stanback (1985b), and Morgan (1989; 1991b) are highly recommended for descriptions of African American women's discourse. Mufwene (1991) is recommended for crucial reading in reconsidering the history of AAVE. Major (1994) and Smitherman (1994) provide the most recent recordings of slang expressions within the general African American populace and the 'hip-hop' culture. Goodwin (1990) provides a new accounting of the social organization of talk among African American children in a Pennsylvania neighborhood.

On Intercultural Communication

Carbaugh (1990) provides an excellent collection of ethnographic studies on culture and communication. For beginners who want to learn more about the ethnography of communication, Hall (1983) is an important culture treatise on the importance of the time dimension for human behavior, and makes excellent use of cultural examples throughout the text. Kim and Gudykunst (1988) is a comprehensive collection of theories in intercultural communication: each chapter contains many testable intercultural ideas. Hofstede (1991) contains an in-depth discussion on the four cultural variability dimensions – individualism–collectivism, power distance, uncertainty avoidance, and masculine–feminine – and offers good integration of conceptual and practical cross-cultural management issues. Ting-Toomey (1994b) provides an in-depth look at cross-cultural facework from both the Eastern and the Western perspectives: theoretical and methodological issues are discussed. Triandis (1995) is a systematic, easy-to-follow discussion on the cultural variability framework of individualism and collectivism: antecedents, consequences, and applications of individualism–collectivism in diverse settings are presented.

On Discourse and Racism

Van Dijk (1984) is among the first studies that examines the interaction between ethnic prejudice and discourse. Van Dijk (1987) specifically focuses on the communication processes of ethnic prejudices in everyday conversations. Van Dijk (1991) deals with the media portrayal of minorities, especially in the British and Dutch press. Van Dijk (1993a) focuses on the role of elite discourse (politics, education, scholarship, media, corporate business) in the reproduction of racism. For analysis of the situation in Germany, the various publications of the Duisburger Institute of Language and Social Research (DISS) headed by Siegfried Jäger are recommended, such as Jäger (1992) on everyday conversations and Jäger and Link (1993) on the media. Within a related framework, Ruth Wodak and her associates at the University of Vienna critically examine antisemitic discourse (Wodak et al., 1990). From a different perspective, that of discursive psychology, Wetherell and Potter (1992) examine the discourse of white New Zealanders.

References

Abrams, D. and Hogg, M.A. (eds) (1990) *Social Identity Theory: Constructive and Critical Advances*. New York: Harvester Wheatsheaf.

Asante, M.K. and Gudykunst, W.B. (eds) (1989) *Handbook of Intercultural Communication*. Beverly Hills, CA: Sage.

Basso, K. (1990) *Western Apache Language and Culture: Essays in Linguistic Anthropology*. Tucson, AZ: University of Arizona Press.

Baugh, J. (1983) *Black Street Speech*. Austin, TX: University of Texas Press.

Blommaert, J. and Verschueren, J. (1992) *Het Belgische Migrantendebat: the Pragmatiek van de Abnormalisering (The Belgian Immigration Debate: The Pragmatics of 'Abnormalization')*. Antwerp: International Pragmatics Association.

Braham, P., Rattansi, A. and Skellington, R. (eds) (1992) *Racism and Antiracism: Inequalities, Opportunities and Policies*. London: Sage.

Brown, P. and Levinson, S.C. (1987) *Politeness: Some Universals in Language Usage*. Cambridge: Cambridge University Press.

Carbaugh, D. (ed.) (1990) *Cultural Communication and Intercultural Contact*. Hillsdale, NJ: Lawrence Erlbaum.

Cocroft, B.A. and Ting-Toomey, S. (1994) 'Facework in Japan and the United States', *International Journal of Intercultural Relations*, 18: 469–506.

Cupach, W.R. and Metts, S. (1994) *Facework*. Newbury Park, CA: Sage.

Dillard, J.L. (1972) *Black English*. New York; Random House.

Dovidio, J.F. and Gaertner, S.L. (eds) (1986) *Prejudice, Discrimination, and Racism*. Orlando, FL: Academic Press.

Erman, B. (1987) *Pragmatic Expressions in English: a Study of 'You Know', 'You See', and 'I Mean' in Face-to-Face Conversation*. Stockholm: Almqvist and Wiksell.

Essed, P.J.M. (1991) *Understanding Everyday Racism: an Interdisciplinary Theory*. Newbury Park, CA: Sage.

Etter-Lewis, G. (1991) 'Black women's life stories: reclaiming self in narrative texts', in Sherna Berger Cluck and Daphne Patai (eds), *Women's Words: the Feminist Practice of Oral History*. New York: Routledge.

Fowler, R., Hodge, B., Kress, G. and Trew, T. (1979) *Language and Control*. London: Routledge and Kegan Paul.

Frye, M. (1983) *The Politics of Reality: Essays in Feminist Theory*. Trumansburg, NY: Crossing Press.

Gallois, C., Barker, M., Jones, E. and Callan, J. (1992) 'Intercultural communication: evaluations of lecturers and Australian and Chinese students', in S. Iwawaki, Y. Kashima and K. Leung (eds), *Innovations in Cross-Cultural Psychology*. Amsterdam: Swets and Zeitlinger. pp. 86–102.

Gallois, C., Franklyn-Stokes, A., Giles, H. and Coupland, N. (1988) 'Communication accommodation theory and intercultural encounters: intergroup and interpersonal considerations', in Y.Y. Kim and W. Gudykunst (eds), *Theories in Intercultural Communication*. Newbury Park, CA: Sage. pp. 157–85.

Gallois, C., Giles, H., Jones, E., Cargile, A. and Ota, H. (1995) 'Accommodating intercultural encounters: elaborations and extensions', in R. Wiseman (ed.), *Intercultural Communication Theory*. Thousand Oaks, CA: Sage. pp. 115–47.

Gates, H.L. (1988) *The Signifying Monkey: a Theory of Afro-American Literary Criticism*. New York: Oxford University Press.

Giddings, P. (1984) *When and Where I Enter: the Impact of Black Women on Race and Sex in America*. New York: William Morrow.

Giles, H. and Coupland, N. (1991) *Language, Context and Consequences*. Pacific Grove, CA: Brooks/Cole.

Giles, H. and Johnson, P. (1987) 'Ethnolinguistic identity theory: a social psychological approach to language maintenance', *International Journal of the Sociology of Language*, 68: 66–99.

Goodwin, M.H. (1990) *He-Said-She-Said: Talk as Social Organization among Black Children*. Bloomington, IN: Indiana University Press.

Gudykunst, W.B. (1988) 'Uncertainty and anxiety', in Y.Y. Kim and W.B. Gudykunst (eds), *Theories in Intercultural Communication*. Newbury Park, CA: Sage. pp. 13–56.

Gudykunst, W.B. (1995) 'Anxiety/uncertainty management (AUM) theory: current status', in R. Wiseman (ed.), *Intercultural Communication Theory*. Thousand Oaks, CA: Sage.

Gudykunst, W.B. and Nishida, T. (1986) 'Attributional confidence in low-context and high-context cultures', *Human Communication Research*, 12: 525–49.

Gudykunst, W.B. and Shapiro, R. (1996) 'Communication in everyday interpersonal and intergroup encounters', *International Journal of Intercultural Relations*, 20 (1): 19–45.

Hall, E.T. (1959a) *The Hidden Dimension*. New York: Fawcett.

Hall, E.T. (1959b) *The Silent language*. New York: Doubleday.

Hall, E.T. (1983) *The Dance of Life*. Garden City, NY: Doubleday.

Harrison, J.A. (1884) 'Negro English', *Anglia 7*. pp. 232–79.

Hartmann, P. and Husband, C. (1974) *Racism and the Mass Media*. London: Davis-Poynter.

Hofstede, G.H. (1980) *Culture's Consequences*. Beverly Hills, CA: Sage.

Hofstede, G.H. (1991) *Cultures and Organizations: Software of the Mind*. New York: McGraw-Hill.

Houston Stanback, M. (1983) 'Code switching in black women's speech'. PhD dissertation, University of Massachusetts.

Houston Stanback, M. (1985a) 'Black women's talk across cultures', paper presented to the Speech Communication Association.

Houston Stanback, M. (1985b) 'Language and black woman's place: evidence from the black middle class', in P.A. Treichler et al. (eds), *For Alma Mater: Theory and Practice in Feminist Scholarship*. Chicago: University of Illinois Press.

Hymes, D. (1962) 'The ethnography of speaking', in T. Gladwin and W.C. Sturtevant (eds), *Anthropology and Human Behavior*. Washington, DC: Anthropological Society of Washington. pp. 13–53.

Hymes, D. (1974) 'Ways of speaking', in R. Bauman and J. Sherzer (eds), *Explorations in the Ethnography of Speaking*. Cambridge: Cambridge University Press. pp. 433–51.

Jäger, S. (1988) *Rechtsdruck: die Presse der neuen Rechten ('Rechtsdruck': the Press and the New Right)*. Bonn: Dietz.

Jäger, S. (1992) *BrandSätze: Rassismus im Alltag ('Brandsätze' [inflammatory sentences, firebombs]: Racism in Everyday Life)*. DISS-Studien. Duisburg: DISS.

Jäger, S. and Link, J. (1993) *Die vierte Gewalt: Rassismus und die Medien*. Duisburg: DISS.

Johnson, K.A. (1987) *Media Images of Boston's Black Community*. Boston, MA: University of Massachusetts, William Monroe Trotter Institute, Research Report.

Jones, E., Gallois, C., Barker, M. and Callan, V. (1994) 'Communication between Australian and Chinese students and academic staff', in A. Bouvy, F. Van de Vijver, P. Boski and P. Schmitz (eds), *Journeys into Cross-Cultural Psychology*. Amsterdam: Swets and Zeitlinger. pp. 184–96.

Katriel, T. (1986) *Talking Straight: Dugri Speech in Israeli Sabra Culture*. Cambridge: Cambridge University Press.

Kim, M.S., Sharkey, W. and Singelis, T. (1994) 'The relationship between individual's self construals and perceived importance of interactive constraints', *International Journal of Intercultural Relations*, 18: 1–24.

Kim, Y.Y. and Gudykunst, W. (eds) (1988) *Theories in Intercultural Communication*. Newbury Park, CA: Sage.

Labov, W. (1972) 'The transformation of experience in narrative syntax', in W. Labov, *Language in the Inner City*. Philadelphia: University of Pennsylvania Press. pp. 354–96.

Langer, E.J. (1989) *Mindfulness*. Reading, MA: Addison-Wesley.

Leeds-Hurwitz, W. (1990) 'Notes in the history of intercultural communication: the Foreign Service Institute and the mandate for intercultural training', *Quarterly Journal of Speech*, 76 (3): 262–81.

Major, C. (1994) *Juba to Jive: a Dictionary of African-American Slang*. New York: Penguin.

McGarry, R.G. (1994) *The Subtle Slant: a Cross-Linguistic Discourse Analysis Model for Evaluating Interethnic Conflict in the Press*. Boone, NC: Parkway.

McMillan, T. (1992) *Waiting to Exhale*. New York: Penguin Viking.

Miles, R. (1989) *Racism*. London: Routledge.

Morgan, M.H. (1989) 'From down South to up South: the language behavior of three generations of Black women residing in Chicago'. PhD dissertation, University of Pennsylvania.

Morgan, M.H. (1991a) 'Indirectness and interpretation in African American women's discourse', *Pragmatics*, 1 (4): 421–51.

Morgan, M.H. (1991b) 'Language and communication style among African American women', *UCLA Center for the Study of Women Newsletter*, 7 (Spring).

Mufwene, S. (1991) 'Ideology and facts on African American English', *Pragmatics*, 2 (2): 141–66.

Philipsen, G. (1987) 'The prospect for cultural communication', in D. Kincaid (ed.), *Communication Theory: Eastern and Western Perspectives*. New York: Academic Press. pp. 245–54.

Philipsen, G. (1989) 'Speech and the communal functions in four cultures', in S. Ting-Toomey and F. Korzenny (eds), *Cross-Cultural Interpersonal Communication*. Newbury Park, CA: Sage. pp. 79–92.

Preiswerk, R. (ed.) (1980) *The Slant of the Pen: Racism in Children's Books*. Geneva: World Council of Churches.

Reeves, F. (1983) *British Racial Discourse*. Cambridge: Cambridge University Press.

Rickford, J.R. (1992) 'Grammatical variation and divergence in vernacular Black English', in M. Gerritsen and D. Stein (eds), *Internal and External Factors in Syntactic Change*. Berlin: Mouton de Gruyter.

Smitherman, G. (1977) *Talkin and Testifyin: the Language of Black America*. Boston: Houghton Mifflin. Reissued, with revisions, Detroit: Wayne State University Press, 1986.

Smitherman, G. (1994) *Black Talk: Words and Phrases from the Hood to the Amen Corner*. New York: Houghton Mifflin.

Smitherman-Donaldson, G. and van Dijk, T.A. (eds) (1987) *Discourse and Discrimination*. Detroit: Wayne State University Press.

Stewart, W.A. (1964) *Nonstandard Speech and the Teaching of English*. Washington, DC: Center for Applied Linguistics.

Stewart, W.A. (1967) 'Sociolinguistic factors in the history of American Negro dialects', *Florida Foreign Language Reporter*, Spring: 2–4.

Sykes, M. (1985) 'Discrimination in discourse', in T.A. van Dijk (ed.), *Handbook of Discourse Analysis. Vol. 4: Discourse Analysis in Society*. London: Academic Press. pp. 83–101.

Tajfel, H. and Turner, J. (1986) 'The social identity theory of intergroup relations', in W. Austin and S. Worchel (eds), *The Social Psychology of Intergroup Relations*. Monterey, CA: Brooks/Cole. pp. 7–17.

Ting-Toomey, S. (1988) 'Intercultural conflict styles: a face-negotiation theory', in Y.Y. Kim and W.B. Gudykunst (eds), *Theories in Intercultural Communication*. Newbury Park, CA: Sage. pp. 13–38.

Ting-Toomey, S. (1994a) 'Managing conflict in intimate intercultural relationships', in Dudley D. Cahn (ed.), *Conflict in Personal Relationships*. Hillsdale, NJ: Lawrence Erlbaum. pp. 47–77.

Ting-Toomey, S. (ed.) (1994b) *The Challenge of Facework: Cross-Cultural and Interpersonal Issues*. Albany, NY: State University of New York Press.

Ting-Toomey, S., Gao, G., Trubisky, P., Yang, Z., Kim, H.S., Lin, S.-L. and Nishida, T. (1991) 'Culture, face maintenance, and styles of handling interpersonal conflict: a study in five cultures', *International Journal of Conflict Management*, 2: 275–96.

Triandis, H. (1995) *Individualism and Collectivism*. Boulder, CO: Westview Press.

Trubisky, P., Ting-Toomey, S. and Lin, S.L. (1991) 'The influence of individualism, collectivism and self-monitoring on conflict styles', *International Journal of Intercultural Relations*, 15 (1): 65–84.

van Dijk, T.A. (1984) *Prejudice in Discourse*. Amsterdam: Benjamins.

van Dijk, T.A. (1987) *Communicating Racism: Ethnic Prejudice in Thought and Talk*. Newbury Park, CA: Sage.

van Dijk, T.A. (1988a) *News Analysis: Case Studies of International and National News in the Press*. Hillsdale, NJ: Lawrence Erlbaum.

van Dijk, T.A. (1988b) *News as Discourse*. Hillsdale, NJ: Lawrence Erlbaum.

van Dijk, T.A. (1991) *Racism and the Press*. London: Routledge.

van Dijk, T.A. (1993a) *Elite Discourse and Racism*. Newbury Park, CA: Sage.

van Dijk, T.A. (1993b) 'Stories and racism', in D. Mumby (ed.), *Narrative and Social Control*. Newbury Park, CA: Sage. pp. 121–42.

Wang, M.L. (1995) 'Talking about other cultures: a discourse analysis', paper presented at the Annual Conference of the International Communication Association, Albuquerque, New Mexico.

Wetherell, M. and Potter, J. (1992) *Mapping the Language of Racism: Discourse and the Legitimation of Exploitation*. Chichester: Columbia University Press.

Williams, J. (ed.) (1995) *PC Wars: Politics and Theory in the Academy*. New York: Routledge.

Williams, R.L. (ed.) (1975) *Ebonics: the True Language of Black Folks*. St Louis: Institute of Black Studies.

Wilson, C.C. and Gutiérrez, F. (1985) *Minorities and the Media*. Beverly Hills, CA and London: Sage.

Wodak, R. (1991) 'Turning the tables: anti-semitic discourse in post-war Austria', *Discourse and Society*, 2: 65–84.

Wodak, R., Nowak, P., Pelikan, J., Gruber, H., de Cillia, R. and Mitten, R. (1990) *'Wir sind alle unschuldige Täter': Diskurshistorische Studien zum Nachkriegsantisemitismus ('We Are All Innocent Perpetrators': Discourse Historic Studies in Post-War Anti-semitism)*. Frankfurt/Main: Suhrkamp.

7

Organizational Discourse

Dennis K. Mumby and Robin P. Clair

This chapter is about the relationship between discourse and organizations. Both authors are scholars in a sub-discipline of communication studies called organizational communication. We are interested in understanding how, through discourse, people accomplish the everyday task of functioning as part of large, coordinated, institutionalized structures. In brief, and for the purposes of this chapter, we can define *organization* as a social collective, produced, reproduced and transformed through the ongoing, interdependent, and goal-oriented communication practices of its members. In this sense, when we speak of organizational discourse, we do not simply mean discourse that occurs *in* organizations. Rather, we suggest that organizations exist only in so far as their members create them through discourse. This is not to claim that organizations are 'nothing but' discourse, but rather that discourse is the principal means by which organization members create a coherent social reality that frames their sense of who they are.

In general terms, the study of organizational discourse allows us to get at the relationship between everyday organizational talk, and larger issues of social structure and meaning. When organizational communication scholars examine the discourse of organization members, they are interested in how communication functions simultaneously as both an expression and a creation of organizational structure. The range of communication phenomena that are studied from this perspective is quite large, and includes metaphors (Deetz and Mumby, 1985; Koch and Deetz, 1980; Salvador and Markham, 1995; Smith and Eisenberg, 1987), storytelling (Boje, 1991; Brown, 1985; Clair, 1993; Helmer, 1993; Mumby 1987), and rituals (Rosen, 1985; 1988; Trice and Beyer, 1984). In each case, the communicative practices of members are examined for the ways that they contribute to the ongoing (and sometimes rather precarious) process of organizing and constituting social reality. As Boden states, 'It is through the telephone calls, meetings, planning sessions, sales talks, and corridor conversations that people inform, amuse, update, gossip, review, reassess, reason, instruct, revise, argue, debate, contest, and actually *constitute* the moments, myths and, through time, the very *structuring* of the organization' (1994: 8, emphasis in original).

Within this rather general framing of the study of organizational discourse, we can identify two main perspectives that characterize current lines of research: the cultural, or interpretive, approach, and the critical approach (the emergence of postmodern thought in the last few years has somewhat muddied this distinction, but that is a topic for another paper). Both of these perspectives are concerned with the relationship between discourse and the creation of social reality. However, the cultural approach tends to operate at a largely descriptive level, and focuses on the ways in which organization members' discursive practices contribute to the development of shared meaning. As such, the principal goal of this research is to demonstrate the connection between the shared norms and values of an organization on the one hand, and the means by which these norms and values are expressed on the other. Thus Trice and Beyer (1984: 654) state that, 'In performing the activities of a rite or ceremonial, people make use of other cultural forms – certain customary language, gestures, ritualized behaviors, artifacts, other symbols, and settings – to heighten the expression of shared meanings appropriate to the occasion.'

On the other hand, the critical approach to organizational discourse is interested in different issues. Although it shares the concern of the cultural approach with exploring how social reality is created through discourse, the critical approach focuses more closely on the question of power and control in organizations. Critical discourse studies see organizations not simply as social collectives where shared meaning is produced, but rather as sites of struggle where different groups compete to shape the social reality of organizations in ways that serve their own interests. For example, it is in the interests of management to articulate a social reality for employees that emphasizes commitment to the organization, working hard, accepting economic hardship, and so forth. Employees, on the other hand, want better working conditions, shorter hours and more pay and benefits. Clearly, these two sets of interests are at odds with each other. However, it is not simply on the terrain of economics that such issues are addressed. Many organization scholars are concerned with examining how these competing interests get resolved through the control of symbolic and discursive resources. As with economic resources, symbolic resources are not distributed equally amongst the various competing organizational interest groups. Those organizational groups with more economic power are generally able to wield more power through various discursive and symbolic means. Indeed, the ongoing control of economic resources may well depend on how well a particular interest group is able to shape social reality. For example, while management imposing a pay cut on workers is clearly not in the best interests of the latter, it can be discursively shaped as such by appealing to employees' ability to make sacrifices 'for the good of the company'. Management might invoke a 'family' metaphor, for instance, in order to create a social reality that obscures the possibility that the organization is making a purely economic decision ('We in the ACME Corp. family know that in times of hardship our members will pull together and make the sacrifices necessary for our continued success together').

While this example is very much oversimplified (most organizations are characterized by multiple interest groups, including shareholders, grass roots activists, trade unions, customers, etc.) it points to the important (and relatively underexplored) idea that an organization's power and politics are frequently exercised through the discourse of its members. The critical perspective on organizational discourse is concerned not only with examining the relationship between discourse and power, but also with addressing the inequities that are produced, maintained, and reproduced as a result of this relationship. In the next section, we discuss in more detail the major currents and directions in contemporary research.

Critical Organizational Discourse Analysis

Following van Dijk (1993a: 132), we can say that critical discourse analysts explore the connection between everyday talk and the production of, maintenance of, and resistance to systems of power, inequality, and injustice. In our own work, then, we are concerned with the relationship between organizational talk and the exercise of power and resistance, both in organizations and in larger social structures. Fairclough provides us with a useful definition of critical discourse analysis:

> By 'critical' discourse analysis I mean analysis which aims to systematically explore often opaque relationships of causality and determination between (a) discursive practices, events and texts, and (b) wider social and cultural structures, relations and processes; to investigate how such practices, events and texts arise out of and are ideologically shaped by relations of power and struggles over power; and to explore how the opacity of these relationships between discourse and society is itself a factor securing power and hegemony. (1993: 135)

There is a lot of information incorporated into this definition, so it is worth unpacking it a little. First, critical discourse analysts argue that, although there is a connection between discourse and power/inequality, this relationship is often obscured and not readily apparent. In this sense, one of the goals of critical analysis is to move beyond a surface-level examination of discourse and to show how it simultaneously produces and hides 'deep structure' relations of power and inequality. For example, Mumby (1987) provides a deep structure analysis of an organizational story to show how the story is not simply a useful way to impart organization rules but rather functions *ideologically* to produce, maintain, and reproduce organizational control.

Second, then, when Fairclough refers to texts being ideologically shaped by power relations he – like other critical discourse analysts – is using the notion of 'ideology' in a particular fashion. The term refers not simply to the ideas, beliefs, and values that individuals take on, but rather to the process by which social actors, as part of larger social collectives, develop particular identities and experience the world in a particular way. As such, we can say that ideology, through its expression in various forms of discourse, constitutes who people are as thinking, experiencing social actors.

Third, and most importantly for critical discourse analysts, ideology does not emerge in a neutral fashion, but is tied up with the relations of power and control that characterize society. Ideology functions to maintain and reproduce existing relations of power (Giddens, 1979). Thus a three-way relationship emerges among discourse, ideology, and power. Put simply, discourse reproduces, creates, and challenges existing power relations; ideology is the mediating factor in this relationship, providing an interpretive frame through which discursive practices are given meaning.

Finally, power is generally exercised not coercively, but subtly and routinely. The most effective use of power occurs when those with power are able to get those who have less power to interpret the world from the former's point of view. Power is thus exercised through consent rather than coercion. This is referred to by critical discourse analysts as the process of *hegemony* (Gramsci, 1971). In the rest of this section, we present some of the recent developments in critical analyses of organizational discourse. The goal of this research is to get beneath the surface level of organizational discourse, and to show how larger, macro-social issues are at stake in the ways in which organization members go about their routine practices.

Recent critical studies of organizational discourse seem to be developing in two related directions. First, there is the approach described above, which is basically concerned with understanding and critiquing the relationships among discourse, ideology, and power (Helmer, 1993; Huspek and Kendall, 1991; Mumby, 1987; Mumby and Stohl, 1992; van Dijk, 1993b; 1993c; Witten, 1993). Here, the goals are critique and emancipation – critiquing existing power relations and suggesting possibilities for alternative organizational forms. Second, and more recently, there has emerged a critical feminist perspective on organizational discourse (Ferguson, 1984; Gherardi, 1994; Martin, 1990; Pringle, 1988). This approach problematizes the notion of gender, arguing that issues of discourse, power, and control can only be understood by examining the ways in which talk socially constructs definitions of masculinity and femininity, and male–female interactions.

For the remainder of this section we will focus on these two recent developments in the study of organizational discourse. In the final section of the chapter, we will provide a concrete analysis of the relationships among discourse, gender, and sexual harassment.

Critical Studies of Organizational Discourse

The last ten years has seen a significant growth in the study of power in organizations – a topic that, until recently, was taboo amongst organizational researchers. Traditionally, scholars have studied how power (authority) is legitimately exercised in organizations, but the idea that organizations are sites of hegemony and coercion has, for the most part, been off limits as an area of research. Much of this has to do with economic connections between universities and corporations. Many organizational scholars fund their research through corporate grants, so doing research that depicts organizations as characterized by inequity, lack of democracy, etc., is rather like biting the hand that feeds you. No knowledge is 'pure' knowledge, and so there are good political reasons why certain kinds of research trends develop rather than others. Even today, there are, relatively speaking, only a small number of studies that involve researchers actually going into organizations and studying first hand the ways in which power functions as control.

Two classic early 'critical ethnographies' did much to provide the impetus for future critical discourse studies. First, Burawoy (1979) employed participant-observer methods to study the workers in a machine shop. Reversing the usual management question of 'Why don't workers work harder?', he instead used as his starting point the question, 'Why do workers work as hard as they do?' By studying the workers' (and his own) behaviors, rituals, and talk about their jobs at close hand over a period of several months, Burawoy was able to show that workers internalized and continually reproduced a system of consent that served the interests of management in maintaining production levels. While workers experienced 'small wins' through shop-floor games such as 'making out' (in which they produced an excess over required output on easy jobs in order to build up a 'kitty' for more difficult jobs where it was harder to meet the required bonus rate), they generally reproduced the logic of capitalism, in effect maintaining their own subordination through active consent to the system in place. The second study is Stewart Clegg's (1975) critical ethnography of a building site in the North of England. Using participant-observer methods and drawing on interviews, field notes, and transcriptions of meetings, he shows how power is exercised through a set of interpretive frames that each worker incorporates as part of his or her organizational identity. The interpretive procedures that are used to make sense of everyday organizational life serve to perpetuate inequitable working conditions and reproduce managerial definitions of what counts as appropriate behavior.

Since around 1985, the critical study of organizational discourse has developed into an influential body of research in the fields of organizational communication and management studies. Michael Rosen's (1985; 1988) critical ethnographic research is a good example of work that combines participant observation with close textual analysis. In his study of a Philadelphia advertising agency, Rosen interprets 'text' very broadly, examining various discursive practices such as a Christmas party skit, an annual corporate breakfast, and speeches by corporate vice-presidents. His analyses attempt to show the relationship between these various discursive practices and the ideological production and reproduction of capitalist relations of domination (Rosen adopts an explicitly Marxist perspective). Rosen's texts and subsequent analyses are too long to be reproduced in full here, but a short extract might help to suggest the tenor of his work.

Rosen (1988) provides an extended analysis of the company Christmas party, demonstrating how it functions as a 'social drama'. He argues that 'social drama provides a possibility for reproducing an organizational consciousness, which is a consent to the social relations of the organization. The degree to which symbols evoke emotion is crucial in this process of reproduction. If the Christmas party fails to access the emotive pole . . . this event is likely to be less operationally efficacious in reproducing consent' (1988: 469). An extract from his interpretation of one of the Christmas skits illustrates this process at work:

> One [skit] included a telephone receptionist on stage answering outside calls. In response to a caller's supposed questioning of the changing agency personnel she said, 'Well honey, I can't tell you myself what's going on around here. Things change a lot. The associates don't associate much. The place should be called Shoenman and Company.' . . . Later she was paging someone for Barry Kassian, 'Mr Quenzel, get your ass in Mr Kassian's office!' Under the veneer of corporate politeness the raw authoritarian nature of relations exists. And another phone message: 'Mr Ebert [research director], yes, a guy on 15th Street is calling, says he's your bookie.' According to agency lore, Harry loves to gamble: cards, horses, whatever. The surface image of a managerial elite Brahmanism, an unreachableness due to status, is mocked. (1988: 473)

Rosen's article continues in this way, using a strong, narrative form to paint a vivid picture of the Christmas party as an organizational event that plays an important role in the structuring of social reality at Shoenman and Associates. Notice that Rosen does not subject carefully, literally transcribed discourse to micro-analysis, as a conversation analyst might (see Pomerantz and Fehr, Chapter 3 in this volume), although his means of data collection and analysis are no less rigorous. While a conversation analyst attempts to uncover the micro-structures and patterns of everyday talk, Rosen is more interested in larger units of analysis, examining how complex communicative behaviors (rituals, speeches, breakfast etiquette, party skits, etc.) can be connected to the production and reproduction of capitalist economic relations. Although this may seem a large conceptual leap (discourse to capitalism), Rosen develops a sophisticated interpretation to show how the Christmas party functions ideologically to simultaneously secure and obscure the economic foundation of all relationships within the organization (particularly those between management and lower-level employees). As Rosen states, 'In Shoenman and Associates a moral community is systematically cultivated, enabling and obscuring an underlying network of instrumental relationships' (1988: 479).

A key trend, then, in the critical approach to organizational discourse is that everyday talk is political in nature. This does not mean that people talk explicitly about political issues, but that all discourse potentially structures relations of dominance and subordination in organizations. As we discussed above, this structuring of relations of domination and subordination takes place through the ideological structuring of discourse. We must be careful, however, not to simplify the relationships among discourse, ideology, and power. There are no one-to-one, fixed relationships between discourse, what it means, how it functions ideologically, and the effects of power. As Stuart Hall states, 'There is "no necessary corre-spondence" between the conditions of a social relation or practice and the number of different ways in which it can be represented' (1985: 104). In analysing the discursive construction of his own identity as a person of color he explains:

> At different times in my thirty years in England, I have been 'hailed' or inter-pellated [addressed] as 'coloured', 'West-Indian', 'Negro', 'black', 'immigrant'. Sometimes in the street; sometimes at street corners; sometimes abusively; sometimes in a friendly manner; sometimes ambiguously. (A black friend of mine was disciplined by his political organization for 'racism' because, in order to scandalize the white neighbourhood in which we both lived as students, he would ride up to my window late at night and, from the middle of the street, shout 'Negro!' very loudly to attract my attention!) All of them inscribe me 'in place' in a signifying chain which constructs identity through the categories of color, ethnicity, race . . . It is the position within the different signifying chains which 'means', not the literal, fixed correspondence between an isolated term and some denotated position in the color spectrum. (1985: 108)

Although Hall is not an organizational communication researcher, his work provides important insight into the relationship among discourse, ideology, and power. First, he is able to demonstrate the complexity of the relation-ships among these terms. Power is not simply expressed and reproduced through discourse; rather, there is a complex and dynamic process of ideological struggle in which different and competing groups attempt to shape and influence the way in which social reality is constructed. Thus in speaking of race, Hall says, 'The effect of the struggle over "black", if it becomes strong enough, is that it stops the society reproducing itself functionally, in *that* old way. Social reproduction itself becomes a contested process' (1985: 113). Second, Hall shows that even the most apparently natural human characteristic – one's race – is subject to social construction through discourse. Racial identity as such is not fixed, but is constructed through the complex set of signifying practices that position each of us discursively. As Hall argues, 'there is no essential, unitary "I" – only the fragmentary, contradictory subject I become' (1985: 109).

   Critical analysis of organizational discourse thus provides insight into the processes through which struggles over competing interests are discursively shaped. Organizations don't simply reproduce themselves; they exist precariously as symbolic structures shot through with competing interests, struggles, and contradictions. A few more examples will help to illustrate this process at work (so to speak!).

   Mumby's (1987; 1988) analysis of organizational storytelling is a good example of how stories as discursive practices are powerful devices for structuring organizational reality. Following and expanding upon Giddens (1979), Mumby argues that organizational storytelling functions ideologi-cally in four different ways: (1) through representing sectional interests as universal; (2) by obscuring or transforming structural contradictions;

(3) through the process of reification (that is, making human constructions seem natural and objective); (4) as a means of control, or hegemony (Gramsci, 1971). By way of explicating these four ideological functions of organizational stories, Mumby (1987: 120–5) subjects a single story to close textual analysis. The story is as follows:

> [Tom Watson Jr, chairman of the board of IBM, is challenged by] a twenty-two-year-old bride weighing ninety pounds whose husband had been sent overseas and who, in consequence, had been given a job until his return . . . The young woman, Lucille Burger, was obliged to make certain that people entering security areas wore the correct clear identification.
>   Surrounded by his usual entourage of white-shirted men, Watson approached the doorway to an area where she was on guard, wearing an orange badge acceptable elsewhere in the plant, but not a green one, which alone permitted entrance at her door. 'I was trembling in my uniform, which was far too big,' she recalled. 'It hid my shakes, but not my voice. "I'm sorry," I said to him. I knew who he was alright. "You cannot enter. Your admittance is not recognized." That's what we were suppose to say.'
>   The men accompanying Watson were stricken; the moment held unpredictable possibilities. 'Don't you know who he is?' someone hissed. Watson raised his hand for silence, while one of the party strode off and returned with the appropriate badge. (1987: 121)

While space does not permit a full analysis of this story here, a couple of issues are worth addressing. From an ideological perspective, there are many elements of the story that function to reify and hence naturalize the complex social relations that are embedded in the story. Part of the power of the narrative is derived from the ways in which it draws upon audience understandings of class and gender issues. Thus, not accidentally, Lucille Burger is 'interpellated' (addressed) as twenty-two, a bride, weighing ninety pounds, and as wearing a uniform that's too big for her. Her organizational identity is therefore defined patriarchally, in relationship to her absent husband and the men present in the story: her youth, innocence (connoted by the term 'bride'), diminutive stature (associated in Western society with lack of power), and ill-fitting uniform (which functions symbolically to show how 'ill-suited' she is for her position), all situate her in sharp contrast with the ominous white-shirted men, headed by the embodiment of white, male corporate elitism, the IBM CEO. The story only makes sense and is worth telling because of these embedded assumptions about class and gender that give it narrative force. The story has a paternalistic air to it, suggesting that everyone should respect IBM's rules, from the lowliest employee to the top executive; as a narrative, it works precisely because of the huge gulf that exists in terms of class, gender, and corporate position between the two protagonists. Ideologically, the story plays up the theme of democracy, while drawing on characteristics of the social structure that are decidedly anti-democratic (that is, inequities of class, gender, and wealth).

From a critical perspective, then, the story is not simply an interesting expression of a unique corporate culture (as some culture theorists would explain it), but is rather a discursive practice that is meaningful only within a complex set of class- and gender-based social relations. Paraphrasing Stuart Hall, we can say that Lucille Burger is not an 'essential, unitary I', but a subjectivity that is partially constituted out of the complex and contradictory discourses of gender and class. Discursively speaking, gender and class become 'differences that make a difference' in terms of their importance in symbolically constructing relations of domination and subordination. Let us explore two more examples before moving on to our discussion of feminist critical discourse analysis.

Helmer (1993) provides an interesting critical ethnography of a horse-racing track. Again focusing on storytelling, Helmer shows how three organizational tensions and oppositions – administration versus horsemen, 'chemists' versus honest horsemen, and men versus women – are produced and reproduced through the stories that organization members tell. He argues that 'storytelling creates and sustains symbolic oppositions that enable members to position themselves and others in the organization.' As such, narrative 'serves to stratify the organization along lines of power and authority, gender, and ethics' (1993: 34). In the tradition of critical organization studies, Helmer is more interested in the divisive than the cohesive elements of organizational life. One important dimension of Helmer's study – and one that represents an advance over the work of Martin et al. (1983) and Mumby (1987; 1988) – is that he studies organizational storytelling as it occurs naturally in actual organizational settings. As Helmer states, 'the analysis of storytelling as an organizing process requires close attention to context, including time and place, [and] communicator roles and characteristics . . . Not all research on storytelling has met this requirement, with the result that *stories-as-artefacts* are often mistaken for *storytelling-as-process*' (1993: 35). This is an important critique of existing work in discourse analysis (whether in organizational contexts or not), which tends to focus largely on interview data, brief extracts of discourse taken out of their original context, archival material, and so on. The tendency is to reify the written text and hence lose the sense of discourse as communication, that is, as a dynamic, complex, ongoing process.

Again, it is not possible to do justice to the complexity of Helmer's analysis here, but a brief extract should help to convey the general flavor of his study. In the following example, his concern is with the organizational stratification of men and women at the track. Historically, women have not been allowed to occupy positions of responsibility in horse-racing and, despite advances in the last twenty years, men still vastly outnumber women in terms of the most visible and financially rewarding positions. It is within this historical and political context, then, that women must discursively construct their place/space in the organization. Based on his field research and analysis, Helmer suggests that storytelling plays an important role in maintaining the male–female tension. He provides the following example:

A groom named Sue described a relationship that commonly develops between a male trainer and a female groom:

'A lot of the girls are known as "trainer-fuckers", you know what I mean? They won't go out with other grooms, they won't go out with anybody but trainers. So the girls talk about the other girls – you know, "she's just a trainer-fucker, that's all." There are so many girls – grooms – that will go in that direction.'

Why?

'They're getting taken out to lavish dinners, they go for weekends, stay at motels, they're seen at parties. I'd say it's more for the status of it. There's so many that couldn't care whether it's a serious relationship or not. You know, your big trainers always have money, they've got credit cards – dining and dancing is all on the credit card. You stay in motels as compared with staying in the shedrow. It all comes down to that.' (1993: 41–2)

Helmer argues that 'girls talking about other girls' through storytelling contributes to maintenance of the opposition between men and women. This opposition, he suggests 'is both the medium and the outcome of a form of everyday interaction that both expresses and preserves part of the cultural system of power and privilege' (1993: 42). At one level, it's hard to know where to start in providing a critical analysis of this story, such is its richness. Helmer's principal interpretation is that the story has embedded in it an opposition between women who are 'trainer-fuckers' and those who are not, hence allowing the latter (including the storyteller) to distinguish themselves from the former, and thus to discursively construct 'an ethical orientation toward male trainers and other women' (1993: 42).

Although this is a legitimate interpretation, we would argue that other issues make this story fascinating. The story is structured around the basic contradiction that women face in a society where it is predominantly men who control the economic, cultural, and sexual capital. Women are disadvantaged both economically and politically, but in order to gain some of that economic and political capital they are frequently required to subordinate themselves to men. This subordination process can involve women taking on 'male' characteristics to compete in corporate life, or adopting behavioral and discursive practices that are deferential toward men, or selling their sexual capital in return for economic capital. It seems to us that this story is, at one level, an expression of the frustration that the speaker feels about women (or, as she calls them, 'girls') who, in order to be successful, subordinate themselves to men perceived as having power. The term 'trainer-fucker' functions ideologically as a pungent metonymic device, interpellating (addressing) the women purely in terms of their sexuality and their ability to use it to advance themselves. In this context, the speaker uses an interpretive frame that connects the deployment of sexuality with power ('the big trainers'), having a good time (lavish dinners, dining and dancing, motels), and money (symbolically embodied in the almighty credit card, suggesting potentially unlimited resources, expense accounts, etc.). As such, one senses a tension between the desire for success – and the rewards that accompany it – and the condemnation of a woman for being 'just a trainer-fucker'. At this level, both Martin et al. (1983) and Helmer seem correct in suggesting that organizational tensions and contradictions are both constituted and resolved through storytelling; while women who use their sexuality to gain advancement (economically, at least) may be successful at one level, discursively they are marginalized, positioned as 'other' by the 'legitimate' female grooms. Finally, and following from this analysis, this story is significant as an example of the process through which members of subordinate groups (in this case, women disenfranchised from equal participation in organizational power) discursively position *each other* as marginalized. As the philosopher-historian Michel Foucault (1979) has argued, this suggests that power is not simply exercised from the top down (in a repressive fashion), but rather pervades social structures such that it is continually produced and reproduced by the most mundane social practices (such as telling a story).

A final example gets at the close relationships among organizational discourse, power, and identity. Collinson (1988) provides an interesting participant-observer study of social interaction in an engineering plant. He examines the ways in which the excusively male, working class workforce employs humor as a discursive practice that functions in multiple ways to: (a) resist management ideology; (b) produce conformity to working class norms of masculinity; and (c) control fellow workers who shirk their job responsibilities.

Collinson provides several pithy examples of both verbal and nonverbal humor to illustrate the intense pressure that workers place on each other to conform to a culture in which one's masculine identity is strongly associated with the ability to both give and receive jokes. Thus, 'Defensively engaged in the mock battles of male sparring, bluff and bravado, it was expected that these workers would be aggressive, critical and disrespectful, so as to create embarrassment in others' (1988: 187). Some examples of workers' accounts of shop-floor humor include:

> You've got to give it or go under. It's a form of survival, you insult first before they get one back. The more you get embarrassed, the more they do it, so you have to fight back. It can hurt deep down, although you don't show it.

> I detest being embarrassed, so I take the piss out of the others.

> I like shocking apprentices. A classic is sending one of the lads for 'a long stand'. They go over and say, 'Bob sent me for a long stand.' The other bloke'll say 'OK' and then after a while he'll say, 'Is that long enough?' 'Fucking hell' the apprentice will think.

Collinson's analysis of such workplace humor is particularly interesting because of his attempts to show the relationships among humor, masculine identity, and collective resistance to management and the capitalist relations of production that they represent. He suggests, for example, that the strong workplace culture that is both manifest in, and reproduced through, humor, actually works against the chances for genuine, collective resistance to management. In his critical interpretation, Collinson shows that humor expresses and reproduces a masculine identity composed of sexual aggressiveness, independence, personal freedom, and a strong focus on the workers' roles as 'breadwinners' for their families. This conception of identity, while useful in holding one's own and 'having a laff' on the shop-floor, is rooted in a strongly individualistic ideology that does not lend itself easily to a *collective* sense of identity that might lead to more effective forms of workplace resistance. Collinson thus warns against the tendency to romanticize working class resistance, and shows the importance of examining the relationships among discourse, identity, and power in the workplace.

Both Helmer's and Collinson's studies provide us with interesting insights into the relationships between gender, power, and discourse. In the next section we look more closely at the issue of gender by turning to a discussion of the growing body of feminist research on organizational discourse.

Feminist Studies of Organizational Discourse

If there is an issue that organization researchers have been even slower to consider than power, it is gender (with race lagging even further behind). While there are plenty of studies around that focus on gender as an organizational variable (for example, examining the effects of gender on subordinates' perceptions of supervisors), relatively little work exists that treats organizations as fundamentally gendered social structures. In the last few years, however, a body of work has emerged that examines how we 'do gender' (West and Zimmerman, 1987) in organizations (Acker, 1990; Alvesson and Billing, 1992; Collinson, 1992; Gherardi, 1994). Such work is interested in how everyday talk and behavior constitute and reproduce masculine and feminine identities. Gender, its formation, and its role in organizational structuring, are what is problematized in this research.

Feminist organizational research makes the assumption that organizations are largely patriarchal, and therefore privilege masculine ways of thinking and organizing the world. In this context, feminist research takes place on two different, but related, fronts. First, there is work that critiques that are perceived as masculine, instrumental biases in the ways in which organizations are studied; from this perspective, the knowledge and discourse produced by scholars about organizations is viewed as fundamentally reflecting a male vision of the world, focusing on efficiency, rationality, control, and so forth (Mumby and Putnam, 1992; Calás and Smircich, 1991). This vision, it is argued, contributes to the ongoing production of a male-defined way of doing work. Second, feminist researchers have focused on the everyday practices of organizational life, attempting to make sense out of the processes through which the work of 'doing gender' is accomplished. We briefly discuss a few examples of this second line of research below.

Joanne Martin's (1990) analysis of a story told by the CEO of a large, multi-national corporation, is a good illustration of the issues that feminist researchers address in examining organizational discourse. The story told by the CEO is as follows:

> We have a young woman who is extraordinarily important to the launching of a major new (product). We will be talking about it next Tuesday in its first world wide introduction. She has arranged to have her Caesarian yesterday in order to be prepared for this event, so you – We have insisted that she stay home and this is going to be televised in a closed circuit television, so we're having this done by TV for her, and she is staying home three months and we are filling in to create this void for us because we think it's an important thing for her to do. (1990: 339)

Martin analyses this story (told by the CEO to illustrate his corporation's benevolent attitude toward child care, maternity leave, etc.) as a means of getting at suppressed gender conflicts that are implicit in the story and which, she argues, characterize much of contemporary organizational life. Thus, while organizations are increasingly recognizing the socially and legally inappropriate nature of gender inequality, organizational talk is still very much gendered. Martin engages in a form of analysis called 'deconstruction' (a form of literary textual analysis developed by the French philosopher, Jacques Derrida), examining the story in terms of the oppositions and contradictions that are embedded in it, as well as in terms of what is absent from, but implicit in, the text.

Martin is principally concerned in her analysis with the way the story addresses the split between the public and private spheres of life. She argues that this organizational pregnancy represents an intrusion of the private into the public domain, and that the CEO's telling of the story represents an attempt to deal with the juncture of the public and private realms embodied in gender and sexuality. An employee's pregnancy, Martin argues, reveals organizational taboos associated with the private and the sexual realms, and tests the limits of 'an unstated sexual ideology that undergirds current norms of organizational functioning' (1990: 348). Some of the violated norms that Martin deals with are as follows. (1) A pregnant belly becomes visible; thus, ignoring a woman's gender and conducting 'business as usual' are not possible. (2) Effective infant care involves emotion and nurturance; outside prescribed organization norms, emotion and nurturance are usually taboo. (3) Pregnancy is caused by sexual intercourse. While sex is not completely taboo in organizations, who has sex with whom is implicitly dictated by organizational norms: generally speaking, taboos about voluntary sexual behavior are more limiting for women (particularly those in the higher echelons of organizations) than for men.

In general terms, Martin's analysis is intended to challenge the traditional dichotomies (particularly the public/private split) that characterize organizational thought and behavior. By examining discourse in terms of both its (present) text and (absent) sub-text, we can begin to understand how existing organizational structure is perpetuated through talk, and how alternative, more participatory structures might be realized. As Martin states, 'If feminist perspectives were fully incorporated [into organizational thought], the usual emphases on rationality, hierarchy, competition, efficiency, and productivity would be exposed as only a very small piece of the organization puzzle' (1990: 357).

Finally, an important and growing area of research addresses the intersection of gender, race, and sexuality. Through a focus on discourse, feminist scholars are beginning to explore systematically the ways in which, through everyday talk, people construct themselves and others in relation to race and gender. For example, Frankenberg's (1993) *White Women, Race Matters*, while not about organizations *per se*, is a fascinating study in (following the black feminist writer bell hooks) 'interrogating whiteness'. Drawing on data collected from dozens of lengthy interviews of white women from various socio-economic backgrounds, Frankenberg analyses the ways in which these women construct race through their discourse. With great insight, she shows how white women struggle with the process of positioning themselves in relation to people of color, and how this enables them to implicitly construct various understandings of 'whiteness' versus 'blackness'. Her point is that 'white' and 'black' are not natural categories with intrinsic significance, but rather are socially constructed through discourse.

Essed's (1991; 1992) research similarly examines the discursive processes through which racism and sexism are institutionalized. For example, in a series of 55 interviews with women of color from both the USA and Holland, Essed systematically analyses narrative accounts provided by these women of their experience of racism and sexual harassment. Such narratives, she demonstrates, are not *ad hoc*, but rather follow a specific structure that reflects the women's knowledge about the nature of racism. Her analysis provides insight into both the varying degrees of 'discursive consciousness' (Giddens, 1979) that these women exhibit regarding racism and sexism, and the ways in which 'individual dominant group members participate in practices through which structures of racial domination are reproduced' (Essed, 1992: 222). The generally higher level of awareness of what constitutes racist/sexist behavior in the former group of women is arguably a reflection of their double subordination as *women* of *color*.

Finally, and of particular relevance for our interest in the ways in which dominant organizational groups reproduce those relations of domination, van Dijk's (1993d) study of corporate managerial discourse demonstrates how the managerial elite reproduces, through talk, racist views of subordinate, minority groups. Van Dijk's work is particularly interesting in so far as it is concerned not with blatant forms of racism and discrimination, but rather with the subtle linguistic moves that discursively construct minorities and position them as different and, by implication, inferior to the white 'norm'. For example, van Dijk (1993d: 151–7) shows how managers' stories about experiences with minorities can function simultaneously to prove the positive attributes of the manager/employer, and the negative attitudes and attributes of minority personnel. Van Dijk, like Essed, demonstrates that such stories and accounts are not structured in an *ad hoc* fashion, but rather reflect larger, societal-level systems of meaning regarding racial minorities in Dutch and US societies. Thus, with topics such as equal opportunities and discrimination 'a number of standard subtopics, standard arguments, and even standard moves of defense, face-keeping, and positive self-presentation' occur (1993d: 156).

In the study of the relationships among discourse, organization, and domination, we can thus identify three (and perhaps other) research possibilities: (1) the study of how members of oppressed groups can discursively penetrate the institutionalized form of their oppression (for example, Essed, Hall); (2) the examination of how members of the dominant group(s) discursively construct and reproduce their own positions of dominance (van Dijk); and (3) the analysis of the ways in which subordinated individuals discursively frame their own subordination in ways that can perpetuate it (Helmer, Clair). It is the third possibility that is taken up in the final section of this chapter with a detailed discussion of research on sexual harassment as a discursive practice, conducted by Robin Clair. Our intent is both to further understanding of the extent to which discourse can create, reproduce, or challenge embedded social structures, and to provide a detailed explication of how a particular theoretical framework can be applied to actual discourse.

Sexual Harassment as a Discursive Practice

Sexual harassment is without doubt a widespread and serious problem (Clair, 1994; Clair et al., 1993; Fairhurst, 1986; Gutek, 1985; Loy and Stewart, 1984; Paludi, 1990). It is beyond the scope of this chapter to review all of the literature that documents the physical, emotional, and economic repercussions of sexual harassment (for example, MacKinnon, 1979). Instead, we focus on sexual harassment as a discursive practice of domination, one that contributes to controlling marginalized members of the workforce.

'Sexual harassment is not "personal": it is violence out of history' (Taylor and Conrad, 1992: 414), violence that creates and perpetuates oppression. The violence of sexual harassment is discursively enacted on several levels (Clair, 1993; Strine, 1992; Taylor and Conrad, 1992; Wood, 1992). First, if we look at sexual harassment as verbal and nonverbal messages of physical force, threat, and intimidation we readily see how sexual harassment violates the 'personal' rights of individuals being harassed. Yet, when we look at sexual harassment as a pervasive condition in society we recognize that the deeper-level message is intended not for a single individual, but for an entire group of people, usually women. Thus, sexual harassment helps to create a social reality at both the micro-level and the macro-level of society. The micro-level exchanges support the macro-level system and the macro-level system legitimates acts of sexual harassment against individuals.

With these thoughts in mind, we turn our attention to how the individuals who report encountering sexual harassment frame their experiences. How the victims of sexual harassment talk about their experiences can provide valuable information about how an oppressive system is discursively maintained.

A Critical Interpretation of Victims' Discourse: Framing

We have detailed the theoretical assumptions of critical discourse studies as it is applied to organizational communication in the previous sections of this chapter. Now we will focus in more detail on how talk can be interpreted to reveal the deep-level meanings of power and dominance. One way to examine the discourse is to address how it is framed.

The concept of framing communication was originally developed by Gregory Bateson (1972) and further developed by Erving Goffman (1974). Framing has been defined as a 'kind of metanarrative that influences interpretation but is not part of the content' (Stahl, 1989: 49). As Clair explains, 'framing devices are rhetorical/discursive practices that define or assign interpretation to the social event' (1993: 118). Several scholars suggest that frames are critical to disguising the deep-level power structures that sustain a dominant ideology. Most recently, scholars have used the concept of framing to help them interpret talk about such organizationally related concepts as negotiation (Putnam and Holmer, 1992), leader–member exchange (Fairhurst, 1993), sexual harassment (Chapman, 1994; Clair, 1993; Williams, 1994), and racism (Essed, 1991; van Dijk, 1993d). The following discourse analysis explores how speakers frame their stories and in turn how these frames can be explicated to illuminate ideological implications of the discourse.

Critical interpretation of discourse through frame analysis examines the deeper-level meanings embedded in the discourse to understand how these meanings are created and sustained and how such meaning systems perpetuate oppression or encourage emancipation. Power relations are frequently sustained by framing discourse in ways that partially fix certain meanings about our social reality. Therefore, in order to discover how oppression is maintained we need to look at how the discourse is framed, what frames are used to perpetuate the dominant ideology, and what frames allow us to see that alternative social realities are possible.

The Framing of Sexual Harassment

Following the theoretical premises set forth by critical scholars, Clair (1993) conducted a critical interpretive analysis of women's narratives about their experiences with sexual harassment. Clair argued that the women might be discursively participating in their own domination (that is, hegemony) by framing their experiences in certain ways. Specifically, Clair suggested that six frames might be used that would contribute to the women's oppression through sexual harassment. The frames were generated based upon theoretical positions and used as a guide to see if the discourse supplied by the women could be described according to the frames. The six framing devices proposed relied primarily on the theoretical insights of Giddens (1979) and Mumby (1987; 1988). The six frames are: (1) accepting the dominant interests; (2) simple misunderstanding; (3) reification; (4) trivialization; (5) denotative hesitancy; and (6) personalizing the public. Each of the frames is briefly described below.

Accepting the Dominant Interests   The notion that the dominant group's interests are universalized translated into a frame that Clair (1993) called 'accepting the dominant interests'. If this frame were used by victims of sexual harassment, then one would expect victims to describe their own concerns about the harassment as less important than management's interests. Management's interests would become universalized and take precedence over self-interests. A victim might conclude that it is more important to protect the company from bad publicity than to protect victims from sexual harassment. Victims, framing sexual harassment in this way, might offer to quit their jobs or ask for transfers rather than insist that the harasser be fired or transferred.

Simple Misunderstanding   The second frame is based on the notion that contradictions in the system must be disguised if the status quo is to be maintained. One way to disguise sexual harassment is to frame it as 'flirting', 'joking', or some other innocuous behavior. When stories of sexual harassment are framed in this way, they are called 'simple misunderstanding'. Victims who frame their encounters with sexual harassment as a simple misunderstanding might say something like 'I'm not sure if that was sexual harassment or a bizarre request for a date.'

Reification   A third framing device, reification, relies on interpreting the encounter with sexual harassment as natural and immutable. A victim who invokes reification may claim that 'boys will be boys and you can't change biology.' This kind of frame suggests that nothing can be done about sexual harassment because it is an inevitable and natural consequence of male–female interaction.

Trivialization   Trivialization is similar to, yet distinct from, accepting the dominant interests. One might accept that management's concerns must be considered uppermost without denying that the sexual harassment is in itself also a serious concern. Yet, when one frames sexual harassment as a trivial thing one automatically accepts the dominant interests and dilutes the seriousness of sexual harassment. The trivialization frame occurs when the victim makes light of the situation even though it has damaging effects. A victim of sexual harassment that invokes a frame of trivialization may make light of the situation or turn it into a joke.

Denotative Hesitancy   Wood (1992) explains that when we 'name' an issue we give it a certain legitimacy that it did not have before the 'naming'. Yet, every practice that is named achieves its 'name' or definition through deliberations (Schiappa, 1991). Naming goes through a process of deliberation where 'experts' often receive a privileged status in the process of naming and defining (Schiappa, 1991). When victims of sexual harassment fail to name their experience as 'sexual harassment' they are displaying a hesitancy to use the new term. Clair (1993) discusses denotative hesitancy as a frame used by some victims of sexual harassment who avoid labeling their experiences as 'sexual harassment'.

Personalizing the Public   Feminists challenged the taken-for-granted dichotomy between public and private domains when they argued that the 'personal is political'. To frame issues as personal rather than public or political is to relegate these issues to the position of the unspoken. If an issue is personal then it will be dealt with at an interpersonal level and not discussed in terms of how it relates to the community at large. With respect to framing sexual harassment, Clair (1993) suggests that personalizing the public/political can occur in at least one of two ways. First, although sexual harassment is a public concern, the victim may frame the act or the solution to it in an interpersonal way. For example, rather than seeking public support to fend off sexual harassment a harassed individual may call upon a friend or relative. Second, the victim of harassment may frame the incident as so 'personal' that they are too embarrassed to talk about it in any detail.

Clair (1993) provides several stories of workplace sexual harassment as told by the victims. Of the fifty women interviewed, nearly half told stories of encountering sexual harassment. Each of these stories was critically analysed for the framing devices employed. Given space limitations, we provide examples of the enactment of only three of the frames discussed above. Interested readers are referred to Clair (1993) for a more in-depth discussion.

Example 1: Reification

Elizabeth, who works as a cashier in a gift shop, reported a story of sexual harassment that occurred when she was younger:

> [My boss] did not treat me like a person . . . He used to touch me in the back room and he used to rub my back and hug me . . . [He asked me] When are you going to be old enough to go to a hotel room with me? [The woman was 16 years old at the time and working at a family owned restaurant. She summarized the situation in the following way] I felt bad. I was close to the family. And I thought it was normal, but it was very, very abnormal. And it used to make me so mad inside.

Franny, who worked as an assistant to several men in a large company, told us that:

> [We live in a] very egocentric, very male-dominated [country and] that's just the way it is . . . [However] There are other countries that do not have that mentality.

Critical Interpretation of the Discourse   Elizabeth's story indicates that the sexual harassment was perceived as both normal and abnormal; both an inevitable and immutable part of life and something that was not right. Furthermore, Elizabeth begins her story by telling us that her boss did not treat her like a person. In other words, she does not automatically accept the notion that this is the way she should be treated. Instead Elizabeth recognizes that she is not being treated like a human being, that instead she is being objectified. Elizabeth's recognition implies that some resistance to reification is occurring. Franny's story also indicates a mixture of reification and resistance, or at least hope that things can change. First, Franny says of sexual harassment 'That's just the way it is.' However, Franny also suggests that it is not like this in all countries of the world and maybe Americans could look to other societies for different ways of dealing with issues of sexuality. She too suggests then that this is an immutable part of American society, but she does not frame the story exclusively in terms of reification. Neither of these women is willing to give up hope that sexual harassment can be stopped.

Example 2: Trivialization

Cassie describes her feelings about sexual harassment in the following way:

> Well, if it's subtle, and it's jokingly, and it's not hurting me or my position, I'm okay with it, because it's not harming me. And it's nothing really direct. But then it annoys you and you say something about it. You almost want to dish it back, really bad.

Gabriella, a waitress, tells of her experiences in the restaurant where both managers and cooks sexually harassed the waitresses. One boss in particular,

> used to come to all the girls and put his arm around them and schmooze them. But he never really, I mean he never really, you know, never really tried anything.

Irene also told a story about her boss:

> My former boss would come up behind me and rub against me . . . it got to be kind of a joke.

Helen, a medical technician, describes her response to her boss's unwanted touching:

> [My boss] kept wanting to, I don't know, touch you . . . I would joke with him about it and make light of it and just kind of blow him off.

Critical Interpretation of the Discourse   Joking, making light of the situation, and 'blowing off' the harasser were common responses to sexual harassment. These responses frame the experience in a way that reduces their intensity and importance. It should be noted that one woman who was harassed actually filed charges against the man, but when no one would support her she rescinded the charge, redefined or reframed the harassment as 'just touchy feely' and 'made a joke of it'. These discursive techniques frame sexual harassment as a trivial matter. In addition, Gabriella's explanation that 'he never really tried anything' suggests that sexual harassment is perceived in degrees of severity. Putting one's arms around a subordinate may be less offensive than threatening a subordinate with the loss of her job if she does not engage in sexual activity with the man. By excusing the 'lesser offense' it is more easily trivialized and less likely to receive serious consideration as a problem. However, it is important to note that trivializing the harassment may also provide a coping mechanism for the victim.

Example 3: Personalizing the Public

Uta, a registered nurse (RN), recounts an experience of sexual harassment that she encountered as a nursing student:

> When I was in nursing school I was in surgery and I was extremely nervous, the surgeon was one of the big guys on the staff. They were doing surgery on a woman; and they were cutting her abdomen open; and, they got down to her pubic hair and were joking about it. They looked at me and made some comment about my red hair and then made a comment about whether my pubic hair matched the hair on my head. I thought I would die.

Vanessa, who is also a nurse, told the following story:

> [A doctor] came up to me a couple of days ago and said he gets turned on by pregnant women [the respondent was pregnant at the time]. I told him I felt sorry for him . . . It was really an injustice to his wife.

Yvonne also describes a sexual harassment situation that she encountered:

> I had an operator . . . who would constantly ask me for sex. Every morning he be waiting to ask me for sex; and, he would always tell me he'd pay me, that he'd give me his check. Whatever it took for me to have sex with him. I brought my boyfriend on the job and he stopped [respondent laughed].

Critical Interpretation of the Discourse   The first story, about the nurse who is questioned about whether the color of her pubic hair matches the color of the hair on her head, demonstrates personalizing the public in two ways. First, the story is framed in such a way that the woman depicts herself as embarrassed nearly to death. This type of embarrassment can silence a story because the embarrassed individual is fearful of losing face or is too overwhelmed to discuss the issue in public. The second way that the story reflects personalization is that the nurse takes the comments as though they are directed at her personally. Although another woman is also being demeaned, the nurse does not frame the story as though the doctors are belittling women in general. In another scenario provided by Clair (1993), a female surgeon, Melissa, witnessed a similar situation. Unlike the nurse, however, the surgeon frames the issue quite differently:

> When you're a surgeon and you do surgery on women, and there are male surgeons, there are lots of inappropriate comments made – often sexually based, often degrading comments that they would never make if the woman patient was awake, and that as a woman surgeon bothers you a lot . . . [Some men] have preconceived notions of women as people and how they are as patients that I don't consider to be valid.

The surgeon's encounter is similar yet different from the nurse's encounter. Although both witness male surgeons making inappropriate sexual comments about the patient, the nurse seems to have encountered only one such incident that is directed at the patient and at herself. Because only one incident is discussed and the nurse does not speculate upon the commonness of this practice, the discourse reinforces a personal, singular, isolated frame around the subject of sexual harassment. On the other hand, the surgeon implies that this sort of sexual commentary is common practice in the operating room, which may contribute to her framing the issue as directed at 'women' in general rather than at any single individual.

A second way that personalizing can be achieved is by framing the situation as an interpersonal encounter rather than an organizational or socio-political encounter. For example, the pregnant nurse, who is told by the doctor that he is 'turned on' by pregnant women, suggests that the doctor's behavior is an 'injustice to his wife'. To frame the behavior as an injustice to the doctor's wife, rather than an injustice to the nurse or to women in general, relegates the sexual harassment to a violation of the man's commitment to his wife.

A similar framing is evident in the story of the operator who continually asked for sex from his co-worker. She tells us that he even offered his paycheck for sexual services. This woman tells us that she brought her 'boyfriend on the job' and this was enough to make the operator stop sexually harassing her. Once again the sexual harassment is framed as a matter of interpersonal concern. In other words, the woman allows the boyfriend to take action rather than a more public institution. As Clair suggests, 'By calling on the boyfriend or husband to protect the interests of the woman, they make those interests separate from organizational interests. Consequently, the organization is relieved of its accountability/ responsibility in the matter and the dominant ideology remains undamaged' (1993: 131).

These three examples of framing devices show how women discursively participate in the current patriarchal system. However, as mentioned earlier, exceptions do exist. They might also be explored via similar or inverted frames. For example, those women who did not hesitate to name sexual harassment, exemplify the opposite of denotative hesitancy. One might seek out empowering or counter-hegemonic frames by inverting the current frames or by looking for new and different frames.

Pragmatic Implications

Conducting a discursive frame analysis concerning sexual harassment is more than an academic exercise. Clair's (1993) study indicates that a few women are moving toward new definitions of sexual harassment. Some women are talking about hiring attorneys. Others are telling harassers 'that is sexual harassment.' As sexual harassment receives more attention from the public (for example, the Clarence Thomas/Anita Hill Senate hearings or the US Navy's Tailhook scandal of sexual harassment) and is less sequestered, its framing becomes of crucial interest to individuals, marginalized groups, organizational management, and the public at large.

Discussions of sexual harassment have moved beyond the geographical boundaries of the United States. Exposés of the subject have appeared in mainland China's newspapers. In a global community of technology the media provide their account of sexual harassment in society and that means that the frames they use will reflect certain interests. Discursive analyses of news events covered by the media contribute to an understanding of how people come to view a topic (van Dijk, 1991). By exploring the frames that are used we can come to understand whose interests are being served.

In addition, definitions of sexual harassment are being argued in courtrooms and debated among legislators. Policies and procedures for dealing with sexual harassment are being written by organizational managers. As laws are enacted concerning sexual harassment it is paramount that citizens keep a watchful eye on how these laws, policies, and procedures are being framed. Exactly whom do the laws and policies protect? Discursive frame analysis can help to answer these questions and open the dialogue concerning issues of power and domination.

Conclusion

In this chapter we have tried to provide a sense of how critical discourse analysts study everyday organizational life. The focus has been on illustrating how such discourse studies make explicit the connections among everyday discourse, sense-making practices, larger social structures, and the enactment of power relations. Critical discourse studies of organizations are characterized by the development of robust theoretical perspectives which are applied, sometimes intuitively, to 'real life' data. In many respects, discourse analysts are involved in a creative construction of meaning, attempting to construct a sensible, insightful reading out of data that are frequently incomplete and obscure. The work is important, however, because organizations pervade every dimension of our lives, strongly shaping our identities and our experience of the world. Understanding how organizations work is fundamental to maintaining a critical impulse to how we view the world. In a very real sense, figuring out the relationships among discourse, organizations, and power is fundamental to the maintenance of a democratic society, because it is at the level of everyday life that participatory practices are either maintained or eroded. It is our hope that everyone adopts a communication ethic, critical or otherwise, that serves to critique authoritarianism and preserves and enhances everyday democracy.

Recommended Reading

Boden (1994): a conversation analysis approach to the study of organizational talk. Stresses the notion of organizations as constantly produced and reproduced through the everyday discourse of its members. Uses Anthony Giddens's 'structuration theory' as its conceptual framework.

Boje (1991): argues that organizational stories must be studied not as self-contained entities that a teller relates to an audience, but rather as discursive acts that are co-produced by multiple organization members. A good example of the relationship between discourse and organization as process.

Clair (1993): a more detailed account of the research on sexual harassment discussed in the final section of this chapter.

Collinson (1988): examines the relationship between humor, class, power, and the construction of masculine identity in an organizational setting. One of the few studies that employs qualitative methods to examine the social construction of *masculinity* rather than femininity.

Helmer (1993): one of the relatively few critical organization studies that examines the relationship between power and storytelling in its naturalistic context.

Mumby (1987): an early example of the attempt to make explicit the relationships among discourse, ideology, and power in organizations through the analysis of a single organizational story.

Rosen (1988): a Marxist analysis employing ethnographic methods that examines how organizational rituals can function to reproduce the political and economic relations in an organization. Places the office Christmas party in a new light!

van Dijk (1993c): an excellent overview of the theoretical principles that underlie a critical approach to discourse analysis.

References

Acker, J. (1990) 'Hierarchies, jobs, bodies: a theory of gendered organizations', *Gender and Society*, 4: 139–58.

Alvesson, M. and Billing, Y. (1992) 'Gender and organization: towards a differentiated understanding', *Organization Studies*, 13: 73–102.

Bateson, G. (1972) *Steps to an Ecology of Mind*. New York: Ballantine.

Boden, D. (1994) *The Business of Talk: Organizations in Action*. Cambridge: Polity Press.

Boje, D. (1991) 'The storytelling organization: a study of performance in an office-supply firm', *Administrative Science Quarterly*, 36: 106–26.

Brown, M.H. (1985) 'That reminds of a story: speech action in organizational socialization', *Western Journal of Speech Communication*, 49: 27–42.

Burawoy, M. (1979) *Manufacturing Consent: Changes in the Labor Process under Monopoly Capitalism*. Chicago: University of Chicago Press.

Calás, M. and Smircich, L. (1991) 'Voicing seduction to silence leadership', *Organization Studies*, 12: 567–602.

Chapman, P. (1994) 'Sexual harassment, bureaucratic silence: implications for organizational communication'. Unpublished MA thesis, Department of Communication, Purdue University, West Lafayette, IN.

Clair, R.P. (1993) 'The use of framing devices to sequester organizational narratives: hegemony and harassment', *Communication Monographs*, 60: 113–36.

Clair, R.P. (1994) 'Resistance and oppression as a self-contained opposite: an organizational communication analysis of one man's story of sexual harassment', *Western Journal of Communication*, 58: 235–62.

Clair, R.P., McGoun, M.J. and Spirek, M.M. (1993) 'Sexual harassment responses of working women: an assessment of current communication oriented typologies and perceived effectiveness of response', in G.L. Kreps (ed.), *Communication and Sexual Harassment in the Workplace*. Cresskill, NJ: Hampton. pp. 209–33.

Clegg, S. (1975) *Power, Rule, and Domination*. London: Routledge and Kegan Paul.

Collinson, D. (1988) 'Engineering humor: masculinity, joking and conflict in shop-floor relations', *Organization Studies*, 9: 181–99.

Collinson, D. (1992) *Managing the Shopfloor: Subjectivity, Masculinity, and Workplace Culture*. New York: Walter de Gruyter.

Deetz, S. and Mumby, D.K. (1985) 'Metaphors, information, and power', in B. Ruben (ed.), *Information and Behavior 1*. New Brunswick, NJ: Transaction. pp. 369–86.

Essed, P. (1991) *Understanding Everyday Racism*. Newbury Park, CA: Sage.

Essed, P. (1992) 'Alternative knowledge sources in explanations of racist events', in M.L. McLaughlin, M.J. Cody and S.J. Read (eds), *Explaining One's Self to Others: Reason-Giving in a Social Context*. Hillsdale, NJ: Lawrence Earlbaum. pp. 199–224.

Fairclough, N. (1993) 'Critical discourse analysis and the marketization of public discourse: the universities', *Discourse and Society*, 4: 133–68.

Fairhurst, G.T. (1986) 'Male–female communication on the job: literature review and commentary', in M.L. McLaughlin (ed.), *Communication Yearbook 9*. Beverly Hills, CA: Sage. pp. 83–116.

Fairhurst, G.T. (1993) 'The leader–member exchange patterns of women leaders in industry: a discourse analysis', *Communication Monographs*, 60: 321–51.

Ferguson, K. (1984) *The Feminist Case against Bureaucracy*. Philadelphia: Temple University Press.

Foucault, M. (1979) *Discipline and Punish: the Birth of the Prison* (trans. A. Sheridan). New York: Vintage.

Frankenberg, R. (1993) *White Women, Race Matters: the Social Construction of Whiteness*. Minneapolis, MN: University of Minnesota Press.

Gherardi, S. (1994) 'The gender we think, the gender we do in our everyday organizational lives', *Human Relations*, 47: 591–610.

Giddens, A. (1979) *Central Problems in Social Theory: Action, Structure, and Contradiction in Social Analysis*. Berkeley, CA: University of California Press.

Goffman, E. (1974) *Frame Analysis: an Essay on the Organization of Experience*. Cambridge, MA: Harvard University Press.

Gramsci, A. (1971) *Selections from the Prison Notebooks* (trans. Q. Hoare and G. Nowell Smith). New York: International Publishers.

Gutek, B.A. (1985) *Sex and the Workplace: Impact of Sexual Behavior and Harassment on Women, Men, and Organizations*. San Francisco: Jossey-Bass.

Hall, S. (1985) 'Signification, representation, ideology: Althusser and the post-structuralist debates', *Critical Studies in Mass Communication*, 2: 91–114.

Helmer, J. (1993) 'Storytelling in the creation and maintenance of organizational tension and stratification', *The Southern Communication Journal*, 59: 34–44.

Huspek, M. and Kendall, K. (1991) 'On withholding political voice: an analysis of the political vocabulary of a "nonpolitical" speech community', *Quarterly Journal of Speech*, 77: 1–19.

Koch, S. and Deetz, S. (1980) 'Metaphor analysis of social reality in organizations', *Journal of Applied Communication Research*, 9: 1–15.

Loy, P. and Stewart, L. (1984) 'The extent and effects of the sexual harassment of working women', *Sociological Focus*, 17: 31–43.

MacKinnon, C.A. (1979) *Sexual Harassment of Working Women*. New Haven, CT: Yale University Press.

Martin, J. (1990) 'Deconstructing organizational taboos: the suppression of gender conflict in organizations', *Organization Science*, 1: 339–59.

Martin, J., Feldman, M., Hatch, M.J. and Sitkin, S.B. (1983) 'The uniqueness paradox in organizational stories', *Administrative Science Quarterly*, 28: 438–53.

Mumby, D.K. (1987) 'The political function of narrative in organizations', *Communication Monographs*, 54: 113–27.

Mumby, D.K. (1988) *Communication and Power in Organizations: Discourse, Ideology and Domination*. Norwood, NJ: Ablex.

Mumby, D.K. and Putnam, L.L. (1992) 'The politics of emotion: a feminist critique of bounded rationality', *Academy of Management Review*, 17: 465–86.

Mumby, D.K. and Stohl, C. (1992) 'Power and discourse in organization studies: absence and the dialectic of control', *Discourse and Society*, 2: 313–32.

Paludi, M.A. (ed.) (1990) *Ivory Power: Sexual Harassment on Campus*. Albany, NY: State University of New York Press.

Pringle, R. (1988) *Secretaries Talk: Sexuality, Power, and Work*. London: Verso.

Putnam, L.L. and Holmer, M. (1992) 'Framing, reframing, and issue development', in L.L. Putnam and M.E. Roloff (eds), *Communication and Negotiation*. Newbury Park, CA: Sage. pp. 128–55.

Rosen, M. (1985) 'Breakfast at Spiro's: dramaturgy and dominance', *Journal of Management*, 11 (2): 31–48.

Rosen, M. (1988) 'You asked for it: Christmas at the bosses' expense', *Journal of Management Studies*, 25: 463–80.

Salvador, M. and Markham, A. (1995) 'The rhetoric of self-directive management and the operation of organizational power', *Communication Reports*, 8: 45–53.

Schiappa, E. (1991) 'Defining reality: the politics of meaning', unpublished manuscript, Department of Communication, Purdue University, West Lafayette, IN.

Smith, R.C. and Eisenberg, E. (1987) 'Conflict at Disneyland: a root-metaphor analysis', *Communication Monographs*, 54: 367–80.

Stahl, S.D. (1989) *Literary Folklorists and the Personal Narrative*. Bloomington, IN: Indiana University Press.

Strine, M.S. (1992) 'Understanding "how things work": sexual harassment and academic culture', *Journal of Applied Communication Research*, 20: 391–400.

Taylor, B. and Conrad, C.R. (1992) 'Narratives of sexual harassment: organizational dimensions', *Journal of Applied Communication Research*, 20: 401–18.

Trice, H. and Beyer, J. (1984) 'Studying organizational cultures through rites and ceremonials', *Academy of Management Review*, 9: 653–69.

van Dijk, T.A. (1991) *Racism and the Press*. London: Routledge.

van Dijk, T.A. (1993a) 'Editor's foreword to critical discourse analysis', *Discourse and Society*, 4: 131–2.

van Dijk, T.A. (1993b) 'Stories and racism', in D.K. Mumby (ed.), *Narrative and Social Control: Critical Perspectives*. Newbury Park, CA: Sage. pp. 121–42.

van Dijk, T.A. (1993c) 'Principles of critical discourse analysis', *Discourse and Society*, 4: 249–83.

van Dijk, T.A. (1993d) *Elite Discourse and Racism*. Newbury Park, CA: Sage.

West, C. and Zimmerman, D. (1987) 'Doing gender', *Gender and Society*, 1: 125–51.

Witten, M. (1993) 'Narrative and the culture of obedience at the workplace', in D.K. Mumby (ed.), *Narrative and Social Control: Critical Perspectives*. Newbury Park, CA: Sage. pp. 97–118.

Williams, D. (1994) 'The discursive politics of sexual harassment: a feminist poststructuralist reading of the Hill–Thomas hearings', unpublished doctoral dissertation, Department of Communication, Purdue University, West Lafayette, IN.

Wood, J.T. (1992) 'Telling our stories: narratives as a basis for theorizing sexual harassment', *Journal of Applied Communication*, 20: 349–62.

8

Discourse and Politics

Paul Chilton and Christina Schäffner

Discourse and Politics: Introduction

Some philosophers – Descartes is the best known – have defined humans as essentially linguistic animals. Aristotle, on the other hand, famously defined humans as political animals. No doubt both definitions contain a germ of the truth. What political discourse analysts would probably have to claim, if they were to think philosophically, would be that the one definition necessarily involves the other. It is surely the case that politics cannot be conducted without language, and it is probably the case that the use of language in the constitution of social groups leads to what we call 'politics' in a broad sense.

Although the study of language has never been central to the academic disciplines concerned with politics, some political philosophers have from time to time made clear their awareness of the question. In the disciplines concerned with language, it is worth noting that the study of rhetoric – the art of verbal persuasion – was thought of by Greek and Roman writers as a sort of 'political science'. In the Greek polis and in the Roman empire the rhetorical tradition played a part in the training of orators who fulfilled important public functions, including political functions, and to a certain extent provided an apparatus for the critical observation of political verbal behaviour.

In the late twentieth century the massive expansion of print and electronic media means that people are exposed to verbal messages of many kinds, a large proportion of which can be thought of as political in nature, though as we shall note below, what is 'political' is a matter of interpretation. The increased mediation of political messages has important implications. One is that the opportunity for the reception, interpretation and critique of political texts and talk has vastly increased. Another is that the need for awareness and critical evaluation has correspondingly increased. It might be argued that the ability to deal critically with political discourse is natural and need not be studied in depth by academics or anyone else. Against such a view two arguments can be made. The first applies to criticisms of many in-depth studies of human behaviour. Human learning, for instance, is natural in some sense of the term, but this does not preclude the interest and utility of psychological studies of cognition or the education process.

Similarly, political discourse is a complex form of human activity which deserves study in its own right. The second kind of argument is of an ethical nature. Many commentators, and indeed many ordinary people in everyday life, have the feeling that politicians and political institutions are sustained by 'persuasive' or 'manipulative' uses of language of which the public is only half-aware. Such a view was in fact upheld by some of the early rhetors, Isocrates, Plato, Cicero, for example, who suspected that public speakers were able to hoodwink citizens by specious talk. In the twentieth century the notion of total linguistic manipulation was developed into the nightmare political discourse fictionalized in Orwell's *Nineteen Eighty-Four* (1949). Together, these two rationales for political discourse analysis (PDA) contribute not only to intellectual curiosity but also to the concerns of all political animals.

Politics and Political Discourse

Political Science and the Philosophy of Language

In political philosophy the meaning of words has traditionally raised problems and caused anxieties. For instance, questions about the meaning of 'democracy', 'equality', 'freedom', and the like, have been recurrent subjects of debate. Earlier studies assumed that there were 'true' meanings for such terms (Sir George Lewis, 1898), and this tendency has been strong throughout most of the twentieth century. Many 'political scientists', influenced by logical positivism and the Vienna Circle, desired to rid political language of confusion and ambiguity. Interestingly, a similar view was held also in the seventeenth century by Thomas Hobbes, who can be viewed as the founder of modern political science. In the last third of the twentieth century a more relativistic approach emerged. Sartori (1984) has a more flexible approach, while the notion that political concepts may be relative to the 'language' of the polity, and thus 'contestable', comes into clear focus in Gallie (1956), Connolly (1974), Lukes (1975), and Ball et al. (1989). This development was also influenced by the later Wittgenstein (1953) and the work of Austin (1962) and Searle (1969), and the increasing recognition that language was in fact a form of action.

Post-Structuralism and Deconstruction

In the 1980s Anglo-Saxon departments of politics and international relations were influenced by 'continental' philosophy. A key influence was the French social philosopher Michel Foucault, who worked with a notion of 'discourse' which, though it included language practices, did not provide precise linguistic descriptions. The work of Jacques Derrida fostered a notion of 'deconstruction', which pushed relativist interpretations still further. While 'text' is crucial to Derrida, he does not use the theoretical framework of linguistics. There are many books and articles in this vein, but Shapiro (1981; 1984) and der Derian and Shapiro (1989) illustrate the evolution of approaches. What is important is that many political 'scientists' have moved towards the view that both the terms of political debate and the political processes themselves are constituted and communicated through text and talk.

Social-Psychological Approaches

Not entirely incompatible with the above developments, approaches deriving from social psychology have included both qualitative and quantitative methods that aimed to demonstrate the non-rational and non-explicit aspects of political behaviour. Harold Lasswell, influenced by Sapir's anthropological linguistics, held a view of language which, together with the view that the 'science' of politics was the 'science of power', led him to quantitative investigations of the political 'functions' of language. He also distinguished analytically between *syntax*, *style* and *semantics*, concentrating on the last, which he defined in terms of political slogans and symbols (Lasswell et al., 1949). Another important approach has been the study of political myths, and the symbolic and ritual dimension of political processes (Edelman, 1964; 1971).

In the 1960s and 1970s some political scientists sought quantifiable empirical accounts of political verbal behaviours. They thought of communication as a simple encoding–decoding process (for example, Graber, 1976). A quantitative semantic approach has also been attempted in the case of political ideologies and international conflict (Osgood, 1979; Leites, 1963; Tetlock, 1985). Though such studies use the psychologist's rather than the linguist's methods, they do seek a descriptive precision absent in approaches influenced by the philosophical perspective.

Linguistics and Political Discourse

Linguists have shared some of the above perspectives – for instance, the critical perspective and the general epistemological stance according to which political realities are constructed in and through discourse. Some, however, would insist on political objectivity (Wilson, 1990). Where linguists most obviously differ from their colleagues in departments of politics is in the way their research is informed by theories and methods derived from linguistics. The variety of approaches they have utilized may indeed appear quite bewildering. Furthermore, they have been interested in an extraordinary variety of political issues and phenomena. In order to convey some of this variety, we consider three broad 'literatures' in PDA, which are discourses in their own right and are related, in part at least, to the historical specificities of particular countries and cultures.

French Approaches

What is noteworthy about the 'French school' is its combination of political scientists, political philosophers (principally *marxisants*), and a characteristically French brand of linguistics. Two main methodological tendencies are apparent.

The first is 'political lexicometry', a computer-aided statistical approach to the political lexicon, developed by the Laboratoire lexicométrie et textes politiques, founded in 1967 and based at the École Normale Superieure at Saint-Cloud. The method establishes a corpus (for example, texts produced by the French Communist Party) consisting of separate texts and makes comparisons on the basis of relative frequencies (see Bonnafous and Tournier, 1995 for summary). Broadly speaking, such a methodology can only be related to macro-sociological and historical questions of political discourse. For example, one study shows how the relative frequency of the words *travailleur* and *salarié* varies significantly between French trade unions, reflecting different political ideologies, and how also the frequency changes over time (early 1970s to late 1980s), reflecting chronologic shifts in political ideologies (Groupe de Saint-Cloud, 1982; Bonnafous and Tournier, 1995). As the Saint-Cloud group themselves acknowledge, quantitative studies provide only the raw data for interpretive political analysis.

The second methodological tendency amongst political discourse analysts, overlapping with the Saint-Cloud group, is diverse. One strand was influenced by Althusser's (1970) Marxist analysis of society emphasizing the notion of the 'state apparatus' (Pêcheux, 1975; 1990). This is congenial to a discourse approach that sees the political phenomenon of the state as involving a complex set of discourses creating political 'subjects'. Another guiding notion was 'discourse formation', taken from Foucault (1971). These abstract notions, however, mesh with methods of detailed linguistic analysis. Some researchers investigate detailed rhetorical patterns, for example in the presidential campaigns of 1988 and 1995 (Groupe de Saint-Cloud, 1995). The influence of Anglo-Saxon pragmatics (speech acts, conversational implicature, relevance) is also prominent, alongside that of the French linguist Benveniste (1966/1974), whose work on *énonciation* (utterance or discourse) focused on deictic phenomena. This framework enables a sophisticated analyst like Achard, who retains some of the general Althusserian framework, to produce detailed accounts of the political functioning of a very wide range of text types (Achard 1995).

German Approaches

Analysis of political language, political texts and political vocabulary in Germany was largely motivated by specifically German political interests and issues, particularly the historical past of fascism and the subsequent political division into two German states.

In studies of the language of fascism, the focus was originally on words, that is on specific meanings that they had developed and their use or misuse (for example, Klemperer, 1975). More recently, it has been argued that the language of the Third Reich cannot be defined by the linguistic forms but only by their functions. National Socialist language is treated as a social phenomenon, characterized by specific discursive practices (for example, Ehlich, 1989; for a comprehensive survey of the variety of approaches cf. Sauer, 1995). Within the framework of a discursive-historical analysis, persistent argumentation patterns (such as allusions, denial, mitigation) can be seen in, for instance, the discourse of Austrian politicians in speaking about the Nazi past (for example, Wodak, 1989; Wodak and Menz, 1990).

The development from a word-centred linguistic analysis to a text- and action-oriented communicative analysis is also evident in studies on the language (use) of the two German states. In order to compare the semantic structure of the political vocabulary in East and West Germany, the concepts of *Ideologiegebundenheit* (the phenomenon of being ideology-bound) and *ideologische Polysemie* (ideological polysemy) were introduced (Schmidt, 1969; Dieckmann, 1969; 1981) and dominated much of the research in the 1960s and 1970s.

One focus of research has been a critical reflection on the strategic use of political keywords for achieving specific political aims. Under the headings of 'semantic battles' and 'annexation of concepts', strategic operations with words have been analysed: for instance, 'hijacking' terms of political opponents in order to give them a new meaning, or linking a basic value (such as 'solidarity', 'freedom') to a political party in such a way that ultimately the party will be identified with the value (cf. Klein, 1989; Burkhardt et al., 1989; Liedtke et al., 1991).

Some researchers, influenced by Anglo-Saxon pragmatics, conversation analysis, and media studies, have studied organizational principles of linguistic actions (such as turn-taking strategies, schema orientation, speech acts, conversational implicatures) occurring, for example, in interviews with politicians, political speeches and TV debates (Holly, 1990; Grewenig, 1993; Schäffner and Porsch, 1993; Sucharowski, 1985). Heringer (1990) and Krebs (1993) link structures of a political speech to the effects it had had on the hearers.

The process of political transformation in East Germany in 1989–90 and the subsequent German unification offered vast scope for political discourse analysis. A wide spectrum of (mainly pragmatic, sociolinguistic, cognitive linguistic) approaches are applied to study, for example, the changing political lexicon, ritualistic discourse in the former German Democratic Republic, and changes in text types and discursive strategies (for example, Lerchner, 1992; Burkhardt and Fritzsche, 1992; Reiher and Läzer, 1993).

Anglophone Approaches

In this section we include not only British, American and Australian work, but also other work that has been disseminated in English, especially that which originates from the Netherlands and Belgium.

Orwell's informal critical stance toward political discourse was recognized by some British linguists (Fowler, Kress, Hodge, Fairclough), who sought to apply the insights of modern linguistics. Following the linguistic trends of the times, transformational-generative models were influential and provided means of describing certain syntactic forms that had politically pragmatic implications (Fowler et al., 1979). More important, however, in the British and Australian approaches was the 'functional' linguistics of Halliday (1973). This framework made it possible to link linguistic form to social and hence also to political activity. But the tools of anglophone political discourse analysis have been essentially eclectic, drawing particularly on pragmatics, especially the theory of speech acts, implicit meaning of various types (Richardson, 1985; Wilson, 1990; 1991; Blommaert and Verschueren, 1991; 1993), cognitive linguistics (Chilton, 1985), Brown and Levinson's (1987) 'politeness phenomena' (Chilton, 1990), conversation analysis (Atkinson, 1984), and European text analysis as developed by van Dijk (1980). Van Dijk himself applies a range of analytic methods, including textual, pragmatic, ethnomethodological and cognitive approaches, to political discourse and to the critique of racist discourse in the media and elsewhere (van Dijk, 1989; 1994; 1995).

In the United States Chomsky's critique of American foreign policy has been trenchant and controversial. Although he has referred to what are essentially discourse processes, such as 'the manufacture of consent' and 'propaganda', he has not sought to apply linguistic theory in order to analyse them (see, for example, Chomsky, 1988a; 1988b). Chomsky's revolutionary contribution to the discipline of linguistics has no *direct* application to the study of discourse or politics. Those American scholars who have sought to apply linguistic analysis to political discourse have lacked the Marxist perspective of some of the more radical European researchers, and their work often appears to be predicated on a form of linguistic idealism. Bolinger (1980) examines a range of linguistic devices from the point of view of their potential distorting or manipulative effects, a standpoint shared by American rhetorical criticism. Developments in semantic theory have provided insights into an aspect of political discourse which has concerned rhetoricians of all periods – the disturbing role played by metaphor. Lakoff (1996), for instance, examines the metaphorical basis of the different systems of 'morality' assumed by 'conservatives' and 'liberals' in American political culture.

The Linguistic Analysis of Political Discourse

Political Texts and Strategic Functions

The task of political discourse analysis is to relate the fine grain of linguistic behaviour to what we understand by 'politics' or 'political behaviour'. There are two problems that might strike the reader immediately. (1) What is 'political' depends on the standpoint of the commentator. (2) The multiplicity of acts that are performed through language (that is, discourse), can be interpreted as serving many different purposes – not only political, but also heuristic, ludic, informative, etc. Both these problems could be the subject of lengthy discussion, but here we have to limit ourselves to the following points.

With regard to the first problem, we will define as potentially 'political' those actions (linguistic or other) which involve power, or its inverse, resistance. Of course 'power' is a concept that has no accepted definition amongst political theorists, and we do not attempt to resolve the matter here.

With regard to the second problem, we link political situations and processes to discourse types and levels of discourse organization by way of an intermediate level, which we call strategic functions. The notion of *strategic functions* enables analysts of text and talk to focus on details that contribute to the phenomena which people intuitively understand as 'political', rather than on other functions such as the informational, the ludic, etc.

The following strategic functions[1] are proposed for discussion, and are certainly not definitive.

Coercion   Clear examples are speech acts backed by sanctions (legal and physical): commands, laws, edicts, etc. Less obvious forms of coerced behaviour consist of speech roles which people find difficult to evade or may not even notice, such as spontaneously giving answers to questions, responding to requests, etc. Political actors also often act coercively through discourse in setting agendas, selecting topics in conversation, positioning the self and others in specific relationships, making assumptions about realities that hearers are obliged to at least temporarily accept in order to process the text or talk. Power can also be exercised through controlling others' use of language – that is, through various kinds and degrees of censorship and access control.

Resistance, Opposition and Protest   Many of the discourse strategies used by the powerful for coercion may be counter-deployed by those who regard themselves as opposing power. However, there may be specific forms of discourse characteristic of the relatively powerless. Such forms include media (*samizdat* under the Soviet empire, *graffiti* amongst marginalized ethnic groups, posters, etc.) and specific linguistic structures (such as slogans, chants, petitions, appeals, rallies, etc.).

Dissimulation   Political control involves the control of information, which is by definition a matter of discourse control. It may be quantitative or qualitative. Secrecy is the strategy of preventing people receiving information; it is the inverse of censorship, which is the preventing of people giving information. In another mode of dissimulation, information may be given, but be quantitatively inadequate to the needs or interests of hearers ('being economical with the truth', as British politicians put it). Qualitative dissimulation is simply lying, in its most extreme manifestation, but includes various kinds of verbal evasion and denial ('I am not opposed to benefits, but . . .'), or the omission of reference to actors. Euphemism has the cognitive effect of conceptually 'blurring' or 'defocusing' unwanted referents, be they objects or actions. Implicit meanings of various types also constitute a means of diverting attention from troublesome referents.

Legitimization and Delegitimization Political actors, whether individuals or groups, cannot act by physical force alone – except in the extreme case, where it is questionable that one is still in the realm of what is understood by 'politics'. This function is closely linked to coercion, because it establishes the right to be obeyed, that is, 'legitimacy'. Why do people obey regimes that are very different in their policies? Reasons for being obeyed have to be communicated linguistically, whether by overt statement or by implication. The techniques used include arguments about voters' wants, general ideological principles, charismatic leadership projection, boasting about performance, and positive self-presentation. Delegitimization is the essential counterpart: others (foreigners, 'enemies within', institutional opposition, unofficial opposition) have to be presented negatively, and the techniques include the use of ideas of difference and boundaries, and speech acts of blaming, accusing, insulting, etc.

The four strategic functions listed above are closely related to functions found throughout social life, not simply in 'politics'. However, to look at linguistic behaviour and other kinds of communicative behaviour in terms of the four strategic functions is to view those behaviours politically, to politicize them. Throughout this century diverse areas of social life have been rendered political in this fashion. For example, for people in many societies up till relatively recently it appeared natural (not political) to assume that 'foreigners', women, homosexuals, disabled people were inferior or sick as the case may be. Such groups have, however, come to view themselves and to be viewed by others politically. Such politicization has eroded the boundaries between institutional and non-institutional politics.

The four functions can be viewed as interpretive or productive, and in different ways. That is, they can be treated as strategies of political interpretation – in the sense that they can be so used by an analyst, or in the sense that an analyst attributes such functions, as a hypothesis, to the (unconscious) interpretive strategies of hearers. Alternatively, they can be regarded as productive, in the sense that the analyst can attribute them, again as a hypothesis, to the strategies used by speakers in the production of coherent discourse in a given society.

How are the strategies enacted by choice of language? Such a question can only be answered by close participatory analysis of the linguistic detail. It is important to remember that we are concerned with text structure, syntax and lexis not for their own sake, but only in so far as they are the means by which speakers and hearers interactively produce complex and diverse meanings. This implies that we are interested in wordings and phrasings because they can be given meanings that are consistent with our background knowledges and values, given the anglophone political culture we the authors and you the readers inhabit. It also means that political discourse analysis, despite the importance of precise and rigorous linguistic description, is an activity in which the analyst is engaged.

Granted that what is 'political' depends on the participants, societies generally have institutionalized discourses communicated through a cluster of different types of texts and forms of talk. Such a cluster can be seen from two perspectives. A first group comprises texts that discuss political ideas, beliefs, and practices of a society or some part of it (text producers need not be politicians only). Strictly speaking, this is 'metapolitical discourse'. And a second group consists of texts that are crucial in giving rise to – or, to use the political term, constituting – a (more or less coherent) political or ideological community or group, or party. Such texts may function to constitute and maintain the institutions of an entire polity, or they may operate (also) in some part of the whole, say a political party, or indeed at an individual level. Within this second group one may draw finer distinctions: inner-state (domestic) discourse and inter-state (foreign policy and diplomacy) discourse; internal-political discourse (politicians talking, planning, deciding, etc. among themselves) and external-political discourse (politicians communicating with the public). Different forms of text and talk correspond to these different discourse distinctions.

Linguistic Levels

In linking the strategic functions to linguistic analysis of texts and talk, all levels and aspects of language need to be borne in mind. An analyst of political discourse needs to refer to:

1 *pragmatics* (interaction amongst speakers and hearers)
2 *semantics* (meaning, structure of lexicon)
3 *syntax* (the internal organization of sentences).[2]

The task that political discourse analysis sets itself is to relate the detailed linguistic choices at these levels to the four categories of political interpretation which we have referred to as 'strategic functions'.

There are two paths for investigating the political functioning of linguistic choices. First, one can work from the general linguistic levels, asking the question: what strategic functions are typically fulfilled by, for example, falling intonation, passive syntax, lexical antonyms, presupposed meanings, in discourse? Such a question draws on one's knowledge of the language (and political culture), but can also be the goal of empirical investigation (informed of course by knowledge of the language and culture) of instances of texts and talk.

Second, one may work from texts and transcriptions, using one's understanding of the language and political culture to make clear the links between linguistic choices and strategic functions. This corresponds simply to the question that any citizen under ideal conditions of time and reflective capability might ask: 'Why has X chosen (or why is X obliged) to use such-and-such a pronunciation, intonation, wording, phrasing, text type rather than some other possible one?'

Analysing Political Text and Talk: an Example

In this section we illustrate some selected aspects of the analysis of a transcribed text, namely a speech by the British Prime Minister John Major. In analysing this text, we work from the fine linguistic detail, and ask: 'In which ways can the linguistic choices of the speaker be interpreted as functioning in a politically strategic manner, given the wider political culture and the narrower political context?' Not all relevant phenomena can be commented on directly here, and in particular the important phenomenon of indirectness in meaning is referred to only in passing.

The speech was delivered at the 11th Conservative Party Congress in Bournemouth, England, on 14 October 1994.[3] These annual party conferences are internal events; their main addressees are thus UK nationals, and specifically loyal party members. The Conservative conference took place shortly after the conference of the Labour Party under Labour's new reforming leader, Tony Blair. The Labour Party had moved ideologically towards the political right during the preceding decade, in terms of its economic and social policy, as evidenced in such measures as the acceptance of privatization of public industries and the restriction of the trade unions within the Labour Party conference itself. The ideological convergence of Western political parties had become marked following the collapse of communist regimes and socialist ideologies in the late 1980s and early 1990s. The Tory conference can be seen as a reaction to this changed wider context, and in the narrower context as a turn in the ongoing 'macroconversation' of domestic politics.

Pragmatics

Language as Action   Conversation analysis (CA) has shown the subtlety of the management of talk. Participants have turns and variable rights to speak and intervene, depending on the genre and their own status. Such rights or duties to speak or to listen, and the way they are assigned, imposed or claimed in face-to-face interaction, suggest a political dimension in everyday linguistic encounters. And what is more usually thought of as 'political' can be understood in such terms also – that is, as the distribution of rights and duties to speak or listen, give orders or obey, make laws or be law abiding, make broadcasts or be an audience, etc. More generally, democracies and totalitarian regimes can be thought of in terms of their characteristic means of the control of discourse. From city states to large modern states the organization of the political 'conversation' defines the nature of the polity.

The linguistic details of talk can be seen to be far from accidental, but delicately structured and functional in the management of social, and thus potentially political, relationships. Given a particular setting or purpose, one turn will have an unmarked and marked, or 'preferred' and 'dis-preferred' response. Speech acts (offers, orders, admissions, etc.), capable of being understood as threatening to one or the other of the participants ('face threatening acts'), will be mitigated or disguised in various linguistic ways, including euphemisms, justifications ('accounts'), appeal to common interests, to authority, and so forth. Even when a stretch of talk or text is apparently monologic, it usually involves implicit dialogic organization, reflecting oppositional discourses in the surrounding political culture.[4]

The notion of speech acts is central to political discourse analysis, because it dissolves the everyday notion that language and action are separate. Among many attempts at classifying speech acts, Searle (1969) usefully distinguished the following, which can be seen to have direct relevance to political discourse: *representatives* (truth claims), *directives* (commands, requests), *commissives* (promises, threats), *expressives* (prais-ing, blaming), *declaratives* (proclaiming a constitution, announcing an election, declaring war). Speech acts can only be effectively performed under certain conditions ('felicity conditions'), which in the case of politically relevant speech acts may include complex conditions such as the power or status of the speaker, the institutional location, the holding of an election, and the style of language used.

Neither conversational dialogue nor speech acts occur without the participants being assigned particular speaking and hearing roles, which may involve a social and political 'role', or 'place', or 'position', in a broader sense. You may be 'positioned' as someone who speaks, gives orders, gives advice, or gives the 'facts'; or you may be 'positioned' as someone who listens, takes orders, takes advice, or accepts the 'facts'. Analysts of political discourse frequently find that pronouns and the meanings associated with them give a kind of map of the socio-political relationships implicit in a discourse.[5]

The Leader and Other Subjects   The speaker in our sample text, John Major, engages in (and reproduces) a genre which constitutes very par-ticular relationships that are not only linguistic, but also social and political. This works in two ways: on the one hand, there is the set of relationships between addresser, addressees, and third-party 'overhearers' or observers; and on the other hand, there is the set of political actors in his political universe, and their interrelationships, referred to or presupposed by the speaker, though not necessarily addressed. These relationships are most obviously mediated by pronouns, which delineate a social or political 'space' in which people and groups have a 'position'.

Amongst the resources of English it is the pronouns *I, you, we, they* (and their variants) that have a special function in producing a social and political 'space' in which the speaker, the audience, and others are 'positioned'. Simple frequency of occurrence of the pronouns *I* (*me, my*) and *we* (*our*) can be indicative: 112 occurrences of *I*, 35 of *my/me*, 125 of *we*, 45 of *our*.

The primary addressees are the delegates present at the conference: 'I can tell the Conference this', 'I'll tell you why'. What is the function of such apparently redundant formulae? Apart from simply preparing hearers to focus on a particular stretch of talk, they simultaneously define the speaker as authoritative source of information or knowledge and define the (potentially critical) audiences as subordinate, uninformed and unknowledgeable ('I wonder how many of you know exactly how many . . . hospital projects have been built . . . I have the latest bulletin', 'I know', 'I understand'. They *coerce* the hearers into certain communication roles and political roles, and they *legitimize*, or rather presuppose the legitimacy of, the speaker. Of course, there are also addressees, members of the party, who are critical (especially with regard to the debate on Europe), and who would need to be persuaded and convinced of the firmness of the leader. Hence the need for the prefatory expressions, and the aggressive perlocutory effect they may have.

In establishing the leader–led, speaker–spoken to, and teacher–taught relationships, Major's text presents him in certain roles, by making 'I' the subject of particular verbs. These verbs belong to semantic fields associated with speaking, feeling, and action. That is, they position Major in the discourse as truthful narrator or messenger on the one hand, and man of action on the other. Thus, there are 25 references to acts of speaking, such as 'I just want to say', 'I'll tell you', 'my message to you'. The role of the politician is almost oracular. He is a guardian of truth, a seer of the future, and a bringer of good tidings: 'Let me give you some good news.' The acts of speaking include the right to criticize and condemn kinds of speaking allegedly indulged in by others: 'take care not to confuse travesty with truth.' They also include the power to utter certain kinds of speech acts, as we will see below.

Above all, and partly in response to criticisms of 'dithering', there are 44 expressions of decision-taking, order-giving, and action: for example, 'I have asked Gillian Shepherd to . . .', 'I asked for a fresh look at . . .', 'I will not tarry . . . But I will take it in my own time.' Some actions, positioning Major on a geopolitical map, are related to movement and travel to places of historic danger, and are embedded in mini-narratives: 'I was in Warsaw – where the first bombs fell in 1939 . . . I flew to Berlin . . . I was in South Africa . . . I spoke to [the South African] Parliament . . . I flew from South Africa to Chequers . . . Boris Yeltsin was my guest.'

In order to demarcate the Conservatives as a party distinct from other parties, the speaker has to assume or manufacture internal consensus – a collective understanding that certain concepts, actions, and relationships are true or correct. The corollary is the assuming or manufacturing of external dissensus, here *vis-à-vis* Labour. In addition, for any party, but especially for the Conservatives, it is important also (though contradictorily, since national dissensus is also necessary to their position) to claim that the consensus extends to the nation as a whole. This is a *legitimizing function* in the narrow as well as in the broader context. One of the principal ways in which politicians position themselves and others in relation to their parties, their government, their potential electors, and their nation is the use of the pronoun *we/us/our/ours*. In ordinary conversation *we* would usually include the speaker and the hearer(s); in Major's speech, and in political discourse generally, *we* (and its related forms) is often open to several different understandings of its intended referents.

Thus, 'we' may include the speaker, the hearers in the hall, and conceivably other hearers who consider themselves to be either members of the party or its supporters. It is given sentence-initial position, or syntactic focus, and/or (phonetic) stress. Contextually it excludes Labour ('they', 'them'). And the associated verbs come from lexical fields concerned with belief, conflict, moral rectitude, and provision (giving the good life to others). It is also striking, and consistent with other ideological elements of this discourse, that property and ownership concepts are involved in the use of the possessive form ('our', etc.). The following is a sample (underlining as in the original):

> how wrong they have been . . . and how right we have been . . . it is we who have . . . We have won . . . we've beaten . . . we are the Party of the Union . . . they are our issues . . . This is our ground [not Labour's] . . . let me tell them what we stand for . . . our philosophy . . . our opponents.

However, the referents of 'we' can overlap or coincide with at least two other groups. The first is the government, which, in the context, may be conceived as having opponents or dissenters within the Party, whence the exclusive meanings of *we* that apparently refer to the government as distinct from the Conservative hearers as a whole: for example, 'we've listened . . . we've changed our minds.' The second group that 'we' can designate is the entire country: 'we are now doing well as a country.' The *we* forms following this sentence then have an indeterminate meaning that could refer just to Conservatives or to the country, or in some cases to the government, or some combination of any of these. It is unclear what category hearers will conceptualize in these instances, but one possibility is a vague category in which 'the country' and 'the Conservatives' are in some way conflated. Thus Major goes on: 'we have a recovery built to last.' But the pronoun then shifts to a mixture of plausible referents – the Conservatives, the country as a whole, or some indefinite equivalent of the pronoun 'one' – as in the following:

> We [one? the Conservatives? the British?] were told unemployment would go on rising . . . We [Conservatives? government? British?] were told we [Conservatives? government?] wouldn't get interest rates down. We have.

The pronoun's role in blending the references to Conservatives, government and country as a whole is particularly clear in the area of foreign policy, where there are indirect implications that the Labour Party does *not* coincide with national interest. For example:

> That's Britain today. So let's [the audience, all British?] recognise what we [British] are . . . put our own distinctive British mark [on the world] . . . there were appeasers and accommodators [during the Cold War]. But not in our [Conservatives] Party. We [Conservatives] can say with pride. We never heard their voices in this hall [invites inference: unlike the Labour Party conference where some people argued for unilateral nuclear disarmament].

Such utterances are obviously not simply statements of policy. The main function of the speech is to achieve unity within the party at a time of decreasing public support for the Conservatives and decreasing internal party support for the leader John Major. Positioning of this kind can be seen as serving a *legitimizing function* with respect to the leader's authority within the party, but also a *delegitimizing function*, since it draws boundaries between groups, one of which is claimed to be right and the other wrong.

Speech Acts   The 'positioning' of the speaker as an authoritative narrator and messenger and as a decisive actor is crucial.[6] Certain kinds of speech act, for example orders, requests, advisings, warnings, promises, commitments, etc., can only be performed 'felicitously' on the basis of recognized powers. Others, such as explicit or implicit claims to truthfulness, knowledge, or accurate assessment, depend partly on being empirically refutable in the light of events, but many bald assertions appear to be 'felicitous' on no other basis than the authority of the speaker. Let us consider the role of just three of the five types of speech act mentioned above.

The first type of speech act which we may consider is *representatives.* Conservative policy is presented by simple statements and claims, often claims to the truth. These are by far the most numerous types of speech acts, and their typical form is: 'we *are* now doing well . . . Britain is making more, selling more, exporting more.' No evidence is given and the references, especially for 'making' and 'more,' are undecidable for the hearers. This seems prima facie like a flouting of Grice's maxims (Grice, 1975), but in practice the hearers in such situations conventionally tolerate lower levels of information and evidence: challenges or questions are not in the rules of the current game, and the authority of the speaker is paramount. Assertions are in many cases 'boasts' – problematic though essential acts of political rhetoric which have to be hedged or mitigated by politeness devices, and which often also serve the function of obscuring the grounds of exaggerated or over-general claims. A further important point is the following: the assertions only have relevance, in Grice's sense, in relation to background propositions that Major and his audience mutually know have been made in Labour discourse.

The second type of speech act is *directives.* Orders are probably the most power-dependent and the most obvious linguistic realization of the coercion function. It would of course be very odd, given the genre, if explicit orders were instantiated in Major's speech. There are only three marginal examples of the basic imperative form, one being Major's 'order' to 'whisper it gently', mitigating with irony the boast that 'we *are* now doing well as a country', and the imperative 'hang on a minute.' The latter is an order to the audience to delay its response to a boast about hospital provision – an example of the speaker's right to control turn-taking but which may be perceived as friendly interaction with the audience. And it is followed almost immediately in the speech by its counterpart – a pseudo-order to the Labour health spokesman (absent, of course): 'junk it, Blunkett!' This is intended primarily for the immediate audience: a virtual play-acting of the tough boy standing up to his opponent. The purpose here can be understood not merely as refuting criticisms of Conservative health policy, but as expressing the opposition and difference between the parties.

Although there are no genuine orders enacted during the speech there are certainly constative mentions of orders being given to ministers. There are also perhaps examples of indirect speech acts which might be taken by the immediate hearers as requiring some action or change of behaviour on their part: 'it's time to put the marker down', 'it's time for this country to set its sights high again', 'it's time to accelerate this trend.' This may or may not be true for more distant hearers: 'Schools . . . must open up their facilities', 'I don't want councils selling off school playing fields.'

Closely related to these examples are numerous speech acts in Major's discourse using the phrase 'let's' (not 'let us,' which is open to interpretation as a request for permission, as in 'let me,' which he does use quite frequently): 'So let's have the courage to look forward', 'So let's recognize what we are. Look with confidence at the new world.' The negative form is: 'don't let us fool ourselves.' The processes referred to here are mental, and not susceptible to being ordered in any case. The speech act in question here might be called an 'urging', and is characteristically performed by leaders.

The third type of speech act is *commissives*. Explicit commissives (promises, threats, offerings) will be typically made with great caution, though politicians will certainly want to *appear* to be making them. Such promises are recognized idiomatically as 'empty'. Various forms of pragmatic hedging or semantic vagueness will accompany the most explicitly signalled promise performatives (*dissimulation function*). For example:

> Since we are making a lasting change to pre-school opportunities, we will have to phase in the introduction of this extra provision. But what I am doing today is giving you a cast-iron commitment that it will happen. And I'm giving you that commitment now, so that Gill Shepherd can start consulting on it next week.

A 'cast-iron' commissive is presumably intended to reassure, although, since the phrase is a cliché, an audience may not be convinced. Moreover, the speaker does not indicate what the precise nature of the 'provision' would be, nor does the stressed 'will' in fact specify a precise time in the future, nor is it said that Shepherd will do any more than 'consult on it'.[7]

Promises are the inverse of threats (which are close to warnings), and in political discourse the boundary is fragile, since the future action referred to in both acts may be something desirable to some hearers and something undesirable to others. Now Major is addressing, as we have noted, not just the gathered throng but other mediated hearers, and here specifically the bitterly divided community of Northern Ireland. So what do the different potential hearers make of the following, a speech act which Major, as elsewhere, signals before he performs it?

> But let me give this assurance. For as long as is necessary, as many policemen and troops as are necessary will stay on duty in Northern Ireland to protect all the people of Northern Ireland.

Readers will by now have spotted the hedge 'as are necessary'. One can also note the ambiguity of 'assurance' (something that 'reassures' and also some kind of commitment). But the commitment to the presence of troops in Northern Ireland was not something desirable to 'all the people' – to some it was undesirable. Thus, this 'assurance' is a promise to the 'Loyalists' and a threat or warning to the 'Nationalists' and some moderates.

Semantics

Words and Worlds The vocabularies of languages are commonly taken as neutral 'reflections' of the real world. They may be more accurately regarded, however, as constructions of the real that reflect the interests of a speech community – or perhaps the interests of dominant groups in a community. As national languages become elaborated in their functions,[8] different fields of activity (government, religion, judiciary, education, bureaucracy . . .) elaborate their vocabularies. These vocabularies can often be described in terms of structured 'lexical fields'. Such fields are related to cognitive 'schemata' or 'scripts', which are knowledge bases about objects and activities (for example, scripts for social activities such as 'making a purchase', 'voting'). Languages are historically constituted out of discourses, and are not simply a socially or politically neutral resource. Political discourse is one such discourse, not separate from the others but rather drawing on, corroborating or modifying them. Meanings in and across fields are related in various ways (semantic relations). Sometimes the same word has different meanings ('polysemy'), depending on discourse differentiation (for example, 'the source of power' in technological discourse vs 'the source of power' in political discourse). Antonymy is an important relation in political discourse, enabling speakers to communicate opposition and draw boundaries (*legitimizing, delegitimizing functions*).

A crucial conceptual and semantic mechanism in the production of political meanings is metaphor. It is important to note that metaphors are not merely one-off 'rhetorical flourishes', but cognitive devices for forming and communicating conceptualizations of reality which may be in some way problematic. From the interactive perspective, metaphors enable speakers to avoid direct (face-threatening and over-revealing) references. Recurrent metaphors are embedded in languages and cultures and depend both on the human conceptual system and on cultural systems. Selections from these systems may be used to structure particular discourses, and to reproduce those systems symbolically. In political discourse, one may cite two common metaphors: *argument is war* (for example, 'the opposition's claims were shot down in flames'), a metaphor which constitutes adversarial debate as a quasi-natural state of affairs; and *states are containers* (for example, 'the minister for external affairs was concerned about foreign penetration of the security cordon'), which constitutes the geographically and culturally bounded 'sovereign' state as the natural unit of international relations.[9]

Marketing Metaphors: the Real Thing	The lexical fields appearing in John Major's speech are selections from the larger fields available in the language. As one would expect, politics and administration are well instantiated. Equally, the conventional *argument is war* metaphor appears: 'We have won the battle of ideas – it is an astonishing triumph.' Metaphor works by appropriating one taken-for-granted field of knowledge and applying it to another. One frequently used field in Major's speech is the highly lexicalized field of the market economy: this field is projected metaphorically onto other domains, and the metaphorical projection has several ramifications. The following extract is evidence of this:

> What the Labour Party has done is to study our instincts and attitudes, and then go away and **market test** them . . . But it is one thing for the Labour Party to commit grand larceny[10] on our language. It is one thing for them to say what **market research** has told them people would like to hear. But it is quite another to **deliver** it . . .
>
> **Buying** Tory policy from Labour is like **buying a Rolex on the street corner**. It may bear the name. But you know it's **not real**. Our task is to **promote** the **real thing** and expose the **counterfeit** . . . As for this **new, biologically improved** Labour Party. It may well **wash blander**. But I'd give it a **shelf life** of under three years. (bold added)

The bold words belong to the semantic field of the market, and in fact correspond to a structured script (*market research→promotion→sell→ delivery*). Further, the phrases 'a Rolex' and 'on the street corner' are dependent on background knowledge concerning economic value, what is 'real' and what is 'counterfeit'. Understanding the metaphor requires the audience to know and share certain values. Certain consequences follow. If politics is marketing, then policies are saleable commodities, and commodities are by definition a form of property.

This cluster of concepts is linked to another chain of metaphors that are responsible for the coherence of the above passage. Because policies are ideas and ideas are conceived of as the same thing as language, 'policies are commodities' entails 'language is a commodity': hence Major speaks of 'our language', the language that 'belongs to' the Conservatives. This makes it possible to construct an argument against the Labour Party that has the following form:

1 Labour's 'language' is Conservative 'language'.
2 Language is a commodity.
3 Commodities are exclusively owned by someone.
4 To use a commodity owned by someone else is to steal that commodity.
5 Therefore, to use Conservative language is to steal that language.

All this is not 'mere' metaphor. First, it is possible that the commodification of policies really is taken to be a 'fact' of political life in Conservative discourse, or that the metaphor leads people to talk, write and act as if it is. Second, whether that is the case or not, the ontology and deontology of the market, its concepts and potential inferences, are taken for granted as a familiar and natural reality to the hearers, a 'ground' on the basis of which metaphors can be developed without being challenged. Granted the free market model as a premise, an argument can be constructed that represents the Labour Party as performing illicit acts, or as being in some sense 'not for real'. Not only does this metaphorical strategy confirm a particular world view based on the supposed naturalness of the 'market' (*legitimizing function*); it also discredits the opponent (*delegitimizing function*).

Syntax

Agency and Focus Much of syntactic organization has to do with concepts and communicative functions that are not directly encoded in the content words of a language's vocabulary, and is therefore less easy to bring to awareness.

It is often relevant to the analyst to investigate two aspects of sentence organization in political discourse: 'thematic roles' and 'topicalization'. The first have to do with, for example, who (*agent*) is doing what (*processes* of moving, affecting, causing, etc.) to whom (*patient*), where (*location*), why (*cause, purpose*), by what means (*instrument*). The way a speaker assigns such roles can be interpretively linked with particular representations of the political universe, or to claims concerning causation, agency, and responsibility.[11] Consider the examples in Table 8.1, which are simple, hypothetical and context-less, but which indicate some of the potential implications of semantic roles. In the table, *theme* is the term used for an entity caused to move by an agent, and *author* is an entity that appears like an agent but is not the direct cause of the act.

Sentence structure and the semantics of lexical items combine in such a way that they cannot be made sense of without knowing or postulating knowledge of the powers of the governments of sovereign states. Consider, for example, flipping the grammatical subject and object. One can just as well say 'Alf sent Bert to the Balkans' as 'Bert sent Alf to the Balkans', but

Table 8.1

	Subject	Verb	Object	Prepositional phrases
(1)	The government	sent	troops	to the Balkans
	agent	*cause, motion*	*theme*	*goal*
(2)	Troops	were sent		by the government
	theme	*cause, motion*		*agent*
				to the Balkans
				goal
(3)	Troops	were sent		to the Balkans
	theme	*cause, motion*		*goal*
(4)	Troops	went		to the Balkans
	author (or *agent*)	*motion*		*goal*

what about 'troops sent the government to the Balkans'? Some might say that the latter is in some way 'ungrammatical'. Or one might say that it is still grammatical, but that the semantic roles are anomalously assigned, given the current real world in which the sovereignty of states includes the power of governments to order troops. This relationship, although essential for understanding the sentence, may be made in varying degrees implicit (*dissimulation function*). Sentence (1) in Table 8.1 seems to make the relationship clearest in the most syntactically neutral form. The passive sentences (2) and (3) may be felt to express the same relationship less directly (although the end position may, in context, give special emphasis). But in English the passive construction can omit overt reference to the agent completely, as in (3). In (4) 'troops' may be implicitly understood as the agent of their own actions, contrary to background knowledge, and though both causality and agency may be understood, neither is *overtly* expressed. Thus an event can be syntactically encoded in various ways.

The second dimension of sentence structure has to do with what the speaker wishes to indicate as the 'topic' in the ongoing universe of discourse, and with what he or she wishes to present as 'new information'. 'Topics' tend to be the first element in English sentences; 'new information' tends to be phonologically stressed or in end position. The word order of sentences interacts with intonation and stress, and enables speakers to selectively focus on elements of the political universe, and in this fashion to constrain the real-time processing of the hearers.

The political functions of such choices will vary according to context, but it is clear for instance that sentence (1) might be used when claiming credit, or apportioning blame, according as the speaker is or is not the government itself (*legitimizing, delegitimizing function*).

Agents of Change   Concepts of temporal stability are coded into the basic grammatical categories: nouns tend to refer to more static, atemporal, and discrete phenomena, verbs to the fleeting, the temporal, and the dynamic. Speakers of English have certain choices as to the encoding of the involvement of agents in acts of causation.

Traditional Conservative ideology in general gravitates around the concept of *change*. It is opposed to planned attempts to alter the status quo and impose preconceived models. However, more recent forms of Conservatism have not opposed certain forms of change and have represented themselves as dynamic. A discourse problem for a Conservative speaker is to reconcile the opposites of change and tradition, movement and stability.

Let us consider the use of the word *change* in Major's speech, comparing intransitive uses (no agency), transitive uses (with a causing agent), and nominalization (not explicitly expressing either):

Intransitive (no agency)
> The political landscape has **changed** in the last few years and it's **changed** again in the last few months . . . Britain has **changed**.
> Foreign affairs: the world **has changed** . . .
> Hope had flowered and the world **had changed** . . .[12]
> Things **are changing** [with reference to Northern Ireland] . . .

Transitive (agency asserted)
> . . . it is we who have **changed** the whole thrust of politics and moved it in our direction . . .
> if we are to **change** the climate against crime . . .
> we have to **change** attitudes . . .
> Lech Walesa, a shipyard worker who helped **change** history . . .

Nominalization
> That's what **our changes** are all about . . .
> after the **Curriculum changes** of recent years, teachers deserve stability . . .
> The **changes** taking place are truly awesome . . .
> Harold Macmillan spoke of the **wind of change** . . .
> Four snapshots of **change** . . .
> I will just say 'no' to **change** which would harm Britain . . .
> **Change** for the sake of **change** would never appeal to any Conservative . . .
> In a world of **bewildering change**, this Party must stand for continuity and stability, for home and health . . .

What is the significance of such patterns of occurrence? A full analysis shows that the transitive expressions of agency are significantly less frequent than the other two groups. Also, they are qualified in various ways (cf. the use of 'if' above). One refers interestingly in quasi-Marxist terms to the Polish leader, and another refers to changes in Conservative education policy. What explains this? Although it is important for Major to claim intention, responsibility and action, it is equally important for him to avoid charges of being 'interventionist'. It is also important for a Conservative leader to maintain a Conservative ideological premise: that planned social and political change in general is not desirable. There is another premise that explains the prevalence of intransitivity and nominalization: that there is a 'natural' order of things and a 'natural' course of events. Thus, intransitive constructions encode the notion that the universe changes independently, and also makes it possible to avoid complex controversial issues of blame and responsibility. Nominalization, as the reader can verify, either performs similar functions (changes just 'take place') or makes Conservative agency indirect or non-specific, while claiming credit ('our changes'). The functions served by such grammatical choices may be interpreted as self-legitimizing, combining with dissimulation.

Conclusion

By showing some of the pragmatic, semantic and syntactic choices made in the text, analyses such as the above bring to conscious consideration the conceptual world constructed in the text, as well as the relationships between the speaker and others that are established during the actual utterance of the text. On the conceptual level, though, such analyses are capable of indicating the current preoccupations of a political actor (whether an individual or a group) in terms of the issues and ideological assumptions that are selected for expression at a particular historical moment. On the interactive level, the analysis shows what the text is *doing* – what social and political positions and relationships it is assuming or producing between actors such as the leader and the conference, the party and the public, the party and the opposition, the country and other countries.

To sum up, the analysis of the sample text illustrates the procedure for interpretively linking linguistic details on the levels of pragmatics, semantics and syntax to the strategic political functions of coercion, resistance, opposition, protest, dissimulation, legitimization and delegitimization. We propose the notion of 'strategic functions', and the particular four 'functions' we have labelled, purely by way of hypothesis. Our claim is that these strategies are enacted by the speaker – as a social actor in the political and cultural context – through linguistic choices. It is for the readers to evaluate the hypothesis in the light of their own social and political experience.

Recommended Reading

Burkhardt et al. (1989)
Chilton (1985)
Chilton (1996)
Ehlich (1989)
Fairclough (1989)
Hodge and Kress (1993)
Klein (1989)
Liedtke et al. (1991)
Mehan and Wertsch (1988)

Van Dijk (1989)
Wilson (1990)
Wodak (1989)
Wodak and Menz (1990)

Notes

1 For 'functions' cf. Jakobson (1960), Halliday (1973); for 'strategic' cf. Habermas (1979, 1981).
2 Phonetics and phonology are excluded for reasons of space, although in political discourse analysis it is important in general to consider (i) the phonetic resources for oratorical delivery (pauses, stress, volume, pitch) and (ii) the regional and class associations of particular accents, reproducing social and geographical structures of the polity.
3 The transcription used here is the official text issued by the Conservative Party News Department of the Conservative Central Office. Only illustrative passages are quoted here.
4 This point was made by Volosinov (1973).
5 Cf. Althusser's (1970) notion of 'interpellation of the subject'.
6 Such authority is of course also established by virtue of his different concurrent roles defined by the particular speech situation (not just the man John Major, but also Prime Minister, Conservative Party Leader, conference speaker).
7 As it turned out, in summer 1995 the Conservative government announced a controversial 'voucher' scheme for pre-school education.
8 Cf. Haugen (1966).
9 For research on metaphors in political discourse see, for example, Chilton (1985; 1996), Chilton and Lakoff (1995), Schäffner (1991), and from the perspective of a political scientist, Opp de Hipt (1987).
10 'Grand larceny' is defined by the *OED* as theft of 'property . . . of more than 12 pence in value'.
11 Cf. Hodge and Kress (1993), Kress and Trew (1978), van Dijk (1995).
12 The formulation 'the world has/had changed' is actually used three times in the section on foreign affairs.

References

Achard, P. (1995) 'Formation discursive, dialogisme et sociologie', *Langages*, 117: 82–95.
Althusser, L. (1970) *Essays on Ideology*. London: Verso.
Atkinson, M. (1984) *Our Masters' Voices*. London: Methuen.
Austin, J. (1962) *How To Do Things with Words*. The William James Lectures, 1955. Oxford: Clarendon Press.
Ball, T., Farr, J. and Hanson, R.L. (1989) *Political Innovation and Conceptual Change*. Cambridge: Cambridge University Press.
Benveniste, E. (1966/1974) *Problèmes de linguistique générale*, 2 vols. Paris: Gallimard.
Blommaert, J. and Verschueren, J. (1991) 'The pragmatics of minority politics in Belgium', *Language in Society*, 20: 503–31.
Blommaert, J. and Verschueren, J. (1993) 'The rhetoric of tolerance or, what police officers are taught about migrants', *Journal of Intercultural Studies*, 14 (1): 49–63.
Bolinger, D. (1980) *Language – the Loaded Weapon: the Use and Abuse of Language Today*. London and New York: Longman.
Bonnafous, S. and Tournier, M. (1995) 'Analyse du discours, lexicométrie, communication et politique', *Mots*, 117: 67–81.
Brown, P. and Levinson, S. (1987) *Politeness: Some Universals in Language Usage*. Cambridge: Cambridge University Press.

Burkhardt, A. and Fritzsche, K.P. (eds) (1992) *Sprache im Umbruch: Politischer Sprachwandel im Zeichen von 'Wende' und 'Vereinigung'*. Berlin: de Gruyter.

Burkhardt, A., Hebel, F. and Hoberg, R. (eds) (1989) *Sprache zwischen Militär und Frieden: Aufrüstung der Begriffe?* Tübingen: Narr.

Chilton, P. (1985) 'Words, discourse and metaphors: the meanings of *deter, deterrent* and *deterrence*', in P. Chilton (ed.), *Language and the Nuclear Arms Debate*. Pinter: London. pp. 103–27.

Chilton, P. (1990) 'Politeness and Politics', *Discourse and Society*, 1 (2): 201–24.

Chilton, P. (1996) *Security Metaphors: Cold War Discourse from Containment to Common House*. New York: Peter Lang.

Chilton, P. and Lakoff, G. (1995) 'Foreign policy by metaphor', in C. Schäffner and A. Wenden (eds), *Language and Peace*. Aldershot: Dartmouth. pp. 37–59.

Chomsky, N. (1988a) 'Political discourse and the propaganda system', in N. Chomsky (ed.), *Language and Politics* (ed. C.P. Otero). Montreal: Black Rose Books. pp. 662–97.

Chomsky, N. (1988b) 'Politics and language', in N. Chomsky (ed.), *Language and Politics* (ed. C.P. Otero). Montreal: Black Rose Books. pp. 610–31.

Connolly, W. (1974) *The Terms of Political Discourse*. Lexington, MA: D.C. Heath.

Der Derian, J. and Shapiro, M.J. (1989) *International/Intertextual Relations*. Lexington, MA: Lexington Books.

Dieckmann, W. (1969) *Sprache in der Politik: Einführung in die Pragmatik und Semantik der politischen Sprache*. Heidelberg: Sprachwissenschaftliche Studienbücher.

Dieckmann, W. (1981) *Politische Sprache: Politische Kommunikation*. Heidelberg: Carl Winter Universitätsverlag.

Edelman, M. (1964) *The Symbolic Uses of Politics*. Chicago: Chicago University Press.

Edelman, M. (1971) *Politics as Symbolic Action*. New York: Academic Press.

Ehlich, K. (ed.) (1989) *Sprache im Faschismus*. Frankfurt: Suhrkamp.

Fairclough, N. (1989) *Language and Power*. London: Longman.

Foucault, M. (1971) *L'Ordre du discours*. Paris: Gallimard.

Fowler, R., Hodge, B., Kress, G. and Trew, T. (1979) *Language and Control*. London: Routledge and Kegan Paul.

Gallie, W.B. (1956) 'Essentially contested concepts', *Proceedings of the Aristotelian Society*, New Series, 56: 167–98.

Graber, D.A. (1976) *Verbal Behaviour and Politics*. Urbana, IL: University of Illinois Press.

Grewenig, A. (ed.) (1993) *Inszenierte Information: Politik und strategische Kommunikation in den Medien*. Opladen: Westdeutscher Verlag.

Grice, P. (1975) 'Logic and conversation', in P. Cole and J. Morgan (eds), *Syntax and Semantics 3: Speech Acts*. New York: Academic Press. pp. 41–58.

Groupe de Saint-Cloud (1982) *La Parole syndicale: étude du vocabulaire confédéral des centrales ouvrières françaises (1971–1976)*. Paris: Presses Universitaires de France.

Groupe de Saint-Cloud (1995) *Présidentielle: regards sur les discours télévisés*. Paris: INA-Nathan.

Habermas, J. (1979) *Communication and the Evolution of Society*. London: Heinemann.

Habermas, J. (1981) *Theorie des kommunikativen Handelns*. Frankfurt: Suhrkamp.

Halliday, M.A.K. (1973) *Explorations in the Functions of Language*. London: Edward Arnold.

Haugen, E. (1966) 'Dialect, language, nation', *American Anthropologist*, 68: 922–35.

Heringer, H.J. (1990) *'Ich gebe Ihnen mein Ehrenwort': Politik, Sprache, Moral* (Beck'sche Reihe BSR 425). Munich: Beck'sche Verlagsbuchhandlung.

Hodge, R. and Kress, G. (1993) *Language as Ideology*, 2nd edn. London, New York: Routledge.

Holly, W. (1990) *Politikersprache: Inszenierung und Rollenkonflikte im informellen Sprachhandeln eines Bundestagsabgeordneten*. Berlin: de Gruyter.

Jakobson, R. (1960) 'Closing statement: linguistics and poetics', in T.A. Sebeok (ed.), *Style in Language*. Cambridge, MA: MIT Press; New York: Wiley. pp. 350–77.

Klein, Josef (ed.) (1989) *Politische Semantik: Beiträge zur politischen Sprachverwendung*. Opladen: Westdeutscher Verlag.

Klemperer, V. (1975) *LTI: Notizbuch eine Philologen*. Leipzig: Reclam.

Krebs, B.-N. (1993) *Sprachhandlung und Sprachwirkung: Untersuchungen zur Rhetorik, Sprachkritik und zum Fall Jenninger*. Berlin: Erich Schmidt Verlag.

Kress, G.R. and Trew, A.A. (1978) 'Ideological transformation of discourse; or how *The Sunday Times* got its message across', *Journal of Pragmatics*, 2 (4): 311–29.

Lakoff, G. (1996) *Moral Politics: What Conservatives Know that Liberals Don't*. Chicago: Chicago University Press.

Lasswell, H.D. and Leites, N. et al. (1949) *Language of Politics: Studies in Quantitative Semantics*. New York: G.W. Stewart.

Leites, N. (1963) *A Study of Bolshevism*. Glencoe, IL: Free Press.

Lerchner, G. (ed.) (1992) *Sprachgebrauch im Wandel: Anmerkungen zur Kommunikationskultur in der DDR vor und nach der Wende*. Frankfurt am Main: Peter Lang.

Lewis, Sir G. (1898) *Remarks on the Use and Abuse of Political Terms*. Oxford: Clarendon Press.

Liedtke, F., Wengeler, M. and Böke, K. (eds) (1991) *Begriffe besetzen: Strategien des Sprachgebrauchs in der Politik*. Opladen: Westdeutscher Verlag.

Lukes, S. (1975) *Power: a Radical View*. Atlantic Highlands, NJ: Humanities Press.

Mehan, H. and Wertsch, J. (1988) *Discourse of the Nuclear Arms Debate*, special issue of *Multilingua*, 7 (1–2).

Opp de Hipt, M. (1987) *Denkbilder in der Politik: Der Staat in der Sprache von CDU und SPD*. Opladen: Westdeutscher Verlag.

Orwell, G. (1949) *Nineteen Eighty-Four*. New York: Signet.

Osgood, Ch. E. (1979) 'Conservative words and radical sentences in the semantics of international politics', *Studies in the Linguistic Sciences*, 8 (2): 43–61.

Pêcheux, M. (1975) *Les Vérités de la Palice: linguistique, sémantique, philosophie*. Paris: Maspéro.

Pêcheux, M. (1990) *L'Inquiétude du discours: textes choisis et présentés par Denise Maldidier*. Paris: Editions des Cendres.

Reiher, R. and Läzer, R. (eds) (1993) *Wer spricht das wahre Deutsch? Erkundungen zur Sprache im vereinigten Deutschland*. Berlin: Aufbau.

Richardson, K. (1985) 'Pragmatics of speeches against the peace movement in Britain: a case study', in P. Chilton (ed.), *Language and the Nuclear Arms Debate: Nukespeak Today*. London: Pinter. pp. 23–44.

Sartori, G. (1984) *Social Science Concepts: a Systematic Analysis*. Beverly Hills, CA: Sage.

Sauer, C. (1995) 'Sprachwissenschaft und NS-Faschismus. Lehren aus der sprachwissenschaftlichen Erforschung des Sprachgebrauchs deutscher Nationalsozialisten und Propagandisten für den mittel- und osteuropäischen Umbruch?', in K. Steinke (ed.), *Die Sprache der Diktaturen und Diktatoren*. Heidelberg: Carl Winter Universitätsverlag. pp. 9–96.

Schäffner, C. (1991) 'Zur Rolle von Metaphern für die Interpretation der außersprachlichen Wirklichkeit', *Folia Linguistica*, 25 (1–2): 75–90.

Schäffner, C. and Porsch, P. (1993) 'Meeting the challenge on the path to democracy: discursive strategies in governmental declarations', *Discourse and Society*, 4 (1): 33–55.

Schmidt, W. (1969) 'Zur Ideologiegebundenheit der politischen Lexik', *Zeitschrift für Phonetik, Sprachwissenschaft und Kommunikationsforschung*, 22 (3): 255–71.

Searle, J. (1969) *Speech Acts*. Cambridge: Cambridge University Press.

Shapiro, M.J. (1981) *Language and Political Understanding: the Politics of Discursive Practices*. New Haven and London: Yale University Press.

Shapiro, M.J. (ed.) (1984) *Language and Politics*. Oxford: Basil Blackwell.

Sucharowski, W. (ed.) (1985) *Gesprächsforschung im Vergleich: Analysen zur Bonner Runde nach der Hessenwahl*. Tübingen: Niemeyer.

Tetlock, P. (1985) 'Integrative complexity and Soviet foreign policy rhetoric: a time-series analysis', *Journal of Personality and Social Psychology*, 49 (6): 156–85.

van Dijk, T.A. (1980) *Macrostructures: an Interdisciplinary Study of Global Structures in Discourse, Interaction and Cognition*. Hillsdale, NJ: Erlbaum.

van Dijk, T. A. (1989) 'Structures of discourse and structures of power', in J.A. Anderson (ed.), *Communication Yearbook 12*. Newbury Park, CA: Sage. pp. 18–59.

van Dijk, T.A. (1994) 'Discourse analysis and social analysis', *Discourse and Society*, 5 (2): 163–4.

van Dijk, T.A. (1995) 'Discourse semantics and ideology', *Discourse and Society*, 6 (2): 243–89.

Volosinov, V.N. (1973) *Marxism and the Philosophy of Language*. Cambridge, MA: Harvard University Press.

Wilson, J. (1990) *Politically Speaking: the Pragmatic Analysis of Political Language*. Oxford: Basil Blackwell.

Wilson, J. (1991) 'The linguistic pragmatics of terrorist acts', *Discourse and Society*, 1 (2): 29–45.

Wittgenstein, L. (1953) *Philosophical Investigations* (trans. G.E.M. Anscombe). Oxford: Basil Blackwell.

Wodak, R. (ed.) (1989) *Language, Power and Ideology: Studies in Political Discourse*. Amsterdam, Philadelphia: Benjamins.

Wodak, R. and Menz, F. (eds) (1990) *Sprache in der Politik – Politik in der Sprache: Analysen zum öffentlichen Sprachgebrauch*. Klagenfurt: Drava.

9

Discourse and Culture

Cliff Goddard and Anna Wierzbicka

Discourse and Culture Studies

In different societies people not only speak different languages and dialects, they use them in radically different ways. In some societies, normal conversations bristle with disagreement, voices are raised, emotions are conspicuously vented. In others, people studiously avoid contention, speak in mild and even tones, and guard against any exposure of their inner selves. In some parts of the world it is considered very bad to speak when another person is talking, while in others, this is an expected part of a co-conversationalist's work. In some cultures, it is *de rigueur* to joke and banter obscenely with some people but to go through life not saying a single word to others.

Describing and explaining such culture-specific ways of speaking is the task of 'discourse and culture' studies. It is a task which can be approached from many different directions, using many different methods, but most scholars agree that it goes beyond merely describing speech patterns in behavioural terms. The greater challenge is to show the links between particular ways of speaking and the culture of the people involved. To do this, of course, we have to be able to establish the relevant cultural values and priorities independently of the speech patterns themselves. Such evidence can come from many sources, including surveys or interviews about attitudes, observations of child-raising practices, the proverbs and common sayings of the culture, semantic analysis of cultural key words, and wider cultural analysis.

As in all cross-cultural research, the overriding methodological problem is ethnocentric bias, that is, the danger that our understanding of the discourse practices of other cultures will be distorted if we view them through the prism of our own culture-specific practices and concepts. There is a need to find a universal, language-independent perspective on discourse structure and on cultural values.

In this chapter we first survey a variety of different approaches to culture and discourse studies, then take a close look at cultural aspects of discourse in five unrelated cultures (Japanese, Malay, Polish, Yankunytjatjara, Ewe). In this way, we can draw out some of the main dimensions of cross-cultural variation in discourse.

An Overview of the Field

This section describes different approaches to discourse and culture studies, suggesting that they can be integrated within the 'cultural scripts' framework which has its roots in cross-cultural semantics.

The Ethnography of Communication

The most influential approach to discourse and culture studies is known as the 'ethnography of communication'. It was founded by Dell Hymes (1962) and was further developed by him, John Gumperz, and others in the 1970s (Gumperz and Hymes, 1986, first published 1972; Bauman and Sherzer, 1974). This was a time when linguistic theorizing was dominated by Chomsky's concepts of grammar and of linguistic competence, notions focused on the structural aspects of language rather than on language in use. Hymes emphasized that to be a competent speaker calls for much more than grammatical knowledge. It means knowing how to speak in culturally appropriate ways to different people about different things in different settings. He coined the term 'communicative competence' to take in all these things, along with the knowledge of language structure (see Blum-Kulka, Chapter 2 in this volume).

As a way of studying communicative competence, Hymes suggested research should focus on what he called the 'speech events' of different cultures. These are culturally recognized activities involving speech; for instance, in English, a gossip session, a sermon, a job interview, or a cross-examination in court. Actually, activities like these don't merely involve speaking, but are constituted by speaking in appropriate ways and settings to certain kinds of people. Hymes reasoned that part of being a culturally competent speaker is understanding the speech events recognized by that culture, and he laid out a framework of the dimensions of a communicative event. It is called the SPEAKING framework because the letters in that word can be used as a mnemonic; but note that the components don't follow in order of importance.

S   setting and scene (where and when does it happen?)
P   participants (who is taking part?)
E   ends (what do the participants want to achieve?)
A   act sequence (what is said and done?)
K   key (what is the emotional tone, for example serious, sorrowful, light-hearted?)
I   instrumentalities (what are the 'channels', for example verbal, written, and the 'codes', for example languages, speech styles?)
N   norms of interaction and interpretation (why 'should' people act like this?)
G   genre (what kind of speech event is it?)

Ethnographers of communication have documented the patterning of speech events in a wide range of cultures. Their favoured methods of gathering data are participant observation and consultation with native speakers. Often they uncover striking differences from European norms. For example, among the Wolof of West Africa (Irvine, 1974) exchanging greetings (*nuyyu* or *dyammantë*) is a highly structured routine. Behind the formulaic salutations, the praising of God, the questions and answers about the whereabouts and health of family members, there are complex cultural assumptions about social rank and appropriate behaviour between unequals. A cultural outsider would never realize it, but each greeting exchange establishes the relative rankings of the participants. As a Wolof proverb puts it: 'When two persons greet each other, one has shame, the other has glory.'

Among the Apache (Basso, 1970), greeting behaviour takes a radically different form. Instead of a cascade of verbal formulae, the proper form is a long period of motionless silence. Silence provides an excellent example of the fact that similar verbal forms may have radically different functions in different cultures. Silence sounds the same in any language, but its interpretation differs widely.

To take another example, in Japan there is a belief that as soon as an experience is expressed in words, the real essence disappears. Thus, at any time of emotional climax, whether it be the death of one's parents, the happy news that one's son has passed his university entrance examination, or the sight of something extremely beautiful, the appropriate thing to say is nothing (Williams, cited in Saville-Troike, 1989: 167).

Though Hymes's work inspired many valuable studies, few actually use the SPEAKING framework to organize their descriptions. This is not really as strange as it might seem. What Hymes was trying to do was lay out a framework for gathering data on speech events across cultures (a so-called 'etic' framework). To explain discourse phenomena in cultural terms, however, the crucial components are the N (norms) components. In practice, most studies in the ethnography of communication devote most of their time to explaining these. 'Norms of interaction' refers to the rules for how people are expected to speak in particular speech events; often these are unconscious and can only be discovered by indirect means, for instance, by observing reactions when they are violated. All other cultural knowledge needed to understand a communicative event falls under 'norms of interpretation'. The main difficulty with the ethnography of communication approach is the lack of a principled method for describing cultural norms; in practice, each ethnographer falls back on his or her own devices.

Contrastive Pragmatics

Under this broad heading we can identify several research traditions directed toward understanding cultural variation in patterns of conversation. One tradition has been provoked by the proposal of the philosopher H.P. Grice (1975) that all human communication is mediated by universal principles known as 'maxims of conversation'; for instance, 'be brief', 'be informative', 'be relevant', 'be clear'. The basic idea is that exchanging information is the prototypical function of conversation. It is now known, however, that Grice's maxims do not operate in the same fashion in all cultures. In Malagasy village society (Ochs Keenan, 1976), for instance, people are not expected to satisfy the informational needs of co-conversationalists because, firstly, withholding information brings a degree of status, and, secondly, there is a fear of committing oneself to particular claims lest any resulting unpleasantness bring *tsiny* ("guilt") to oneself and one's family.

Another seminal work is Brown and Levinson's (1978) on universals of politeness. They proposed that all cultures provide a speaker with two broad kinds of strategy to offset the imposition involved with any communicative act: 'positive politeness' strategies appeal to shared identity and common interests, while 'negative politeness' strategies emphasize the autonomy and independence of speaker and addressee (see Blum-Kulka, Chapter 2 in this volume). It is clear, however, that any putative universal strategies of politeness must be culturally relativized.

Independently of such 'universals oriented' research, there is a strain of contrastive pragmatics which concentrates on the cultural realization of speech acts (see Blum-Kulka, Chapter 2 in this volume). One of the largest of such studies is the Cross-Cultural Speech Act Realization Project (CCSARP) which contrasted preferred modes of issuing requests and apologies (or their near-equivalents) in Argentinian Spanish, Australian English, Canadian French, German, and Israeli Hebrew (Blum-Kulka et al., 1989). A number of important studies in this vein have examined interlanguage pragmatics, that is, the discourse of non-native speakers in a second language (Blum-Kulka and Kasper, 1993), and a few (notably Clyne, 1994) have studied people from different cultural and linguistic backgrounds interacting in a lingua franca.

Research in contrastive pragmatics tends to use different methods to those employed in the ethnography of communication, such as questionnaires, surveys, role-plays, and discourse completion tasks. Such tightly controlled data elicitation techniques lend themselves to statistical analysis, though at the cost of under-representing (and possibly at times misrepresenting) spontaneous authentic speech.

Culture Studies

Two further approaches to studying the cultural aspects of discourse are linguistic anthropology and intercultural communication studies. Linguistic anthropology is conducted within the discipline of anthropology. It is directed toward understanding how language use fits in with, and indeed helps to constitute, the larger culture. This work often looks at cultural practices in superb detail, as for instance in the works in Watson-Gegeo and White (1990) on conflict resolution in the Pacific, or those in Schieffelin and Ochs (1986) on socialization strategies.

Intercultural studies and cultural commentaries (for example, Mitzutani and Mitzutani, 1987) usually focus on national-level societies such as Japan or China, comparing them with mainstream Anglo-American culture. Often the motivation is a desire to reduce culturally based misunderstandings in business or international relations. The best of this work contains valuable insights for discourse and culture studies, albeit often in a somewhat anecdotal form.

The 'Cultural Scripts' Approach

Although the approaches described so far have turned up a wealth of evidence testifying to the importance of the 'culture–discourse' connection, the field as a whole continues to labour under some serious difficulties as to how cultural rules (norms, strategies, etc.) of discourse should be stated. The normal practice is to use technical (or semi-technical) labels such as 'direct' vs 'indirect' and 'formal' vs 'informal' as the descriptive meta-language, but it is not difficult to see that such terms are used with different meanings by different authors. For instance, when Japanese speech patterns are contrasted with English ones, the Japanese are described as 'indirect' and the English as 'direct', but when English is compared with Hebrew, it is the English speech patterns which are 'indirect' and the Hebrew 'direct'. Nor are these differences merely quantitative. They are qualitative. Cultures differ on what one should be 'indirect' about, on how to be 'indirect', and, most importantly perhaps, on why to be 'indirect'. A similar critique can be made of the notions of 'formality' (Irvine, 1979), 'politeness' (Janney and Arndt, 1993), 'involvement' (Besnier, 1994), and so on.

Another problem is that if our metalanguage for cross-cultural comparison consists of terms like 'directness', 'deference', 'face', 'politeness', 'hierarchy', and so on, our analyses can easily slip into ethnocentrism because the relevant concepts are not found in the cultures being described and usually cannot even be translated easily into the languages involved. Ethnographic studies often attempt to overcome this by incorporating indigenous terms into their descriptions, for instance, Malagasy *tsiny* "guilt", Japanese *enryo* "restraint", Yankunytjatjara *kunta* "shame" (we use double quotation marks to draw attention to the fact that these glosses are only approximate). But then the same difficulty of translation arises in reverse. Without a sound methodology for lexical semantic analysis, the ethnographer seldom succeeds in explaining the full conceptual content of the indigenous terms.

To a large extent, these problems can be overcome by using the 'natural semantic metalanguage' (NSM) developed by Anna Wierzbicka and colleagues over many years of cross-linguistic semantic research (cf. Wierzbicka, 1992; 1996; Goddard and Wierzbicka, 1994). This metalanguage consists of a small set of simple meanings which evidence suggests can be expressed by words or bound morphemes in all languages; for example, PEOPLE, SOMEONE, SOMETHING, THIS, SAY, THINK, WANT, KNOW, GOOD,

BAD, NO. These appear to be lexical universals, that is, meanings which can be translated precisely between all languages. They combine according to a small set of universal grammatical patterns, comprising a mini-language which is an ideal tool for cross-linguistic semantics. A large body of empirical semantic research has been conducted using the NSM approach, much of it focusing on cultural 'key words', speech acts, and discourse particles – all language elements with an obvious relevance to discourse and culture.

The metalanguage of lexical universals can be used not only for semantic analysis, but also to formulate cultural rules for speaking, known as 'cultural scripts' (Wierzbicka, 1991; 1994a; 1994b; 1994c). Such scripts can capture culture-specific attitudes, assumptions and norms in precise and culture-independent terms. To take a simple example, the script below is intended to capture a cultural norm which is characteristically (though not exclusively) Japanese.

if something bad happens to someone because of me
I have to say something like this to this person:
    'I feel something bad because of this'

This describes the often noted tendency of the Japanese to "apologize" very frequently and in a broad range of situations, but it does not rely on the English speech-act verb 'apologize'. To do this would be both ethnocentric and misleading. A culture-bound concept like 'apology' is inappropriate as a descriptive and analytical tool in the cross-cultural field. The English term would also be misleading in implying a meaning component like 'I did something bad to you.' The so-called 'Japanese apology' does not pre-suppose such a component. One is expected to do it whenever one's action has led to someone else suffering harm or inconvenience, no matter how indirectly. The script above is therefore more accurate, as well as being readily translatable into Japanese.

The cultural scripts approach complements the other traditions in discourse and culture studies by providing an improved method for stating 'rules for speaking'. It is equally compatible with the search for broad generalizations about discourse strategies (contrastive pragmatics) and with a focus on the particularities of individual cultures (ethnography of communication and intercultural studies). It is compatible with data-gathering techniques of any kind. We will also see that the semantic basis of the cultural scripts approach enhances our capacity to articulate the links between speech practices, on the one hand, and culture-specific values and norms, on the other.

Case Studies of Discourse in Culture

We now look into discourse phenomena in five culturally different and geographically separated societies. Among the main phenomena we will see are different discourse preferences in relation to the expression of desires, opinions, and emotions, different conventions for participating in the work of conversation, specialized 'speech styles', and culture-specific conversational routines and genres.

In terms of linguistic texture, recurrent differences include the frequency of imperatives and questions, forms of address and vocatives, special forms of self-reference, the acceptability of overt negation, the use of imprecision and non-specificity, exclamations and discourse particles, and the use of vocabulary which is 'socially marked' in various ways.

Discourse Styles: Japanese, Malay and Polish

To some extent it is possible to speak of the preferred 'discourse style' of a culture as a whole, at least if we confine ourselves to the public sphere, that is to say, to situations where the participants do not know each other very well and are being observed by others as they speak. It is common in the literature to find terms like 'indirectness' and 'restraint' applied to whole cultures in this way. In this section we firstly compare two unrelated cultures (Japanese and Malay) which are often described in this way. How similar are they really? And what is the 'cultural logic' behind the discourse preferences? We then look at a culture (Polish) which can be said to actively encourage 'directness' of expression, at least in certain respects.

For good descriptions of yet other cultural discourse styles, see Schiffrin (1984) and Tannen (1981) on contemporary American Jewish culture, Wikan (1990) on the Balinese, Scollon and Scollon (1981) on the Athabaskan, Harkins (1994) on Australian Aborigines, Matisoff (1979) on traditional East European Jewish culture, and Kochman (1981) on Black Americans.

Japanese Japanese culture is often characterized by its suppression or distrust of verbalism. For instance, Doi notes that

> Western tradition is suffused with an emphasis on the importance of words. In Japan, this tradition does not exist. I do not mean to suggest that traditional Japanese thought makes light of words, but it seems to be more conscious of matters that words do not reach. (1988: 33)

Other writers have pointed to the Zen Buddhist emphasis on the 'inutility' of linguistic communication and to the Japanese preference for non-verbal communication in traditional pedagogy and even in mother–child interaction.

One important cultural source of verbal restraint is the Japanese ideal of *enryo*, usually translated as 'restraint' or 'reserve'. As pointed out by Smith, 'much of the definition of a "good person" involves restraint in the expression of personal desires and opinions' (1983: 44–5). *Enryo* inhibits Japanese speakers from saying directly what they want, and it also makes it culturally inappropriate to ask others directly what they want. Mizutani and Mizutani (1987: 49) explain that except with family and close friends it is impolite to say such things as *Nani-o tabetai-desu-ka 'What do you want to eat?' and *Nani-ga hoshii-desu-ka 'What do you want to have?' A guest in Japan is not constantly offered choices by an attentive host, as in the United States. It is the responsibility of the host to anticipate what will please the guest and simply to present items of food and drink, urging that they be consumed, in the standard phrase, 'without enryo'.

The same cultural constraint prevents people in Japan from clearly stating their preferences, even in response to direct questions. Many Japanese, when asked about their convenience, decline to state it, using expressions like those in (1a) instead. A related phenomenon is the deliberate use of imprecise numerical expressions; when wanting to buy three apples, a Japanese person would prefer to ask for 'about three', as in (1b). And when making a suggestion, open-ended expressions like demo and nado (among others) are favoured, as in (1c). (Examples from Mizutani and Mizutani, 1987: 117–18.)

(1a)   Itsu-demo kekkoo-desu. 'Any time will do.'
       Doko-demo kekkoo-desu. 'Any place will be all right with me.'
       Nan-demo kamaimasen. 'Anything will be all right with me.'

(1b)   Mittsu-hodo/gurai/bakari kudasai. 'Please give me about three.'

(1c)   Eiga-demo mimashoo-ka? 'How about seeing a movie or something?'

As with one's wants, so with one's thoughts and feelings. It is not only a question of when to express them, but whether one should express them at all, a fact which has led some observers to describe the Japanese self as a 'guarded self'. Barnlund (1975) illustrates this restraint about self-exposure with statistical data showing enormous differences between Japanese and Americans not only in the range of topics they are prepared to talk about, but also in the range of persons to whom they are prepared to reveal their thoughts and intentions. If one is to speak, it is important to premeditate in order to avoid saying anything which could hurt or offend somebody or which could embarrass the speaker him/herself.

All these observations suggest that among the cultural scripts of Japan are the following:

(2)   often it is good not to say anything to other people

(3)   it is not good to say things like this to other people:
      'I want this', 'I don't want this'
      'I think this', 'I don't think this'
      if I say things like this, someone could feel something bad

(4)   before I say something to someone
      it is good to think something like this:
         I can't say all that I think
         if I do, someone could feel something bad

Another Japanese ideal relevant to discourse preferences is *omoiyari*, identified by numerous cultural commentators as one of the key personal virtues of Japan. Lebra describes it as follows:

> *Omoiyari* refers to the ability and willingness to feel what others are feeling, to vicariously experience the pleasure or pain that they are undergoing, and to help them satisy their wishes . . . without being told verbally. (1976: 38)

Certainly it is not hard to find evidence to support Lebra's characterization of Japanese culture as a whole as an '*omoiyari* culture' (cf. Travis, 1992). For instance, in a reader's column in the newspaper *Shikoku Shimbun*, where readers place a photo of their child and state their hopes and expectations, one of the most common is *Omoiyari no aru hitoni nattene* 'Please become a person with *omoiyari*.' In education guidelines for teachers, the first one is *Omoiyari no kokoro o taisetsuni shimashoo* 'Let's treasure the mind/heart of *omoiyari*'. In the *sempai/koohai* 'senior/junior' relationship in Japanese companies, *omoiyari* plays a key role: the *sempai* is expected to be able to anticipate the needs of the *koohai* and to satisfy them, for which he or she is rewarded with absolute loyalty.

It has also been observed that the ideal of wordless empathy is carried over into everyday interaction. For example, speaking of the 'ingroup' Nakane says:

> Among fellow-members a single word would suffice for the whole sentence. The mutually sensitive response goes so far that each easily recognises the other's slightest change in behaviour and mood and is ready to act accordingly. (1970: 121)

The high sensitivity to other people's feelings is linked with the often noted tendency for the Japanese to withhold explicit displays of feeling. Honna and Hoffer (1989: 88–90) observe that Japanese who cannot control their emotions are considered 'immature as human beings'. This applies not only to negative or unsettling emotions such as anger, fear, disgust, and sorrow. Even the expression of happiness should be controlled 'so that it does not displease other people'.

These complementary attitudes can be captured in the scripts below. According to (5a) and (5b), Japanese cultural attitudes discourage one from verbalizing about one's own emotions but at the same time encourage emotional sensitivity toward other people. The final, reasonably self-explanatory, script (6) enjoins the Japanese conversationalist both to avoid overt disagreement and to positively express agreement.

(5a) when I feel something
       it is not good to say anything about it to another person
       if I do, this person could feel something bad
       I can't say what I feel

(5b) it is good if I can know what another person feels
       this person doesn't have to say anything to me

(6)   when someone says something to me about something
       I can't say something like this:
          'I don't think the same'
       it is good to say something like this:
          'I would say the same'

Other aspects of Japanese discourse style also make sense in the light of these cultural scripts. For instance, turn-taking follows quite different patterns from those of Anglo-American society. Japanese conversation is expected to be, to a large extent, a collective work of the interlocutors and relies heavily on 'response words', known in Japanese as *aizuchi*. Mizutani and Mizutani explain that this term is built up from *ai*, meaning 'doing something together', and *tsuchi* 'a hammer': 'Two people talking and frequently exchanging response words is thus likened to the way two swordsmiths hammer on a blade' (1987: 18–20). In line with this cooperative image of conversation, a Japanese speaker will often leave sentences unfinished so that the listener can complete them: 'always completing one's sentences can sound as if one is refusing to let the other person participate' (1987: 27).

Finally, there are devices like the ubiquitous particle *ne*, which according to Cook (1992) 'invites the conversational partner to become an active and emotionally supportive co-conversationalist'. For instance, *ne* occurs four times in the following brief passage, sometimes in the middle of a sentence in combination with the non-finite -*te* verb form. The speaker is talking about his experiences with his host family when he travelled to the United States.

(7)   *Boku wa sono inu o ne.*   *Eeto nan dakke?*
       'I, that dog NE   Well, what (am I) talking about?'

       Omae shigoto suru katte kikarete ne.   *Nan no shigoto ka wakannai to*
       omotte ne
       '(I) was asked if I would work and NE (I) thought (I) would not know what work it would be and NE'

       so-soto ittara ne   *Sono inu no sooji ya ara-*
       'when (I) went out- outside NE   cleaning of that dog and wash-'

The literal meaning conveyed by *ne* (Wierzbicka, 1994b: 73–7) can be represented as follows: 'I think you would say the same.' By constantly repeating this message, the *ne* particle contributes powerfully toward forging conversation according to Japanese cultural norms.

Malay (Bahasa Melayu)   The traditional culture of the Malay people places great emphasis upon 'proper conduct' and, as an integral part of this, upon speaking in the proper way. The norms of refined (*halus*) speech in Malay somewhat resemble those of Japanese, but on closer examination the similarities turn out to be superficial (Goddard, 1996; 1997), making the comparison a valuable exercise in our exploration of cultural differences in discourse.

Observers generally describe Malay culture as valuing 'refined restraint', cordiality, and sensitivity, and Malays themselves as courteous, easy-going, and charming. Traditionally, they are a village people, relying on fishing, market gardening and rice cultivation, though present-day Malaysia is one of the most industrialized countries in South East Asia. The Malay people have long been Muslims, though Malay traditions (*adat*) nuance their Islamic practices considerably. The culture is richly verbal, with a large stock of traditional sayings (*peribahasa*), short evocative verses (*pantun*), and narrative poems (*syair*). The importance of speech (*bahasa*) to proper conduct is attested by the fact that *bahasa* has a secondary meaning of 'courtesy, manners'.

One concept fundamental to Malay interaction is the social emotion of *malu*. Though it is usually glossed as 'ashamed', 'shy', or 'embarrassed', these translations don't convey the fact that Malays regard the capacity to feel *malu* as a social good, akin to a sense of propriety. Swift (1965: 110) describes it as 'hypersensitiveness to what other people are thinking about one' (though note the ethnocentric perspective reflected in the prefix 'hyper-'). Desire to avoid *malu* is the primary force for social cohesion – not to say conformism – in the Malay village. Two related social concepts are *maruah*, roughly "dignity, honour", and *harga diri* "self-esteem" (*harga* 'value', *diri* 'self'), both of which are threatened by the prospect of being disapproved of by others, that is, by *malu*. Vreeland et al. emphasizes the importance of these concepts for Malay behaviour generally:

> The social value system is predicated on the dignity of the individual and ideally all social behaviour is regulated in such a way as to preserve one's own *amour propre* and to avoid disturbing the same feelings of dignity and self-esteem in others. (1977: 117)

As in Japan, one is expected in Malay society to think before one speaks. There is a common saying to this effect: *Kalau cakap fikirlah sedikit dulu* 'If you're going to speak, think a little first.' But the underlying cultural attitude is somewhat different to that in Japan. As well as wanting to avoid the addressee feeling something bad (cf. the saying *jaga hati orang* 'mind people's feelings'), Malay verbal caution is motivated by wanting to avoid the addressee's thinking anything bad about one.

(8)   before I say something to someone, it is good to think:
          I don't want this person to feel something bad
          I don't want this person to think something bad about me

Another difference is the value Malay culture places on verbal skill. A refined (*halus*) way of speaking is universally admired, bringing credit to oneself and one's upbringing. It is a skill learnt in the home, and not necessarily connected with wealth, noble birth, or formal education. As

Asmah remarks: 'A rice farmer with only six years of primary education may be found to speak a more refined language than a clerk in a government department' (1987: 88).

Halus speech is especially valued in formal situations, or when talking with *orang lain* 'other/different people', that is, people outside the immediate family circle. One always feels such people are liable to be watching and passing judgment, ready to disparage those without verbal finesse as *kurang ajar* 'uncouth, lit. under-taught'. On the other hand, a cultivated way with words wins admiration. This complex of cultural attitudes can be captured as follows:

(9)   when people hear someone saying something
        sometimes they think something like this:
            'this person knows how to say things well to other people,
            this is good'
        sometimes they think something like this:
            'this person doesn't know how to say things well to other people,
            this is bad'

Aside from courtesy and considerateness, the linguistic features of *halus* speech include the use of elegant phrases instead of mundane vocabulary, careful attention to forms of personal reference (for example, avoiding first and second person pronouns), and recourse to the large inventory of traditional sayings (*peribahasa*) to allude to potentially sensitive matters. A soft (*lembut*, also 'gentle, tender') voice is also important.

Before leaving the topic of *halus* behaviour, we should note that it applies not just to speaking, but to a whole range of non-verbal behaviour as well: for instance, removing the shoes before entering a home, consuming at least some of whatever refreshment is offered, adopting a specific posture when passing between people who are seated, using only the right hand in eating or in passing things, avoiding any physical contact with a member of the opposite sex, pointing and beckoning in a certain way.

In general, Malay culture discourages people from directly expressing how they feel, the ideal demeanour being one of good-natured calm (*senang hati*, lit. 'easy heart'). It is preferable to express feelings with more subtlety, through one's facial expressions and other actions. There is an underlying assumption that people can be relied upon to be sensitive to such non-verbal manifestations. The cultural script can be written as follows:

(10) when I feel something
        it is not good to say something like this to another person:
            'I feel like this'
        if the other person can see me, they will know how I feel

The use of 'meaningful looks' (*pandangan bermakna*) is a favoured non-verbal strategy. For instance, the verb *tenung* (cf. *bertenung* 'to divine') depicts a kind of glare used to convey irritation with someone else's behaviour, such as a child misbehaving or someone in the room clicking a pen in an irritating way. Widening the eyes *mata terbeliak* (lit. 'bulging eyes') conveys disapproval. Lowering the eyes and deliberately turning the head away (*jeling*) without speaking can convey that one is 'fed up' with someone. Pressing the lips together and protruding them slightly (*menjuihkan bibir*) conveys annoyance. Non-verbal expression is critical to the closest Malay counterpart of English 'angry', namely *marah* "offended, angry", which is associated not with scenes of 'angry words' (as sanctioned by Anglo cultural scripts of free self-expression) but with the sullen brooding performance known as *merajuk*.

Polish To round out our picture of cultural variation in discourse style, we now turn to one of the many cultures which encourage the expression of emotionality and disagreement. The central place of warmth and affection in Polish culture (as in Slavic cultures generally) is reflected in many ways in the Polish language, for instance, in the rich system of expressive derivation. Terms of endearment are widely used in everyday speech, especially to children: *ptaszku* 'dear little bird', *kotku* 'dear little cat', *słoneczko* 'dear little sun', *skarbie* 'treasure', *złotko* 'dear little gold', and so on. Personal names can have as many as ten different derivates, each implying a slightly different emotional attitude and 'emotional mood'. For example, all the following could be commonly used with respect to the same person, *Maria: Marysia, Marysieńka, Maryśka, Marysiuchna, Marychna, Maryś, Marysiulka, Marycha, Marysiątko.*

Warm hospitality in making an offer is expressed by the use of diminutives and imperatives together. Similarly, during leave-taking a good host will insist that the guest stay longer, showering them with 'you musts' and with diminutives. Requests between intimates such as husband and wife, or requests directed to children, also typically use both diminutives and imperatives. Examples follow:

(11a) *Weź jeszcze śledzika! Koniecznie!*
'Take some more dear-little-herring (DIM). You must!'

(11b) *Ale jeszcze troszeczkę! Ale koniecznie!*
'But [stay] a little-DIM more! But you must!'

(11c) *Jureczku, daj mi papierosa!*
'George-DIM-DIM, give me a cigarette!'

(11d) *Monisieńko, jedz zupkę!*
'Monica-DIM-DIM, eat your soup-DIM!'

Wierzbicka (1991) argues that Polish culture values uninhibited expression of both good and bad feelings, and that it accords special value to communicating good feelings towards the addressee.

(12a) I want people to know how I feel
when I feel something good I want to say something
when I feel something bad I want to say something

(12b)   if I feel something good when I think about you, I want you to know
       it

A similar complex of attitudes concerns the free expression of opinions, endorsing extreme frankness, 'saying exactly what one thinks', even at the cost of expressing a hurtful truth.

(13a)   I want people to know what I think
       when I think that someone thinks something bad, I want to say it to
       this person

(13b)   if I think that you think something bad, I want to say it to you
       I don't want you to think something bad

Needless to say, such communicative norms clash with those of mainstream Anglo-American society, which encourage a balanced expression of views and the pursuit of compromise and which discourage 'emotionality' (even the word has a pejorative ring) except in exceptional circumstances. The following comments come from the American writer Eva Hoffman, whose family migrated from Poland and settled in North America when she was a girl. The Polish teenager soon made certain discoveries.

> I learnt that certain kinds of truth are impolite. One shouldn't criticise the person one is with, at least not directly. You shouldn't say 'You are wrong about that' though you might say, 'On the other hand, there is that to consider'. You shouldn't say, 'This doesn't look good on you', though you may say, 'I like you better in that other outfit'. (Hoffman, 1989: 146)

Consistent with Polish cultural values, the Polish language contains a large number of discourse particles (such as *ależ*, *skądże*, and *przecież*) and exclamatory phrases (such as *ależ skądże*, *skądże znowu*, and *cóż znowu*) expressing disagreement, exasperation, and impatience with the views expressed by one's interlocutor. For instance, *ależ* signals violent disagreement and is often used in combination with a person's name, showing exasperation at the addressee's wrongness and dumbness. The particle *skądże* means something like: 'Where did you get such an idea from?! You are wrong!' The two are often combined, intensifying the message even further. The paraphrase in (14) gives some idea of the overall effect. Notice the presence of the component: 'I feel something bad when I hear you say this.'

(14)   *Ależ   skądże!*
       but-EMPH   where-from-EMPH

       'But (how can you say that)!
       Where did you get such an idea from?
       You are wrong
       I feel something bad when I hear you say that'

It should be evident from this comparison of Japanese, Malay, and Polish that discourse preferences vary widely from culture to culture. What is an ordinary style in one culture may seem quite shocking and offensive, or quite boring and colourless, from the standpoint of another. To understand such cultural variation it is necessary to go below the surface of the speech patterns themselves and uncover the values and norms which explain them. It must not be forgotten that speech patterns which are superficially similar (for instance, a preference for 'verbal restraint') may spring from different cultural values and be associated with different social meanings in different cultural settings. To bring these connections to light, and even to describe the speech patterns themselves without ethnocentric distortion, requires careful attention to the metalanguage of description and analysis.

Speech Styles in Traditional Yankunytjatjara Society

In this section we look at two specialized and very different 'speech styles' traditionally used by the Yankunytjatjara people of Central Australia. An 'oblique' style *tjalpawangkanyi* (*wangkanyi* 'talk') is used between people in highly constrained relationships, while boisterous 'joking' styles are used by people whose kinship standing implies complete mutual acceptance and a lack of any power relationships.

The Yankunytjatjara are Australian Aborigines whose traditional territory includes Uluṟu (Ayers Rock) and the area to the south-east of this well-known symbol of Australia. It is one of the many dialects of the far-flung Western Desert Language which is spoken over a vast area of the arid western interior of Australia (Goddard, 1986; 1992a; 1992b). The traditional economy was one of hunting and gathering, with small bands of people ranging widely around their territory. Like the other Aboriginal peoples of Australia, the Yankunytjatjara have an intimate knowledge of the land and profound religious connections with it. Their society is small and kin-based; in the traditional lifestyle one would seldom encounter a complete stranger. Everyone is regarded as having some *walytja* ('kin') relationship to everyone else, through a system which extends the terms applying within the close family (such as *mama* 'father', *ngunytju* 'mother', *katja* 'son', *untal* 'daughter', *kami* 'grandmother', *tjamu* 'grandfather') to take in the whole social universe (a so-called classificatory kin system).

First let's see a few examples of ordinary, relaxed Yankunytjatjara speech between people who know each other well. If one person has come to the other's camp hoping to be given something to eat, the request may be made as in (15a). If the two are out driving through the country and one wants the other to stop to gather some firewood, this can be conveyed as in (15b). If one calls at the other's camp wanting to find a third person who lives there, the information could be sought as in (15c).

(15a) *Mai nyuntumpa ngarinyi? Ngayulu mai wiya.*
       food yours   liePRES   I   food NEG

'Any food of yours lying around? I don't have any food.'

(15b) *Ngayulu waru̲ wiya. Nyinatjura ka-n̲a waru̲ urara̲   utitjura.*
      I   wood NEG stopIMP   and-I wood gatherSERIAL loadIMP

      'I haven't got any firewood. Stop and I'll load some on.'

(15c) *Tjilpinya   nyinanyi?*
      old manNAME sitPRES

      'Is the old man around?'

Corresponding 'oblique speech style' *tjalpawangkanyi* versions are shown in
(16). These have a distinctive vocal delivery (softer, slower, and at a higher
pitch than usual) and an exaggerated rising intonation, as if to give the
impression that the speaker is just musing aloud.

(16a) *Aya, anymatjara kutu-n̲a. Mai-nti   wampa   ngarinyi?*
      Oh hungry   really-I food-maybe don't know liePRES

      'Oh, I'm so hungry. I wonder if there might be any food around?'

(16b) *Munta, waru̲-mpa-l.   Nguwan-ampa-n̲a   mana-nyi.*
      oh   wood-INTEREST-I see almost-INTEREST-I getPRES

      'Oh, some firewood, I see. I'd rather like to get some.'

(16c) *Munta, panya   palu̲ru-nti nyanga-kutu?*
      oh   that one DEF-maybe this-towards

      'Oh, could that one be around here somewhere?'

Direct references to the addressee are carefully avoided in *tjalpawangkanyi*,
as are imperatives and vocatives. Overt expressions of denial, refusal, or
disagreement are also scrupulously avoided. The particles *-nti* 'maybe',
munta 'oh, sorry', *wampa* 'don't know', and *wanyu* 'just let' are sprinkled
through sentences, expressing uncertainty, hesitation, and minimization.
Also common is the particle *-mpa* whose full meaning is something like
'one could say more about this'; it acts as a linguistic marker of insinuation
or implication. Another striking feature, reported also of respectful speech
styles in many other places, is generality of reference: speakers avoid using
specific forms which unambiguously indicate a person, place or thing,
preferring vague locutions like *panya palu̲ru* 'that one (person)' and
nyangakutu 'around here', as in (16c).

   To understand the social meaning of *tjalpawangkanyi* calls for a knowledge of Yankunytjatjara culture and, in particular, of the socio-emotional
concept *kunt̲a*. This is usually glossed in bilingual dictionaries as 'shame',
'embarrassment', or 'respect', but *kunt̲a* does not correspond precisely to
any of these English concepts. Essentially, it involves a sense of social
difference, discomfort with being in the other person's presence, and the

desire to avoid acting in any way which might cause the other person to think anything unfavourable about one.

The strongest *kunta* is evoked by the *umari* ('avoidance') relationship between a man and his father-in-law and mother-in-law, which has its basis in secret male rituals whereby a youth becomes an initiated man. Though this is a relationship of the highest respect, the individuals involved must strictly avoid personal contact. One must not speak to an *umari*; nor can one touch, sit near, or even look directly at him or her. Less severe *kunta* is felt in the presence of the siblings or cousins of *umari*, and in other relationships where propriety is important, for instance, between brother- and sister-in-law *inkani*, co-parents-in-law *inkilyi*, and unmarried cousins of the opposite sex *nyarumpa*. These are the very relationships for which *tjalpawangkanyi* is appropriate. *Tjalpawangkanyi*, in other words, can be seen both as a kind of partial avoidance and as a way of giving voice to *kunta*.

By using the *tjalpawangkanyi* style, a speaker expresses the social messages summarized in (17a). Notice that these are framed in the 'third person', in accordance with the perspective of *tjalpawangkanyi* itself. Example (17b) summarizes some of the stylistic rules the speaker attempts to follow.

(17a)   this person is not someone like me
I don't want this person to think anything bad about me
I don't want to be near this person
I don't want to say anything to this person
if I have to say something, I have to think how to say it

(17b)   I can't say things like these to someone like this:
'this person', 'this place', 'this thing'
'I don't want this', 'I don't think the same'
'I want you to do something', 'I want you to say something'

At the other end of the spectrum from *tjalpawangkanyi* are *inka-inkangku wangkanyi* 'talking in fun', *wangkara inkanyi* 'joking around', *wangkara inkatjingani* 'teasing talk', and *warkira inkatjingani* 'teasing swearing'. These joking styles, largely reserved for kin whose relationship is genealogically distant, bend the normal conventions of interaction, or, in more extreme cases, flaunt or even parody them. Yankunytjatjara people find this a rich source of amusement.

Within this domain of 'fun-talk' flourish all the linguistic forms excluded from *tjalpawangkanyi* – including imperatives, vocatives, contradiction, exclamations, and sensitive vocabulary items. Example (18a) illustrates a joking approach for the loan of some sugar; notice how the person positively flaunts his personal wishes. In the response, given in (18b), there is mock hostility. Banter like this might continue for some time before the requester gets the sugar, if he ever does.

(18a) A: *Awai! Tjukaku-na ngalya-yanu.   Tjuka-tja ngalya-yuwa!*
           hey   sugarPURP-I this way-came sugar-me this way-giveIMP

           'Hey! I came here for sugar. Give me some sugar!'

(18b) B: *Tjuka wanyu nyuntu yaalara payamilara nyangangka tjunu?*
           sugar just let you   when   buySERIAL here   putPAST

           'Just when did you ever buy any sugar and bring (put) it here?'

In joking styles the participants delight in making the most of any chance
to playfully defy, challenge, or demean each other. The exchange in (19)
illustrates good-natured teasing *inkatjingani*, in which the nominally senior
kin chides or insults the junior, generating an amusing parry and thrust.
The first speaker is an uncle agreeing to loan his nephew an axe.

(19a) A: *Uwa, kati,   punytjulwiyangku kati!*
           yes   takeIMP bluntNEG.ERG   takeIMP

           'OK take it, but don't blunt it!'

(19b) B: *Wati, nyaaku-na tjitjingku palku   punytjanma? Yuwa-ni*
           man   why-I   childERG not really bluntPOT   giveIMP-me
           ka-na kati!
           and-I takeIMP

           'Man, why would I blunt it as if I were a child? Give (it to) me,
           and I'll be off with it.'

Example (20) is a routine exchange between a pair of distant male cousins
(nominally older and younger brother, *kuta* and *malany*, respectively) who
have become *inkankara* 'joking partners'. Similar joking occurs between
distant female cousins. The sexual innuendo and *risqué* comments consciously 'play' with kin-role expectations. Normally, older brothers and
sisters are expected to monitor and regulate any sexual misbehaviour by
their juniors.

(20a) A: *Wati, nyangangi-na-nta! Wati, nyaa manti-n   yanu?*
           man   seePAST.IMPF-I-you man   what probably-you goPAST

           Kulakula-mpa,   kungka-kutu-mpa.
           randy-INTEREST woman-towards-INTEREST

           'Man, I've been watching you. Man, what would you've been
           after? Randy was it? Off to see a woman, was it?'

(20b) B: *Wiya, wati ngayulu kungka wiya! Wantinyi-na   ngayulu,*
           no   man I   woman NEG leave alonePRES-I I
           palu   nyuntu panya-nku   watjanma, kuta,
           but of course you   ANAPH-REFL sayPOT   senior brother
           wati panya kurangku.
           man ANAPH badERG

'No man, I don't have any woman! I leave them alone, I do. But of course you could be talking to yourself, big brother, (you) bad one.'

Joking can also involve mock abuse with both mild and sexually explicit epithets, such as *mamu* 'monster' and *kalutjanu* 'dickhead' (related to *kalu* 'prick'). But even when the language becomes blatantly obscene, bystanders are far from offended. They just enjoy a good laugh.

Joking relationships, which exist in many societies in Aboriginal Australia (Thompson, 1935), are usually said to embody 'solidarity', 'intimacy', or the like, but the rich social meanings involved cannot really be summed up in a few words. Examples (21a) and (21b) state the social assumptions and stylistic conventions, respectively, of light-hearted speech in Yankunytjatjara.

(21a)   I know you will not think anything bad about me
        I don't have to think how to say things to you

(21b)   I can say things like this to you:
           'I don't want this', 'I don't think the same'
        I can say things like this about you:
           'you are bad', 'you do bad things'
        you can say the same things to me
        when we say things like this to each other, we feel something good

Yankunytjatjara *tjalpawangkanyi* plays much the same social role as the specialized 'avoidance vocabularies' found in other Australian Aboriginal languages such as Dyirbal (Dixon, 1972) and Guugu-Yimidhirr (Haviland, 1979). Good descriptions of speech styles in other societies can be found in Grobsmith (1979) on the Lakota, Albert (1986) on the Burundi, and Keenan (1974) on Malagasy.

Routines and Genres

So far we have looked at cultural variation in discourse at a fairly broad level of description. In this section we look at two discourse phenomena which are much more specific in their scope, namely, linguistic routines and speech genres.

Linguistic Routines in Ewe   Linguistic routines are fixed, formulaic utterances or sequences of utterances used in standardized communicative situations, for example, greetings and partings as well as (to use potentially misleading English labels) thanks, excuses, condolences, compliments, jokes, curses, small-talk, and so on. They may range in size from a single word to lengthy interchanges. The overall meaning of a routine cannot be 'read off' from the literal meaning of the individual words involved; to use a familiar example, *How do you do?* is not a question about health. In general, routines are highly culture-specific both in form and in the way they relate to the sociocultural context. To illustrate, we will compare some fixed expressions in English and Ewe (Ghana and Togo, West Africa).

In many societies, when one realizes that something good has happened to another person, it is usual to say something expressing one's own good feelings at the news. In English, for instance, one would be expected to say *Congratulations!* to someone who has had a baby and *Well done!* (or something similar) to someone who has won an important and difficult contest. Both expressions imply that the addressee is responsible to some extent for the happy event. In Ewe, appropriate things to say in such situations are listed in (22a) and (22b). These data, and the analysis which follows, are from Ameka (1987).

(22a) *Máwú sẽ ŋú!*   *Tɔgbéwó sẽ ŋú!*   *ŋúwò núwó sẽ ŋú!*
       'God is strong'   'Ancestors are strong!' 'Beings around you
                                                     are strong!'

(22b) *Máwú wɔ dɔ́!*   *Tɔgbéwó wɔ dɔ́!*   *ŋúwò núwó wɔ dɔ́!*
       God has worked!'   'Ancestors have worked' 'Beings around you
                                                     have worked!'

These expressions reflect the religious belief system of the Ewe people (and many other African peoples), which holds that every aspect of the universe is permeated by the influence of the Supreme Being *Máwú* and other supernatural beings. As Ameka says: 'for the Ewes, anything that happens to you is the work ultimately of God who may work in diverse ways through the ancestors or other spirits and divinities' (1987: 308).

Ewe cultural values explain why the formulae for acknowledging good events are not explicitly focused on the individuals concerned. Even so, as with the comparable English expressions, the interpersonal function is to register my assumption that you are pleased by what has happened and to display my own happiness at the outcome. Similarly, it is recognized by all concerned that the particular words used comprise a set utterance, appropriate for such occasions. With all this in mind, the meaning of the Ewe fixed expression *Máwú sẽ ŋú!* 'God is strong' can be formulated as follows (adapted from Ameka, 1987).

(23)   *Máwú sẽ ŋú!*
       I now know this: something good happened to you
       I think you feel something good because it happened
       I feel something good because of this
       I want you to know this
       everyone knows good things like this don't happen to people
         if a being of another kind does not do something

because of all this I say:
  'God is strong' (≈ God can do many things, people can't do these
     things)
  everyone knows it is good if people say these words when something
     good happens

This formulation is consistent with the range of situations in which such Ewe expressions are appropriate. For example, they are not used at weddings, since getting married is viewed by the Ewe not as a good thing which happens to a person but as the beginning of a process aimed at something else, namely, procreation. On the other hand, they are appropriate for someone who has come through a dangerous situation, as when someone gets out of hospital.

Another significant cultural dimension emerges when we consider appropriate responses. An expected English response to congratulation is *Thank you!*, which focuses on what is happening between the speaker and addressee. In contrast, the Ewe responses shown in (24) portray the communality of the happy event.

(24) *Yoo, miawóé dó gbe ɖá!*   *Yoo, miatɔwó hɑ̃́!*
      'OK, you all have prayed!'   'OK, yours (pl.) too!'

Such responses register the speaker's appreciation of the religious efforts or ancestor spirits of the addressee and of the whole community.

Another simple example of a linguistic routine which can only be understood in cultural terms is the Ewe exchange in (25).

(25) Speaker A: *Mia (ló)!*   Speaker B: Asíé!
                  'The left hand!'   'It is a hand'

The basis for this routine is the extreme social prohibition on using the left hand in social interaction. In Ewe society, as in many other African societies, one cannot pass an object to a person using one's left hand, nor may one point at or wave to another person with it. The reason is that this hand is reserved almost exclusively for the performance of ablutions. Using the 'dirty' hand in social intercourse normally implies an insult. Nevertheless, it is recognized that at one time or another, one might not be able to use the right hand to do everything. In such situations, it is permissible to use the left, but only after notifying the interlocutor and, so to speak, gaining an indemnity to violate the norm, as in (25).

It should be clear that the apparent simplicity of linguistic routines is deceptive. A proper communicative understanding of a routine involves knowing not only the words, but the cultural assumptions at work in daily interaction. It can even be argued that because of their standardized nature and very high frequency, routines are a good place to begin a study of cultural aspects of discourse. A number of interesting descriptions of linguistic routines can be found in Coulmas (1981).

Polish Speech Genres Bakhtin (1986: 81) defined speech genres as 'relatively stable and normative forms of the utterance', and stressed that the
repertoire of genres available to a speech community changes according to
social and cultural conditions. This important point can be readily
illustrated with the Polish genres of the *kawał* and the *podanie*.

The *kawał* (plural *kawały*) is, roughly speaking, a kind of 'conspiratorial
joke'. Most such jokes are political, expressing national solidarity *vis-à-vis*
foreign powers: the Nazi occupation during World War II, the Soviet-
imposed communist regime in post-war Poland, the foreign partitioning
powers in the nineteenth century.

Kawały circulate widely, the anonymous creations of an oral culture. One
values a *kawał* not for its ingenuity or sophistication (as one does *dowcipy*
'witty jokes'), but for the feeling it gives of belonging to an ingroup.
The implication is: I can tell you, but there are people who I couldn't tell.
Like English 'jokes', however, *kawały* are intended to promote pleasant
togetherness, that is, they are meant to make the speaker and the addressee
feel good together. Normally, a *kawał* requires some kind of introduction
('Do you know this *kawał*?'), reflecting the assumption that since they
circulate so widely this one may already be known to the addressee.

The example in (26) comes from the period in 1981 when martial law
had been imposed in an effort to suppress the Solidarity movement. Every
new demonstration, strike or protest was ascribed to 'Solidarity extremists'.
As with this example, a *kawał* always has an implicit and amusing 'point'
which has to be grasped by the addressee.

(26) The 'TV Dictionary':
       2 Poles: an illegal gathering
       3 Poles: an illegal demonstration
       10 million Poles: a handful of extremists

A semantic analysis of the meaning of the Polish genre term *kawał* would
include the following components, some shared with the English genre
'joke' and others not.

(27) I want to say something to you that many people say to each other
       I say it because I want you to laugh
       when I say it I want you to think of something that I don't say
       when you think of this you will laugh
       we will both feel something good because of this
       I can say this to you because we think the same about things like this

Our second example of a Polish genre is the *podanie*, which was one of the
central written genres of communist Poland. It is a special, written communication between an ordinary person and the 'authorities', in which the
author asks for favours and presents him or herself as dependent on their
goodwill. Needless to say, the very existence of this genre reflects the
dominance over ordinary people of a communist bureaucracy notorious for

the arbitrariness of its decisions. Hardly any aspect of people's lives in communist Poland, no matter how trivial, could be conducted without the need to write *podanie* – and to wait for the response, hoping that it might be benevolent. For example, a university student asking for an extension of the deadline for submitting a thesis, or an employee asking for permission to take annual leave at a particular time, submitted a *podanie*.

In Anglo-Saxon society these intentions might be pursued by way of a 'letter' or an 'application'. But the nearest Polish equivalent to 'letter', namely *list*, could never be used to refer to a formal petition to an institution. And there is no Polish equivalent to the English 'application', which presupposes a certain standard situation with clear guidelines to be followed by both the institution and the applicant. The *podanie* typically starts with such phrases as *Uprzejmie proszę* ('I ask politely') or *Niniejszym zwracam się z uprzejmą prośbą* ('hereby I address you politely to request a favour'), which would be quite out of place in an 'application'.

The supplicant aspects of the Polish *podanie* can be captured in the following semantic formula:

(28)   *podanie*
       I say: I want something to happen to me
       I know it cannot happen if you don't say you want it to happen
       I say this because I want you to say you want it to happen
       I don't know if you will
       I know many people say things like this to you
       I know you don't have to do what people want you to do

Clearly, the *kawał* and the *podanie* are, or rather were, forms of discourse well suited to the particular social and cultural conditions of communist Poland.

Other interesting genre studies include Abrahams (1974) on Black American rapping and capping, Basso (1979) on a form of satirical joking among the Apache, and Sherzer (1974) on Cuna chanting and speech-making.

Conclusions

Even from these five unrelated cultures (Japanese, Malay, Polish, Yankunytjatjara, Ewe), it is possible to draw out some conclusions about major dimensions of variation in discourse style, about the kinds of evidence which may help establish relevant cultural values and attitudes, and about methodological pitfalls involved in such research.

In terms of attitudes to the sheer quantity of words, there may be a preference for verbose as opposed to terse forms of expression, or even a preference for non-verbal expression. The cultural meaning of silence varies widely.

People everywhere adjust their speech according to how they view those they are speaking with, and although some dimensions of social identity (such as gender and age) are of near-universal relevance, the social construals involved vary enormously. In some societies, such as Yankunytjatjara, kin and ritual relationships are crucial. In Japan, the main social dimensions determining discourse style are 'ingroup' vs 'outgroup' and status differences between interlocutors. In Malay society, the most important dimension is whether the individuals belong to the same household. In other places, clan, ethnicity, caste, or rank determine different discourse styles.

At the functional or illocutionary level of discourse, important parameters of variation include how often and in what fashion the speaker expresses his or her own wants, thoughts, and feelings, how often and in what fashion the speaker attempts to influence the interlocutor's wants, thoughts, and feelings, whether or not it is alright to draw attention to differences between speaker and interlocutor, and the place of spontaneous as opposed to regulated expression. Cultures also differ markedly in their conventions for how people participate in the work of conversation, for example by turn-taking, overlapping, or even joint construction of sentences, and in their range of linguistic routines.

One notable generalization is that there is almost always a correlation between patterns of verbal behaviour and patterns of non-verbal behaviour. Thus, where broad cultural preferences or the conventions of a specific speech style inhibit people from expressing interpersonal emotions, we can expect the interlocutors to 'keep their distance' from one another physically as well, for instance, to refrain from touching or directly looking at one another. Conversely, when there is little or no verbal etiquette at work, more intimate and exuberant physical behaviour can be expected.

We have seen that many different kinds of evidence can be used to argue for cultural values and attitudes which can help make sense of discourse phenomena. These include semantic analysis of cultural 'key words', the proverbs and other embodiments of the conventional wisdom of a culture, common socialization routines, direct or indirect elicitation of speakers' attitudes, and even the judicious use of literature.

The biggest methodological problem in discourse and culture studies is the need to find a framework for comparing discourse preferences and cultural values with precision, and one which is resistant, so far as possible, to ethnocentrism. The common practice of using labels such as 'indirectness', 'politeness', 'respect', and 'solidarity', as an informal metalanguage for cross-cultural comparison, cannot really meet this need. A promising approach illustrated in this chapter is the use of cultural scripts written in lexical universals. This provides a framework in which findings from anthropological linguistics, contrastive pragmatics, linguistic anthropology, and cultural studies can be integrated and synthesized. At the same time, the semantic basis of the scripts approach makes it possible to draw links between speech practices, on the one hand, and cultural values and emotions, on the other, thereby facilitating the development of a genuinely cross-cultural pragmatics.

Recommended Reading

Duranti (1988): surveys key concepts in the ethnography of speaking (ES), such as communicative competence, context, speech community, speech event and speech act. Considers the relationship of ES to sociolinguistics and to conversational analysis.

Gumperz and Hymes (1986): a classic collection originally published in 1972. It consists of 19 empirical studies on a variety of European and non-European languages, and an influential introduction by John Gumperz. Though the dominant approach is ethnographic, other influences represented include ethnomethodology, sociology of language, and cognitive anthropology.

Kochman (1981): a study of clashes between the cultural communicative styles of African Americans and middle-class Anglo-Americans. Focuses on black speech acts and events such as argument, cursing, boasting, rapping, sounding and loud-talking.

Saville-Troike (1989): a broad-ranging textbook. Aside from introductory material, major chapters focus on varieties of language, ethnographic analysis of communicative events, attitudes to language use, and the acquisition of communicative competence.

Tannen (1986): a popular exposition of linguistic analysis of conversational style, aiming to help the ordinary reader understand and improve communication in private and public life.

Wierzbicka (1991): a major collection of studies showing how the 'natural semantic meta-language' approach can help achieve a universal, language-independent perspective on communicative styles and cultural norms. Describes discourse phenomena in many languages including Italian, Russian, Polish, Japanese, Chinese, and Hebrew, as well as different varieties of English.

Notes

This chapter has benefited from comments from Felix Ameka, Michael Cooke, Michael Clyne, Diana Eades, Norlinda Hasan, Tony Liddicoat and Teun van Dijk.

References

Abrahams, R. (1974) 'Black talking on the streets', in R. Bauman and J. Sherzer (eds), *Explorations in the Ethnography of Speaking*. London: Cambridge University Press. pp. 240–62.

Albert, E.M. (1986 [1972]) 'Culture patterning of speech behavior in Burundi', in J. J. Gumperz and D. Hymes (eds), *Directions in Sociolinguistics: the Ethnography of Communication*. New York: Holt, Rinehart and Winston. pp. 72–105.

Ameka, F. (1987) 'A comparative analysis of linguistic routines in two languages: English and Ewe', *Journal of Pragmatics*, 11: 299–326.

Asmah Haji Omar (1987) *Malay in its Sociocultural Context*. Kuala Lumpur: Dewan Bahasa dan Pustaka.

Bakhtin, M. (1986) 'The problem of speech genres', in C. Emerson and M. Holquist (eds), *Speech Genres and Other Late Essays*. Austin, TX: University of Texas Press. pp. 60–112.

Barnlund, D. (1975) *Public and Private Self in Japan and the United States: Communicative Styles of Two Cultures*. Tokyo: Simul.

Basso, K.H. (1970) 'To give up on words: silence in Western Apache culture', *Southwest Journal of Anthropology*, 26: 213–30.

Basso, K.H. (1979) *Portraits of 'The Whiteman': Linguistic Play and Cultural Symbols among the Western Apache.* London: Cambridge University Press.

Bauman, R. and Sherzer, J. (eds) (1974) *Explorations in the Ethnography of Speaking.* London: Cambridge University Press.

Besnier, N. (1994) 'Involvement in linguistic practice: an ethnographic appraisal', *Journal of Pragmatics*, 22: 279–99.

Blum-Kulka, S., House J. and Kasper, G. (1989) *Cross-Cultural Pragmatics.* Norwood, NJ: Ablex.

Blum-Kulka, S. and Kasper G. (1993) *Interlanguage Pragmatics.* Oxford: Oxford University Press.

Brown, P. and Levinson S. (1978) *Politeness: Some Universals of Language Use.* Cambridge: Cambridge University Press.

Clyne, M. (1994) *Inter-Cultural Communication at Work.* Cambridge: Cambridge University Press.

Cook, H.M. (1992) 'Meanings of non-referential indexes: a case study of the Japanese sentence-final particle *ne*', *Text*, 12 (4): 507–39.

Coulmas, F. (ed.) (1981) *Conversational Routine.* The Hague: Mouton.

Dixon, R.M.W. (1972) *The Dyirbal Language of North Queensland.* Cambridge: Cambridge University Press.

Doi, T. (1988) *The Anatomy of Self.* Tokyo: Kodansha.

Duranti, A. (1988) 'Ethnography of speaking: towards a linguistics of the praxis', in F.J. Newmeyer (ed.), *Language: the Socio-Cultural Context (Linguistics: the Cambridge Survey,* vol. IV). Cambridge: Cambridge University Press. pp. 210–28.

Goddard, C. (1986) *Yankunytjatjara Grammar.* Alice Springs: Institute for Aboriginal Development.

Goddard, C. (1992a) *Pitjantjatjara/Yankunytjatjara to English Dictionary,* 2nd edn. Alice Springs: Institute for Aboriginal Development.

Goddard, C. (1992b) 'Traditional Yankunytjatjara ways of speaking – a semantic perspective', *Australian Journal of Linguistics*, 12: 93–122.

Goddard, C. (1996) 'The "social emotions" of Malay (Bahasa Melayu)', *Ethos*, 24 3: 426–64.

Goddard, C. (1997) 'Cultural values and cultural scripts in Malay (Bahasa Melayu)', *Journal of Pragmatics*, 27 (2): 183–201.

Goddard, C. and Wierzbicka A. (eds) (1994) *Semantic and Lexical Universals.* Amsterdam: John Benjamins.

Grice, H.P. (1975) 'Logic and conversation', in P. Cole and J.L. Morgan (eds), *Speech Acts.* New York: Academic Press. pp. 41–58.

Grobsmith, E.S. (1979) 'Styles of speaking: an analysis of Lakota communication alternatives', *Anthropological Linguistics*, 21 (7): 355–61.

Gumperz, J.J. and Hymes, D.H. (eds) (1986) *Directions in Sociolinguistics: the Ethnography of Communication* (1972). Oxford: Basil Blackwell.

Harkins, J. (1994) *Bridging Two Worlds.* St Lucia: Queensland University Press.

Haviland, J. (1979) 'Guugu-Yimidhirr brother-in-law language', *Language in Society*, 8: 365–93.

Hoffman, E. (1989) *Lost in Translation.* New York: Dutton.

Honna, N. and Hoffer, B. (eds) (1989) *An English Dictionary of Japanese Ways of Thinking.* Tokyo: Yuhikaku.

Hymes, D.H. (1962) 'The ethnography of speaking'. Reprinted in Joshua Fishman (ed.), *Readings on the Sociology of Language.* The Hague: Mouton, 1968. pp. 99–138.

Irvine, J.T. (1974) 'Strategies of status manipulation in the Wolof greeting', in R. Bauman and J. Sherzer (eds), *Explorations in the Ethnography of Speaking.* London: Cambridge University Press. pp. 167–90.

Irvine, J.T. (1979) 'Formality and informality in communicative events', *American Anthropologist*, 81 (4): 773–90.

Janney, R. and Arndt, H. (1993) 'Universality and relativity in cross-cultural politeness research: a historical perspective', *Multilingua*, 12 (1): 13–50.

Lebra, T.S. (1976) *Japanese Patterns of Behaviour*. Honolulu: University of Hawaii Press.

Keenan, E. (1974) 'Norm-makers, norm-breakers: uses of speech by men and women in a Malagasy community', in R. Bauman and J. Sherzer (eds), *Explorations in the Ethnography of Speaking*. London: Cambridge University Press. pp. 125–43.

Kochman, T. (1981) *Black and White Styles in Conflict*. Chicago: Chicago University Press.

Matisoff, J. (1979) *Blessings, Curses, Hopes, and Fears: Psycho-Ostensive Expressions in Yiddish*. Philadelphia: Institute for the Study of Human Issues.

Mizutani, O. and Mizutani, N. (1987) *How to be Polite in Japanese*. Tokyo: Japan Times.

Nakane, C. (1970) *Japanese Society*. London: Weidenfeld and Nicolson.

Ochs Keenan, E. (1976) 'The universality of conversational postulates', *Language in Society*, 5: 67–80.

Saville-Troike, M. (1989) *The Ethnography of Communication*, 2nd edn. Oxford: Basil Blackwell.

Schieffelin, B.B. and Ochs E. (eds) (1986) *Language Socialization across Cultures*. Cambridge: Cambridge University Press.

Schiffrin, D. (1984) 'Jewish argument as sociability', *Language in Society*, 13: 311–35.

Scollon, R. and Scollon, S.B. (1981) *Narrative, Literacy and Face in Interethnic Communication*. Norwood, NJ: Ablex.

Sherzer, J. (1974) '*Namakke, sunmakke, dormakke*: three types of Cuna speech event', in R. Bauman and J. Sherzer (eds), *Explorations in the Ethnography of Speaking*. London: Cambridge University Press. pp. 263–82.

Smith, R.J. (1983) *Japanese Society: Tradition, Self and the Social Order*. Cambridge: Cambridge University Press.

Swift, M.G. (1965) *Malay Peasant Society in Jelebu*. London: Atholone Press.

Tannen, D. (1981) 'New York Jewish conversational style', *International Journal of the Sociology of Language*, 30: 133–49.

Tannen, D. (1986) *That's Not What I Meant!* Norwood, NJ: Ablex.

Thompson, D. (1935) 'The joking relationship and organized obscenity in North Queensland', *American Anthropologist*, new series, 37: 460–90.

Travis, C. (1992) 'How to be kind, compassionate and considerate in Japanese'. Honours thesis, Department of Linguistics, Australian National University.

Vreeland, N., Dana, G.B., Hurwitz, G.B., Just, P., Moeller, P.W. and Shinn, R.S. (1977) *Area Handbook for Malaysia* (microfilm), 3rd edn. Glen Rock, NJ: Microfilming Corporation of America.

Watson-Gegeo, K.A. and White, G.M. (eds) (1990) *Disentangling: Conflict Discourse in Pacific Societies*. Stanford: Stanford University Press.

Wierzbicka, A. (1990) 'Antitotalitarian language in Poland: some mechanisms of linguistic self-defence', *Language in Society*, 19 (1): 1–59.

Wierzbicka, A. (1991) *Cross-Cultural Pragmatics: the Semantics of Human Interaction*. Berlin: Mouton de Gruyter.

Wierzbicka, A. (1992) *Semantics, Culture, and Cognition*. Oxford: Oxford University Press.

Wierzbicka, A. (1994a) '"Cultural scripts": a semantic approach to cultural analysis and cross-cultural communication', in L. Bouton and Y. Kachru (eds), *Pragmatics and Language Learning*. Urbana–Champaign, IL: University of Illinois. pp. 1–24.

Wierzbicka, A. (1994b) '"Cultural scripts": a new approach to the study of cross-cultural communication', in M. Pütz (ed.), *Language Contact and Language Conflict*. Amsterdam: John Benjamins. pp. 67–87.

Wierzbicka, A. (1994c) 'Emotion, language and cultural scripts', in S. Kitayama and H. Markus (eds), *Emotion and Culture*. Washington: American Psychological Association. pp. 130–98.

Wierzbicka, A. (1996) *Semantics, Primes and Universals*. Oxford: Oxford University Press.

Wikan, U. (1990) *Managing Turbulent Hearts: a Balinese Formula for Living*. Chicago: University of Chicago Press.

10

Critical Discourse Analysis

Norman Fairclough and Ruth Wodak

Critical Discourse Analysis: a Preliminary Description

Like other approaches to discourse analysis, critical discourse analysis (henceforth CDA) analyses real and often extended instances of social interaction which take a linguistic form, or a partially linguistic form. The critical approach is distinctive in its view of (a) the relationship between language and society, and (b) the relationship between analysis and the practices analysed. Let us take these in turn.

CDA sees discourse – language use in speech and writing – as a form of 'social practice'. Describing discourse as social practice implies a dialectical relationship between a particular discursive event and the situation(s), institution(s) and social structure(s) which frame it. A dialectical relationship is a two-way relationship: the discursive event is shaped by situations, institutions and social structures, but it also shapes them. To put the same point in a different way, discourse is socially *constitutive* as well as socially shaped: it constitutes situations, objects of knowledge, and the social identities of and relationships between people and groups of people. It is constitutive both in the sense that it helps to sustain and reproduce the social status quo, and in the sense that it contributes to transforming it. Since discourse is so socially influential, it gives rise to important issues of power. Discursive practices may have major ideological effects: that is, they can help produce and reproduce unequal power relations between (for instance) social classes, women and men, and ethnic/cultural majorities and minorities through the ways in which they represent things and position people. So discourse may, for example, be racist, or sexist, and try to pass off assumptions (often falsifying ones) about any aspect of social life as mere common sense. Both the ideological loading of particular ways of using language and the relations of power which underlie them are often unclear to people. CDA aims to make more visible these opaque aspects of discourse.

CDA sees itself not as dispassionate and objective social science, but as engaged and committed. It is a form of intervention in social practice and social relationships: many analysts are politically active against racism, or as feminists, or within the peace movement, and so forth. But CDA is not an exception to the normal objectivity of social science: social science is inherently tied into politics and formulations of policy, as for instance Foucault's (1971, 1979) work convincingly demonstrated. What is distinctive about CDA is both that it intervenes on the side of dominated and oppressed groups and against dominating groups, and that it openly declares the emancipatory interests that motivate it. The political interests and uses of social scientific research are usually less explicit. This certainly does not imply that CDA is less scholarly than other research: standards of careful, rigorous and systematic analysis apply with equal force to CDA as to other approaches.

CDA in Context

The current interest in critical discourse analysis as a field corresponds to, contributes to but also draws upon an upsurge of critical interest in language in contemporary society. There is for instance widespread cynicism about the rhetoric of commodity advertising, or about the simulated personalness of the language of people working in impersonal service industries (the 'have-a-nice-day' phenomenon). And in a different direction there is a high level of consciousness and self-consciousness about sexist and racist ways of using language,[1] and the critique and change of language are central concerns in contemporary feminist and anti-racist political movements.[2] This critical consciousness about the language practices in which people are involved in their ordinary lives is a response to important shifts in the function of language in social life, of which some are longer term and characterize modern societies, while others are more recent and characterize 'late modernity' (Giddens, 1991).

In broad terms, language has become more salient and more important in a range of social processes. The increased economic importance of language is striking. It is well known for instance that the balance of economic life has shifted increasingly from production to consumption and from manufacturing industries to service, culture and leisure industries. In many service contexts, a key factor in the quality of the 'goods' produced and therefore in profitability is the nature of the language that is used in 'delivering' services. Hence the preoccupation with the 'design' of spoken and written language used by service personnel (air hostesses, shop assistants, etc.). The increasing marketization of public services – the way they are required to operate on a market basis – has entailed a large-scale extension of these design concerns (on universities, for instance, see Fairclough, 1993).

At the same time, key areas of social life are becoming increasingly centred on the media, especially television. This is notably the case with politics. Politicians now have unprecedented access on a regular basis to huge audiences, providing both better opportunities for them to shape opinion and win support, and greater risks of public exposure and discredit. The calculated design of political language is one crucial factor in success in political struggle. Also, the whole process of political struggle and the struggle for political legitimacy is becoming inextricably bound up with media economics and the pursuit of audiences and profitability. This further increases the design pressure on political discourse.

As these examples suggest, the increased importance of language in social life has led to a greater level of conscious intervention to control and shape language practices in accordance with economic, political and institutional objectives. This has been referred to as the 'technologization of discourse' (Fairclough, 1992a), a distinctive characteristic of the contemporary linguistic and discursive order. Technologization of discourse involves systematic, institutionalized integration of: research on language; design and redesign of language practices; and training of institutional personnel in these practices. But technologization of discourse can be seen as just one aspect of a more general characteristic of late modern orders of discourse and late modern social life overall: a peculiarly modern form of 'reflexivity'. As Giddens (1991) puts it, contemporary life is reflexive in the sense that people radically alter their practices – the ways in which they live their lives – on the basis of knowledge and information about those practices. Technologization of discourse is the 'top-down', institutional side of modern reflexivity, but there is also a 'bottom-up' side appertaining to the everyday practices of ordinary people. A critical awareness of discursive practices and an orientation to transforming such practices as one element in social (class, feminist, anti-racist, green, etc.) struggles – or in Giddens's terms, in the reflexive construction and reconstruction of the self – is a normal feature of everyday life. The critical analysis of discourse is therefore firstly a feature of contemporary social life, and only secondly an area of academic work. And critical discourse analysis as an academic pursuit is firmly rooted in the properties of contemporary life.

Theoretical Origins of CDA

Critical discourse analysis applies to language types of critical analysis which have developed within 'Western Marxism'. In broad terms, Western Marxism has given considerably more emphasis than other forms of Marxism to cultural dimensions of societies, emphasizing that capitalist social relations are established and maintained (reproduced) in large part in culture (and hence in ideology), not just (or mainly) in the economic 'base'. Western Marxism includes key figures and movements in twentieth century social and political thought – Antonio Gramsci, the Frankfurt School (including Jürgen Habermas), the Louis Althusser. Critical discourse analysts do not always explicitly place themselves within this legacy, but it frames their work nevertheless.

Gramsci argued that the continuing power of the capitalist class depended upon a combination of 'political society' and 'civil society' – the former being the domain of coercion, the latter being the domain of 'hegemony' where the consent or acquiescence of the majority to the status

quo is won. The emphasis on hegemony entailed an emphasis on i(
and on how the structures and practices of ordinary life routinely n(
capitalist social relations (Forgacs, 1988).

Althusser (1971) made a major contribution to the theory of i(
He viewed ideologies not as a nebulous realm of 'ideas' but as tied to
material practices embedded in social institutions (how teaching is
organized in classrooms, for instance). He also saw the central effect of
ideologies as positioning people in particular ways as social 'subjects',
though he tended to an overly deterministic (structuralist) version of this
process which left little room for action by subjects. Gramsci and Althusser
have inspired a great deal of work in critical analysis, some of which has
influenced critical discourse analysis, including the work of Stuart Hall and
the Centre for Contemporary Cultural Studies at Birmingham in the UK
(Hall et al., 1980).

Michel Foucault's work on discourse was explicitly directed against
Marxism and theories of ideology. For Foucault discourses are knowledge
systems of the human sciences (medicine, economics, linguistics, etc.) that
inform the social and governmental 'technologies' which constitute power
in modern society. They are partly realized in ways of using language, but
partly in other ways (for example, ways of designing prisons or schools).
Foucault's work has generated immense interest in discourse analysis
amongst social scientists, but analysis of a rather abstract sort that is not
anchored in close analysis of particular texts. Some critical discourse
analysts (Courtine, 1981; Fairclough, 1992a) attempt to incorporate a
Foucaultian perspective into ways of analysing texts. (See discussions of
Maas and Jäger below.)

The term 'critical' is particularly associated with the Frankfurt School of
Philosophy. The Frankfurt School returns to the foundations of Marx's
thought and seeks to reexamine the philosophical heritage from which it
arose (in Kant, Hegel, etc.). Frankfurt School philosophers argue that
cultural products cannot be treated as mere epiphenomena of economy.
Instead, they regard such products as relatively autonomous expressions of
contradictions within the social whole, and they perceive within some of
them expressions of both the social physiognomy of the present, and the
critical forces which negate the existing order. They emphasize the
importance of subjective conditions for revolutionary transformation (see
Thompson, 1988: 71ff.; Fay, 1987: 203). According to Jürgen Habermas, a
critical science has to be self-reflexive (reflecting on the interests that
underlie it) and it must consider the historical context in which linguistic
and social interactions take place. Jürgen Habermas developed the concept
of the 'ideal speech situation', to be understood as the utopian vision of
interaction taking place without power relations intruding into it. Rational
discourse could, he argues, overcome distorted communication, that is
opaque and ideological discourse which deviates from the ideal speech
situation. Habermas's approach has influenced German sociolinguistics,
pragmatics, and some studies in CDA (see Wodak et al., 1990).

Another important influence from within linguistics and literary studies has been Mikhail Bakhtin (1981; 1986). Books published under the name of V.I. Volosinov may also have been written by Bakhtin, or were at least heavily influenced by him. Volosinov (1973, written 1928) is the first linguistic theory of ideology. It claims that linguistic signs (words and longer expressions) are the material of ideology, and that all language use is ideological. Linguistic signs are regarded as 'an arena of class struggle': one focus of class struggle is over the meanings of words. Bakhtin's work emphasizes dialogical properties of texts, their 'intertextuality' as Kristeva (1986) has put it: the idea that any text is a link in a chain of texts, reacting to, drawing in, and transforming other texts. Bakhtin also developed a theory of genre, according to which any text is necessarily shaped by socially available repertoires of genres (for example, the genre of scientific articles, or the genre of advertisements), but may creatively mix genres. There are pressures for texts to follow conventional genres, but also pressures to innovate by mixing genres.

Approaches to CDA

In the following we want to give a short overview of some of the most important theoretical approaches to CDA, by comparing them in terms of a number of key features. For example, some of the approaches include a *historical perspective*, in theory and methodology; others do so less or not at all. The centre of attention may be either on the repetition, predictability and *reproduction* of practices, or on *creativity* and innovation. The approaches also differ in how they see the *mediation between the text and the social*. On the one hand, sociocognitive processes are seen as controlling discursive realizations; on the other hand, specific genres are assumed to mediate between social and discursive practices. Some studies in CDA view the *multifunctionality of texts* as a central and important feature. Following the Hallidayan tradition, texts are believed to fulfil and represent several functions at once (ideational, interpersonal, and textual; see below). In contrast, some researchers focus on the discursive level only without taking a functional approach as their point of departure. Lastly, approaches differ in the way discursive events are interpreted. More hermeneutic, interpretative procedures stand in opposition to more text-oriented *interpretations*.

French Discourse Analysis

Althusser's ideological theory and Foucault's theory of discourse were major points of reference for French discourse analysis, notably the work of Michel Pêcheux (1982). Discourse in Pêcheux's theory is the place where language and ideology meet, and discourse analysis is the analysis of ideological dimensions of language use, and of the materialization in language of ideology. Both the words used and the meanings of words vary according to the position in class struggle from which they are used – according to the 'discursive formation' they are located within. For instance, the word *struggle* itself is particularly associated with a working class political voice, and its meaning in that discursive formation is different from its meanings when used from other positions. Pêcheux's main focus was political discourse in France, especially the relationship between social-democratic and communist discourse within left political discourse.

Pêcheux stresses the ideological effects of discursive formations in positioning people as social subjects. Echoing Althusser, he suggests that people are placed in the 'imaginary' (illusory) position of sources of their discourse, whereas actually their discourse and indeed they themselves are effects of their ideological positioning. The sources and processes of their own positioning are hidden from people. They are typically not aware of speaking/writing from within a particular discursive formation. Moreover, the discursive formations people are positioned within are themselves shaped by the 'complex whole in dominance' of discursive formations, which Pêcheux calls 'interdiscourse' – but people are not aware of that shaping. Radical change in the way people are positioned in discourse can only come from political revolution.

Pêcheux and his colleagues changed their views on this and other issues in the late 1970s and early 1980s (Pêcheux, 1988; Maingueneau, 1987). The influence of Foucault increased, as did that of Bakhtin. Studies began to emphasize the complex mixing of discursive formations in texts, and the heterogeneity and ambivalence of texts (see, for example, Courtine, 1981). In addition to its interest in political discourse, French discourse analysis has produced analyses of various other types of written discourse (including religious discourse and school textbooks), and more recently a good deal of work has been done on both spoken and written discourse in the workplace.

Critical Linguists

The 'critical linguistics' (CL) which developed in Britain in the 1970s (Fowler et al., 1979; Kress and Hodge, 1979) was closely associated with 'systemic' linguistic theory (Halliday, 1978; 1985), which accounts for its emphasis upon practical ways of analysing texts in contrast with Pêcheux's more abstract focus on discursive formations, and the attention it gives to grammar in its ideological analysis. Features of the grammatical form of a text are seen as meaningful choices from within the possibilities available in grammatical systems. For instance, if a documentary on the 'Third World' consistently positions poor people in Third World countries as objects of actional (transitive) verbs and never as subjects of such verbs, that may contribute to the construction of the poor overall in the text as passive victims, rather than (say) engaged in struggle (see Fairclough, 1995a). Moreover, in so far as the representations implicit in such meaningful grammatical choices contribute to reproducing relations of domination, grammar works ideologically.

Another focus is the ideological import of systematic ways in which texts are transformed into other texts over time, for instance in the production of news stories in the press, or in the production of medical records from doctors' notes about consultations with their patients. Critical linguistics also drew attention to the ideological potency of systems of categorization which are built into particular vocabularies – particular ways of 'lexical-izing' experience. Critical linguistic analysis was applied to a variety of types of discourse, but the most salient was the discourse of the press (see Fowler, 1991). More recently, it has been applied for instance to various types of educational text and to spoken dialogue, including interview (Kress, 1985).

Social Semiotics

Some of the major figures in critical linguistics have more recently been involved in developing a 'social semiotics' (Hodge and Kress, 1988). Social semiotics draws attention to the multi-semiotic character of most texts in contemporary society, and explores ways of analysing visual images (from press photographs and television images to Renaissance art) and the relationship between language and visual images (Kress and van Leeuwen, 1990). Kress and van Leeuwen explore the value of categories in systemic linguistics for the analysis of visual images, and how these categories are materially realized in pictures. For example, the systemic textual categories of 'given' versus 'new' are realized through the compositional structures of pictures, with the given located on the left and the new on the right. Kress and van Leeuwen also suggest that insights from the analysis of visual images may lead us to rethink our theories of language. Social semiotics also gives more attention than critical linguistics to productive and interpretative practices associated with types of text as well as texts *per se*, and there is a new orientation to struggle and historical change in discourse. The concept of genre, viewed dynamically in a Bakhtinian way, has become central, as well as intertextual analysis of texts alongside more conventional linguistic analysis (Kress and Threadgold, 1988; Fairclough, 1992b; Lemke, 1995; Thibault, 1991). Other English language work includes generic analyses of media discourse which bridge the divide between linguistics and cultural studies.

Sociocultural Change and Change in Discourse

Fairclough (1989; 1992a) has focused upon relationships between socio-cultural change and discursive change, for instance in the commodification of public services in the UK – the process through which services are treated as if they were commodities, for instance in the marketing of them. Discursive change is analysed in terms of the creative mixing of discourses and genres in texts, which leads over time to the restructuring of relationships between different discursive practices within and across institutions, and the shifting of boundaries within and between 'orders of discourse' (structured sets of discursive practices associated with particular social domains). For example, a major change in discursive practices affecting many public institutions in contemporary society is the 'conversationalization' of public discourse, the simulation of conversational practices in public domains, shifting the boundary between the orders of discourse of public life and ordinary life. A major restructuring of the boundary between public and private social life is partly constituted through these shifts in discursive practices. The objective of analyses of tendencies such as conversationalization (Fairclough, 1994) is to draw CDA closer to recent sociological and other social scientific research on social and cultural change, so that CDA can be an effective method within such research. This approach has been applied for instance to consultations between doctors and patients, university prospectuses, and media interviews. Fairclough and his colleagues have also stressed the educational implications of CDA, advocating 'critical language awareness' as a key component of language education in schools and other educational institutions (Fairclough, 1992c).

Socio-cognitive Studies

Most of van Dijk's critical work of the 1980s focuses on the reproduction of ethnic prejudices and racism in discourse and communication, starting out with a critical analysis of news on the coverage of squatters, refugees etc. (van Dijk, 1980). Another initial study examined the ways white Dutch and Californians talk about minorities (van Dijk, 1985a; 1987). Van Dijk (1991) examined the role of the news media in the reproduction of racism. Combining quantitative and qualitative analyses of thousands of news reports in the British and Dutch press, van Dijk discovered that the most frequent topics in the press corresponded to prevailing ethnic prejudices expressed in everyday talk: immigration as invasion, immigrants and refugees as spongers, crime, violence and problematic cultural differences. In his latest book on discourse and racism, van Dijk (1993a) investigated a hypothesis which increasingly suggested itself in the previous studies, namely, that the elites play a crucial role in the reproduction of racism.

More recently, van Dijk has turned to more general questions of abuse of power and the reproduction of inequality through ideologies. In his view, which integrates elements from his earlier studies on cognition, those who control most dimensions of discourse (preparation, setting, participants, topics, style, rhetoric, interaction, etc.) have the most power. He argues that no direct relation can or should be constructed between discourse structures and social structures, but that they are always mediated by the interface of personal and social cognition. Cognition, according to van Dijk, is the missing link of many studies in CL and CDA, which fail to show how societal structures influence discourse structures and precisely how societal structures are in turn enacted, instituted, legitimated, confirmed or challenged by text and talk.

Discourse-Historical Method

The group in Vienna around Ruth Wodak (1975; 1986; Lutz and Wodak, 1987; Wodak et al., 1990; Wodak and Matouschek, 1993) were educated as sociolinguists in the Bernsteinian tradition and Wodak herself was influenced by the Frankfurt School, especially by Jürgen Habermas's critique of formal linguistics. After conducting studies on institutional communication and speech barriers in court, in schools and in hospital clinics,[3] she has increasingly turned her attention (within the framework of interdisciplinary research teams) towards sexism, and contemporary antisemitism and racism in settings of various degrees of formality. One of the major aims of this kind of critical research has been its practical application (see below).

In an interdisciplinary study of post-war antisemitism in Austria completed in 1990, Wodak and her colleagues devised what they have termed a 'discourse-historical method'. The distinctive feature of this approach is its attempt to integrate systematically all available background information in the analysis and interpretation of the many layers of a written or spoken text (see below). The study in which and for which this approach was developed attempted to trace in detail the constitution of an antisemitic stereotyped image, or *Feindbild*, as it emerged in public discourse in the 1986 Austrian presidential campaign of Kurt Waldheim.

Several other studies on prejudice and racism followed this first attempt and have led the group in Vienna to more general and theoretical considerations on the nature (forms and contents) of racist discourse (about foreigners, indigenous minorities, immigrant workers, etc.) (Matouschek et al., 1995; Wodak and Menz, 1990). Fundamentally, they elaborate van Dijk's sociocognitive approach by assuming different types of schemata which are important for text production and text comprehension (sociopsychological theories of text planning and text comprehension; see Wodak, 1992). Although the forms of racist and prejudiced discourse may be similar, the contents vary according to the stigmatized groups as well as to the settings in which certain linguistic realizations become possible. The discourse-historical methodology is designed to enable the analysis of implicit prejudiced utterances, as well as to identify and expose the codes and allusions contained in prejudiced discourse. Thus, typically, text producers use allusions which readers can only understand if they know the objects or background which are referred to. This strategy enables the writers/speakers to back away from responsibility easily as they have not made their statements explicit.

Reading analysis

The linguist Utz Maas (1985; 1989a; 1989b) refers to central ideas of Michel Foucault and combines these with a hermeneutic methodology which he labels *Lesartenanalyse* (reading analysis). He defines discourse 'as linguistic forms correlating with social practice which has to be investigated sociologically and historically'; 'Text analysis becomes discourse analysis whereby discourse correlates to a historically formed social practice' (1984: 18). In other words, a discourse is not an arbitrary corpus of texts, extensionally (objectively) defined by time and space, but rather is intensionally defined by its content, as for example 'fascist discourse' is a correlate of German fascism. Discourse analysis, then, studies the 'rules' which constitute a specific discourse, which thus make a certain text a fascist text. Each text relates to other texts, synchronically and diachronically. And these relationships are also necessarily involved in the definition of the specific discourse. Basically, therefore, he turns away from the pure formal analysis of texts (text linguistics), because such an analysis would only capture immanent aspects of the text and could not, in Maas's opinion, make the specificities of political discourse explicit. As political discourse can only be defined as such through the socio-historical context (social practice of politics), a non-context-oriented analysis, he notes, is doomed to fail.

Utz Maas is known as a major expert on the discourse of National Socialism. His extensive study (1984) was the first analysis of the rhetorics and the discourse of Nazi leaders, but also of everyday discourse, like slogans, newspapers, speeches of student leaders (see also 1989), and even recipes. In the thorough and very detailed analyses of discourse sequences, Maas presents a simple methodology (*Lesartenanalyse*). The importance of the historical dimension and of hermeneutics is particularly apparent in this approach, especially in the analysis of allusions which relate to background knowledge and cannot really be understood without taking this knowledge into account.

Duisburg School

The Duisburg School is also massively influenced by Michel Foucault's theories. Siegfried Jäger is concerned with linguistic and iconic characteristics of discourse, as well as with 'collective symbols' (topoi) (like house, car, waves of immigrants) which possess important cohesive functions in texts. Discourses are, in Jäger's opinion, institutionalized, conventionalized speech modes which relate to behaviour and also to dominance (Jäger and Jäger, 1993: 5). Discourse is seen as the flow of text and speech through time (1993: 6). Any discourse has historical roots, has an impact on the present and also determines the future. The different discourses are all interwoven in texts (*diskursives Gewimmel*)[4] and only explicit discourse analysis can disentangle this chaos. Like Utz Maas, Jäger has developed an explicit methodology in several steps which serves to analyse discourse fragments (sequences) systematically and allows one to cover intertextuality. In contrast to Maas, Jäger focuses his micro-analysis of text on collective symbols, metaphors, and agentive structures.

Margret Jäger and Siegfried Jäger have undertaken a lot of research on the new right in Germany (1993). They analysed all the newspapers and journals which are edited by right wing groups and showed both major common characteristics – certain symbols, 'ethnopluralism' (apartheid), aggressiveness, anti-democratism etc. – and important differences in linguistic elements and styles due to the specific audience addressed.

CDA in Action

Our aim in this section is to give an example of CDA. We shall work with a version of CDA based upon eight principles of theory or method, and we shall show how each affects the practice of CDA through an analysis – necessarily partial – of the following extract from a radio interview with Margaret Thatcher, former Prime Minister of Britain.[5] Some of the principles represent common ground for all approaches within CDA, while others are more controversial.

```
 1   MC:   Prime Minister you were at Oxford in the nineteen
            forties and after the war Britain would embark on a
            period of relative prosperity for all the like of which it
            had hardly known but today there are three and a
 5          quarter million unemployed and e:m
            Britain's economic performance by one measurement
            has fallen to the rank of that of Italy now can you
            imagine yourself back at the University today what
            must seem to be the chances in Britain and the
10          prospects for all now
      MT:   they are very different worlds you're talking about
            because the first thing that struck me very forcibly as
            you were speaking of those days was that now we do
            enjoy a standard of living which was undreamed of
15          then and I can remember Rab Butler saying after we
            returned to power in about 1951–52 that if we played
            our cards right the standard of living within twenty
            five years would be twice as high as it was then and
            em he was just about right and it was remarkable
20          because it was something that we had never thought
            of now I don't think now one would necessarily think
            wholly in material terms indeed I think it's wrong to
            think in material terms because really the kind of
            country you want is made up by the strength of its
25          people and I think we're returning to my vision of
            Britain as a younger person and I was always brought
```

up with the idea look Britain is a country whose
people think for themselves act for themselves can act
on their own initiative they don't have to be told
30   don't like to be pushed around are self-reliant and
then over and above that they're always responsible
for their families and something else it was a kind of
em I think it was Barrie who said do as you would be
done by e: you act to others as you'd like them to act
35   towards you and so you do something for the
community now I think if you were looking at
another country you would say what makes a country
strong it is its people do they run their industries well
are their human relations good e: do they respect law
40   and order are their families strong all of those kind of
things

       ⌈ and you know it's just way beyond economics
MC: ⌊ but you know people still   people still ask
though e: where is she going now General de Gaulle
45   had a vision of France e: a certain idea of France as he
put it e: you have fought three major battles in this
country the Falkland Islands e:m against the miners
and local councils and against public expenditure and
people I think would like to hear what this vision you
50   have of Britain is it must be a powerful one what is it
that inspires your action

MT: I wonder if I perhaps I can answer best by saying how
I see what government should do and if government
really believes in people what people should do I
55   believe that government should be very strong to do
those things which only government can do it has to
be strong to have defence because the kind of Britain I
see would always defend its freedom and always be a
reliable ally so you've got to be strong to your own
60   people and other countries have got to know that you
stand by your word then you turn to internal security
and yes you HAVE got to be strong on law and order
and do the things that only governments can do but
there it's part government and part people because
65   you CAN'T have law and order observed unless it's
in partnership with people then you have to be strong
to uphold the value of the currency and only
governments can do that by sound finance and then
you have to create the framework for a good
70   education system and social security and at that point
you have to say over to people people are inventive
creative and so you expect PEOPLE to create thriving

industries thriving services yes you expect people
each and every one from whatever their background
75   to have a chance to rise to whatever level their own
abilities can take them yes you expect people of all
sorts of background and almost whatever their
income level to be able to have a chance of owning
some property tremendously important the
80   ownership of property of a house gives you some
independence gives you a stake in the future you're
concerned about your children

MC: but could ⌈ you sum this vision up
MT: ⌊ (   ) you said my vision
85   please let me just go on and then that isn't enough
if you're interested in the future yes you will
probably save you'll probably want a little bit of
independent income of your own and so constantly
thinking about the future so it's very much a Britain
90   whose people are independent of government but
aware that the government has to be strong to do
those things which only governments can do

MC: but can you sum it up in a in a in a phrase or two the
aim is to achieve what or to restore what in Britain
95   when clearly risking a lot and winning in a place like
the Falkland Islands is just as important in your
philosophy ⌈ for Britain as as
MT: ⌊ I think
MC: restoring sound money reducing the money supply in
100   the Bank of England

MT: but of course it showed that we were reliable in the
defence of freedom and when part of Britain we: was
invaded of course we went we believed in defence of
freedom we were reliable I think if I could try to sum
105   it up in a phrase and that's always I suppose most
difficult of all I would say really restoring the very
best of the British character to its former
preeminence.

MC: but this has meant something called Thatcherism now
110   is that a description you accept as something quite
distinct from traditional conservatism in this country

MT: no it is traditional conservatism

MC: but it's radical and populist and therefore not
115   conservative

MT: it is radical because at the time when I took over we
needed to be radical e: it is populist I wouldn't call it
populist I would say that many of the things which
I've said strike a chord in the hearts of ordinary

120   people why because they're British because their
             character IS independent because they DON'T like to
             be shoved around coz they ARE prepared to take
             responsibility because they DO expect to be loyal to
             their friends and loyal allies that's why you call it
125   populist. I say it strikes a chord in the hearts of
             people I know because it struck a chord in my heart
             many many years ago

1 CDA Addresses Social Problems

CDA is the analysis of linguistic and semiotic aspects of social processes and problems. The focus is not upon language or the use of language in and for themselves, but upon the partially linguistic character of social and cultural processes and structures. For example, a critical discourse analysis of the extract above might be seen as a contribution to the analysis of Thatcherism – or, in more international terms, the new right in politics. As this example suggests, CDA is by its nature interdisciplinary, combining diverse disciplinary perspectives in its own analyses, and being used to complement more standard forms of social and cultural analysis. Such an analysis might be linked to particular problems and struggles of dominated groups under Thatcherite governments, such as those of the miners and other trade unionists. It could help develop a critical awareness of the discursive strategies of Thatcherism which might be one resource in struggles against it.

Seen in this context, the key claim of CDA is that major social and political processes and movements such as Thatcherism (Fairclough, 1993) have a partly linguistic-discursive character. This follows from the fact that social and political changes in contemporary society generally include a substantive element of cultural and ideological change. This is certainly true of Thatcherism, which has been described as being an attempt to construct a new hegemony, a new basis for winning popular consent, as well as being a set of free market economic strategies, and a political project for strengthening and centralizing the state, pushing back the structures and institutions of social democracy, weakening the trade unions, and so forth (Hall and Jacques, 1983).

Thatcherism as an ideological project for building a new hegemony can be seen as an attempt to restructure political discourse by combining diverse existing discourses together in a new way. This is evident in the extract above. There is a characteristic combination of elements of traditional conservative discourse (the focus on law and order, the family, and strong government, for example *do they respect law and order are their families strong*) and elements of a liberal political discourse and economic discourse (the focus on the independence of the individual, for example *because their character IS independent because they DON'T like to be shoved around coz they ARE prepared to take responsibility*; and on the individual entrepreneur as the dynamo of the economy, for example *you expect PEOPLE to create thriving industries thriving services*).

These are mixed with elements from discourses of ordinary life and ordinary experience which give Thatcher's discourse the populist quality referred to by the interviewer – for example, the expressions *stand by your word, shoved around,* and *strikes a chord in [people's] hearts.* This novel combination of discourses is associated with distinctive representations of social reality and distinctive constructions of social and political relations and identities (see below). It achieved a dominant position in the field of political discourse, though it is arguable to what extent it became hege-monic in the sense of winning widespread acceptance.

2   Power Relations Are Discursive

CDA highlights the substantively linguistic and discursive nature of social relations of power in contemporary societies. This is partly a matter of how power relations are exercised and negotiated in discourse. One issue that receives a great deal of attention is power relations between the media and politics – whether in broad terms mediatized political discourse is the domination of the media over politicians, or the exploitation of the media by politicians. Close analysis of power relations in political interviews in the media can cast some light on this issue (Bell and van Leeuwen, 1994). On the face of it, interviewers exercise a lot of power over politicians in interviews: interviewers generally control the way in which interviews begin and end, the topics which are dealt with and the angles from which they are tackled, the time given to politicians to answer questions, and so forth. In the case of the Thatcher interview, Michael Charlton's questions do set and attempt to police an agenda (see for instance lines 83, 93–4). However, politicians do not by any means always comply with interviewers' attempts to control interviews, and there is often a struggle for control. Charlton for instance in line 83 tries to bring Thatcher back to the question he asked in lines 49–51, but she interrupts his attempt at policing her talk, and carries on with what is effectively a short political speech. The fact that Thatcher makes speeches in her answers to Charlton's questions – or perhaps better, interprets Charlton's questions as opportunities to make speeches rather than requiring answers – points to another dimension of power relations in discourse. Thatcher tries to exercise what we might call rhetorical power, the power which comes from a facility in the rhetoric of political per-suasion, a form of 'cultural capital' which according to Bourdieu (1991) is the prerogative of professional politicians in contemporary societies. This power – in so far as it is effective – is primarily power over the radio audience, but it is also germane to power relations between Thatcher and Charlton in that it circumvents and marginalizes Charlton's power as interviewer. Thatcher's rhetorical power is realized for instance in the large-scale linguistic devices which organize her contributions, such as the triple parallel structure of lines 56–67 (*it has to be strong to have defence,* *you HAVE got to be strong on law and order*, 62; *you have to be str* *uphold the value of the currency*, 66–7).

In addition to the question of power in discourse, there is the question of power over discourse (Fairclough, 1989). This is partly a matter of access. As Prime Minister, Mrs Thatcher could use the media largely on her own terms. Less powerful politicians have access that is more limited and more on the media's terms, while most people have no access whatever. But power over discourse is also a matter of the capacity to control and change the ground rules of discursive practices, and the structure of the order of discourse. We have already referred above to the Thatcherite project for a reconstructed hegemony in the field of political discourse, involving novel combinations of existing discourses. The extract above also illustrates, as we have just indicated, a reconstruction of genre: the genres of political speech and media interview are articulated in a way which makes this interview a powerful political platform for the distinctive Thatcherite style of authoritative and 'tough' but populist political rhetoric.

These examples suggest that discursive aspects of power relations are not fixed and monolithic. Much work in CDA has been characterized by a focus upon the discursive reproduction of power relations. We also need a focus on discursive aspects of power struggle and of the transformation of power relations. It is fruitful to look at both 'power in discourse' and 'power over discourse' in these dynamic terms: both the exercise of power in the 'here and now' of specific discursive events, and the longer-term shaping of discursive practices and orders of discourse, are generally negotiated and contested processes. Thatcherism can for instance be partly seen as an ongoing hegemonic struggle in discourse and over discourse, with a variety of antagonists – 'wets' in the Conservative Party, the other political parties, the trade unions, the professions, and so forth.

3 Discourse Constitutes Society and Culture

We can only make sense of the salience of discourse in contemporary social processes and power relations by recognizing that discourse constitutes society and culture, as well as being constituted by them. Their relationship, that is, is a dialectical one. This entails that every instance of language use makes its own small contribution to reproducing and/or transforming society and culture, including power relations. That is the power of discourse; that is why it is worth struggling over.

It is useful to distinguish three broad domains of social life that may be discursively constituted, referred to as representations, relations and identities for short: representations of the world, social relations between people, and people's social and personal identities (Fairclough, 1992a). In terms of representations, for instance, lines 11–21 of the example incorporate a narrative which gives a very different representation of history to the one in the interviewer's question: the latter's contrast between prosperous past and depressed present is restructured as a past Conservative government creating present prosperity.

The extract constitutes social relations between Thatcher as a political leader and the political public contradictorily, as in part relations of solidarity and in part relations of authority. Thatcher's use of the indefinite pronoun *you*, which is a popular colloquial speech form (in contrast to *one*), implicitly claims that she is just an ordinary person, like her voters (this is the populist element in her discourse). So too does some of her vocabulary: notice for instance how she avoids the interviewer's term *populist* and the interviewer's technical use of *radical* as a specialist political term in lines 113–20, perhaps because their intellectualism would compromise her claims to solidarity. Thatcher's deployment of political rhetoric referred to above is by contrast authoritative. So too is her use of inclusive *we*: she claims to speak for the people. Similar are the passages (including 27–36 and 119–23) in which she characterizes the British, claiming the authority to articulate their self-perceptions on their behalf.

These passages are also interesting in terms of the constitution of identities: a major feature of this discourse is how it constitutes 'the people' as a political community (note Thatcher's explicit foregrounding of the project of engineering collective identity – *restoring the very best of the British character to its former preeminence*), and the listing of characteristics in these examples is a striking discourse strategy. Notice that these lists condense together, without explicit connections between them, the diverse discourses which we have suggested (principle 1) are articulated together in Thatcherite political discourse: conservative and liberal political discourses, liberal economic discourse, discourses of ordinary life. Since the connections between these discourses are left implicit, it is left to audience members to find ways of coherently articulating them together.

Notice also the vague and shifting meanings of the pronoun *we* (lines 13–25, 101–4) in Thatcher's talk. *We* is sometimes what is traditionally called 'inclusive' (it includes the audience and the general population, for example *we do enjoy a standard of living which was undreamed of then*, 13–14), and sometimes 'exclusive' (for example, *after we returned to power*, 15–16, where *we* refers just to the Conservative Party). In other cases, it could be taken as either (for example, *if we played our cards right*, 16–17; *we went we believed in defence of freedom we were reliable*, 103–4). Even if we take the first of these examples as exclusive, it is still unclear who the *we* identifies: is it the Conservative Party, or the government? Also, calling *we* 'inclusive' is rather misleading, for while *we* in for instance *we do enjoy a standard of living which was undreamed of then* does identify the whole community, it constructs the community in a way which excludes those who have not achieved prosperity. Similarly, *we went we believed in defence of freedom we were reliable*, on an 'inclusive' reading, may leave those who opposed the Falklands adventure feeling excluded from the general community. The pronoun *you* is used in a similarly strategic and manipulative way on lines 59–88. We are not suggesting that Thatcher or her aides are consciously planning to use *we* and *you* in these ways, though reflexive awareness of language is increasing among politicians. Rather, there are broader intended strategic objectives for political discourse (such as building a popular base for political positions, mobilizing people behind policy decisions) which are realized in ways of using language that are likely themselves to be unintended.

Finally, the discourse also constitutes an identity for Thatcher herself as a woman political leader who has political authority without ceasing to be feminine. Notice for example the modality features of lines 52–92. On the one hand, there are a great many strong obligational modalities (note the modal verbs *should, have to, have got to*) and epistemic ('probability') modalities (note the categorical present tense verbs of for instance lines 80–2), which powerfully claim political authority. On the other hand, this section opens with a very tentative and hedged expression (*I wonder if I perhaps I can answer best by saying how I see* . . .) which might stereo-typically be construed – in conjunction with her delivery at this point, and her dress and appearance – as 'feminine'.

A useful working assumption is that any part of any language text, spoken or written, is simultaneously constituting representations, relations, and identities. This assumption harmonizes with a multifunctional theory of language and text such as one finds for instance in systemic linguistic theory (Halliday, 1994; Halliday and Hasan, 1985). According to this theory, even the individual clauses (simple sentences) of a text simul-taneously function 'ideationally' in representing reality, and 'interperson-ally' in constructing social relations and identities, as well as 'textually' in making the parts of a text into a coherent whole.

4   Discourse Does Ideological Work

Ideologies are particular ways of representing and constructing society which reproduce unequal relations of power, relations of domination and exploitation. The theory of ideology developed as part of the Marxist account of class relations (Larrain, 1979), but it is now generally extended to include relations of domination based upon gender and ethnicity. Ideol-ogies are often (though not necessarily) false or ungrounded constructions of society (for example, gender ideologies which represent women as less emotionally stable than men). To determine whether a particular (type of) discursive event does ideological work, it is not enough to analyse texts; one also needs to consider how texts are interpreted and received and what social effects they have.

In our example, the political and economic strategies of Thatcherism are an explicit topic, and are clearly formulated, notably in lines 52–92, including the central idea of strong government intervention to create conditions in which markets can operate freely. But Thatcher's formu-lation is actually built around a contrast between government and people which we would see as ideological: it covers over the fact that the 'people' who dominate the creation of 'thriving industries' and so forth are mainly the transnational corporations, and it can help to legitimize existing relations of economic and political domination. It is a common feature of Thatcherite populist discourse. The opposition between government and people is quite explicit here, but ideologies are typically more implicit. They attach for instance to key words which evoke but leave implicit sets of ideological assumptions – such as *freedom, law and order* or *sound finance*. Notice also *thriving industries thriving services*. This is another instance of the list structure discussed above, though it is a short list with just two items. *Thriving industries* is a common collocation, but *thriving services* is an innovation of an ideologically potent sort: to achieve a coherent meaning for the list one needs to assume that services can be evaluated on the same basis as industries, a truly Thatcherite assumption which the listener however is left to infer. Note that not all common-sense assumptions in discourse are ideological, given our view of ideology.

Ideology is not just a matter of representations of social reality, for constructions of identity which are linked to power are (as Althusser emphasized) key ideological processes too. It is useful to think of ideology as a process which articulates together particular representations of reality, and particular constructions of identity, especially of the collective identities of groups and communities. In this case, the ideological work that is going on is an attempt to articulate Thatcherite representations of and strategies for the economy and politics with a particular construction of 'the people' as a political community and base for Thatcherism. Thatcher is simultaneously discursively constructing a political programme and a constituency for that programme (Bourdieu, 1991).

5 Discourse is Historical

Discourse is not produced without context and cannot be understood without taking the context into consideration (Duranti and Goodwin, 1992; Wodak et al., 1990; 1994). This relates, on a metatheoretical level, to Wittgenstein's (1967) notion of 'language game' and 'forms of life': utterances are only meaningful if we consider their use in a specific situation, if we understand the underlying conventions and rules, if we recognize the embedding in a certain culture and ideology, and most importantly, if we know what the discourse relates to in the past. Discourses are always connected to other discourses which were produced earlier, as well as those which are produced synchronically and subsequently. In this respect, we include intertextuality as well as sociocultural knowledge within our concept of context.

Thus, Thatcher's speech relates to what she and her government have said earlier, to other speeches and proclamations, to certain laws which have been decided upon, to reporting in the media, as well as to certain actions which were undertaken.

This becomes very clear if we consider allusions which occur in the text and which presuppose certain worlds of knowledge, and particular intertextual experience, on the part of the listeners. For example, to be able to understand and analyse Thatcher's responses profoundly and in depth, we would have to know what the situation in Britain in the *nineteen forties* (1–2) was like, who Rab Butler (15) or Barrie (33) were, what kind of *vision* de Gaulle had (44–5), why the war in the Falkland Islands was important and what kind of symbolic meaning it connotes (58), etc. It becomes even more difficult when Thatcher alludes to *traditional conservatism* (111) and to what is meant by this term within the Thatcherite tendency in contrast to other meanings.

In the study of antisemitic discourse during the Waldheim affair in Austria (1986) a method was developed which allows the inclusion of layers of historical knowledge (Wodak et al., 1990): the discourse-historical approach. Thus were analysed documents on the Wehrmacht, Waldheim's own speeches as well as those of his opponents, newspaper reports on Waldheim in Austria and abroad, and finally also *vox populi*, conversations on the street by anonymous participants. The discourse history of each unit of discourse had to be uncovered. This naturally again implies interdisciplinary analysis; historians have to be included in such an undertaking.

6   The Link between Text and Society is Mediated

Critical discourse analysis is very much about making connections between social and cultural structures and processes on the one hand, and properties of text on the other. But these connections are rather complex, and are best seen as indirect or 'mediated' rather than direct. One view of this mediated relationship is that the link between text and society is mediated by 'orders of discourse' (see earlier). In the Thatcher example, this approach would aim to show that changes in British policies, in the relationship between politics and media, and in British culture at a more general level (some of which we have pointed to above) are partly realized in changes in the political order of discourse, and in how texts draw upon and articulate together discourses and genres which had traditionally been kept apart. Such new articulations of discourses and genres are in turn realized in features of language, making an indirect, mediated link between sociocultural processes and linguistic properties of texts.

We have already indicated some of this articulatory work in the Thatcher interview: it hybridizes discourses which are traditionally kept apart in the political order of discourse (conservative and liberal discourses), and in its populist features hybridizes the political order of discourse with orders of discourse of ordinary life. We have also suggested that it hybridizes the genre of media interview and the genre of political speaking, drawing together the media and political orders of discourse. However, the mixing of genres needs to be more carefully formulated. The Charlton–Thatcher interview was one of a series of in-depth interviews with prominent figures in public life. Its conventions are those of a 'celebrity interview'. Questions probe the personality and outlook of the interviewee, and answers are expected to be frank and revelatory. Audience members are constructed as overhearers listening in on a potentially quite intense interaction between interviewer and interviewee. The programme should at once be educative and entertaining. However, while Charlton is working according to these ground rules, Thatcher is not. She treats the encounter as a political interview. As politicians commonly do, she therefore uses the interview as an occasion for political speech making, constructing the audience rather than the interviewer as addressee, not answering the questions, and avoiding the liberal intellectual discourse of the questions in favour of a populist discourse. The interaction thus has rather a complex character generically: there is a tension between the participants in terms of which media genre is oriented to (celebrity interview versus political interview), and Thatcher's recourse to political interview entails a further tension between media practices and the rhetorical practices of political discourse.

There are other views of mediation of the link between text and society. The emphasis in Smith (1990) for example is upon the practices of social actors in producing links between society and text in the enactment of local relations, drawing together aspects of ethnomethodological and Marxist theories. Van Dijk on the other hand stresses the sociocognitive mediation of the text–society link (van Dijk, 1985a; 1989; 1993b; Wodak, 1992; Mitten and Wodak, 1993) and sets out to specify the cognitive resources social actors draw upon in their practice, and the relationship between individual meanings or interpretations and group representations (in the case of racist discourse, for instance). On the one hand these different views of mediation indicate contrasting priorities of different theories, but on the other hand they might be regarded as complementary, as pointing to the need in the long run for a complex and multi-sided theory of text–society mediation which gives due weight to orders of discourse, practices of social actors, and sociocognitive processes.

7 Discourse Analysis is Interpretative and Explanatory

Discourse can be interpreted in very different ways, due to the audience and the amount of context information which is included. In a study of the comprehension and comprehensibility of news broadcasts, for example, Lutz and Wodak (1987) illustrate typical but different interpretations of the same text, depending on emotional, formal and cognitive schemata of the reader/listener (*Soziopsychologische Theorie des Textverstehens* (SPTV), sociopsychological theory of text comprehension). Class-, gender-, age-, belief- and attitude-specific readings of the texts occurred which demonstrate that understanding takes place not through a *tabula rasa*, but against the background of emotions, attitudes and knowledge. The same is even more true for complex texts like the Thatcher interview where we deal with historical and synchronic intertextuality, the hybridization of genres and the opaqueness of certain elements and units. Several important issues have to be raised at this point. What are the limits of the discourse unit under investigation: what are the limits of the sign (Kress, 1993)? How much contextual knowledge do we need for an interpretation? Are the critical readings provided by CDA privileged, better, or just more justifiable? For example, the meaning of *you have to say over to people people are inventive creative and so you expect PEOPLE to create thriving industries thriving services yes you expect* (lines 72–3) is certainly opaque. Who is meant by *people*: all British subjects, government included or excluded? Human beings *per se*, or people in the sense of citizens, of the German *Volk*? People who vote Conservative, who are ideologically committed to Thatcherism, or everybody? The group is not clearly defined, which allows readers to include or exclude themselves according to their own ideologies and beliefs. If we continue in the text, it becomes clearer that these *people* have to be able to influence the growth of industries and services in a positive way (*thriving*). But only powerful people are able to do this – elites, managers and politicians. If that is the case, the use of *people* is certainly misleading; it suggests participation where there is none. It mystifies the influence ordinary men and women might have on decisions of the government, an influence which they actually do not have and never would have. This piece of text exemplifies a contradiction which only a CDA might deconstruct and in doing so show the different implications of different readings for social action. Knowledge of Thatcherite argumentation structures and politics (using a discourse-historical methodology) would make it much easier to disentangle manifest and latent meanings and to find out more about the political rhetorics which are used in this interview. Critical reading thus implies a systematic methodology and a thorough investigation of the context. This might narrow down the whole range of possible readings. The heterogeneity and vagueness of the text condenses contradictions which only become apparent through careful analysis. The text is thus deconstructed and embedded in its social conditions, is linked to ideologies and power relationships. This marks the point where critical readings differ from reading by an uncritical audience: they differ in their systematic approach to inherent meanings, they rely on scientific procedures, and they naturally and necessarily require self-reflection of the researchers themselves. In this point, they differ clearly from pure hermeneutics (in this respect see the 'objective hermeneutics' of Ulrich Oevermann and his group: Oevermann et al., 1979). We might say they are explanatory in intent, not just interpretative. We also have to state that interpretations and explanations are never finished and authoritative; they are dynamic and open, open to new contexts and new information.

8   Discourse is a Form of Social Action

We stated at the beginning of our chapter that the principle aim of CDA was to uncover opaqueness and power relationships. CDA is a socially committed scientific paradigm, and some scholars are also active in various political groups. In contrast to many scholars, critical linguists make explicit interests which otherwise often remain covered.

The Thatcher example we have analysed arguably has such applicability in political struggles. But there exist also other examples of important applications of CDA. Wodak and De Cillia (1989) published the first official school materials dealing with post-war antisemitism in Austria. These materials are now used in schools and accompany an exhibition about antisemitism in the Second Austrian Republic. Both the exhibition and the book are used by teachers who want to discuss the different ranges and variations of antisemitic discourse in their classrooms. Similarly, van Dijk (1993a) has analysed Dutch schoolbooks in terms of their potential racist implications. This led to the production of new school materials. Similar educational applications have taken place in the UK under the heading of 'critical language awareness' (Fairclough, 1992c), and the term 'critical literacy' is also widely used especially in Australia. CDA is also used for expert opinions in court. Gruber and Wodak (1992) wrote an expert opinion on a column in the biggest Austrian tabloid which denied the Holocaust (this can be punished with up to seven years in prison). They were asked for their analysis by the Jewish community. The expert opinion showed – through the analysis of many other columns in this paper and by the same author – that the one racist column was not accidental, but was consistent with the usual practice of the newspaper. Unfortunately, the case was lost due to the tremendous power of this tabloid and its financiers, but the expert opinion was published and widely read and cited, and influenced public opinion.

Non-discriminatory language use is widely promoted in different domains. One important area is sexist language use. Guidelines for non-sexist language use have been produced in many countries (Wodak et al., 1987). Such guidelines serve to make women visible in language, and thus also socially, in institutions. Different discourse with and about women can slowly lead to changes in consciousness. Finally, CDA has had much success in changing discourse and power patterns in institutions. For example, while analysing doctor–patient communication, it became apparent that on top of their expert knowledge doctors use many other strategies to dominate their clients (Lalouschek et al., 1990; Mishler, 1977; West, 1990). The critical analysis of such communication patterns led to guidelines for different behaviour patterns, which were and are taught in seminars for doctors. The same is true for other institutions, for bureaucracies, legal institutions and schools (Gunnarsson, 1989; Danet, 1984; Pfeiffer et al., 1987).

Conclusion

We suggested earlier in the chapter that late modern society is characterized by enhanced reflexivity, and that a critical orientation towards discourse in ordinary life is one manifestation of modern reflexivity. A key issue for critical discourse analysts is how the analyses which they produce in academic institutions relate to this critical activity in ordinary life. There is no absolute divide between the two: critical discourse analysts necessarily draw upon everyday critical activities (associated for instance with gender relations, patriarchy and feminism) including analysts' own involvement in and experience of them, and these activities may be informed by academic analysis (as feminism has been). Yet critical discourse analysis is obviously not just a replication of everyday critique: it can draw upon social theories and theories of language, and methodologies for language analysis, which are not generally available, and has resources for systematic and in-depth investigations which go beyond ordinary experience. We think it is useful to see the relationship between everyday discourse critique and academic CDA in terms of Gramscian perspectives on intellectuals in contemporary life, and the relationship of intellectuals on the one hand to the state and the dominant class, and on the other hand to struggles against domination on the basis of class, gender, race, and so forth. Critical discourse analysts ought in our view to be aiming to function as 'organic intellectuals' in a range of social struggles (not forgetting 'new social movements' such as ecological movements or anti-road-building alliances), but ought at the same time to be aware that their work is constantly at risk of appropriation by the state and capital.

Recommended Reading

The following list is for readers who wish to find out more about CDA. It includes some relatively accessible books (such as Fairclough, Kress, van Dijk) and some more difficult books (Pêcheux, Volosinov).

Fairclough (1995a, 1995b)
Fowler et al. (1979)
Kress (1985)
Maas (1989)
Pêcheux (1982)
van Dijk (1991)
Volosinov (1973)
Wodak et al. (1990)

Notes

1 Although critical feminist studies would certainly belong to CDA, we do not have the space here to cover them (see also Wodak and Benke, 1996).

2 We would like to mention the International Association for the Study of Racism (IASR), which many critical linguists belong to. This association gathers over 200 European scholars and – among other activities – reacts to racist discourse in the public sphere through resolutions, letters, expertise, etc.

3 In this chapter, we focus on the analysis of political discourse. Again, we do not want to

exclude critical studies on institutional discourse and power in institutions (see Mumby, 1988; Wodak, 1996), but the elaboration of this domain would exceed the scope of this contribution.

4 This could be translated as 'discursive chaos'.

5 The interview was conducted by Michael Charlton, and was broadcast on BBC Radio 3 on 17 December 1985. For a fuller analysis, see Chapter 7 of Fairclough (1989).

References

Althusser, L. (1971) 'Ideology and ideological state apparatus', in *Lenin and Philosophy and Other Essays*. London: New Left Books.

Bakhtin, M. (1981) *The Dialogical Imagination*. Austin, TX: University of Texas Press.

Bakhtin, M. (1986) *Speech Genres and Other Late Essays*. Austin, TX: University of Texas Press.

Bell, P. and van Leeuwen, T. (1994) *Media Interview*. Sydney: University of New South Wales Press.

Bourdieu, P. (1991) *Language and Symbolic Power*. Cambridge: Polity Press.

Courtine, J.-J. (1981) 'Analyse du discours politique', *Languages*, 62.

Danet, B. (ed.) (1984) *Legal Discourse*, special issue of *Text*, 4.

Duranti, A. and Goodwin, C. (eds) (1992) *Rethinking Context: Language as an Interactive Phenomenon*. Cambridge: Cambridge University Press.

Fairclough, N. (1989) *Language and Power*. London: Longman.

Fairclough, N. (1992a) *Discourse and Social Change*. Cambridge: Polity Press.

Fairclough, N. (1992b) 'Text and discourse: linguistic and intertextual analysis within discourse analysis', *Discourse and Society*, 3.

Fairclough, N. (ed.) (1992c) *Critical Language Awareness*. London: Longman.

Fairclough, N. (1993) 'Critical discourse analysis and the marketization of public discourse: the universities', *Discourse and Society*, 4 (2): 133–68.

Fairclough, N. (1994) 'Conversationalization of public discourse and the authority of the consumer', in R. Keat, N. Whiteley and N. Abercrombie (eds), *The Authority of the Consumer*. London: Routledge.

Fairclough, N. (1995a) *Media Discourse*. London: Edward Arnold.

Fairclough, N. (1995b) *Critical Discourse Analysis*. London: Longman.

Fay, B. (1987) *Critical Social Science*. London: Polity Press.

Forgacs, D. (1988) *A Gramsci Reader*. London: Lawrence and Wishart.

Foucault, M. (1971) *L'Ordre du discours*. Paris: Gallimard.

Foucault, M. (1972) *The Archaeology of Knowledge*. London: Tavistock.

Foucault, M. (1979) *Discipline and Punish: the Birth of Prison*. Harmondsworth: Penguin.

Fowler, R. (1991) 'Critical linguistics', in Kirten Halmkjaer (ed.), *The Linguistic Encyclopedia*. London, New York: Routledge. pp. 89–93.

Fowler, R. and Kress, R. (1979) 'Critical linguistics', in R. Fowler et al., *Language and Control*. London: Routledge. pp. 185–213.

Fowler, R., Kress, G., Hodge, R. and Trew, T. (eds) (1979) *Language and Control*. London: Routledge.

Giddens, A. (1991) *Modernity and Self-Identity*. Cambridge: Polity Press.

Gruber, H. and Wodak, R. (1992) *Ein Fall für den Staatsanwalt?* Institut für Sprachwissenschaft Wien, *Wiener Linguistische Gazette*, Beiheft 11.

Gunnarsson, B.-L. (1989) 'Text comprehensibility and the writing process', *Written Communication*, 6 (1): 86–107.

Hall, S. and Jacques, M. (1983) *The Politics of Thatcherism*. London: Lawrence and Wishart.

Hall, S., Hobson, D., Love, A. and Willis, P. (eds) (1980) *Culture, Media, Language: Working Papers in Cultural Studies 1972–79*. London: Hutchinson.

Halliday, M.A.K. (1978) *Language as Social Semiotic*. London: Edward Arnold.

Halliday, M.A.K. (1994) *Introduction to Functional Grammar*, 2nd edn. London: Edward Arnold.

Halliday, M.A.K. (1985) *Introduction to Functional Grammar*. London: Edward Arnold.

Halliday, M.A.K. and Hasan, R. (1985) *Language, Context and Text*. Oxford: Oxford University Press.

Hodge, R. and Kress, G. (1988) *Social Semiotics*. Cambridge: Polity.

Jäger, S. and Jäger, M. (1993) *Aus der Mitte der Gesellschaft*. Duisburg: Diss.

Kress, G. (1985) *Linguistic Process in Sociocultural Practice*. Oxford: Oxford University Press.

Kress, G. (1993) 'Against arbitrariness: the social production of the sign as a foundational issue in critical discourse analysis', *Discourse and Society*, 4 (2): 169–91.

Kress, G. and Hodge, R. (1979) *Language as Ideology*. London. Routledge, 2nd edn 1993.

Kress, G. and Threadgold, T. (1988) 'Towards a social theory of genre', *Southern Review*, 21.

Kress, G. and van Leeuwen, T. (1990) *Reading Images*. Geelong, Vic.: Deakin University Press.

Kristeva, J. (1986) 'Word, dialogue and novel', in T. Moi (ed.), *The Kristeva Reader*. Oxford: Blackwell.

Lalouschek, J., Menz, F. and Wodak, R. (1990) *Alltag in der Ambulanz*. Tübingen: Narr.

Larrain, J. (1979) *The Concept of Ideology*. London: Hutchinson.

Lemke, J. (1995) *Textual Politics*. New York: Taylor and Francis.

Lutz, B. and Wodak, R. (1987) *Information für Informierte*. Vienna: Akademie der Wissenschaften.

Maas, U. (1984) *Als der Geist der Gemeinschaft seine Sprache fand*. Opladen: Westdeutscher Verlag.

Maas, U. (1989) *Sprachpolitik und politische Sprachwissenschaft*. Frankfurt am Main: Suhrkamp.

Maingueneau, D. (1987) *Nouvelles Tendances en analyse du discours*. Paris: Hachette.

Matouschek, B., Wodak, R. and Januschek, F. (1995) *Notwendige Maßnahmen gegen Fremde*. Vienna: Passagen.

Mishler, E. (1977) *The Discourse of Medicine*. Norwood, NJ: Ablex.

Mitten, R. and Wodak, R. (1993) 'On the discourse of racism and prejudice', *Folia Linguistica*, XXVII (3–4): 192–215.

Mumby, D.K. (1988) *Communication and Power in Organizations: Discourse, Ideology and Domination*. Norwood, NJ: Ablex.

Oevermann, V., Allert, T., Konau, E. and Krambeck, J. (1979) 'Die Methologie einer "objectven Hermeneutik"', in H.G. Soeffner (ed.), *Interpretative Verfahren in den Sozial- und Textwissenschaften*. Frankfurt am Main: Metzler. pp. 352–434.

Pêcheux, M. (1982) *Language Semantics and Ideology*. London: Macmillan.

Pêcheux, M. (1988) 'Discourse – structure or event?', in C. Nelson and L. Grossberg (eds), *Marxism and the Interpretation of Culture*. London: Macmillan.

Pfeiffer, O.E., Strouhal, E. and Wodak, R. (1987) *Rechtaufsprache*. Vienna: Orac.

Scannell, P. (ed.) (1992) *Broadcast Talk*. London: Sage.

Smith, D. (1990) *Texts, Facts and Femininity*. London: Routledge.

Thibault, P. (1991) *Social Semiotics as Praxis*. Minneapolis, MN: University of Minnesota Press.

Thompson, J.B. (1988) *Critical Hermeneutics*, 4th edn. Cambridge: Cambridge University Press.

van Dijk, T. (1980) *Macrostructures: An Interdisciplinary Study of Global Structures in Discourse, Interaction and Cognition*. Hillsdale, NJ: Erlbaum.

van Dijk, T. (1985a) *Prejudice in Discourse*. Amsterdam: Benjamins.

van Dijk, T. (ed.) (1985b) *Discourse and Communication: New Approaches to the Analysis of Mass Media Discourse and Communication*. Berlin: de Gruyter.

van Dijk, T. (1987) *Communicating Racism*. London: Sage.

van Dijk, T. (1989) 'Structures of discourse and structures of power', in J.A. Anderson (ed.), *Communication Yearbook 12*. Newbury Park, CA: Sage. pp. 18–59.

van Dijk, T. (1991) *Racism and the Press*. London: Routledge.

van Dijk, T. (1993a) *Discourse and Elite Racism*. London: Sage.

van Dijk, T. (1993b) 'Principles of critical discourse analysis', *Discourse and Society*, 4 (2): 249–83.

van Leeuwen, T. (1993) 'Genre and field in critical discourse analysis', *Discourse and Society*, 4 (2): 193–223.

Volosinov, V.I. (1973) *Marxism and the Philosophy of Language* (1928). New York: Seminar Press.

West, C. (1990) 'Not just "doctor's orders"; directive–response sequences in patients' visits to women and men physicians', *Discourse and Society*, 1 (1): 85–112.

Wittgenstein, L. (1967) *Philosophische Untersuchungen*. Frankfurt am Main: Suhrkamp.

Wodak, R. (1975) *(=Leodolter): Das Sprachverhalten von Angeklagten bei Gericht*. Kronberg IT: Scriptor.

Wodak, R. (1986) *Language Behavior in Therapy Groups*. Los Angeles: University of California Press.

Wodak, R. (1992) 'Strategies in text production and text comprehension: a new perspective', in Dieter Stein (ed.), *Cooperating with Written Texts: the Pragmatics and Comprehension of Written Texts*. Berlin, New York: Mouton de Gruyter.

Wodak, R. (1996) *Disorders of Discourse*. London: Longman.

Wodak, R. and Benke, G. (1996) 'Gender as a sociolinguistic variable', in F. Coulmas (ed.), *Handbook of Sociolinguistics*. Oxford: Oxford University Press. pp. 127–50.

Wodak, R. and De Cillia, R. (1989) 'Sprache und Antisemitismus', *Hitteilungen des Instituts für Wissenschaft und Kunst*, 3.

Wodak, R., De Cillia, R., Blüml, K. and Andraschko, E. (1989) *Sprache und Macht*. Vienna: Deuticke.

Wodak, R. and Matouschek, B. (1993) '"We are dealing with people whose origins one can clearly tell just by looking": critical discourse analysis and the study of neoracism in contemporary Austria', *Discourse and Society*, 2 (4): 225–48.

Wodak, R. and Menz, F. (eds) (1990) *Sprache in der Politik – Politik in der Sprache: Analysen zum öffentlichen Sprachgebrauch*. Klagenfurt: Drava.

Wodak, R., Menz, F., Mitten, R. and Stern, F. (1994) *Die Sprachen der 'Vergangenheiten': Gedenken in österreichischen und deutschen Medien*. Frankfurt am Main: Suhrkamp.

Wodak, R., Moosmüller, S., Doleschal, U. and Feistritzer, G. (1987) *Das Sprachverhalten von Frau und Mann*. Vienna: Ministry for Social Affairs.

Wodak, R., Pelikan, J., Nowak, P., Gruber, H., De Cillia, R. and Mitten, R. (1990) *'Wir sind alle unschuldige Täter': Diskurshistorische Studien zum Nachkriegsantisemitismus*. Frankfurt am Main: Suhrkamp.

11

Applied Discourse Analysis

Britt-Louise Gunnarsson

Applied discourse analysis (ADA) is not an established field, although much of the discourse analysis that is being carried out is applied. In modern and postmodern society, there is a growing awareness of the importance of effective communication among professionals in different sections of society, which indeed can be related to the ongoing differentiation and specialization of the academic and non-academic worlds. Language has become one of the most important tools of many professions, with meetings, proceedings, and conferences as a cornerstone of professional contacts. The ability to communicate, not only within one's own group, but also between different specialist groups and between experts and lay people, is absolutely vital if society is to function properly. In many professions, oral and written contact with the general public forms the core of professional work. At the same time, the development of new communication technology has created new forms for professional interaction. Many people's professional work consists of an intricate interaction between people and advanced technical equipment and systems.

This societal development is reflected in interest among researchers, where the last decade has seen a clear increase in studies of different problem areas within society. What characterizes applied discourse analysis is a concern with various areas of real life, where discourse is essential to the outcome of interaction between individuals. The focus within ADA is thus on language and communication in real-life situations, and the goal is to analyse, understand or solve problems relating to practical action in real-life contexts. The focus is not on language *per se* – whatever that might be – but on language in use in authentic contexts.

Basing my approach on a broad definition of what applied studies are, I will in this chapter give examples of analyses relating to a variety of problem areas within society. My discussion of ADA will cover both the spoken and the written sides of discourse. From a theoretical and methodological perspective this means that I will have to cover a wide range of research traditions, as the spoken and written sides of communication – though in real life strongly intertwined – have been studied by different research groups within different research traditions.

From Applied Linguistics to Applied Discourse Analysis

A central issue for a discussion of applied discourse analysis is indeed how ADA relates to its mother field of applied linguistics (AL). Another is how these applied subfields differ from the corresponding general fields, that is what the term 'applied' refers to.

Over the years, the term 'applied linguistics' has been given a wide variety of interpretations. The traditional and most widespread use of the term is also the narrowest one, restricting AL to the application of linguistic research to mother tongue education and to the teaching and learning of foreign and second languages. According to this interpretation, the central issues are language acquisition and learning, testing, error analysis, and teaching methodology and technology. Gradually, however, applied linguistics has been given a broader definition, and by most scholars AL is now used to refer to different types of problem areas within society, not only educational problems, but practical and social problems of all kinds.

At a theoretical level, early AL studies reflect the situation in linguistics and its adjacent fields at the time. Work carried out in the 1950s, 1960s and 1970s is clearly indebted to structuralism and to functional stylistics. What has taken place in the last ten to fifteen years is a broadening of the scope of AL. As focus has gradually shifted towards pragmatics, text linguistics, discourse analysis, psycholinguistics, sociolinguistics, social constructivism, and critical linguistics, AL too has undergone changes. The study of smaller units, of words and sentences, has yielded ground to studies of larger units, of texts and discourse. An interest in more global text patterns and in spoken discourse, combined with a growing awareness of the relationship between text and context, has changed the subject-matter of linguistic investigation. As theoretical and methodological interests and insights have evolved, linguistic analysis has been able to solve new types of problems, and along with this widening of the perspective, new areas have become central to those interested in applied research. Medical discourse, communication in social welfare settings, workplace interaction, institutional discourse, intercultural negotiations, courtroom interaction, bilingualism, writing in non-academic settings and gender issues in different settings are examples of applied research areas in the 1990s.

Disciplines like socio- and psycholinguistics have brought a multidisciplinary approach to the study of language and discourse, as has cross-disciplinary collaboration between linguists on the one hand and anthropologists, sociologists, ethnomethodologists, psychologists and educationalists on the other. In theoretical terms, AL has travelled from structuralism to social constructivism, and the longer the journey has lasted the more AL has come to be integrated with ADA.

This new situation for linguistic research has blurred the boundary between general and applied linguistics and discourse analysis and also between pure research and its application. The traditional view that AL is a matter of applying linguistic research to problem areas is misleading as a description of modern AL and ADA. Applied studies play their own part in the development of linguistic theory and methods. A good deal of theoretical knowledge has grown out of contact with real-life problems. And many theoretical insights obtained through 'pure' research are found to be irrelevant to the study of real-life problems. Applied linguistics and applied discourse analysis are involved in general theory building. Through its problem-oriented studies, theory is developed, evaluated and revised.

The subject-matter of applied linguistics is language and communication in real-life situations, and the link with real life steers the selection of questions to be asked and also the methods by which answers are sought. It does not, though, limit the theoretical aspirations of the applied subfields. Applied linguistics has thus come to be more and more integrated with applied discourse analysis along with the increasing awareness of the importance of context for our understanding of language and linguistic practice. This evolving subfield, ADA, comprises studies relating to a wide range of different settings and problem areas within society. And depending on the problem area in focus, the theoretical and methodological basis has varied.

It would be giving a false picture of ADA to describe it as a homogeneous field, undergoing one unifying line of development. My ambition here is instead to give a picture of ADA research in its variety. To cover all this variation in one chapter would indeed be impossible, and I am forced to limit my discussion to a few settings and to a presentation of a few representative studies.

The Educational Setting

The educational setting is, as has been mentioned above, the traditional applied research arena, and my discussion of ADA will start there.

A wide variety of studies have been carried out. Owing a debt to the developmental perspective of Piaget and Vygotsky, many studies have been devoted to literacy problems and to early development of talking and writing skills in children. In particular, mother–child interaction has been recorded and analysed (Snow and Ferguson, 1977). Söderbergh (1977), for instance, has been able to describe the child's successive breaking of the language code through analyses of a child's talk to herself and to her mother. Barnes and Todd (1977) studied the gradual and differentiated acquisition of the skill of expressing oneself orally and participating in conversation. The preschool child's efforts to learn to write have been the focus of many studies, as has writing development in older pupils.

Much research has also been undertaken from a sociological perspective. Basil Bernstein's (1971; 1973) work on the importance of class and early socialization has, although criticized by many, served as a basis for a great deal of research with a sociological perspective. Reading and writing, language learning and teaching have been studied from a sociolinguistic angle (see Stubbs, 1980; Pride, 1979). Gardner (1985), for instance, pointed to the important roles played by attitudes and motivation in second language learning. Others have viewed educational discourse from a macro perspective. Schools are societal institutions, which reproduce the social structure and the established order (Bourdieu and Passeron, 1970; Mehan, 1991).

A large group of studies have been devoted to problems relating to second language acquisition. In the late 1950s and early 1960s a major concern was to determine the influence on learning and use of the first language (L1) on the second language (L2). The predominant method was *contrastive analysis*, that is L1 and L2 were compared and areas of similarity and difference were identified. Another early approach was known as the *study of errors*. A more interactional angle is taken in Færch and Kasper (1983), where the focus is on different communication strategies revealed in communication. In Færch and Kasper (1987), the methods introduced are based on introspection. Verbal reports, think-aloud protocols etc. are used for the study of learners' performances and abilities.

Other studies have more directly focused on interaction in the classroom, both teacher–pupil and pupil–pupil interaction. In the 1960s Bellack and his colleagues (1966) studied the language of the classroom, describing educational activity as related to three interactive moves: *soliciting*, *responding* and *reacting*.

Sinclair and Coulthard (1975) used the classroom situation as a step towards the development of a model for discourse analysis. An essential feature of their model is an analysis of the *situation*, for which they found it relevant to distinguish three sets of categories: *discourse categories* (informative, elicitation, directive); *situational categories* (statement, question, command); *grammatical categories* (declarative, interrogative, imperative). The following piece of classroom discourse demonstrates the crucial role of the situation in the analysis of discourse. (T = teacher, P = pupil.)

T: What kind of a person do you think he is? Do you –
     what are you laughing at?
P: Nothing

The pupil interpreted the teacher's 'interrogative' as a 'directive' to stop laughing. The teacher, however, had abandoned his first question, 'What kind of a person do you think he is?', because he realized that the pupil's laughter was an indication of her attitude. The teacher asked why she was laughing, as he saw a chance to use her laughter as an opening of the topic for discussion. He continues and the pupil realizes her mistake, which in this case lay in misunderstanding the situation, not the sentence. The pupil then tells the teacher why she was laughing.

T: Pardon?
P: Nothing

T: You're laughing at nothing, nothing at all?
P: No.
      It's funny really 'cos they don't think as
      though they were there they might not like it.
      And it sounds rather a pompous attitude.

(Sinclair and Coulthard, 1975: 30)

The approach of Sinclair and Coulthard has been quite influential and their framework has been elaborated to suit language classes (Lörscher, 1983).

The component of classroom interaction that has most interested researchers is the exchange, that is (teacher's) *initiative*, (pupil's) *response* and (teacher's) *feedback*. This tripartite structure is studied in depth by Mehan (1979) and found to be an organization principle in classroom interaction. Mehan sees this structure as constitutive of the event of a lesson, that is as constitutive of a social reality in interaction. He talks about a 'constitutive ethnography' of the classroom.

The *conversational analysis* (CA) paradigm has been used for the analysis of dialogue processes in the classroom. Gustavsson (1988), for instance, analysed eight lessons of Swedish as a second language in grades 4–6 of the Swedish comprehensive, compulsory school. Using an initiative–response (IR) analysis (Linell et al., 1988), he studied the dialogue dynamics and coherence as well as dominance relations. Among other things he investigated the types of questions and the relation between interactional dominance and amount of speech. The language lessons were compared with non-didactic conversations, the pupil talking to his/her teacher and to a class-mate. The language lessons emerged as an extremely asymmetric situation, where the pupil's role in the inter-action is reduced to that of a passive follower, given – and taking – very few opportunities to influence the course of the talk. The degree of asymmetry was shown to be systematically related to the kind of lesson activities going on; the more focus on language *per se* and the more abstract the aspects of language brought into focus, the smaller the pupil's share of the interactional territory. The following sequence (here only presented in English translation) is an example of this typical interactional dominance maintained by the teacher in the second language acquisition classroom.

117 T: yeah! Listen, Yousuf, what was it that Eta was going to do this
         evening
118 P: (3s)
119 T: you try and tell me /P:oh/ what you remember now, what was
         she going to do this evening
120 P: she ran to er down to er the newsagent's
121 T: to do what
122 P: to buy cigarettes for her Mum

123 T: very good, er listen now it . . . what's it like out there, how's the
         weather this evening
124 P: ah cold, it was er wait, it was about thirteen degrees . . . below
125 T: yes, it's cold 'cause what season is it
126 P: it was <u>sixteen</u> degrees below
127 T: /LAUGHING A LITTLE/ yes it was, more precisely it was
         sixteen degrees below, and what season is that then
128 P: well February
129 T: yes but what season, that's the month that's right /P:mm/ but
         what season, is it summer, winter or
130 P: well winter

                                        (Gustavsson, 1988: 126, L6)

Within the terms of the initiative–response analysis, this sequence can be
analysed as follows. After the vocative, the teacher in 117 takes a *soliciting
initiative*. When P does not answer, T makes explicit what she wants P to
do. In line 119 T renews her initiative, *repeated initiative*, thus signalling
that P's silence in line 118 was an *inadequate response*. In line 120 follows a
minimal, adequate response from P. Lines 121 to 123 are a typical classroom sequence, a *soliciting initiative* followed by a *minimal adequate
response* followed by a positive evaluation. In line 124 we find an expanded
response, that is P's utterance is more than minimally adequate. In this case
it can also be seen as an *assertive initiative*. In 126 P ignores T's current
initiative, and in the terms of the IR analysis, his conversational contribution this time is *self-linked*, as opposed to *alter-linked*: 126 contains a self-
linked assertive initiative. In 127 T first responds to P's contribution, before
renewing her own initiative. Her turns are thus *alter-linked* as well as self-
linked (1988: 128–31).

Legal and Bureaucratic Settings

A certain branch within the study of written professional discourse has
been devoted to the study of legal and bureaucratic language. Common to
a large proportion of these studies has been the focus on the reading and
comprehension processes. Taking its base in the many descriptive studies of
the characteristics of legislative language, in terms of vocabulary, syntax,
and textual patterns (Mellinkoff, 1963; Gustafsson, 1984; Kurzon, 1986;
Bhatia, 1987), as well as in analyses of the functions of laws and other
legal texts (Danet, 1980; Gunnarsson, 1984), the ultimate aim of these
studies has been to find more adequate writing strategies and to reform
language.

In the 1960s texts were analysed and assessed in relation to their
readability, and 'readability formulae' were devised as a mechanical way of
analysing documents at a surface level. An analysis of jury instructions by

Charrow and Charrow (1979) represented a step forward. Their ideas for reform derived from various linguistic factors: nominalizations, prepositional phrases, misplaced phrases, 'whiz' and complement deletion, lexical items, modals, negatives, passives, embeddings, etc. However, these studies, though certainly of practical interest, were not based on any theory of text comprehension or on a very searching analysis of the societal function of the texts.

Other studies have had a more theoretical foundation. On the basis of a critique of previous research, Gunnarsson (1984) rejected the concern with lexis or syntax, which went no further than memorization or ability to paraphrase, and developed a theory of functional comprehensibility focusing on perspective and function orientation (implications for action). One starting point for this theory was taken from an analysis of the functions of laws and legislative texts in society. These were seen on the one hand to have a steering function related to the direction of the actions of citizens, groups and organizations in society – *action-directing function* – and on the other hand a controlling function related to the control of this by courts – *control-directing function.*

The second starting point of this study derived from theories about comprehension within cognitive psychology and in research about reading, schema theories and theories about task-directed top down text processing. Based on an analysis of the reading and use of law texts, a theory of the comprehensibility of language was developed where the reading purpose was seen to steer the process towards a focus on the perspective and the function orientation of the text. A *court perspective* and a court orientation were discerned on the one hand and a *citizen perspective* and citizen orientation on the other.

Based on this theory of law text reading and comprehension, a Swedish Act of Parliament, the Joint Regulation Act, was systematically rewritten.[1]

The alternative law text consists of a collection of clearly expressed rules, mainly of action rules for parties, with the framework situation, the acting party, the other party and the action explicitly stated. The rules are structured into a framework situation – in the text marked by the use of italics – and a directive part. This content structuring is done to facilitate the reading process, which was analysed as consisting of four steps: (1) looking for the relevant part and section of the law, (2) looking for the relevant rule, (3) realizing what is laid down in the law, (4) realizing the consequence this will have for an action. For the same reader-directed purpose, the text also has headings in the margin.

In the alternative text, the cases are clearly stated. Incomplete descriptions of the framework situation, like expressions in the original law text such as 'otherwise' and 'in a case other than those mentioned' (see extract from original §16 below) were avoided. More complete descriptions of the conditions of the framework situation were used instead, such as 'If a request for negotiations has been made to an organization of employers' and 'Where the parties are to negotiate under

§10' (see alternative §16). Cases where conflict arises as well as conflict-free cases, normal cases as well as exceptions, primary-party cases as well as secondary-party cases, and initiatives as well as obligations are explicitly mentioned. Cases more central to the action-directing function have, however, been highlighted.

Conflict-free cases as well as cases of conflict are clearly stated in the alternative text. Conflict-free cases are, however, given greater emphasis. These cases, beginning with the conjunction 'Where', are thus mentioned first, while the cases involving conflict, beginning with the conjunction 'If', follow (see alternative §16).

In the alternative text, the primary-party cases are stressed. In the case of symmetrical action rules, where one party can be considered as the primary party and the other as the secondary, we thus find that the primary party case is described first and fully, while the secondary party is only mentioned afterwards and incompletely, for example: 'An employer has a corresponding right' (see alternative §7).

The alternative text can also be described at more superficial text levels. The intention was to use 'normal' vocabulary, thus avoiding legal terms wherever possible. Following the analysis schema, passives and complicated syntax were avoided. The sentences follow a subject-verb-object (SVO) structure. The typography marks the content structure. The extracts on page 293 from both original and alternative texts are illustrative of this approach. (For further examples in English, see Gunnarsson, 1984.)

The comprehensibility of the rewritten text and of the original text were then tested on different groups of people. They were given legal problems to solve with the aid of either text. The test showed the rewritten text to be clearly more comprehensible than the original one for all groups.[2] The results of this experiment with legislative texts were, at the time they were presented, widely debated in the press and among lawyers. Though not immediately accepted among the professionals, the results have in the long run come to have a certain impact on legislative and bureaucratic writing in Sweden.

Other legal areas which have been studied by ADA scholars are courtroom proceedings and police encounters. Linguists, sociologists and ethnographers have in their studies focused on different types of content and argumentative features, in order to reveal how utterances are part of a prior and anticipated context. Cross-examination, question–answer patterns, topic progression and recycling, argumentative structure, and story patterns have been analysed. This research has emanated from different traditions, ranging from speech act theory to an ethnomethodological tradition comprising micro-analysis of varying elements in dialogue. The most recent works within the CA tradition include studies on courtroom interaction (Atkinson, 1992; Drew, 1992; Philips, 1992). By means of the close reading methodology of this tradition, new light can be shed on problems relating to the interactive asymmetries of courtroom practice.

Alternative version

§7

Meaning of   An employee has a right to
the right to   –   belong to an organization of employees
organize   –   take advantage of membership of this organization
    –   lend active support to the organization
    –   attempt to establish an organization
    An employer has a corresponding right.

§16 (extract)
. . .

Time and   *Where the parties are to negotiate under §10:*
place for   The parties may together decide on a time for the negotiations.
negotiations   *If the parties have not agreed on a time:*
    If a request for negotiations has been made to an individual
    employer or a local organization of employees, the parties
    shall meet to negotiate within two weeks of that party having
    received the request.
    If a request for negotiations has been made to an organization
    of employers or a central organization of employees, the
    parties shall meet to negotiate within three weeks of that party
    having received the request. The parties shall decide on a time
    and place for the negotiations.
    *Where the parties are to negotiate prior to a decision of the
    employer under §§11–13:*
    The parties shall together decide on a time for negotiations
    and should in doing so take into account how long the
    employer's decision can be postponed.
. . .

Original version

§7   By right of association is meant a right for employers and
employees to belong to an organization of employers or an
organization of employees, to take advantage of that
membership, and to work for the organization or in order
to establish an organization.

§16   (extract) . . . In a case other than those mentioned in
§§11–13, a meeting for negotiations shall, if the parties are not
otherwise agreed, be held within two weeks of the other party
having received a representation concerning negotiations,
where the other party is an individual employer or a local
organization of employees, and otherwise within three weeks
of such representation having been received by the other
party. In addition, it shall be for the parties to decide on a
time and place for a negotiation meeting.

(Gunnarsson, 1984: 87–9)

In his analysis of recorded data from an Anglo-American rape trial, Drew (1992) focuses on phenomena associated with 'contrasting versions' which are produced by the participants in the courtroom cross-examination. We shall here look closer at one scene, in which the attorney (A) cross-examines the witness (W), who claims that she has been raped.[3]

1	A:	An' at that time (0.3) he asked ya to go
2		out with yu (0.4) isn't that c'rect
3		(2.1)
4	W:	Yea h
5	A:	With him (.) izzn'at so?
6		(2.6)
7	W:	Ah don't remember
8		(1.4)
9	A:	W'l didn:'e ask you if uh (.) on that night
10		that uh (.) he wanted you to be his girl
11		(0.5)
12	A:	Didn'e ask you that?
13		(2.5)
14	W:	I don't remember what he said to me that night.
15		(1.2)
16	A:	Well yuh had som uh (p) (.) uh fairly lengthy
17		conversations with thu defendant uh did'n you?
18		(0.7)
19	A:	On that evening uv February fourteenth?
20		(1.0)
21	W:	Well we were all talkin.
22		(0.8)
23	A:	Well you knew at that time that the
24		defendant was interested (.) in you (.)
25		did'n you?
26		(1.3)
27	W:	He asked me how I'(d) bin en
28		(1.1)
29	W:	J-just stuff like that
30	A:	Just asked yuh how (0.5) yud bin (0.3) but
31		he kissed yuh goodnight (0.5) izzat right=
32	W	=Yeah=he asked me if he could?
33		(1.4)
34	A:	He asked if he could?
35		(0.4)
36	W:	Uh hmmm=
37	A:	=Kiss you goodnight
38		(1.0)
39	A:	An you said (.) ho kay (0.6) izzat right?
40	W:	Uh hmmm

41   (2.0)
42   A: An is it your testimony he only kissed yuh
43   (t') once?
44   (0.4)
45   W: Uh hmm
46   (6.5)
47   A: Now (.) subsequent to this . . .

                                        (Drew, 1992: 478–9)

Using this scene as an example, Drew is able to explore two senses of the phenomenon of 'contrasting versions'. The first sense concerns the alternative and competing versions which the attorney (A) and then the witness (W) produce to describe the 'same' action or event. In lines 1–2 the attorney proposes that the defendant asked her to go out. She first seems to confirm this (line 4), but then changes her confirmation by answering that she does not remember (line 7). When the attorney proposes that the defendant asked her if she wanted to be his girl, she answers again that she does not remember: 'I don't remember what he said to me that night' (line 14).

In the following part of the scene, lines 16–30, we can follow the thread of contrasting versions in the courtroom discourse. In lines 16–19, the attorney proposes a first version of what happened on 14 February. He proposes that the defendant and the witness had fairly lengthy conversations. The witness, in her subsequent answer, line 21, produces an alternative description, 'Well we were all talkin', by which she is heard to dispute or challenge the attorney's version. Similarly, in lines 23–5, the attorney proposes a first version of an event: 'Well you knew at that time that the defendant was interested in you, did'n you?' Without directly rejecting and contradicting the attorney's version, in lines 27–9 the witness disputes it by giving her own description of what happened that night: 'He asked me how I'd bin . . . just stuff like that.' Her version gives quite a different characterization of the event. According to Drew, the listeners, such as the jury, are likely to interpret this response as if the witness was presenting the 'maximum property' of what happened, that is, as if she was claiming that the defendant said nothing more than that.

The last part of the scene demonstrates a second sense of 'contrasting versions'. In lines 30–47, we can follow how the attorney manages to convey to the jury a contrast between the witness's account of what happened, and what is likely in fact to have happened. The attorney designs a pair of adjacent questions in such a way as to juxtapose facts. In lines 30–1, the attorney makes explicit the contrast between the witness's previous statement that the defendant had asked her how she had been and an earlier statement that he had kissed her goodnight. The contrast between these statements implies a version which is at odds with the witness's version of events. The attorney thus uses this technique as a means to discredit the witness. In response to her attempts to rebut his versions, he produces contrasts which in turn are designed to damage her rebuttals.

Another line of research has focused on the understanding and interpretation of utterances. Within a sociolinguistic theoretical framework, experiments have been carried out with different versions of utterances, in order to test powerful and powerless speech, gender differences, etc., in style, self-presentation, tone of voice, etc. (O'Barr, 1982; Adelswärd et al., 1987). O'Barr investigated the effects of *powerless* and *powerful speech* on jurors' attribution of credibility and competence to witnesses. The use of intensifiers, hedges, hesitation forms, witness-asks-lawyer-questions, gestures, polite forms, 'sir' and direct quotations were considered as features of powerless speech. O'Barr taped fictive witness reports, where the female and male witnesses were distributed on a scale from powerless to powerful speech in relation to these features. The tapes with the reports were given to jurors who were asked to grade each witness as to convincingness, truthfulness, competence, intelligence and trustworthiness. The results clearly point to a lower grading of those witnesses, males and females, whose speech could be characterized as powerless. Female and male witnesses who used features relating to powerless speech were interpreted as less truthful, competent, trustworthy, etc. than those whose speech could be characterized as powerful (O'Barr, 1982).

In another experiment the interpretation of persons with no legal training and with legal training as regards witnesses using a *narrative style* (powerful speech) was compared to their interpretation of witnesses using a *fragmented style* (powerless speech). The two extracts below illustrate this style difference; the same testimony is presented in fragmented style and narrative style (Q = question, A = answer).

Fragmented style

Q: What happened after you first saw him?
A: He walked into the store, and I was still talking.
Q: What was he doing?
A: He just walked in and he was walking around like he was going to buy something.
Q: You remained on the phone?
A: Well he never did come to the counter or anything, so I just kept talking to my sister.
Q: Were you still the only persons in the store?
A: No, a couple of minutes later, this, uh, two people came in the store.
Q: What did you do then?
A: I told my sister I had to go because I had some customers.
Q: So did you hang up the phone?
A: Yes
Q: And then what happened?
A: Well I waited on the couple and they went on out.

(O'Barr, 1982: 139–40)

Narrative style

Q: Alright, now please tell the court and members of the jury what happened after you first saw him?

A: Well, he walked into the store, and I was still talking. He just walked in and he was walking around like he was going to buy something. And, he never did come to the counter or anything, so I just kept talking to my sister. And then a couple minutes later, this, uh, two people came in the store and I told my sister I had to go because I had some customers. So him and I were still in there, and I hung like I hung up the phone and went to the counter and waited on the couple and they went on out.

(O'Barr, 1982: 145–6)

The results of this experiment are more complex. On the whole, narrative testimonies were interpreted more positively than fragmented ones. Interpretations, however, were also related to the listeners' expectations of the behaviour of men and women as witnesses and of the attorney–witness relationship. O'Barr argues that the fact 'that the testimony type affected not only evaluations of the witness but also perceptions of the attorney–witness relationship shows that listeners use court observations to arrive at rather complex beliefs about those they hear' (1982: 82).

Police interrogation has also been the subject of ADA research. Cicourel (1968) analysed the part played by police questioning in the long bureaucratic judicial process. In this pioneering work, he studied the social construction of 'cases', particularly the formation and transformation of the images of young delinquents as the cases pass through the legal system (police, social workers, probation officers, prosecutors, courts).

Jönsson (1988) focused on another problem associated with the bureaucratic routine. Her interest was not only in the dialogue between policeman and suspect but also in the interplay between police interrogation and the written police report. Comparing the content of the reports with the dialogues in order to find the origin of each piece of information, she discovered that about as much as 40–50 per cent of the information in the report originated from the policemen, that is the policemen had made statements presented to the suspects in the form of yes/no questions, which they had to confirm or not confirm.

Jönsson also analysed the use of quotation marks and *verba dicendi* in the police reports. She wanted to find out who was presented as the narrator to the reader. She then found that quotation marks were used quite frequently but not always to show real quotations. She also found that verbs like 'say', 'state', 'report' with complements involving an expression referring to the suspect as grammatical subject were very often used even if the source of the information was not the suspect's own utterance. Jönsson does not interpret this as signs of conscious attempts to mislead the reader. Instead she believes her findings reveal to what extent policemen are bound by conventions for police reporting.[4] She concludes:

However, these findings, together with the results of the analyses of the origins of the information, clearly show that the suspects have limited influence on the final shape of the report, though to the reader they may seem to be the narrator. The suspects are supposed to verify the report, but this is done in a cursory way. (Jönsson, 1988: 106)

The Medical-Social Setting

Another ADA area that has been studied extensively is medical discourse. Both a sociological tradition and a discourse-oriented tradition ranging from a more traditional pragmatic approach to a more CA approach are represented here.

The problems that arise between doctors and patients have been seen to a large extent as interactional, and it has been assumed that it is possible to do something about them. The asymmetries between doctor and patient have been analysed in various ways. Elliot Mishler (1984) talked about the two different voices in doctor–patient interaction, the *voice of medicine* and the *voice of the lifeworld*, which represent different ways of conceptualizing and understanding patients' problems.

The different perspectives in medical interaction have also been the concern of Aaron Cicourel, one of the founding fathers of doctor–patient research. By means of conversational analysis of extracts from doctor–patient encounters he was able to reveal important sources of miscommunication (Cicourel, 1981). In Cicourel (1983) miscommunication is discussed in relation to differences as regards *structure of belief*. Using recordings not only of doctor–patient interaction, but also of later interviews with the patient, Cicourel can reveal what set of beliefs relating to the disease is held by the patient. On the one hand the patient, who is suffering from cancer, thinks that cancer is contagious and that she has caught the disease from her husband who died some time ago. She is also afraid that her children have been contaminated: 'maybe, the cancer is contagious and nobody warned us, and my, me dear son, he always kissed his dad on the forehead, and uh my daughter did too, and you know that last three weeks, or so, they really perspire and I wonder if the germs don't come out with the perspiration' (1983: 234). On the other hand she doubts that she really has cancer and thinks that the operation which she has undergone might have been performed on the wrong person. What arouses this suspicion in particular is a letter she has received from the hospital without any date or name on it. In the extract below, taken from one of the interviews with this patient, she talks about this (P = patient, R = Researcher).

P: I had two thoughts, was this somebody else's letter stuck in my envelope, or uh . . . or was that normal and somebody in, along the line somewhere said it wasn't normal and I, as I say, then I, I just didn't know what to think. When you get, open up a letter like that . . . see . . . it's a shock particularly I think I hadn't gotten over the shock of my husband's death yet and all this kep, came upon me

R: Okay . . . okay . . . and you did speak to the doctor . . .

P: Apparently he said something to them, so I'm getting a date on it now but still as you see I don't have a name on it.

R: Yeah.

P: What's so hard about typing in a name? I think this is an important procedure that we do these Pap tests and I think

R: yes

P: they should be

R: I agree

P: covered well instead of just haphazardly.

(Cicourel, 1983: 229)

The dissatisfaction of the patient in this case could be related to the bureaucratic procedures involved. However, it also points to a wider problem relating to *asymmetrical communicative power* in general. The professional-bureaucratic setting of a hospital creates informational constraints and resources which work for the doctor, but weaken the patient's communicational capabilities. When a person, like the patient here, feels that the bureaucratic setting places constraints on their scope to express their views, feelings and emotions, they are likely to feel doubt as to what they are told.

A more directly institutional approach to the study of discourse in the medical setting is taken in Lalouschek et al. (1990) and in Wodak (1997). The actual discourse between the medical actors – doctor, nurse, patient and relatives – is analysed in relation to a macro description of the institution as a working organization. In one study the morning sessions of an out-patients' clinic of an Austrian hospital are analysed. The research team was there to observe what took place and the conversation was recorded. Their interest was in the interactive process. They analysed the role of the setting, that is the routines of the institution and the particular events taking place on this particular morning. They also considered the role of the professionals, that is that of the individual doctors and nurses with their particular personality and experience. This study reveals a clear relationship between the setting, the professionals' state of art and the actual conversation. The doctors' behaviour towards the patients, for instance the length of the conversation, the tone and degree of mutual understanding, vary with the degree of stress and tension caused by the events occurring. The more tense the situation is, the shorter the conversation, the more irritation in the voice and the more signs of miscommunication between the professionals and the lay people.

The study of the out-patients' clinic showed a complex web of contradicting and overlapping actions: examination, treatment, advice, teaching, learning, organization, reorganization and telephone calls take place at the same time. A variety of professionals are involved in these activities – head doctors, senior doctors, junior doctors, professors, nurses of different kinds, orderlies, porters, ambulance personnel, service personnel – as well as patients, all constantly changing. Treatments and examinations take place one after the other.

To cope with these overlapping and contradictory processes, the institution relies, according to Wodak, on a set of *myths*: the myth of the undisturbed, predictable process, the myth of efficiency, the myth of time, and the myth of the collective knowledge. These myths have been created to cover up and hide the internal contradictions. The myth of time, for instance, presents the doctor as a person who is constantly on call and thus permanently pressed for time. This also means that everyone has to wait for the senior doctor. In this scene, the logic is built around this myth of time. We can here first follow two junior doctors, DF2 a female doctor and DM8 a male doctor, talking over the head of the patient, who is lying half-naked on the examination table:

DF2:   Mhmm - so if you think that there's only /to DM8/
DF2:   ONE result here -- then you're wrong
DM8:   yes well . . well please
DF2:   yes right
DM8:   send him to X (name of senior doctor)

(Wodak, 1997: 194)

Everybody now waits for the senior doctor. Nurses and doctors go on with other tasks (sorting card index, heading results sheets) or start looking for the senior doctor. The patient, who has not been informed, does not understand what is happening. He wonders why he has to go on lying there half-naked and why, suddenly, the focus of interest has turned away from him. After a few minutes he tries to find out:

P: Can I put my clothes on again?
DF2:   No you've still got to wait
DF2:   a little for the senior doctor - you know - because
DF2:   we said your ECG was negative -- and you're anaemic
DF2:   ok

(Wodak, 1997: 195)

This study by the Wodak group was carried out within the framework of the critical discourse analysis paradigm. In this case it meant that the results of the study led to action directed towards practitioners, that is the research team conducted courses for doctors based on their results.

The Workplace

In recent decades considerable interest has been shown in interaction and communication in workplaces and different working life settings.[5]

An anthropological approach to the study of workplace interaction is found in Goodwin and Goodwin (1997). With one foot in the CA tradition, the research couple analysed the interplay between linguistic and non-linguistic means in the construction of facts. They showed, for instance, how the defence in the famous Rodney King trial in Los Angeles in 1992 reconstruct the well-known scene of the video tape showing the policemen's beating of the coloured man lying on the ground. The lawyer in the trial reconstructs this event by focusing not on the policemen's actions but on the movements of Rodney King. The lawyer deliberately places certain elements in the foreground and others in the background using non-verbal as well as verbal means. Visually the body movements of Rodney King are highlighted while the policemen's movements are toned down. The lawyer also breaks down the body movement to a set of small moves explicitly pointing to each one of these. Verbally the lawyer focuses on the threatening character of each body turn. The purpose of this visual and verbal highlighting of certain parts of the scene is to construct and reconstruct the scene to make the jury view it from the perspective of the accused policemen.

Special problems relating to workplace interaction arise when accidents occur, in spite or because of the interaction. In a Labovian tradition, Linde (1988) has analysed interaction in relation to authentic disasters focusing on the role of politeness strategies in aviation discourse. By means of a quantitative measurement of mitigation, Linde analysed discourse failure and success in data from eight aviation accidents and also in data from flight simulator experiments.[6]

Negotiations form another sub-area that has been focused on in relation to the business world and organizations. Considerable practical interest is here of course attached to intercultural negotiations, and many studies have analysed negotiations between individuals from different cultures and with different mother tongues (Firth, 1995).

Applying the technique of discourse analysis to various workplace situations in which negotiations take place, researchers have been able to draw attention to the subtle strategies used by the participants for the purpose of coming to an agreement. In Hazeland et al. (1995), negotiations between a travel agency employee and her customer are analysed. According to Hazeland et al., the main body of these negotiations is accomplished by a process of categorization. By subtly negotiating *categories*, the participants collaboratively try to arrive at descriptions – and thus holiday bookings – that satisfy both parties.

The researchers distinguish between a *scaling-up operation* and *attribute transfer*, two methods by which employee and customer collaboratively achieved a transition from one category to another and thereby negotiated a description that could satisfy the wishes of the customer and the possibilities of the employee.

The *scaling-up operation* is shown in the following extract.[7] The travel agency clerk (A) asks a mother calling on behalf of her daughter where in

Italy the girl wants to go. The mother (B) answers that her daughter would like to go to Venice and Florence and then adds a formulation of a consequence of this preference, 'it should be situated in the vicinity.' The employee then translates this consequence by saying, 'then you get something on the Adriatic coast.'

```
A:  and er where she- where in Italy did she want to go to
       (. . .)
B:  what she's talking about mostly that is e:r
    Venice and Florence that 's where she would like to go
    to=
    =so yes, hh it should be situated in the vi cinity er
A:                it should be si-               in the
    vicinity
B:  yes
A:  hh yes: and then you get Florence
    yes then you get something on the Adriatic coast
    0.4
B:  yes
```

(Hazeland et al., 1995: 279)

The clerk here uses the resources provided by the customer's addition to interpret 'in the vicinity' as a rather large vicinity: she 'scales up' the target region. In order to accept this scaling-up operation, the customer must be willing to stretch her requirements in such a way that the clerk's offer is still compatible with them. When the clerk starts mentioning different towns in the region, the negotiations start. Cattolica is mentioned, but the customer finds this 'rather far from there'. Ravenna is mentioned but dropped as a possibility before Rimini is mentioned. The clerk says 'Rimini then is closest' and the customer seems to agree 'really Rimini'. Rimini is still far from Florence and Venice, but by enlarging the area to be taken into consideration, in this case by hanging up their discussion on the formulation 'in the vicinity', they manage to come up with a solution, that is find a destination which is both included in the agency's range and satisfies the needs of the customer.

The other operation, *attribute transfer*, will be illustrated below. The customer (B) has initially asked for 'a brochure for coach trips to Italy', and when asked what kind of trips she wants, she says 'a teenager trip'. A little later the clerk (A) proposes a shift in categories. We can follow how step by step she informs the customer of the transferability of the relevant category attributes.

```
A:  but er it should specifically be a teenager trip,
    cause you know it- often is
B:  well that's not necessary er (fe)
A:  when you go for example to Italy
    and you just take a er shuttle trip you know
```

B: yes
A: so that me ans hh er the transport back and forth
B: yes
A: and over there er accommodation either an apartment
     or a hotel h h you know then there will of course also
B: yes
A: a lot of young people am ongst them of course right?
B: yes
     so that doesn't make any difference
A: hh right so those real hh you know where you do have
     more older people joining eh that are
     those er excursion trips you know which ev- hh
B: yes

(Hazeland et al., 1995: 283–4)

When the customer has admitted that it is 'not necessary' for it to be specifically 'a teenager trip', the clerk reformulates the category 'teenager trip' by proposing two new categories: 'a shuttle trip' and 'accommodation'. She adds that of course there will be a lot of young people among the travellers on trips characterized by such a combination. The clerk takes the attribute 'young travellers' of the category 'teenager' and attaches to this two categories combined. The employee has steered the negotiation from a teenager trip towards a shuttle and accommodation trip, which is a trip mostly taken by young travellers.

We have here looked closer at workplace negotiations. An adjacent area of concern is that of conflicts and misunderstanding in different working life settings. A special type of problematic talk is that related to *moral discourse*, that is to discourse on shameful subjects like alcoholism, abortion, theft and the like. Discourse analysts have looked at how institutions handle these delicate situations.

Hall et al. (1997), for instance, studied moral construction in social work discourse. The researchers analysed an interview with a social worker where he tells a former colleague about a case of child abuse – 'failure to thrive' – which he had been handling in an inner city public welfare agency in the UK. By analysing these interviews as narratives, the researchers were able to reveal the moral character of the decision making and the rhetorical character of its justification. They looked at the presence of *institutionalized voice* in the social worker's narrative, that is the voice which makes this narrative hearable as a social work story. They also studied how the case was established as a case of 'failure to thrive', and how the narrative makes clear that the parents are responsible for the upcoming situation. They found that the narrative seemed to derive its internal coherence and consistency from the point of view of the social worker's action-logic.

In describing the narrative account of the case given in the interview by the social worker, Hall and his colleagues focused on the specific structural characteristics of the narrative, in particular the accumulative use of a three-stage device by the social worker in building an extreme case in which his last resort was the decision he had taken. The first stage was to show that parental non-cooperation was a cause. In order to justify coercive intervention, the parents' physical aggressiveness is dramatized, and the institutional representative is presented as physically subdued. The selection of lexico-grammatical structures stress the non-physical actions of the institutional representative. So we find institutional agents combined with mental processes: 'the hospital felt', 'the staff found the mother difficult', 'the foster parent found it impossible', 'the assessment went very well.' Of a different character is the description of the physical violence of the parents in relation to the agency: 'the black worker was kicked and punched', 'the mother was so hostile, I was threatened.' The parents are also explicitly held responsible for the failure to apply institutional measures: 'the parents refused to cooperate', 'they just stopped cooperating', 'parents failed to attend', 'the family were not cooperating with them either', 'the mother went off in a temper before we could.'

The second stage relates to the claim that the case in question was an extreme case. The narrative thus contains extreme case formulations such as 'had the situation been left any further the child would have died', 'the situation caused much anxiety', 'it was really a very serious matter and on that basis', 'arrangement of access in area of office was a horrendous task', 'things became extremely difficult, the situation was exacerbated by the birth of another child', 'regrettably I was forced into a situation.' By these formulations, the social worker pictures himself as a victim of circumstances; anyone acting under the same circumstances would have come up with the same conclusion as he did.

The third stage of the narrative claims that his decision was his last resort, in other words that as a professional he had done what he could to prevent the sad outcome: 'we involved the FWA [Family Welfare Association] with two objectives', 'we attempted to hold case conferences where we could review the situation', 'I did a joint home visit with the FWA . . . we went to cover three things', 'we tried very hard to liaise with other agencies and we did this successfully', 'where not only had I to take places of safety that I had to apply a section forty one allowing me to go with the police to get access'. Through his narrative the social worker is trying to suggest that the course of action has more to do with the blameworthiness of his client than with institutional failure.

The researchers' conclusion is that the narrative is a form of social practice, which is instrumental in reproducing social relations and realities within social work discourse, like this case of child abuse (Hall et al., 1997).

Science and the Academic Setting

The scientific arena can be seen as a special kind of workplace. It has, however, followed a tradition of its own, a sociological-rhetorical tradition with a clear basis in the sociology of science (Merton, 1973). Several studies have been devoted to analysis of the role of texts in establishing scientific fact. The scientific field is seen as a workplace, a laboratory where social rules determine the establishing of facts and the rank order of the scientist. Knorr-Cetina (1981) was one of the first to describe the writing up of results as a process of tinkering with facts rather than a knowledge-guided search. Latour and Woolgar (1986) described the *social construction of scientific facts* as an antagonistic struggle among scientists, leading to a purposeful diminishing of the results of others and a levelling up – to a generalized level – of one's own results. Scientific facts are considered as mere works; rhetoric determines what becomes scientific fact.

In Latour (1987), objects are seen as initiating actions as much as human beings. His analysis also points to differences in argumentation and practice at the different stages of the process, at the science-in-the-making stage as compared with the made-science stage.

Bazerman (1988) studied the rise of modern forms of scientific communication, focusing on the historical emergence of the experimental article. A *social constructivist approach* in relation to written texts is also found in Bazerman and Paradis (1991), which examines the important role played by texts in profession building. Textual forms and definitions are found to impose structure on human activity and help to shape versions of reality. Texts are shown to play powerful roles in staging the daily actions of individuals, and to be important factors in the rise of action.

Writing at college and university level and the different academic genres of writing have attracted the attention of many researchers. As within the educational area, much research has been steered by the practical need to improve the teaching of writing in the college classroom. The Freshman Writing Program in the American colleges, which has resulted in academic writing being taught to all college students, has led to a large number of studies on genres and on the writing process. The most recent trends within this field owe a debt to Bakhtin, Leontev and Vygotsky, as well as to Bazerman and other researchers within the sociology of science.

Academic written genres have been studied from different angles. The socio-cognitive perspective is central for many American writing researchers. Working in the competitive society of the US, they have come to focus on the *rhetorical* (persuading) *patterns* used by scientists within their respective *discourse community* (Miller, 1984; Swales, 1990; Berkenkotter and Huckin, 1995). For the rhetorical analysis of article introductions, Swales developed the so-called CARS model (CARS = create a research space). The typical research article (RA) introduction is assumed to focus on three *rhetorical moves* directed towards the creation of a space for the research presented within the scientific discourse community.

Move 1   Establishing a territory
  Step 1   Claiming centrality
           and/or

Step 2   Making topic generalization(s)
           and/or
Step 3   Reviewing items of previous research

Move 2   Establishing a niche
Step 1A   Counter-claiming
           or
Step 1B   Indicating a gap
           or
Step 1C   Question-raising
           or
Step 1D   Continuing a tradition

Move 3   Occupying the niche
Step 1A   Outlining purposes
           or
Step 1B   Announcing present research
Step 2   Announcing principal findings
Step 3   Indicating RA structure

(Swales, 1990: 141)

The European tradition, on the other hand, builds more on a text-linguistic tradition, with a close analysis of the texts at different levels: *pragmatic*, *referential-cohesive, thematic, cognitive* (Schröder, 1991; Gunnarsson, 1992; 1993; Melander and Näslund, 1993).

Originally for the study of the sociohistorical construction of science in medical, economic and technical articles, Gunnarsson (1992) developed a model for the abstract analysis of the cognitive content of texts. Five *cognitive worlds* (knowledge worlds) are discerned: scientific world, object world, practical world, private world and external world. The *scientific world* means that the content relates to theory, classification or experiment/ observation; the *object world* that it relates to a description of the phenom- enon (for example, in medicine, the disease); the *practical world* means that the content describes the work of practitioners or their interaction with clients (in medicine, physicians' work or interaction with patients); the *private world* means that the content focuses on the experience of the individual (in medicine, how a patient feels about a disease), or the per- sonal situation of the individual; the *external world* concerns content relating to conditions or measures taken which regard field-external matters (in medicine, economic, political or social matters). These worlds corre- spond to different sectors of society – academic community, educational sector, professional life, private life and public sector – and the method- ology thus provides a means to study the relationship between text, social group and society.

The extracts below, taken from a corpus of medical articles, show segments of the texts that have been classified as belonging to the five cognitive worlds:

Scientific world
> But pneumothorax is quite commonly regarded as a result of diagnostic or therapeutic measures or as a complication of complicated or advanced lung disease.
> (Scientific world: classification)

Object world
> Tuberculosis is an infectious disease which is caused by a living organism invisible to the naked eye, the tubercle bacillus, and which occurs not only in human beings, but also in animals.
> (Object world: phenomenon)

Practical world
> Insertion of the chest drain was preceded by premedication with pethidine and careful local anaesthesia.
> (Practical world: work)

Private world
> For the first few days after the insertion of the drain, many patients feel considerable pain.
> (Private world: experience)

External world
> Introducing the simplified method of treatment proposed would result in significant savings.
> (External world: measures)

The proportions of texts representing these five worlds have been found to vary from one field to another, and most interestingly, from one period to another. The world character of texts of a certain period reveals the stage of development of the science in question, but also the structure of the scientific community and the roles of scientists within society. We can also say that it is through their texts that scientists create or construct their science and the role patterns within their community, and also their place in society.

Spoken discourse within academia has been studied much less than written discourse. I will, however, conclude by taking up a couple of projects currently in progress, which problem-wise are starting a new tradition rather than following an established one.

One of these studies is a CA-oriented project investigation of scientific discourse from an anthropological point of view and with a focus on the interplay between verbal and non-verbal behaviour (Jacoby and Gonzales, 1991; Ochs et al., 1993).

The other study concerns interaction at academic seminars within three different traditions (humanities, social sciences and natural sciences). The analysis focuses on subculture differences as well as on patterns of dominance and control. Gender, academic status and actual role are further considered. Gunnarsson (1995), for instance, presents an analysis of the chairperson's control of the interaction and content at the seminars. The chairing function entails a possibility to influence and control the students' socialization into the department culture. The chair has a possibility to control what knowledge is accepted, and which attitudes and norms are allowed. S/he has also a possibility to show the accepted hierarchy and the accepted attitudes and norms for behaviour. If the chair's functions are related to the content and interaction within the frame of the seminar, it is clear that the chair can initiate and control the general purpose of the discourse, that is s/he can set the scenario. The chair can of course control the turntaking, determining who is allowed to speak, when and for how long. He or she can also initiate and control the discussion in relation to which topic and what aspect of this topic is to be discussed. The chair can also control the centrality of the topic – how much should be said about it, when it should be dropped and a new one introduced. The chair has also a possibility to control the conclusion, steering the evaluation and attitudes towards the discussed topics.

A comparison of the control executed by a male and a female chair at two seminars within the same department revealed quite remarkable differences in use by the chairs of their possibilities to control the seminar discussion. The male professor studied exerted a more or less total control of the content as well as of the interaction, while the female chair exerted only minimal control of the events. These results are interpreted in a Foucaultian perspective, that is as the interest of the group in power in having control of the knowledge sphere.

Conclusions

Applied discourse analysis encompasses a wide range of studies and a variety of methodologies, and this chapter has not been able to give more than a brief idea of all the research under way. Many areas have not been mentioned, such as work on communication with blind and deaf people, on interaction with the disabled, on bilingualism and on the whole field of language planning. Rather than attempting to cover everything, my aim has been to give a few glimpses of trends and developments within ADA. I have stressed the dynamic and expansive character of ADA, where collaboration cuts across disciplines and where theories and methods are evolved in the search for an understanding of problems relating to written and spoken discourse.

Recommended Reading

As mentioned above, ADA is a growing research area. For further readings, I would therefore like to suggest four anthologies which can be said to present studies in the current front line of applied discourse analysis. The first anthology, *Textual Dynamics of the Professions*, edited by Charles

Bazerman and James Paradis (1991), presents studies with a new and interesting approach to writing in professional communities. *Talk at Work*, edited by Paul Drew and John Heritage (1992), covers studies of spoken discourse undertaken in a variety of professional settings. *The Discourse of Negotiation*, edited by Alan Firth (1995), contains analyses of negotiations in various workplace encounters. The fourth anthology, *The Construction of Professional Discourse*, edited by Britt-Louise Gunnarsson, Per Linell and Bengt Nordberg (1997), includes studies of both spoken and written discourse from a historical as well as a contemporary perspective.

Notes

1 This was done in collaboration with nine legal experts, who scrutinized the alternative law text. From the point of view of legal content and legal function, the original law text and the rewritten text were identical.

2 A similar approach was taken by Austrian researchers, who also included in their model a socio-psychological dimension relating to attitudes towards legal language and law text reading (Pfeiffer et al., 1987).

3 I present here a somewhat simplified version of the discourse transcription in Drew (1992).

4 A more detailed analysis of the perspective setting in police interrogations is presented in Linell and Jönsson (1991).

5 Sometimes distinctions are made between institutions, organizations and workplaces. In this chapter, however, I use 'workplace' in a very wide sense, covering white-collar workplaces, such as institutions and organizations, as well as more traditional blue-collar workplaces.

6 Another study focused on the written discourse surrounding an aircraft accident (Herndl et al., 1991).

7 This and the following extract from Hazeland et al. (1995) are slightly simplified.

References

Adelswärd, V., Aronsson, K., Jönsson, L. and Linell, P. (1987) 'The unequal distribution of interactional space dominance and control in courtroom interaction', *Text*, 7: 313–46.

Atkinson, J. Maxwell (1992) 'Displaying neutrality: formal aspects of informal court proceedings', in Paul Drew and John Heritage (eds), *Talk at Work: Interaction in Institutional Settings*. Cambridge: Cambridge University Press.

Barnes, Douglas and Todd, Frankie (eds) (1977) *Communication and Learning in Small Groups*. London: Routledge and Kegan Paul.

Bazerman, C. (1988) *Shaping Written Knowledge: the Genre and Activity of the Experimental Article in Science*. Madison, WI: University of Wisconsin Press.

Bazerman, C. and J. Paradis (eds) (1991) *Textual Dynamics of the Professions: Historical and Contemporary Studies of Writing in Professional Communities*. Madison, WI: University of Wisconsin Press.

Bellack, A.A., Kliebard, H.M., Hyman, R.T. and Smith, F.L. (1966) *The Language of the Classroom*. New York: Teachers College Press.

Berkenkotter, Carol and Huckin, Thomas N. (1995) *Genre Knowledge in Disciplinary Communication: Cognition/Culture/Power*. Hillsdale, NJ: Erlbaum.

Bernstein, Basil B. (1971) *Class, Codes and Control. Vol. 1: Theoretical Studies towards a Sociology of Language*. London, Boston: Routledge and Kegan Paul.

Bernstein, Basil B. (1973) *Class, Codes and Control. Vol. 2: Applied Studies towards a Sociology of Language*. London, Boston: Routledge and Kegan Paul.

Bhatia, Vijay K. (1987) *Analysing Genre: Language Use in Professional Settings*. London, New York: Longman.

Bourdieu, P. and Passeron, J.-C. (1970) *La Reproduction: éléments pour une théorie du système d'enseignement*. Paris: Minuit.

Charrow, Robert P. and Charrow, Veda R. (1979) 'Making legal language understandable: a psycholinguistic study of jury instruction', *Columbia Law Review*, 79 (7): 1306–74.

Cicourel, Aaron V. (1968) *The Social Organization of Juvenile Justice*. New York: Wiley.

Cicourel, Aaron V. (1981) 'Language and medicine', in Charles A. Ferguson and Shirley Brice Heath (eds), *Language in the USA*. Cambridge: Cambridge University Press. pp. 407–29.

Cicourel, Aaron V. (1983) 'Hearing is not believing: language and the structure of belief in medical communication', in Sue Fisher and Alexandra Dundas Todd (eds), *The Social Organization of Doctor–Patient Communication*. Washington, DC: Center for Applied Linguistics. pp. 221–39.

Danet, Brenda (1980) 'Language in the legal process', *Law and Society Review*, 14 (3): 447–564.

Drew, Paul (1992) 'Contested evidence in courtroom cross-examination: the case of a trial for rape', in Paul Drew and John Heritage (eds), *Talk at Work: Interaction in Institutional Settings*. Cambridge: Cambridge University Press.

Drew, Paul and Heritage, John (1992) *Talk at Work: Interaction in Institutional Settings*. Cambridge: Cambridge University Press.

Færch, Claus and Kasper, Gabriele (eds) (1983) *Strategies in Interlanguage Communication*. London, New York: Longman.

Færch, Claus and Kasper, Gabriele (eds) (1987) *Introspection in Second Language Research*. Clevedon: Multilingual Matters.

Firth, Alan (ed.) (1995) *The Discourse of Negotiation: Studies of Language in the Workplace*. Oxford: Pergamon.

Gardner, R.C. (1985) *Social Psychology and Second Language Learning: the Role of Attitudes and Motivation*. London: Edward Arnold.

Goodwin, Charles and Goodwin, Marjorie Harness (1997) 'Professional vision', in Britt-Louise Gunnarsson, Per Linell and Bengt Nordberg (eds), *The Construction of Professional Discourse*. London: Longman. pp. 292–316.

Gunnarsson, B.-L. (1984) 'Functional comprehensibility of legislative texts: experiments with a Swedish Act of Parliament', *Text*, 4 (1/3).

Gunnarsson, B.-L. (1992) 'Linguistic change within cognitive worlds', in G. Kellermann and M.D. Morrissey (eds), *Diachrony within Synchrony: Language History and Cognition*. Frankfurt am Main: Peter Lang.

Gunnarsson, B.-L. (1993) 'Pragmatic and macrothematic patterns in science and popular science: a diachronic study of articles from three fields', in M. Ghadessy (ed.), *Register Analysis: Theory and Practice*. London, New York: Pinter.

Gunnarsson, Britt-Louise (1995) 'Academic leadership and gender: the case of the seminar chair', in I. Broch, T. Bull and T. Swan (eds), Proceedings of the 2nd Nordic Conference on Language and Gender. Tromsö, 3–5 November. NORDLYD. Tromsö University Working Papers on Language and Linguistics No. 23. pp. 174–93.

Gunnarsson, B.-L., Linell, P. and Nordberg, B. (eds) (1997) *The Construction of Professional Discourse*. London, New York: Longman.

Gustafsson, Marita (1984) 'The syntactic features of binomial expressions in legal English', *Text*, 4 (1/3): 123–42.

Gustavsson, Lennart (1988) *Language Taught and Language Used: Dialogue Processes in Dyadic Lessons of Swedish as a Second Language Compared with Non-Didactic Conversations*. Linköping Studies in Arts and Science 18. University of Linköping.

Hall, Christopher, Sarangi, Srikant K. and Slembrouck, Stefaan (1997) 'Moral construction in social work discourse', in Britt-Louise Gunnarsson, Per Linell and Bengt Nordberg (eds), *The Construction of Professional Discourse*. London, New York: Longman. pp. 265–91.

Hazeland, Harrie, Huisman, Marjan and Schasfoort, Marca (1995) 'Negotiating categories in travel agency talk', in Alan Firth (ed.), *The Discourse of Negotiation: Studies of Language in the Workplace.* Oxford: Pergamon. pp. 271-97.

Herndl, Carl G., Fennell, Barbara A. and Miller, Carolyn R. (1991) 'Understanding failures in organizational discourse: the accident at Three Mile Island and the shuttle *Challenger* disaster', in C. Bazerman and J. Paradis (eds), *Textual Dynamics of the Professions: Historical and Contemporary Studies of Writing in Professional Communities.* Madison, WI: University of Wisconsin Press. pp. 279-305.

Jacoby, Sally and Gonzales, Patrick (1991) 'The constitution of expert–novice in scientific discourse', *Issues in Applied Linguistics,* 2 (2): 149-81.

Jönsson, Linda (1988) *Polisförhöret som kommunikationssituation.* SIC 23. Studies in Communication. University of Linköping.

Knorr-Cetina, K. (1981) *The Manufacture of Knowledge.* Oxford: Pergamon Press.

Kurzon, Dennis (1986) 'It is hereby performed: legal speech acts', *Pragmatics and Beyond,* VII:6. Amsterdam, Philadelphia: John Benjamins.

Lalouschek, Johanna, Menz, Florina and Wodka, Ruth (1990) *Alltag in der Ambulanz.* Tübingen: Gunter Narr.

Latour, Bruno (1987) *Science in Action: How to Follow Scientists and Engineers through Society.* Cambridge, MA: Harvard University Press.

Latour, Bruno and Woolgar, Steve (1986) *Laboratory Life: the Construction of Scientific Facts* (1979). Princeton, NJ: Princeton University Press.

Linde, Charlotte (1988) 'The quantitative study of communicative success: politenesss and accidents in aviation discourse', *Language and Society,* 17: 375-99.

Linell, Per, Gustavsson, Lennart and Juvonen, P. (1988) 'Interactional dominance in dyadic communication: a presentation of the initiative–response analysis', *Linguistics,* 26: 3.

Linell, Per and Jönsson, Linda (1991) 'Suspect stories: perspective-setting in an asymmetrical situation', in Ivana Markova and Klaus Foppa (eds), *Asymmetries in Dialogue.* Hertfordshire: Harvester Wheatsheaf. pp. 75-100.

Lörscher, W. (1983) *Linguistische Beschreibung und Analyse von Fremdsprachenunterricht als Diskurse.* Tübingen: Narr.

Mehan, H. (1979) *Learning Lesson: Social Organization in the Classroom.* Cambridge, MA: Harvard University Press.

Mehan, H. (1991) 'The school's work of sorting students', in Deidre Boden and Don H. Zimmerman (eds), *Talk and Social Structure: Studies in Ethnomethodology and Conversation Analysis.* Oxford: Basil Blackwell.

Melander, Björn and Näslund, Harry (1993) 'Diachronic developments in Swedish LSP texts: a presentation of some of the results from the research project LSP Text in the 20th Century', in *FINLANCE,* vol. XII. Language Centre for Finnish Universities. University of Jyväskylä.

Mellinkoff, David (1963) *The Language of the Law.* Boston: Little, Brown.

Merton, R. (1973) *The Sociology of Science* (ed. Norman Storer). Chicago: University of Chicago Press.

Miller, C.R. (1984) 'Genre as social action', *Quarterly Journal of Speech,* 70.

Mishler, Elliot G. (1984) *The Discourse of Medicine: Dialectics of Medical Interviews.* Norwood, NJ: Ablex.

O'Barr, M. (1982) *Linguistic Evidence: Language, Power and Strategy in the Courtroom.* New York: Academic Press.

Ochs, Elinor, Gonzales, Patrick and Jacoby, Sally (1993) 'Interpretative journey: how physicists talk and travel through graphic space', revised draft. Department of TESL and Applied Linguistics. University of California, Los Angeles.

Pfeiffer, O.E., Strouhal, E. and Wodak, R. (1987) *Recht auf Sprache: Verstehen und Verständlichkeit von Gesetzen.* Vienna: Verlag Orac.

Philips, Susan U. (1992) 'The routinization of repair in courtroom discourse', in Alessandro Duranti and Charles Goodwin (eds), *Rethinking Context: Language as an Interactive Phenomenon.* Cambridge: Cambridge University Press. pp. 311-22.

Pride, J.B. (ed.) (1979) *Sociolinguistic Aspects of Language Learning and Teaching*. Oxford: Oxford University Press.

Schröder, H. (ed) (1991) *Subject-Oriented Texts: Languages for Special Purposes and Text Theory*. Berlin, New York: Walter de Gruyter.

Sinclair, J. McH. and Coulthard, R.M. (1975) *Towards an Analysis of Discourse: the English Used by Teachers and Pupils*. London: Oxford University Press.

Snow, C.E. and Ferguson, C.A. (eds) (1977) *Talking to Children: Language Input and Acquisition*. Cambridge: Cambridge University Press.

Söderbergh, Ragnhild (1977) *Reading in Early Childhood: a Linguistic Study of Preschool Child's Gradual Acquisition of Reading Ability*, 2nd edn. Washington, DC: Georgetown University Press.

Stubbs, Michael (1980) *Language and Literacy: the Sociolinguistics of Reading and Writing*. London: Routledge and Kegan Paul.

Swales, J.M. (1990) *Genre Analysis: English in Academic and Research Settings*. Cambridge: Cambridge University Press.

Wodak, Ruth (1997) 'Discourse-sociolinguistics and the study of doctor–patient interaction', in Britt-Louise Gunnarsson, Per Linell and Bengt Nordberg (eds), *The Construction of Professional Discourse*. London, New York: Longman. pp. 173–200.

Appendix: Transcribing Conventions

The transcript techniques and symbols were devised by Gail Jefferson in the course of research undertaken with Harvey Sacks. Techniques are revised, symbols added or dropped as they seem useful to work. There is no guarantee or suggestion that the symbols or transcripts alone would permit the doing of any unspecified research tasks: they are properly used as an adjunct to the tape-recorded materials.

Brackets   Indicate that the portions of utterances so encased are simultaneous. The left-hand bracket marks the outset of simultaneity, the right-hand bracket indicates its resolution.

$$I \; don' \begin{bmatrix} know \\ you \end{bmatrix} don't$$

Colons   Indicate that the immediately prior syllable is prolonged. The number of colons is an attempt to represent the length of the prolongation.

We:::ll now

Hyphen   Represents a cutting off short of the immediately prior syllable.

But-

Capital letters   Represent increased loudness of the utterances (or parts of utterances) so marked.

CAPS

Italics and underscoring   Used to represent heavier emphasis (in speaker's stress) on utterances or parts of utterances so marked.

italics   underscoring

Equal signs   Used to indicate that no time elapsed between the objects 'latched' by the marks. Often used as a transcribing convenience, these can also mean that a next speaker starts at precisely the end of a current speaker's utterance.

'Swhat I said=
=But you didn't

Period encased in parentheses   Denotes a pause of one-tenth of a second.

(.)

Numbers encased in parentheses   Indicate the seconds and tenths of seconds ensuing between speaker turns. They may also be used to indicate the duration of pauses internal to a speaker's turn.

(1.3)

Score sign   Indicates a pause of about a second that it wasn't possible to discriminate precisely.

(#)

Double parentheses   Enclose descriptions, not transcribed utterances.

((very slowly))

Single parentheses encasing words   Indicate that something was heard, but the transcriber is not sure what it was. These can serve as a warning that the transcript may be unreliable.

(word)

Parentheses encasing an x   Indicate a hitch or stutter on the part of the speaker.

I (x) I did

Punctuation marks   Used for intonation, not grammar. A period represents 'falling' intonation, a question mark represents 'rising' intonation, and a comma represents a 'falling-rising' intonational contour.

.   ?   ,

Degree symbols   Represent softness, or decreased amplitude of the utterances encased by them, with the right-hand symbol marking the move back to a normal level of amplitude.

°So you did.° I see.

Breathing indicators   A period followed by hh marks an inhalation. The hh alone stand for exhalation.

.hh   hh

Laughter particles   The hunh, eh, hengh and heh are laughter particles.

hunh-heh   eh-heh   hengh

Name Index

Subject Index

speech: convergence, 162; divergence, 162;
    event, 58, 95, 232; genre, 252–3; powerful
    vs powerless, 296
speech act theory, 38, 42–4, 59, 152
speech acts, 95, 211, 216, 219, 234; cross-
    cultural studies of, 45; indirect, 44–7; in
    discourse, 47
speech community, 95, 130, 158; African
    American, 152–3, 156
speech style, 131, 136
spoken dialogue, 92
spoken interaction, 4
spontaneity, 4
status, 129
stereotype, 57, 173–4
storytelling, 173–4, 192–4; organizational,
    187–91
strategic functions, in political discourse,
    211–13
strategy, 84, 105; bald-on record, 51;
    negative politeness, 51; off-the-record, 52;
    positive politeness, 51
study of errors, 288
style, 33, 171–2; communication, 95;
    fragmented, 296–7; interactional, 56;
    narrative, 296–7; talk, 130–1, 135
subculture, 130
subordination, 186
symbolic power, 53
syntax, 38, 214, 223

tabloid, 124
tag questions, 128–9
talk, 65; African American, 132; and gender,
    127–36; styles of, 130–1; vs text, 4, 16; *see
    also* discourse, and conversation
talk-in-interaction, 64, 66; and gender, 131–5
tasks, institutional, 111
technical vocabulary, 100–1
technologization of discourse, 260
telephone calls, 68, 70
television soap operas, 123
temporal organization, 66
testimony, 109
textbooks, 280
text: linguistics, 306; and society, 277;
    understanding, 278; *see also* discourse

text–society mediation, 278
textual analysis, of media, 124–6
Thatcherism, 271, 275
thematic roles, 223
Third Reich, 210
time, 12
timing, 73, 77, 84
titles, 121
tjalpawangkanyi, 246–9
topic, 71, 83–4, 224
topical organization, 87; selection, 33;
    transition, 134
topics, 167
transcripts, 70–1, 313–14
transfer, 170
transitives, 225
translation, 56–7
transparency, illocutionary, 44
trial, 294–5
trivialization, 197, 199
turn taking, 73–4, 78–9, 83–4, 102–3, 106

understanding, text, 278
understandings, 73
utterance, 39

variation: contextual, 41; cross-cultural, 56;
    cultural, 41
vocabulary, 291; technical, 100–1

ways of speaking, 146, 231
Western Marxism, 260
Wolof, 233
women, 54, 66, 119–43, 189; African
    American, 148–56; Black, 148–56;
    European American, 150; media images
    of, 122; media language and, 127–8; and
    organizations, 189–91
women's magazines, 122, 126, 221
workers, 185
working class, 191
workplace, 111, 300–4; negotiation, 303
writing, college, 305

xenophobia, 165

Yankunytjatjara, 245–9